THE
ROMAN CATHOLIC CHURCH

and the Creation of

THE MODERN IRISH STATE
1878 - 1886

EMMET LARKIN

THE ROMAN CATHOLIC CHURCH
AND THE CREATION OF
THE MODERN IRISH STATE

Memoirs of the
AMERICAN PHILOSOPHICAL SOCIETY
Held at Philadelphia
For Promoting Useful Knowledge
Volume 108

FIG. 1. Thomas W. Croke, Archbishop of Cashel, 1881.

THE
ROMAN CATHOLIC
CHURCH

and the Creation of

THE MODERN IRISH STATE

1878 - 1886

♀ 21

EMMET LARKIN
Professor of British and Irish History
University of Chicago

THE AMERICAN PHILOSOPHICAL SOCIETY
Independence Square • Philadelphia

1975

To
Desmond Ryan

CONTENTS

ILLUSTRATIONS

Preface

The idea of writing a history of the Roman Catholic Church in Ireland was suggested to me nearly twenty years ago, when I was a graduate student in Dublin, by the late and sincerely lamented Desmond Ryan. My conviction steadily grew, as I continued to research and to write in Irish history, that the history of modern Ireland could not be properly written until the role of the Church in that country was better understood. Finally, in the summer of 1958, I formally began my work on the Church by visiting the various archives and libraries in Dublin, Rome, and London to collect the necessary materials for my history. I have returned nearly every year since then to either Dublin, Rome, or London to continue my research. For all the various opportunities to continue my research I must thank the American Philosophical Society, the Social Science Research Council, the American Council of Learned Societies, and the National Endowment for the Humanities for numerous grants-in-aid. I must also express my appreciation to the Old Dominion Fund of the Massachusetts Institute of Technology, the Howard Foundation of Brown University, and the Division of Social Sciences of the University of Chicago for their generous aid, without which the writing of this volume would not have been possible.

Before proceeding to acknowledging all those who have had a particular share in helping to create this volume, however, I should like to say a few words about the technique adopted as regards style and scholarly apparatus. Inasmuch as history is an art, the historian is perhaps more bound, if not indeed limited, by the materials he works in than by the techniques he works with. His form, therefore, must be appropriate to his substance, and some techniques are obviously more appropriate to certain kinds of evidence than others. The richness in the quality and the quantity of both the general archival materials and the personal papers of the principal characters in this study was indeed very great. In presenting this evidence in this volume, therefore, I have consciously adopted a technique which I should like to call "mosaic." The many varied bits and pieces of evidence have been selected and arranged to create a portrait of the Church between 1878 and 1886. There are, I believe, a number of advantages in using a "mosaic" technique when the material is appropriate. Since the writing of history can never result in more than a representation of what was "true," an historical portrait in "mosaic" is perhaps more "realistic" than might at first be supposed. The technique of "mosaic" allows for the inclusion of a great deal more of the evidence in its original form and contributes, therefore, not only to the immediacy of the actual experience, but to the authority of the representation, thereby enhancing the reality of the historical portrait. As in all representations, and perhaps even more so in a mosaic, the appreciation has a great deal to do with properly relating it to the mind's eye—in a word, in achieving perspective. If I have been successful, then, in constructing my mosaic, the numerous details should integrate and the various parts should harmonize when this volume is read whole.

Since the system of footnoting in this volume is not orthodox, a word of explanation to the reader may also be in order. Most of the ecclesiastical and a few of the lay correspondences quoted from have not been catalogued in any more systematic way than by date. These correspondences, therefore, have been simply footnoted in the text as K (Kirby), Mc (McCabe), C (Croke), S (Smith), M (Manning) and so forth, and the dates and the correspondents of the individual letters used have also been acknowledged in the text. The problem of indicating a break or omission in any particular letter quoted from has been resolved by using the word "then" in the parenthetical interpolation. For example, "The world," Cardinal McCabe wrote Kirby on December 16, "does not seem to be improving"(K). "In any case," he *then* added, "I hope you are well," indicates that between the last sentence and the previous one there has been a break in the text. Sometimes the letter quoted from was a copy rather than the original, and this is resolved in the designation. For example, if McCabe writes Kirby and the designation is Mc rather than K, the letter quoted from is obviously a copy. If there is any variation from this, it has been noted in a footnote. The various abbreviations used in this volume for the respective correspondences in the order of their appearance are listed on page xx.

In turning to the many obligations that I have incurred in the researching and writing of this volume, there is, perhaps, no one I am indebted to more than the Most Rev. Dr. Donal Herlihy, Bishop of Ferns, and formerly Rector of the Irish College in Rome. I can only say that his generosity was as extraordinary as his patience. In the next breath I must also sincerely thank the Most Rev. Dr. Dominic Conway, Bishop of Elphin, and formerly Spiritual Director and then Rector of the Irish College, for all his kindnesses, academic and personal, in helping me find my way in Rome and encouraging me in my work. I am also under considerable obligation to the late Archbishop of Dublin, the Most Rev. Dr. John Charles McQuaid, for granting me permission to research in the archdiocesan archives. I must also thank the Most Rev. Dr. Thomas Morris, Archbishop of Cashel, for his permission to read the Croke correspondence on microfilm in the National Library as well as for his hospitality and generosity in my visit to Thurles. I am also under obligation to the late Bishop of Elphin, the Most Rev. Dr. Vincent Hanly, for his kind permission to read the microfilm copy of the Gillooly correspondence. Finally I must especially thank Dom Mark Tierney, O.S.B., who has arranged and catalogued the Croke papers in the Cashel archives, for his help and advice, and whose hospitality at Glenstal Abbey to this wandering scholar was in the great Benedictine tradition.

To my good friend and mentor, Professor David H. Greene of New York University, who read this manuscript through, I must once again note that words will not make amends. His wise counsel was well taken, and he at least will see the results on almost every page of this volume. To the staff of the National Library of Ireland, and particularly to Mr. Ailfred McLoichlainn, Keeper of Printed Books, I must express my gratitude as well as my appreciation for their unfailing kindness and patience. No words, however, can explain my obligation to the late Mina Carney, whose help and generosity over the past twenty years has been both unstinted and selfless. Without her encouragement it is not too much to say that this book might never have been written. Finally I must acknowledge my great debt to the late Desmond Ryan. He was not only a brave and serene man, but it was he who inspired this book, and that is why, therefore, I have dedicated it to him.

In conclusion I must take this opportunity, inadequate as it is, to thank all those who have hand or part in the making of this book, and especially Sir John Dilke, the Trustees of the British Museum, the Controller of H.M. Stationary Office for the Public Record Office, for their respective permissions to quote from the Dilke, Balfour, and Carnarvon papers. In making all these acknowledgements, I hope it is unnecessary to point out that no one, but myself, is responsible for the errors that may be found in this volume.

Emmet Larkin

University of Chicago
1974

ROMAN CATHOLIC ARCHBISHOPS
AND BISHOPS IN IRELAND, 1878 -1886

Archbishops of Ireland

Armagh:
  Daniel McGettigan, 1870-1887
Dublin:
  Paul Cullen, 1852-1878
  Edward McCabe, 1879-1885
  William J. Walsh, 1885-1921
Cashel:
  Thomas William Croke, 1875-1902
Tuam:
  John MacHale, 1834-1881
  John MacEvilly, 1881-1902

Bishops of the Province of Armagh

Ardagh and Clonmacnoise:
  Bartholomew Woodlock, 1879-1894
Clogher:
  James Donnelly, 1865-1893
Derry:
  Francis Kelly, 1864-1889
Down and Connor:
  Patrick Dorrian, 1865-1885
  Patrick McAlister, 1886-1895
Dromore:
  John Pius Leahy, O.P., 1860-1890
Kilmore:
  Nicholas Conaty, 1865-1886
Meath:
  Thomas Nulty, 1866-1898
Raphoe:
  Michael Logue, 1879-1887

Bishops of the Province of Dublin

Ferns:
    Michael Warren, 1876-1884
    James Browne, 1884-1917
Kildare and Leighlin:
    James Walshe, 1856-1888
    James Lynch, C.M. (Coadjutor) 1869-1896
Ossory:
    Patrick F. Moran, 1872-1884
    Abraham Brownrigg, 1884-1928

Bishops of the Province of Cashel

Cork:
    William Delany, 1847-1886
    T. A. O'Callaghan, (Coadjutor) 1883-1916
Cloyne:
    James MacCarthy, 1874-1893
Kerry:
    Daniel McCarthy, 1878-1881
    Andrew Higgins, 1881-1889
Killaloe:
    Michael Flannery, 1858-1891
    James Ryan, (Coadjutor) 1872-1889
Limerick:
    George Butler, 1864-1886
Ross:
    William Fitzgerald, 1877-1897
Waterford:
    John Power, 1874-1886
    Pierce Power, (Coadjutor) 1886-1889

Bishops of the Province of Tuam

Achonry:
    Francis MacCormack, 1875-1887
Clonfert:
    Patrick Duggan, 1872-1896
    John Healy, (Coadjutor) 1884-1903
Elphin:
    Laurence Gillooly, C.M., 1858-1895
Galway:
    John MacEvilly, 1857-1881
    Thomas Carr, 1883-1886
Killala:
    Hugh Conway, 1873-1893

ABBREVIATIONS

K	—Kirby Papers
F.O.	—Foreign Office Papers
G	—Gillooly Papers
GR	—Granville Papers
OR	—O'Riordan Papers
C	—Croke Papers
S	—Smith Papers
Mc	—McCabe Papers
B	—Balfour Papers
W	—Walsh Papers
M	—Manning Papers
CAR	—Carnarvon Papers

Prologue

In the eight years between the death of Paul Cardinal Cullen, the archbishop of Dublin, in 1878 and the defeat of Gladstone's first Home Rule Bill in 1886, Charles Stewart Parnell created the modern Irish state. This is the story of the part played by the Roman Catholic Church in Ireland in the creation of that state. What makes the telling of this story so difficult is that there were actually two churches and two states in Ireland during this period—an Irish and a Roman church and an Irish and a British state—all in highly complex inter-relationship. These four historical forces, moreover, were not simply discrete quantities involved in a predictable relationship, but they were also always changing in themselves because of internal and external pressures. The Irish state in 1878, for example, was little more than an idea in the minds of some Irishmen. By 1886, however, that idea had been successfully focused, crystallized, and institutionalized by Parnell. Between 1878 and 1886, therefore, the Irish state was the most dynamic, not to say the most volatile element, in the whole complicated relationship between church and state in Ireland. The Irish Church, on the other hand, was a good deal more than an idea in 1878. In the previous twenty-five years, the Irish Church, both at home and abroad, had created a very formidable institutional base, and its particular dynamic, therefore, had less to do with an idea being realized than with an idea already crystallized attempting to change its focus. Before 1878, the Irish Church had concentrated on creating the necessary apparatus for the saving of souls, while after that date the Church's focus was to be centered more and more on how to take effective social and political action in a fundamentally revolutionary situation. In successfully institutionalizing itself before 1878, then, the Church had become a social and economic power in the state; and after 1878, it would not only have to take up its political and social responsibilities in the state, but it would also have to declare that the state was Irish and *not* British.

xxi

This story is primarily concerned, therefore, with how the Irish Church responded to the challenge presented by a revitalized Irish nationalism evoked by the process of creating the modern Irish state. Irishmen had indeed been Irish as long as they had been conscious of it, but more significantly perhaps, they had also been Cork men and Galway men, and Munster men and Connaught men, and some had even become west Britons and ultramontanes. The subtle process by which the Irish finally transcended their local and provincial origins, or even their more cosmopolitan and ideological allegiances between 1878 and 1886, and sublimated their old loyalties in a national political consciousness, certainly owes most to the political genius of Parnell. For it was Parnell who successfully focused that consciousness in the Land League by creating during 1879 a genuinely national grass-roots organization which made every tenant farmer in Ireland realize not only that he had a great deal in common with every other Irishman, but that in their recently acquired conscious unity there was dignity as well as power. In his launching of the Irish National League in 1882, furthermore, Parnell structured that consciousness he had focused in the Land League in a political organization that gave both coherence and substance to the idea of an Irish state. Finally, in the general elections of 1885 and 1886, he crystallized in his person as leader and institutionalized in the Irish Parliamentary party the deep conviction among Irishmen that their state would be soon as legal as it was then real.

The conversion of the Irish clergy in this great political revival was perhaps, after the conversion of the tenant farmers in the Land League agitation, the most significant factor in the creation of the Irish state. They too had not only to transcend their local and provincial origins as well as their cosmopolitan allegiances, but they also had to come to terms with what were deeper and perhaps more profound class and ideological loyalties. Their social and political status in Irish society was in a large measure unilaterally redefined for them between 1878 and 1884, and the adjustment was undoubtedly painful. In their somewhat diminished but more sharply focused social and political situation, the Irish clergy gradually came to realize how great their responsibilities were for maintaining basic order in a society in fundamental political and economic transition. The result of this growing awareness of their responsibilities on the part of the higher clergy, and the increasing sympathy with the developing national consciousness on the part of the lower clergy, was the securing in the autumn of 1884 of a very effective, if informal, clerical-nationalist alliance. The real difficulty in achieving this alliance, and why it took some six years to secure, was not only that the Irish Church had to overcome the reluctance of the majority of the Irish bishops and a large number of the senior clergy to enter even an informal concordat with the Parliamentary party led by Parnell, but it also had to convince the Roman Church that the shift in focus to the social and political needs of the Irish people was as essential to the saving of their souls as the creating of the necessary institutional base had been in the previous generation. Rome was, if anything, even more reluctant than the majority of the bishops about an *entente* with an Irish state that was hardly yet *de facto*, let alone *de jure*, especially when it had its own heart set on the resumption of diplomatic relations with a very real and legal British state. By 1886, however, the Roman Church was much disabused about the willingness of the British government to effect diplomatic relations, and the Irish bishops, after the agreement in the autumn of 1884, had worked out a very satisfactory *modus operandi* with Parnell and his party in regard to the basic rights and privileges of the Irish Church in the new Irish state. The result was that the British state in 1886 was finally faced with a formidable clerical-nationalist alliance, which had the tacit approval, if not the blessing, of Rome.

By 1886, then, the British state had lost the great game it had played for so many centuries in Ireland. An Irish state had been created in the minds of most Irishmen and the national and local political apparatus necessary to the functioning of that state was operative. That apparatus, moreover, was entirely in the hands of Parnell and his party. When Gladstone proceeded to give those executive, legislative, and judicial functions form in the first Home Rule bill, final notice was given that the ratification of the substance of that *de facto* by the British Parliament was really only a matter of time. After 1886, therefore, to talk about a solution to the Irish question, other than self-government, was not to face up to the realities of Irish political life. The crucial point to be made in this story, however, is that the Irish state could not perhaps have been made real and certainly not stable, before 1886 if the Irish Church had not been accommodated. If the Irish Church, moreover, had not accepted the accommodation when it did, the character of the Irish state would have been a great deal different from what it eventually did become. This early and timely definition of the Irish Church's place in the Irish state, in fact, not only contributed very materially to the character of that state, but to its eventual stability as well. For when the Irish state finally emerged in 1921 as legal as it was real, it did enter into its political inheritance with some of the most awkward and vexatious questions in the realm of church and state already long settled, and could proceed with greater confidence, therefore, to the rapid consolidation of the coup so recently made against the remnants of British rule in Ireland.

Part I

NEW DEPARTURES

I. New Departures

November, 1878 - December, 1879

Paul Cardinal Cullen was dead. The critical question now was who would succeed him as archbishop of Dublin. "Only two names," Michael Canon Verdon reported on November 21, 1878, to his old mentor, Tobias Kirby, rector of the Irish College in Rome, "are spoken of here as possible successors i.e. Dr. McCabe and Dr. Moran."[1] "As regards the election on the 28th inst.," Verdon explained, "it seems almost certain that Dr. McCabe will have a *very large* majority of the votes." "It is possible—but by *no means certain*," Verdon added, "that Dr. Moran's name will appear second on the list." "*Many*," he concluded significantly, "*are afraid of him*." Patrick Francis Moran had indeed acquired a forbidding reputation while bishop of Ossory. He was known as a strict, stern, and austere man, who in matters ecclesiastical was a fierce ultramontane. Moran was, in fact, made too much in the image and likeness of his late cousin, Cardinal Cullen, whose protégé and private secretary he had been before his promotion to the see of Ossory. The Dublin clergy were determined, therefore, if their suffrages meant anything at all, that their regret at the passing of the cardinal would not be so soon turned to grief.

The day after the usual celebration of the month's mind Mass in memory of the cardinal, the Dublin clergy, as was the customary procedure, met and commended three names—*dignissimus*, *dignior*, and *dignus*—to Rome as most worthy, more worthy, and worthy for their widowed see. McCabe was, as Verdon had predicted he would be, the overwhelming choice of the Dublin clergy with forty-three votes, while Moran received only seven, and Bartholomew Woodlock, rector of the moribund Catholic University of Ireland, rounded out the *terna* with one vote. Edward McCabe had been appointed auxiliary bishop to Cardinal Cullen in 1877, when it

---

[1] Kirby Papers(K), Archives of the Irish College, Rome.

became apparent that the heavy pastoral and administrative duties were becoming too much for the aging cardinal. McCabe was a conscientious, hard-working, and unassuming man, who seemed unique only in that he was one of the few priests trained in the national seminary at Maynooth ever to find favor with the cardinal. "I am sure," McCabe confessed to Kirby on November 29, enclosing the commendation of the Dublin clergy for Rome, "that the result must have been a surprise to you: It certainly was to me, for I thought the clergy of Dublin would have been too wise and good to place my most unworthy name first on the list"(K). "But I rest easy," he concluded amiably, "that Rome will prove itself wiser than Dublin."

Moran, who had not only been trained in Rome at the Irish College but had served some ten years as Kirby's vice-rector, was also in close touch with his old friend and mentor. The most absurd rumors, Moran had early reported to Kirby, were afloat about the appointment to Dublin.[2] Some newspapers, he explained to Kirby on November 7, had even gone so far as to urge the appointment of Newman(K). Such a thing, Moran argued, obviously somewhat at sea himself, would be ruinous to the best interests of the Holy Faith in Ireland, since Newman was cast in the English mold and did not, therefore understand the Irish. The solitary failure, Moran reminded Kirby, among Irish ecclesiastical institutions was the Catholic University, which had been organized by Newman. "It has no students," he confided revealingly, "and no life and if we continue to uphold it by annual subscriptions it is only through respect for the cause of Catholic Education which it nominally represents." All the great institutions of the Dublin archdiocese, Moran concluded, depended on the voluntary contributions of the faithful, and goodbye to them if Newman were appointed. This account of why Newman would not do for Dublin tells perhaps more about Moran's own lack of confidence in Roman procedures than it does about the inadequacies of Newman.

At first, Moran appeared to accept the overwhelming commendation of the Dublin clergy in favor of McCabe with very good grace. The ususal meeting of the bishops of the

---

[2] K, November 3, 1878.

Dublin province to report to Rome on the commendation of the clergy, Moran informed Kirby on November 29, would be held on December 9, and he also expressed the hope that "we will all unanimously recommend Dr. McCabe"(K). Sometime in the ten-day interval between this letter and the bishops' meeting, however, Moran had a change of heart. When the bishops did convene, on December 9, Moran presented a short statement in which, as he explained to Kirby the following day, though he had the greatest regard for McCabe's humility, zeal, and devotedness, he feared that McCabe "would not be able to carry on the necessary correspondence with the Holy See"(K). Fortunately, McCabe had discreetly absented himself from the meeting. After making his statement, which amounted to an unabashed vote of confidence in himself, Moran withdrew to allow his fellow suffragans to make their report on the clergy's commendation to the Congregation of Propaganda, which would then make its own recommendations to the pope for the appointment to Dublin.

Though Moran, it seems, did not personally interfere further in the matter, he did write Kirby some ten days after the bishops met, warning him that others might be interfering. "The Abp. of Cashel and his suffragans," Moran reported to Kirby on December 20, "are writing to Propaganda about Dublin, but I do not know the purport of their letter"(K). Moran, however, proved to be somewhat overanxious. The archbishop of Cashel, Thomas W. Croke, had, in fact, written Kirby a "confidential" letter only two days before on December 18, explaining that though he had been asked to write by several bishops, he did not like to do so without being invited by Propaganda(K). Croke explained in the course of his letter that, since Dublin was no ordinary see, he felt all the bishops had an interest in it. He also informed Kirby that he thought Moran's fellow suffragans had reported to Propaganda in favor of McCabe. Croke's letter provided Kirby with the opportunity, if indeed he needed one, to exert his not inconsiderable influence at Rome in favor of Moran. Kirby's own position had been greatly improved in Rome when his old friend, Cardinal Pecci, was elevated early in 1878 as Leo XIII. Moreover, the new cardinal prefect and secretary of Propaganda were both old friends as well. Moran was also well known and liked by the new pope. Since Moran not only spoke and wrote Italian fluently, but had been intimately associated with almost all important Irish and British imperial business done at Rome for nearly twenty years, he was in especial favor at the Propaganda.

Kirby soon informed Croke, who had also been his student in the Irish College, that Propaganda would be pleased to have a letter from him about the vacant see of Dublin. "I send off by this post to Propaganda," Croke responded in a letter marked "private," on January 3, 1879, "the strongest letter I could write in favor of Dr. M."(K). "I will now tell you a *secret*," Croke confided to the man who had perhaps done the most to secure his own appointment to the see of Cashel nearly four years before, "Dr. Moran is most unpopular amongst the Bishops, and I do not think a single Irish Bp. but myself would write in his favor." "Personally," continued Croke, "I don't favor him. But I believe he is a good man, and a clever man, and vastly more fitted for Dublin than Dr. McCabe. Hence my support for him." "The Bishops," Croke added revealingly, "would support Dr. McCabe simply because he is a Maynooth man." "I write all this to you," concluded Croke, "in strictest confidence: and, indeed, I do not think I would write as much to any living man." "Let me hear from you," he added finally, "how the land lies as soon as possible."

"What about Dublin," Croke inquired impatiently of Kirby less than two weeks later on January 15, "and what about my letter to Propaganda. Has it arrived safely?"(K). "I was just posting this," he added in a hurried postscript, "when Postman handed me yours of the 11th inst. All right. I sincerely hope Dr. M. will be appointed." Some two weeks later, in early February, Kirby obviously wrote Moran that Rome would not decide about Dublin quickly, for Moran replied on February 7 that a delay would not do much harm(K). Even Croke, whose store of patience was never large, managed to control himself for another five weeks. "Let me have," he finally wrote Kirby on March 14, "just one line by return to say, when Dublin will be decided and *how*"(K). Propaganda did, in fact, decide the question at its next congregation the following week. They finally recommended McCabe to the pope, who then appointed him archbishop of Dublin. Kirby immediately telegraphed the news of the decision on March 23 to both McCabe and Moran. McCabe replied, on March 25, with a simple and dignified thank-you note, while Moran had written the day before that he was pleased that the long period of uncertainty was over(K). Moran, however, had not changed his mind about McCabe's fitness for Dublin. "He will have," Moran had noted a little sourly in his letter to Kirby on March 24, "great difficulties to contend against in Dublin and I fear very much his strength will be unequal to the task"(K).

Commendation by the clergy, report by the bishops, and recommendation by Propaganda to the pope for his authoritative approval had been the formal mode of procedure in appointments to Irish sees for nearly fifty years. Why then did Propaganda delay some four months in making a decision which seemed obvious in the first place? The answer to this question reveals a good deal about the subtleties of Roman ecclesiastical administration. The procedure in Irish episcopal appointments, especially during the ascendancy of Cardinal Cullen, had been attended to more in the breach than in the observance. Scarcely an appointment had been made, in fact, in thirty years which had not passed under the approving eye of the cardinal. A year or two earlier, in the pontificate of Pius IX, when precedent had become stronger than procedure, Moran would have been the much more likely choice than McCabe. The new pope, Leo XIII, however, was cautiously feeling his way and appeared extremely anxious, moreover, to change the image of the Papacy he had inherited from his predecessor.[3] The overwhelming vote of the Dublin clergy, the unanimous report of the provincial bishops, and the general impression abroad that McCabe had, in fact, been the choice of the late cardinal as his auxiliary, all made Propaganda reluctant to violate procedure when there was no good reason or apparent need to do so.[4] The patent superiority of Moran in talent and ability, his Roman connections, and Kirby's exertions on his behalf all had resulted, on the other hand, in that favorite Roman ecclesiastical pastime—delay.

---

[3] Foreign Office Papers(F.O.), 170/258, Great Britain, Public Record Office, London. Sir Augustus Paget to the Earl of Derby, April 1, 1878: "All the acts of the present pontiff show him to be animated as yet by a very different spirit from that of his predecessor and hence much agitation and irritation amongst the Jesuits and ultramontane faction."

[4] K, December 30, 1878. See for comment of John MacEvilly, coadjutor to the archbishop of Tuam: "We were all delighted to see how the Dublin clergy endorsed by their act, the approbation of the Cardinal's administration. For in this light was their act regarded by all the Cardinal's friends and admirers."

When Cardinal Cullen died, the Irish Church lost its great ultramontane anchor. The drift from Rome, which was just perceptible before his death, was only partially corrected by the appointment of McCabe. That good man, whose succession to Dublin seemed to give more satisfaction than joy in Ireland, would not long survive the terrible storms that were about to break on the Irish Church. Whether even so effective a make-weight as the cardinal, in fact, could have counted for much in the powerful currents soon to be set in motion is doubtful. In the next few years, Irish confidence in Rome was to be severely shaken by a series of unexpected shocks from that quarter. The first of these, significantly enough, came shortly after the death of the cardinal. About a year before his death, the Irish Christian Brothers, a very large teaching order, had appealed to Rome about several statutes passed among the many at the Synod of Maynooth in 1875 by the Irish bishops for the good governance of the Irish Church. In their memorial to Rome the Brothers had asked that their houses and internal affairs be exempt from episcopal visitation. They also wanted to exclude the bishops and parish priests from examining in their schools in secular subjects, but were willing to allow them to examine their pupils in the catechism. "Their pretensions on this score," Cardinal Cullen remarked to Laurence Gillooly, the bishop of Elphin, on January 29, 1878, when Propaganda had forwarded him the Brothers' memorial for his reply, "are much higher than those of the government."[5] "The National Board," he pointed out to Gillooly in going to the heart of the matter, "allows the P.P.'s as managers to examine in everything taught in the schools." A few days later Cullen informed Kirby that he and the bishops of his province had drawn up a reply for Propaganda. "I think it is made quite clear," he commented characteristically on February 1, "that nihil innovandum est"(K).

A week later, Pius IX was dead, and the cardinal set out for Rome to attend the conclave. While en route, however, Cardinal Pecci was elevated as Leo XIII, and Cullen decided to pursue a more leisurely pace, not arriving in Rome until early March, when the coronation and the festivities were over. Once he reached Rome, however, the cardinal remained there for nearly three months. There were many reasons why

---

[5] Gillooly Papers(G), Archives of the Diocese of Elphin, Sligo.

Provinces and Dioceses of IRELAND

Raphoe

Derry

Down & Connor

ARMAGH

Dromore

Clogher

Armagh

Killala

Achonry

Kilmore

Ardagh & Clonmacnois

Elphin

Meath

Tuam

TUAM

Galway,

Clonfert

Kildare & Leighlin

Dublin

Kilmacduagh & Kilfenora

Tuam

DUBLIN

Killaloe

Ossory

Ferns

Cashel & Emly

Limerick

Waterford & Lismore

CASHEL

Kerry

Cloyne

Cork

Ross

—— Ecclesiastical Provinces

— Dioceses Boundary

0   60   120
miles

N

MAP 1.

he should have extended his stay for so long a period of time. He was not only in his seventy-fourth year, but his physical stamina of late had been undermined by a nagging and troublesome cough, and Rome was certainly a healthier place than Dublin for him to be in the late winter and early spring. There was also, of course, the inevitable Irish business to be conducted at Propaganda, and there were two items that evidently had priority in the cardinal's mind. The first was how the archbishop of Tuam, John MacHale, was to be persuaded to give over effective control to the coadjutor archbishop recently imposed on him by Rome without creating a public scandal. The other was to block the Christian Brothers' appeal against the statutes of the Synod of Maynooth which concerned them and their schools. The cardinal, moreover, had not only been an acute connoisseur of ecclesiastical power all his life, but what was even more important, he had always realized and understood that Rome had been the real source of his power in Ireland. Rome was, therefore, the critical place for him to be when the new pope might begin to rearrange all the old power relationships. While the cardinal partially managed to recover his health in Rome, as well as reassure himself that his power base there was still secure, neither the Tuam nor the Christian Brothers' cases were settled when he finally set out for Dublin in early June.

"I suppose you will soon be able," Moran hinted broadly to Kirby, some four months later on October 21, and three days before the cardinal died, "to let us know the decision of Propaganda about the Xtian Brothers"(K). "The news," Moran wrote Kirby again, three weeks later on December 11, "which you have given about the Christian Brothers' case is very serious indeed. It will I fear undo in great part the good which was hoped for from the Maynooth Decrees"(K). "I fear too," continued Moran, who did not panic easily, "that the result will be detrimental to the Xtian Brothers themselves, as no Bishop will now be willing to admit them into his Diocese and probably many of their present houses will be closed." "We have been startled here," wrote the late cardinal's secretary, P. J. Tynan, two days after Moran, "by the announcement made by the Christian Brothers that Rome has at last decided altogether in their favour"(K). "As far as I can learn the opinions of the Bishops," he continued, emphasizing Moran's point, "I am sure that a decision in their favour would be the very worst thing that could happen for themselves, as it would be followed in a great many dioceses by their expulsion from their schools, which are parochial property." "There is a rumour, here," wrote the coadjutor to the archbishop of Tuam, John MacEvilly, some two weeks later on December 30, to Kirby, "that the Christian Brothers succeeded [*sic*] in their appeal against the Bishops"(K). "If they did," he warned, "time will tell that they are doomed. Neither the Bishops or P.P. ['s] will have collections for them." "Moreover," he concluded meaningfully, if vaguely, "it would sow the seeds of discord, which, I fear is [*sic*] already appearing."

Three weeks later MacEvilly was both more apprehensive and more explicit. "The rumour about the adverse decision on the subject of the Christian Brothers' appeal," he reported to Kirby on January 23, 1879, "has produced a fearful spirit of discontent among the Bishops and Priests. It *wont end well*"(K). "It is not what we wanted," he added for good measure, "in our unequal struggles with a hostile Government on the vital subject of Education. I gave my views and those of the Province very strongly to the Propaganda some months ago at the instance of our own dear Cardinal when he was last at Rome." A month later, when the Irish bishops assembled on February 17, to protest the government's ignoring the subject of Irish university education in the measures announced for the coming session of Parliament, they also considered the rescript from Propaganda upholding the appeal of the Christian Brothers. "The Bishops," Moran reported to Kirby on February 21, "were unanimous in the Resolution that the Holy See be requested to reconsider the decision forwarded to us"(K). The archbishop of Armagh, Daniel McGettigan, and he, Moran added, were appointed to go to Rome and explain the views of the bishops. Earlier that same week MacEvilly had also written Kirby, though somewhat more heatedly, about both London and Rome. "We have been," he charged on Ash Wednesday, February 19, "treated scandalously by the Government regarding University Education"(K). "Their organs held out every hope to the last moment," he explained, "and then dashed them to the ground. Did any Country ever suffer so much for the faith & attachment to the See of Peter?" "The late decision," he continued, reminded of Rome, "in the case of the Christian brothers and other matters have caused a very ugly feeling among the most devoted children of the H. See in this country. I never knew in my time anything like it. I am no alarmist but I see that *affection* is greatly on the wane, obedience of course must continue." "The knowledge now become general," he added in conclusion, coming finally to what was really on his mind, "that defiance has been effectively hurled at the H. See in a *certain quarter* here regarding which I shall say nothing, has done a world of mischief in this Province to the Sacred cause of authority."

The "*certain quarter*," of course, referred to that other item of Irish business the cardinal had failed to settle on his final visit to Rome. John MacHale, the archbishop of Tuam, who was in his eighty-seventh year in 1878, had been both Rome's thorn and Cullen's cross for well over thirty years. One of the last acts of Pius IX was to impose John MacEvilly as coadjutor with the right of succession on MacHale over his most strenuous protests. From the date of MacEvilly's appointment on February 2, 1878, MacHale studiously ignored him. He refused, in fact, to share any part of his revenue with him, and continued to manage the archdiocese through his very capable vicar general and nephew, Dr. Thomas MacHale. MacEvilly early complained to Kirby, on February 5, that he had acquired only the trappings of power in his elevation and not its substance(K). While in Rome from February to June, therefore, Cullen did his best to persuade Propaganda to force MacHale to retire gracefully in favor of MacEvilly. Cullen obviously thought he had succeeded, for he wrote as much to Laurence Gillooly, bishop of Elphin and senior suffragan in the Province of Tuam. "I may tell your Lordship *in confidence*," he wrote from the Irish College in Paris on his way home on June 8, 1878, "that Propaganda with the sanction of his Holiness wrote to Dr. MacHale to give up all powers to Dr. MacEvilly immediately, adding that if he did not do so, his Holiness will give them himself after 30 days from the date of the letter"(G). "I hope," concluded Cullen, "his Grace will set things right." His Grace of Tuam, however, would not bend, and as the months slipped by, Rome seemed less inclined to proceed with her promise to break him. Cullen obviously counseled patience, for as long as he was alive, MacEvilly did not broach the matter to Kirby. After the cardinal's death, however, MacEvilly's complaints about his anomalous position were less guarded and steadily grew more strident.[6] "As patience has its limits," he finally wrote Kirby in exasperation on April 2, 1879, when MacHale attempted to find another bishop to ordain priests for Tuam, "and as I am sufficiently trampled on already by not being allowed to remedy some abuses from which souls are being eternally lost, and which will soon become irremediable, I certainly will protest against any such treatment any longer, and call for redress from the H. See"(K). From MacEvilly's other remarks to Kirby, it was obvious that Rome was, as usual, attempting to gain time by calling for more information before proceeding to the most unusual course of deposing an archbishop. "The state of that Diocese," MacEvilly then declared, "is something awful. It is simply folly for any other Bishops to give any advice to H. See about it, save the Bishops of Clonfert and Achonry who alone know of these crying evils."

Indeed, the case of the Patriarch of the West, or the Lion of the Fold of Judah, as the admirers of Archbishop MacHale variously liked to refer to him, presented an extraordinary problem for Rome. Why this was so had mainly to do with the fact that for nearly sixty years MacHale had been the most persistent and bitter critic of British rule in Ireland. In consistently supporting at every turn that Irish theme which transcended all others—nationalism—he had built up in the Irish mind at home and abroad the image of a patriot bishop. To depose him in his old age, therefore, would simply antagonize the whole of Irish nationalist opinion at a stroke. Still, from the pastoral point of view and the cure of souls, the condition of the archdiocese of Tuam was nothing less than deplorable. The diocese was understaffed, only relatives of the archbishop received preferment, the diocesan seminary was heavily in debt, Protestant missionaries were making converts in Connemara, the diocese was riddled with secret societies, the clergy were denouncing each other and their parishioners publicly, the archbishop himself was certainly infirm in body and probably in mind.[7] By doing nothing, given the arch-

---

[6] K, December 30, 1878; Ash Wednesday [February 19], 1879.
[7] The evidence of the deplorable state of the archdiocese of Tuam from a pastoral point of view is overwhelming. See K, January 8, 1878, Sister M. Teresa White; January 14, 1878, Mrs. E. M. Forbes; January 14, 1878, John MacEvilly; February 10, 1878, John MacEvilly.

bishop's advanced age, Rome undoubtedly hoped that Providence would soon provide them with the solution. The archbishop, however, defied all expectations, and with each passing month the contending parties only became more vexed with each other and Rome.

Meanwhile, about a month after the news of the Christian Brothers' successful appeal against the bishops reached Ireland, the president of the Peter's Pence Association in Rome, Prince Altieri, circularized the bishops asking them for an extraordinary collection for March in celebration of the first anniversary of the consecration of Leo XIII. This was, unfortunately, a most inopportune time to press for a collection because Ireland had just been through two successive bad harvests and the winter of 1878-1879 was especially severe. "This is the worst year since 50," wrote the newly appointed bishop of Kerry, Daniel McCarthy, from Killarney on February 14, 1879, "crops fallen entirely here. We certainly would have the direst distress—perhaps famine—only that imported meal (Indian) and flour are very cheap"(K). "Our offering," he reassured Kirby, "will be good—considering the times." The new bishop of Kerry, however, proved the exception rather than the rule among the Irish bishops in 1879. "I would make a collection for the Pope this year," T. W. Croke, the archbishop of Cashel, had explained to Kirby on January 15, "were it not for a collection I am making for our Cathedral. I have already laid out nearly £10,000. Of this sum I got £6,000 within the past year"(K). The bishop of Cloyne, James McCarthy, also pleaded poverty to Kirby in the name of his cathedral on February 24 and added that he and the other bishops of the province of Cashel had decided not to make the special collection because of the bad times(K). He did, however, forward some £350 which had been collected as part of the regular collection, reminding Kirby that he had contributed a £1,000 at the pontifical jubilee of Pius IX in 1877, and consoling him with the promise that he would bring another £1,000 when he visited Rome the following year. The crucial decision, however, had come from the vacant see of Dublin, which under Cardinal Cullen had always taken the lead in Peter's Pence by making up at least one quarter of the total Irish contribution in any given year. "I fear very much," McCabe had written Kirby from Maynooth on January 26, 1879, breaking the news gently, "that such an appeal now will injure the regular annual Collection, which in Dublin is now a matter of course. But as I say this in the interest of the general Collection, we will hold a Collection if the Authorities in Rome think it right"(K). Two weeks later on February 12, McCabe wrote again, enclosing a letter from T. J. O'Reilly, president of the St. Peter's Pence Confraternity in Dublin(K). Father O'Reilly had pointed out to McCabe on January 30, that the regular collection, which took place every year in Dublin at the end of June, had yielded over the last ten years some £25,000, and that a special collection in March would certainly injure the annual collection(K). McCabe concurred in Father O'Reilly's opinion and thought that it would be wiser under the circumstances to forego the special collection.

No one realized, of course, the success of the Christian Brothers' appeal, the delay in any decision about the archbishop of Tuam, and the inopportune special collection were but the beginnings of a serious rift with Rome. For thirty years Cardinal Cullen had been the loyal and devoted servant of Pius IX in Ireland. He had managed to impose in those years an authoritative calm on the Irish Church and to create at the same time an ultramontane Catholicism effective enough to contain Irish nationalism. He was able to do this not only because he was prudent, willful, and stubborn, but because he had the almost unqualified support of Rome in all Irish ecclesiastical patronage and especially in episcopal appointments. The price paid for this power, however, was high, for independence gave way to prudence, affection to obedience, and respect to fear. Besides Rome's confidence, and his own ability to persevere, Cullen was also most fortunate in that his thirty years of ascendancy in the Church were accompanied by an unparalleled relative economic prosperity and a comparative political tranquility. Shortly before his death, however, the economic and political situations radically began to change. The economic prosperity of the mid-Victorian heyday in Ireland began to fade as bad harvest succeeded bad harvest and competition from the New World completed the ruin by undermining agricultural prices. At the same time, the Irish nationalism, which the cardinal had done so much to contain, began to find a new meaning and focus in the ambitions of a young politician named Charles Stewart Parnell. Moreover, though the cardinal did not live long enough to appreciate the change, the policy of Leo XIII was not to be the policy of Cullen's old friend and patron, Pius IX. "We live in troubled times," McCabe had written Kirby prophetically on January 17, 1879, less than three months after the death of the cardinal, "and I fear very very much that they are only the precursor of days of greater calamity"(K).

"We have no local news," a friend in Limerick had written a lonely young Irish seminarian in Rome in September, 1877, "that could interest you."[8] "The late obstruction movement in Parliament," he noted, "and the Eastern War monopolize the newspapers." "Farmers," he then added more significantly than he knew, "had never had such a hard tug with the harvest." Indeed, when another bad harvest had followed in 1878, a difficult situation became dangerous. When the winter and spring of 1878-1879 turned unusually cold and then wet, the poor who were already destitute after two bad harvests became desperate at the prospect of a third. The bishop of the very wealthy diocese of Meath, Thomas Nulty, wrote Kirby on May 29, that the last winter was the most severe he could ever remember(K). The cold had been accompanied by drought until the middle of May, and though the rain had finally come, the cold persisted. The result was that the planting was now a month behind. "I never remember," Nulty added to the tale of woe, "to have seen such depression in trade and such universal poverty among the farming and grazing classes in this Diocese." "We have scores," he observed, "of most respectable farmers and Graziers in this Diocese who have become bankrupt." "Only think of plenty of the finest American beef," he exclaimed, "for sale this moment in Mullingar!" "Probably," he noted in an afterthought, "I will dine on some of it today." "Mullingar," Nulty concluded in a futile burst of local patriotism, "was famous for the superiority of its Beef and Mutton and only imagine these Americans under-selling us even here."

"The depression in business," wrote the very shrewd bishop of Cork, William Delany, to Kirby three weeks later, "is so severe, that we have not been able to send our annual tribute

---

[8] O'Riordan Papers(OR), Archives of the Irish College, Rome. September 20, 1877, J. Mulcahy to Michael O'Riordan.

to the Holy Father."[9] "But as we never failed as yet," he promised, "I will make every effort to sustain our character." The promise from Limerick, however, was somewhat less reassuring. John Bourke, the parish priest of Pallaskenry, reported the usual collection for the pope would be taken up on July 6. "I am sorry to tell you," he explained to Kirby, "that I fear it won't be as good as last time for our people are suffering a good deal from the great depression of the times, besides their various ecclesiastical wants which are nowadays very great from the number of Churches that are being built some of them like my own approaching completion."[10] Worse yet was the news from the bishop of Waterford. "The diocese," John Power bluntly informed Kirby on July 3, "having recently contributed a very large offering to his late Holiness, the flock would not feel pleased to be again called on within so short a time"(K). "Besides," he added, attempting to soften his refusal as best he could, "the present year is one of unprecedented depression all over Ireland—town and country." "Since the famine time," he concluded somberly, "there has not been such desponding among all classes [as] at present. Hence the present time would be most unfavourable to appeal to the flock."

"The weather," reported the bishop of Derry on July 10, "has been and is still very cold in Ireland"(K). "The harvest," he warned ominously, "will be late on account of the cold and continual rain." "I trust in God," he concluded hopefully, "we shall soon have a change for the better." "Our weather," the bishop of Kerry explained to Kirby several days later, on July 14, from the other end of Ireland, "is very unfavourable— almost constant rain"(K). "If we have another bad harvest," he concluded in despair, "our hopes will be blighted—and our people obliged to leave the country." "Since the Famine years," wrote Denis Hallinan to Kirby on September 18, from Newcastlewest in the diocese of Limerick, "the prospects of this country were never so hopeless"(K). "There is an appeal," he explained pathetically, "for reduction of rent from one end of the land to the other: to be follwed, I suppose, by the cry of distress and hunger when winter comes round." "May God,"

---

[9] K, June 21, 1879. Delany eventually sent the usual £600 on November 6, 1879.

[10] K, June 30, 1879. John Butler, the Bishop of Limerick, eventually forwarded £681-10-0 on October 29, 1879. The average contribution from Limerick had been about £1,000 annually.

he concluded, "help our poor people." "I fear," the very able and intrepid bishop of Down and Connor, Patrick Dorrian, wrote Kirby from Belfast on September 24, "we are in for a famine in Ireland next year. God's will be done"(K).

Not everyone in Ireland, however, was yet so disheartened that they were willing to resign the fate of the Irish people again into God's hands alone. The emergence of a new leadership at this critical moment, in fact, saved the Irish people from a repetition of that abject submission they had made in their bewilderment forty years before during the Great Famine. The prime mover among these new men was Michael Davitt. He, and most of those who joined him in the land agitation, were or had been members of the secret, oathbound, and revolutionary Irish Republican, or Fenian, Brotherhood. Davitt had, in fact, only recently been provisionally released from Dartmoor Prison where he had served over seven years of a fifteen-year sentence for his Fenian activities. His release had been mainly the result of the efforts of his old friend and fellow Fenian, John O'Connor Power, who with his young parliamentary colleague, Charles Stewart Parnell, had brought the brutalities Davitt had suffered under the penal servitude system to the attention of the House of Commons by obstructing its business. Since his release Davitt had been endeavoring to bring the various nationalist groups, revolutionary and constitutional, together in one united movement. By the spring of 1879 he had convinced all but the most extreme of the Fenians in Ireland and America of the necessity of a "new departure" if British domination in Ireland was ever to be brought to an end. He had been unable, however, to persuade Parnell to take up the leadership of a combined political and agrarian agitation around which he was convinced Irish nationalist opinion could be rallied and united.[11]

The land agitation, of which Davitt was the spark and the organizer, actually began with a formidable protest meeting at Irishtown, on Sunday, April 20, 1879, in County Mayo in the west of Ireland. This meeting was particularly interesting because the landlord who was threatening his tenants with

---

[11] T. W. Moody, "The New Departure in Irish Politics, 1878-9," *Essays in British and Irish History*, ed. by M. A. Cronne, T. W. Moody, and D. B. Quinn (London, 1949), pp. 303-333.

eviction if they did not pay their arrears in rent was a Catholic priest. The tenants explained to Davitt that because Geoffry Canon Burke, who was the executor of the estate under his brother's will, was a clergyman, they could not even obtain a hearing in the local press. The speakers, in shattering the conspiracy of silence at Irishtown, besides protesting the action of Canon Burke, demanded a reduction of rents and denounced the whole landlord system. The meeting was a great success, for Canon Burke capitulated a few days later and reduced the rent on his estate by one quarter, or five shillings in the pound. Naturally, the news spread, and there were immediate requests from other parts of Mayo for protest meetings. Davitt organized another meeting for Westport on Sunday, June 8, 1878, and invited Parnell to attend and speak. Many of the Mayo altars, meanwhile, rang with warnings and denunciations of meetings organized by "irresponsible people," who had demonstrated their "disrespect" for the clergy.[12] The clerical rumbling was finally climaxed three days before the Westport meeting by the following remarkable letter from the archbishop of Tuam to the editor of the *Freeman's Journal:*

Dear Sir, —In a telegraphic message exhibited towards the end of last week in a public room of this town, an Irish member of Parliament has unwittingly expressed his readiness to attend a meeting convened in a mysterious and disorderly manner, which is to be held, it seems, in Westport on Sunday next. Of the sympathy of the Catholic clergy for the rack-rented tenantry of Ireland, and of their willingness to cooperate earnestly in redressing their grievances, abundant evidence exists in historic Mayo, as elsewhere. But night patrolling, acts and words of menace, with arms in hand, the profanation of what is most sacred in religion—all the result of lawless and occult association, eminently merit the solemn condemnation of the ministers of religion, as directly tending to impiety and disorder in Church and in society. Against such combinations in this diocese, organised by a few designing men, who, instead of the well-being of the community, seek only to promote their personal interests, the faithful clergy will not fail to raise their warning voices, and to point out to the people that unhallowed combinations lead invariably to disaster and to the firmer rivet-

---

[12] Michael Davitt, *The Fall of Feudalism in Ireland* (London, 1904), pp. 141-152.

ing of the chains by which we are unhappily bound as a subordinate people to a dominant race. I remain, dear sir,

Faithfully yours,
+ John, Archbishop of Tuam[13]

Whether this letter was written by the archbishop, or his very able vicar general and nephew, is indeed a moot point. There can hardly be any doubt, however, that it was written for Roman rather than Irish consumption. The archbishop and his advisers were only too aware that Rome was eager for an excuse to depose him in favor of his coadjutor. "I am exceedingly rejoiced to learn by your letters," Archbishop McCabe wrote Kirby at the end of June, 1879, "that the S. Congregation is going to send Dr. MacEvilly into the Diocese of Tuam."[14] "From all I can learn," continued McCabe, who was a fair man, "from persons competent to give an opinion of the state of things in that part of the Irish Church, and yet not disposed to exaggerate, the state of Religion is deplorable." "The poor old A.B. is, I expect," McCabe then noted, "a mere automaton in the hands of a Party." "The accounts given," he pointed out, "of the work he is doing are utterly absurd. If he were touching on 50 years of age instead of 90, he could scarcely accomplish them." "I fear," he warned, "if Dr. MacEvilly's translation be much longer deferred he will go to Tuam too late."

Some two months later, armed with a letter from the cardinal prefect of Propaganda, MacEvilly arrived in Tuam. "The letter from the Cardinal," McCabe informed Kirby on September 1, "was very strong and they [sic] may set aside any serious opposition, but I fear if Dr. MacHale is to remain Vicar General or in other words acting Archbishop, that very little will be at the disposal of the Coadjutor"(K). Matters turned out exactly as McCabe feared they would. The archbishop not only refused to see his coadjutor, but informed him through his vicar general that, if indeed he had to resign his see, he felt it incumbent on him to publish the reason for his resignation, and that would be that Rome had forced on him a prelate whose appointment he had

---

[13] *Ibid.*, p. 253. Archbishop MacHale's letter is dated June 5, 1879, from Westport.
[14] K, no date; received June 30, 1879.

opposed.[15] Since Archbishop MacHale refused to give way
quietly before the general mandate in the cardinal prefect's
letter, and threatened, moreover, to create a public scandal if
he were deposed, the next move was up to Rome. As was
usual, however, Rome made no move. "The position of the
Coadjutor of Tuam," McCabe wrote Kirby on December 29,
1879, four months after the cardinal's strong letter, "is almost
untenable. He had no authority to interpose. The Archbishop
will not see him and all his suggestions are disregarded"(K).
"Can nothing more," McCabe inquired discreetly, "be done by
Propaganda?"

Meanwhile, Parnell was not intimidated by either the
clerical or the episcopal injunctions and made a most effective
speech at Westport. "A fair rent," he told the tenants who had
assembled in their thousands to hear him, "is a rent a tenant
can reasonably pay according to the times."[16] "Now, what
must we do," Parnell then asked. "in order to induce the landlords to see the position?" "You must show the landlords," he replied, "that you intend to hold a firm grip on your
homesteads and lands. You must not allow yourselves to be
dispossessed as you were dispossessed in 1847. You must not
allow your small holdings to be turned into large ones." "I
should be deceiving you," he then candidly confessed, "if I
told you that there was any use in relying upon the exertions
of the Irish members of Parliament on your behalf." "I think
that if your members were determined and resolute," Parnell
explained, "they could help you; but I am afraid they won't."
"I hope that I may be wrong, and that you may rely upon the
constitutional action of your parliamentary representatives in
this sore time of your need and trial," he counseled in conclusion, "but above all things remember that God helps him who
helps himself, and that by showing such a public spirit as you
have shown here to-day, by coming in your thousands in the
face of every difficulty, you will do more to show the landlords
the necessity of dealing justly with you than if you have 150
Irish members in the House of Commons."

In noting that some 8,000 tenants had come "in the face of

---

[15] K. Letter dated August 2, 1879, should be September 2, 1879. See also letter
dated September 1, 1879, for MacEvilly's account of his interviews with Dr. Thomas
MacHale.

[16] R. Barry O'Brien, *The Life of Charles Stewart Parnell* (London, 1910), pp. 146-
147.

every difficulty," Parnell was, of course, alluding discreetly to the clerical opposition to the meeting. At this time Parnell, who was ambitious for supreme political power, was attempting to gather all the various strands of that power into his own hands in order to twist them into an Irish nationalist rope. One of the most important of those strands was the Roman Catholic clergy, and only the Irish people could deliver them into his hands. Davitt has reported how Parnell soon learned all the facts concerning the Irishtown meeting. "He was intensely interested," Davitt shrewdly observed, "especially about the clerical opposition, and this hostility may, perhaps, have been one reason why he showed some disinclination for a time to become identified with the movement."[17] Parnell's instincts were supremely political in that power was his end and politics his means. When he asked Charles Kickham, supreme head of the Irish Republican Brotherhood, about this time whether he thought "that the people feel very keenly on the land question,"[18] "Feel keenly on the land question?" Kickham, whose means, as head of the revolutionary party in Ireland, was conspiracy, replied regretfully, "I am only sorry to say that I think that they would go to hell for it."

At the Westport meeting, therefore, Parnell must have realized that in the land agitation he had the possible means of forcing his leadership on a reluctant clergy. He was certainly reassured a month later when a by-election allowed him to test his strength against the clerical opposition in County Clare at Ennis. He crossed over from Westminster and campaigned vigorously for his personal nominee, Lysaght Finegan, who was opposed by William O'Brien, a Whig Catholic barrister and the favorite of the local bishop and priests. "The member for Ennis is dead," wrote a young priest, W. J. Halpin, on July 21, from Limerick to a friend in Rome, "and the election is in full swing there, the bishop and priests making fools of themselves as usual"(OR). "Parnell is down there supporting his candidate," he continued, "who by all account is the right man but the *Clargy* should have their man also. . . ." "In a short time," he concluded dryly, "it will be enough to have any man defeated if the priests go for him." "If Ennis had been lost," Parnell later remarked, "it would have satisfied me that the

---

[17] Davitt, *op. cit.*, p. 151.
[18] O'Brien, *op. cit.*, p. 146.

priests were supreme in Irish politics."[19]

Why then did Parnell still hold back in August when Davitt again offered him the leadership of the agrarian agitation? By June he was the real leader of the Home Rule movement in the country and in Parliament; Davitt had assured him of the support of the Fenian rank and file; John Devoy, head of the powerful Clan na Gael in America, had pledged the necessary financial support; the clergy had been humbled, and still Parnell hesitated. The traditional reasons offered for his hesitation make some superficial sense, but they are not really convincing. Parnell did not want to abandon, it was argued, the various Tenants' Defense Associations and their leaders all over the country which had in recent years supported him through thick and thin. Yet when Parnell finally agreed to become president of the Irish National Land League in late September, the executive of the League was merely enlarged to accommodate the leadership of the various associations. It was also argued that Parnell was reluctant to accept the responsibility that would be attached to him as leader for all the inanities, not to mention outrages, indulged in by individual members of the organization. In September, however, he merely obviated this by imposing the condition that there should be nothing in the League platform that could not be advocated both in the House of Commons and at meetings in Ireland. Davitt was more than right when he remarked, in retrospect, that these reasons were more expedient than determinant on Parnell's part.[20] Why Parnell did not commit himself sooner, of course, to the land agitation was simply that he was waiting to see whether that agitation could be sustained until the next general election when he could then use it as his springboard to political power. When it became evident that the harvest of 1879 was a failure, and that the farming classes and the laborers were facing ruin and famine, he took up the presidency of the Land League because he realized there would be a general election before there would be another harvest.

[19] *Ibid.*, p. 152.
[20] Davitt, *op. cit.*, p. 160.

II.   The Land League

October, 1879 - December, 1880

The conference which founded the Irish National Land League in Dublin on October 21, 1879, included only two young priests. Both curates, however, were prominent in proposing and seconding resolutions, and when the conference appointed a fifty-three man executive committee, thirteen of those who allowed their names to be put forward were priests. They included the dean of Cashel, several very reverends, and a number of prominent parish priests. While it was becoming more and more obvious that a very large number of the second order of clergy were sympathetic to the League, the really crucial question was how many of the bishops were prepared to support it and to what degree. In a hierarchy of twenty-eight in late 1879, five bishops were willing to support the League in private and discreetly encourage it in public, five more were sympathetic, nine were hostile, and nine were neutral.[1] When the nine who were hostile to the League had finally to face the wrath of the people, they were reduced to three or four, and the neutrals tended, as they always do, to go with the majority and the popular party.[2] The bishops who were friendly to the League, while they did not commit themselves publicly, did not interfere with their priests when they organized local branches of the League and

---

[1] Those who supported the League were Croke (Cashel), Dorrian (Down and Connor), Nulty (Meath), MacCormack (Achonry), Duggan (Clonfert).

Those who were sympathetic were Butler (Limerick), Fitzgerald (Ross), Power (Waterford), D. McCarthy (Kerry), J. McCarthy (Cloyne).

Those who were hostile were McCabe (Dublin), MacHale (Tuam), MacEvilly (Galway, and Coadjutor to Tuam), Moran (Ossory), Warren (Ferns), Walshe (Kildare and Leighlin), Delany (Cork), Gillooly (Elphin), Woodlock (Ardagh and Clonmacnoise).

Those who were neutral were McGettigan (Armagh), Donnelly (Clogher), Kelly (Derry), Leahy (Dromore), Conaty (Kilmore), Logue (Raphoe), Ryan (Coadjutor to Killaloe), Conway (Killala), Lynch (Coadjutor to Kildare and Leighlin).

The bishop of Killaloe, Michaen Flannery, is not included because he was mentally incapacitated.

[2] The three or four who held out against the League were McCabe, Gillooly, MacHale, and perhaps Delany.

even became presidents of those branches. The League
spread rapidly and the clergy were soon prominent at nearly
all the League meetings, where they shared the platform with
men who had some very hard things to say about an Irish
propertied class which in their opinion had forfeited its rights
because it had forgotten its duties.

The agrarian agitation, and especially the part played by a
number of the Irish clergy in it, was reported to Rome, and
the pope and several of his cardinals were alarmed. The chief
offender seemed to be the archbishop of Cashel, Thomas W.
Croke, for Kirby wrote to him on November 15 that he had
been cited in Rome for using violent language and giving his
"public support and approbation to a politician known to be a
violent man, and to have used language of a socialistic tendency." Archbishop Croke, who was not and never had been in
the habit of mincing words, wrote Kirby a very carefully
constructed reply by return, which he recommended to the
attention of Cardinal Simeoni, the prefect of Propaganda.

The Palace, Thurles
November 21st, 1879

My dear Monsignor Kirby,

I have duly received your favor of the 15th and lose no time in
replying to it.

As a rule, it is not easy for anyone to answer a general
accusation such as you say has been made against me at the
Propaganda, and it is particularly difficult to do so, when the
author of the accusation is, as in my case, unknown to the
accused.

But, the thing is very simple, so far as I am concerned, for I
emphatically deny that there is any ground whatever for the
complaint that I understand has been lodged against me. I am
not conscious of ever having used language which any bishop in
the church might not have used, and if I have, I claim it as a
right to have the violent language so used by me *specified*.

I cannot say for certain what politician you refer to as "A
person known to be a violent man, preaching socialistic doctrines" but I presume you mean Mr. Parnell. I have never
spoken a word to Mr. Parnell but once: and that casually: nor
have I ever mentioned his name in any public document either
directly or *indirectly* but once, and then I referred to him because
of a mischievous contention that had arisen between him and

Mr. Gray, editor of the "Freeman's Journal," and solely in the interest of peace and charity.

At *that* time, he had held no meeting, and made no pronouncement on the land question, nor did I know anything whatever about his views on the subject. Since that time, or since he commenced the land agitation, I solemnly declare I have never mentioned his name in public. How can anyone, then presume, to report me "as giving public support and approbation to a politician known to be a violent man, and to have used language of a socialistic tendency?"

To the above statement I think it but right and honest to add, that Mr. Parnell's *parliamentary policy* is approved by 99% of the Irish priesthood and people.

There is not in the whole of Ireland, this moment, a diocese in which there is less agrarian crime, or *agitation*, than there is in this; and nothing has ever yet been said by me, or by any Cashel priest, but what was calculated to promote peace and good will between all classes of people.

I preach nearly every Sunday of my life, somewhere; and I defy anyone to point out a word or phrase in my published, or unpublished sermons, that is not sound, and safe, and *irreprehensible*.

I can say no more unless, I get something specific to deal with. This is not, I believe, the first time that *clandestine* charges have been made against me in Rome. Englishmen, I know, do not like me—Irish aristocrats, I know, do not like me; and, perhaps one or two anti-Irish ecclesiastics do not like me. But I have the satisfaction of knowing, that I stand higher in the estimation of the Irish race, at home and abroad, than any living Irish ecclesiastic but one. This is probably the head and front of my offending. May I beg of you to read this letter for His Eminence Cardinal Simeoni, and to assure him, at the same time, that *he* has no more dutiful subject, and Holy Mother the Church no more devoted son, than the much misrepresented Archbishop of Cashel, who has the honor of subscribing himself *his* and *your* most humble and faithful servant.

+ T. W. Croke(K)

Indeed, the archbishop of Cashel was not the only Irish bishop who felt that Rome had been misinformed about the Irish political situation. When Kirby mentioned to the very able and energetic bishop of Down and Connor, Patrick Dorrian, that the pope had expressed his disapproval of Parnell's policy, Dorrian was no less unequivocal in his reply than Croke had been. He not only declared himself in favor of Parnell on November 24, but maintained that the Irish leader was being misrepresented in the English and Irish press, as well as by the landlord party and Whig Catholics in Ireland(K). Dorrian also pointed out to Kirby that Parnell was bringing the misery of the people and misgovernment of the country to the attention of the public, and that in doing so he was "cool, confident and constitutional." If the people, Dorrian further argued, saw the bishops and priests going against them in their misery they would despair and religion would suffer. "But," above all else, he counseled Kirby in conclusion, "priests and people must keep *united* and I hope nothing shall induce the Holy Father to interfere against the friends of the distressed and famishing poor."

That those bishops who openly supported the Land League should express themselves so strongly was perhaps to be expected, but what was more surprising was that even those who were opposed to the land agitation were extremely cautious in reporting their views to Kirby in Rome. The archbishop of Dublin, for example, explained to Kirby on November 27, that he was very sorry to learn that complaints about Irish priests as abettors of communistic agitations had reached the ear of the Holy Father(K). While admitting that some of the clergy had indeed gone a little astray, McCabe assured Kirby that they could be counted on the fingers of one hand, and then abruptly changed the subject. Kirby, however, who was persistent if nothing else, wrote McCabe by return of post sounding him out on the advisability of the pope taking some action in the matter. In again admitting that some priests had gone too far, McCabe pointed out to Kirby on December 7, that the clergy were witnessing every day very great distress which they were powerless to relieve(K). "If it would not be a presumption on my part," he cautiously advised Kirby, "I would wish to say that it will be wise if the authorities in Rome abstain from any action *at least for the present*." "If I felt that the Holy Father should interfere," McCabe further assured Kirby, "I would not hesitate to humbly ask him to do so, but I think the Bishops' hands are strong enough as yet."

The very next day Patrick Moran, the bishop of Ossory who also opposed the agitation, wrote Kirby a long letter in which he minimized both the effect of the agitation and the influence of the agitators(K). Moran maintained that the agitation was confined to Mayo, which had long been a stronghold of disaffection in general and Fenianism in particular. He also characterized the leadership of the Land League variously as "Atheist," "Protestant," "Socialist," "Fenian," and worst of all perhaps, "a clerk from Dublin who was unheard of till the present agitation." Moran further assured Kirby, and obviously alluding to Croke, that all the bishops were quite orthodox in their desire to maintain peace and order, but that it was very difficult to condemn agitators in Ireland when those same men were made great heroes of at meetings of Catholic societies in London. He then artfully suggested to Kirby that Rome should instruct Cardinal Manning to take his lead from the Irish bishops in the matter of Irish agitators, otherwise it would be quite useless for the Irish bishops to raise their voices against such men.

The situation in the West, however, was certainly more serious and widespread than either Moran knew or was willing to admit to Kirby. Both McCabe and Moran must have realized that the tenant farmers all over Ireland were being swept up in the agitation, and to oppose them at that critical moment would indeed jeopardize the influence of the priests with the people. In such circumstances, the prudent course for the bishops who opposed the agitation was obviously to attempt to ride out the storm. McCabe and Moran must have also realized that a pronouncement by the pope would not only further alienate the people, but that such an action would make it impossible for them to ride out the present storm. That is why, for example, McCabe recommended that Roman action should be deferred, while Moran was more artful in wanting to deflect it in the direction of London and Cardinal Manning. If Kirby was confused, however, by the variety and subtlety of the advice he was receiving from Ireland, he must have certainly been sobered by the long and detailed letter he received from John MacEvilly, the coadjutor to the archbishop of Tuam. MacEvilly warned Kirby on December 11, that any pronouncement by the pope at that moment would be fatal to the interests of the Holy See in Ireland(K).

> The facts are these: a dire famine stares us in the face. The new year will open with a general distress throughout the country. The tenant farmers—the real friends of religion, of the priests, & of the H. See—will be sorely pressed for food. The landlords as a class—there are very many noble exceptions—have no sympathy with the people, with the priests, or the Holy See. They never contribute as a class, to our public charities. Cath.

University, Pope, etc. The people alone do so. The Landlords are exceedingly oppressive. As a general rule, the people are oppressed, the rents far too high, and poor tenant robbed of the fruit of the sweat of his brow, obliged to pay double rent for the land his own labor reclaimed from utter barren worthlessness. This is but robbing the laborer of his hire on a general scale. The people are very discontented at this state of things. They are now, as a rule, unable to pay rents, shop and bnk. debts. This year the crops have failed. The price of cattle very low, no employment for the laborers. The result is great depression. This state of things is availed of by some dishonest trading Politicians, who, acting on the credulity of our artless people, have managed to gather them together at large meetings, and in many instances, especially throughout the Co. Mayo—a great part of it in the diocese of Tuam—have managed to hold their meetings without reference to the priests of whom they wish to estrange the people, and I am sorry to say, have succeeded to a great extent. At meetings held without reference to the priests or their presence, the most shocking principles have been enunciated. The priests denounced, as unfeeling without any concern for their suffering flock, and a dreadful feeling against religion got up. In order to meet this evil and knock the wind out ot the sails of these unprincipled ringleaders, it has been deemed prudent for the priests to formulate the restlessness at meetings in the interest of order and religion, to take the lead and keep Godless nobodies in their proper place. In my own opinion, though I have taken no part whatever, this is the wise and proper course(K).

"Whether the priests will it or no," MacEvilly emphasized, "the meetings will be held. Their people will assemble under the pressure of threatened famine to expound their wrongs to landlords and government; if the priests keep aloof, these meetings will be scenes of disorder; if the priests attend they will keep the people attached to them." "I dare say," he admitted, echoing McCabe, "some few may utter sentiments too strong. But certainly the body are for order and proper allegiance. Government, I fear, will do nothing. The landlords, in many instances, will evict for nonpayment of impossible rent." "It would render the H. See," MacEvilly warned, "very odious to seem to be influenced by the English against those who sacrificed everything for the Faith, and when the *general evictions* come, as come they will, in some districts, it would ruin us, if the authorities [in Rome] could be quoted, as against our people." "*Religion in this country*," he prophesied solemnly in conclusion, "*would never get over it.*"

MacEvilly's dilemma was actually that of all those bishops and priests who opposed the Land League. The clergy must either participate in the agitation or they would sacrifice their influence with the people. In recent months public opinion had rapidly shifted to the left, and, if the clergy did not also make the transition, they would be displaced by the new lay leadership that had emerged in the crisis. What made the decision more galling for many of the clergy was not only that the new leadership was more radical with regard to the political spectrum, but that it was also much less "respectable" in terms of the social spectrum. That is why Moran and MacEvilly, for example, were so upset by the prospect of "a clerk from Dublin," or "Godless nobodies" aspiring politically on a national or even local level. Whatever their social prejudices, however, the clergy as a body began to move to the left. Those bishops and clergy, however, who thought they were preserving their political options in temporarily coming to terms with the League, or even by infiltrating it, did not appreciate the fact that there was to be no return to the political *status quo ante*. What was undertaken by Croke and Dorrian out of conviction and by MacEvilly in the name of expediency resulted not only in the further radicalization of Irish politics but in the eventual nationalization of the Irish Church.

Indeed, now that winter had come on in earnest, the problem was much more one of survival than of politics. "Distress," McCabe informed Kirby on December 29, from what was the wealthiest and most economically secure diocese in Ireland, "in its most aggravating form is gathering around us. Even in Dublin it is making itself felt. In the West, North-West, and South-West it is becoming alarming. Our Government is piddling with it. The landlords can borrow money to improve their properties but they seem unwilling to do so. Private charity is doing what it can but private help will not save a Province"(K). On New Year's Day, T. J. O'Reilly, president of the Peter's Pence Confraternity in Dublin, wrote Kirby announcing that a general collection would be made throughout the diocese for the relief of the distressed, and asked whether the pope might be induced to make a contribution(K). "I trust," Monsignor," Father O'Reilly explained further, "that you will forgive this thought of mine if there were anything inconsistent in it, but as having been the medium of transmitting over thirty thousand pounds sterling from this Diocese towards the relief of the necessities of the Holy See, I dare to express it." "It wd. not," Kirby noted in the margin of this letter, "be *prudent*. I send you £5."

As the distress deepened, and since the government chose to do nothing, all that stood between the Irish people and starvation was either emigration or the charity of the Irish in England and America. "I was glad to hear yesterday," Michael Canon Brady informed Kirby on January 12, from Athy in Kildare, "that former parishioners in America are again sending remittances to their poor friends"(K). "I trust," he added pathetically, "the returning prosperity of America may favourably react on poor Ireland." About a week later, on January 20, Patrick Dorrian wrote Kirby from Belfast enclosing £350 Peters Pence for the pope. He also explained that even though there was distress in Belfast he was taking up a collection the following Sunday for those who were worse off elsewhere(K). "Government," Dorrian exclaimed angrily, "yet keeps aloof and does nothing!!!" Early in February, however, the pope was moved to forward each of the four Irish archbishops a contribution of £142-7-0 to be distributed among their suffragan bishops for the relief of the poor and distressed.

One of Archbishop Croke's priests, James J. Ryan, and another former student of Kirby's, wrote his old mentor on February 14, explaining that the pope's gift was most opportune, especially "considering the unfriendly tone which some of the Catholic papers in Rome assumed towards us, about the end of last year, & the comments of the press in this country, & in England on the supposed Vatican utterances, and inspirations"(K). "You will be pleased to know," Ryan added and referring to Croke, "the Archbishop continues to receive large sums of money from France, and America. This week he disbursed £400, though £4,000 would scarcely have been sufficient to meet the applications made on him within the same period." That same day the archbishop of Armagh, Daniel McGettigan, also wrote Kirby asking him to thank the pope for his gift(K). "The contribution from His Holiness and Propaganda," McGettigan remarked, while enclosing some £450 in Peter's Pence, "reminds me of what is taking place at home i.e. 'the *Poor helping* the Poor.'" Besides the large sums of money sent from England and America, and what was collected in Ireland, the French bishops had taken up the lead of the pope and recommended the Irish cause warmly in their Lenten pastorals.[3] The result was that by the end of April the worst was over and the Irish people were saved from famine by what amounted to a generous act of universal charity.

The winter of 1879-1880 was both a severe and a significant experience for the Irish people. Who was indeed responsible for such a state of affairs? All shades of clerical opinion, even the most conservative, had no doubt where the responsibility lay. "Very great distress," Michael Canon Verdon, president of the Dublin diocesan seminary at Clonliffe had explained to Kirby as early as December 2, "prevails in some parts of the Country, and great and probably just indignation is felt against the Government. Many very sensible men think that the Government have acted very badly, and have allowed things to go so far that they will not now be able to prevent a famine during the winter in many parts of the Country"(K). "Some of the Bishops and Archbishops," Verdon added significantly, "went in a deputation to the Lord Lieutenant a short time ago, and I heard they were very indignant on account of the reception they met with." Though private charity did indeed prevent a famine during the winter, these efforts only highlighted how "culpably remiss" the government had been.[4] Irish national consciousness, however, had not only been touched by the universal suffering during the crisis, but it had also been deepened, if not seared, by the shame of the experience. Once again the Irish people had to beg their bread before the world, and large numbers of them had once again to leave their native land simply in order to survive.

Parnell, meanwhile, had sailed from Plymouth for America in late December, 1879. He arrived in New York on January 2, 1880, and began a whirlwind tour of the United States and Canada. In just more than two months he traveled some eleven thousand miles, visited sixty-two cities, and raised two hundred thousand dollars. His message was simple, forceful, and comprehensive. It was not simply enough, he argued, to save the Irish people from starvation, but something must be

[3] K, March 23, 1880, P. J. Tynan. See also Patrick O'Brien to Kirby, April 3, 1880, from Paris: "I find by late news that the Colony of Victoria alone have subscribed over 21,000 pounds. The other Australian colonies have also subscribed largely."

[4] K, February 9, 1880, Henry F. Neville.

done about the root cause of periodic famine in Ireland. The remedy was to be found, he maintained, in the destruction of the cornerstone of English misgovernment in Ireland, the landlord system. "When we have undermined English misgovernment," he told an enthusiastic audience in Cincinnati, Ohio, on February 20, 1880, "we have paved the way for Ireland to take her place among the nations of the earth."[5] "And let us not forget," Parnell emphasized, "that this is the ultimate goal at which all we Irishmen aim." "None of us," concluded the man who was ambitious to be the leader of the Irish nation at home and abroad, "whether we are in America or in Ireland, or wherever we may be, will be satisfied until we have destroyed the last link which binds Ireland to England." On March 8, while in Montreal, Parnell received a telegram from Joseph Biggar, a staunch supporter and parliamentary colleague, announcing that Parliament had just been dissolved and asking him to return at once. Parnell immediately left for New York, and sailed from there on March 12 for Queenstown, leaving in his wake a hurriedly organized American Land League to sustain and consolidate the enthusiasm aroused by his tour.[6]

When Parnell arrived in Queenstown on March 21, it was soon apparent that he was not only determined on all-out political war, but that he was likely to win that war. "I fear very much," Archbishop McCabe wrote Kirby apprehensively from Dublin on March 22, "that this coming Election will result [in] strange things: Mr. Parnell has returned from America as violent as ever, and I fear that the money he brings home for political purposes will be badly employed"(K). "The people," McCabe observed significantly, "are maddened with the want reigning everywhere and are only too well disposed to listen to the most violent doctrines." A prospective candidate for Parliament rather gloomily wrote Kirby the same day confirming the archbishop's fears. "Two friends of Mr. Parnell," Walter Fitzpatrick explained, "quite unknown in the Queens County have been chosen on his recommendation by

[5] R. Barry O'Brien, *The Life of Charles Stewart Parnell* (London, 1910), p. 160. The rest of this "last-link" speech is quoted from Michael Davitt, *The Fall of Feudalism in Ireland* (London, 1904), p. 204. The whole of the "last link" speech may be found in the *Cincinnati Commercial* of Saturday, February 21, 1880. The three other papers that covered the speech, however, did not carry the "last link" reference. I am indebted to James P. McHugh of Cincinnati for sending me this reference.

[6] T. M. Healy, *Letters and Leaders of My Day* (London, 1928), I: p. 83.

the popular Club"(K). "My friends," he added revealingly, "including some of the leading priests, who used formerly in a great measure to guide the choice of the electors, have been overborne by the mob, and they advise me to wait for better times." Parnell and his friends had their way in Queens County because the local clergy did not dare insist on a candidate of their own, which would split the nationalist vote and assure the reelection of the two sitting members who were diehard Tory landlords. In those constituencies, however, where a Tory candidate posed no threat, the local bishops and clergy very often supported the sitting Whig or Liberal in opposition to the Parnellite.

In most constituencies a simple threat by the Parnellites was sufficient to extract a pledge from the Whig or Liberal to support Home Rule and Parnell's "active," or obstructionist, policy in the new Parliament. The Parnellites were determined, however, to punish those members who they claimed had given and then broken their pledges to support Home Rule in the last Parliament. These Whig "pledge-breakers" were opposed in some seven constituencies, and the liveliest of these contests were generally those in which the local bishop and his clergy opposed Parnell and his friends. The strongest clerical opposition came in Wexford, Cork City and County, and Roscommon. The stormiest of these was easily Wexford. When Parnell arrived in Enniscorthy on Sunday, March 28, he could not even secure a hearing on behalf of his nominees. He was, in fact, assaulted, hit with rotten eggs, and covered with slime by the incensed supporters of Keyes O'Clery, a papal chevalier, who had received his title from Pius IX for defending the Temporal Power against the Risorgimento. "Here in the shadow of Vinegar Hill," asked the chevalier's chairman, Father N. Murphy, at the same meeting Parnell was refused a hearing, "is it to be told that the priests and the bishop and the people of Wexford cannot select their own candidate?"[7] Though Father Murphy, who had appeared with his blackthorn to direct the proceedings, seemed to have few doubts about the answer to his rhetorical question, it seems the local bishop, Michael Warren, had some uneasy second thoughts about the candidates and the election. "I take advantage of a few moments," the bishop of Ferns wrote

---

[7] *Freeman's Journal*, March 29, 1880, quoted in Conor Cruise O'Brien, *Parnell and His Party, 1880-1890* (Oxford, 1957), p. 28, n. 1.

Kirby on March 28, from Enniscorthy, shortly before this Sunday meeting, "—which I am not likely to have again for some days, to say, that I am anxious that Mr. O'Clery may be returned again as M.P. for the Co. of Wexford; but there are immense difficulties in the way. The parties which returned him on the former occasion have turned upon him, and for months have been denouncing him as a 'trator' [sic] and as a 'pledge-breaker.' " "My position with regard to this election,"‎ Warren explained prudently, "and with regard to political matters generally is an extremely delicate and difficult one, and after the best and most anxious consideration that I can give them I believe the interests of religion require of me to keep my name from getting mixed up with them." "Poor Ireland," he lamented piously in conclusion, "is passing through a most dangerous crisis but I trust her multitude of ancient saints will obtain protection and guidance for her children." In the end, the pious and prudent bishop of Ferns proved to have had a sounder grasp of political reality than did Father Murphy, for the Chevalier O'Clery was all but annihilated at the polls by Parnell's candidates.

Three days after his temporary humiliation at the Enniscorthy meeting, Parnell was nominated on March 31, at the eleventh hour for Cork City. Though his nomination paper was signed by two young Cork curates, John O'Mahony and Denis McCarthy, the bishop and senior clergy were furious at Parnell's nomination. The Parnellites were determined to defeat the clerical favorite, N. D. Murphy, a wealthy local brewer, who on the testimony of Michael Davitt was an "Irish Whig of the most reactionary kind."[8] "Altars rang," Davitt recounted in his memoirs, "with warnings against Fenianism and socialism, and all the other wicked things which frighten the virtuous political vision of some politicians when a wealthy Catholic is being opposed for his spurious nationalism or some job-finding supporter of a ministry is fought by the people on principle." After a weekend of speaking and canvassing in Cork, Parnell was so confident of victory on the morning of election day, Monday, April 5, that he decided to spring another eleventh hour candidate on the clergy and electorate of Cork County.

Since polling day for the county was April 14, Parnell and

---

[8] Davitt, op. cit., p. 238.

his friends had less than ten days to canvass the largest county in Ireland. Parnell's victory in Cork City, however, which was announced on April 6, had the effect of nerving the clergy, who fought the Parnellites tooth and nail from one end of the county to the other. The bishops of Cork, Cloyne, Ross, and Kerry, all of whom had some ecclesiastical jurisdiction in Cork County, issued a joint manifesto supporting the sitting members, William Shaw and Colonel Colthurst. Parnell, who had been nominated for Meath and Mayo as well, did what he could on flying trips to Cork to support his nominee, A. J. Kettle, but the clergy were reported to be working hard at the polling centers for their candidates. The scrutiny of the ballots took place on April 15, and while it was soon apparent that Shaw would be easily reelected, Colthurst and Kettle were running even all the way. Colthurst finally won by the narrow margin of 151, with 3,581 votes as against 3,430 for Kettle.[9] This election was in truth a moral victory for Parnell because it presented his opponents with some sober thoughts about their prospects at the next election when the Parnellites would certainly be better organized.

Some months after the Cork election, the bishop of Cork explained what had happened in a long letter to Kirby. "I never took a prominent part in such affairs, since my consecration," began William Delany, on July 12, announcing the principles which had governed his political conduct since 1847, "unless in conjunction with other bishops. We almost always concurred and my part was to encourage the Cork clergy to unite with their brethren of the other dioceses in unity of action. Once I did not approve and therefore remained in the background"(K). "In the last elections for our county," he continued, becoming particular, "I joined with the other bishops in stating publicly what we believed the wishes of the clergy or nearly all. In the city election I did nothing for a long time—I did not propose a candidate to the people or clergy. I did not directly or indirectly seek for a candidate."

Two gentlemen of their own proper motion started for the representation. One was chosen by a great majority, Mr. Daly. The other had been our representative for 16 years, the most really useful member we ever had, a good

[9] C. C. O'Brien, *op. cit.*, p. 174.

Catholic and professing all the so-called popular principles, Mr. Murphy, member of a most numerous and generous and most Catholic family.

They issued their addresses and were opposed by one conservative opponent. Meantime I did nothing whatever on the business. Unexpectedly, our community was astonished to find two of our priests, actively engaged in breeding dissension. They were two curates who not long before had to apologize to me for endeavoring to lead their brother priests, to act apart from me and their parish priest in a public affair of temperance, in which however we were actively engaged.

I readily accepted the apology hoping for better. Yet in a brief space, I found that they were actively engaged in bringing Mr. Parnell to disturb our peace and who would have had no chance but for the support of the Fenians. I felt bound to call together the other clergymen of our city, to explain their duty and their right and to enter my protest against the unwarrantable disturbance of our peace(K).

"I feel perfectly persuaded," Delany then explained, giving excellent example, incidentally, why he was denounced as a "Whig" by the Parnellites, "from what I heard in various quarters, that the great body of the intelligent and respectable people were pleased with my proceeding." "It did not take place until the two gentlemen," he added, referring to Fathers O'Mahony and McCarthy, "disregarding the remonstrance of their parish priest canvassed actively and became nominators of Mr. Parnell." "Of this gentleman," the bishop of Cork concluded dryly, "I need say nothing. You will learn all about him from the public journals."

Meanwhile, Parnell had wisely added insult to injury by choosing to sit for Cork, where the clerical opposition to him had been strongest, though he had also been elected for Mayo and Meath. Almost everywhere his nominees were elected, and only the lack of time, money, and candidates prevented a more comprehensive Parnellite sweep in Ireland. In Britain, Gladstone had humbled the Conservatives with his "Midlothian" campaigns, and when the returns were finally in, the Liberals were in a majority of 137 in the new House of Commons. "All the great furor of the elections," wrote Patrick Moran to Kirby from Kilkenny on April 19, "has now past. The political parties fought a pitched battle with the greatest possible obstinacy, and the result has been a most complete

Liberal victory"(K). "No where have the Tories," Moran emphasized, "got such a telling defeat as in Ireland. Out of 103 constituencies, they have been able to return only 25 members, whilst the Liberals returned 78, and of these we may reckon on 63 being Catholics." "Some of the elections," Moran then explained, "where the Parnellites or extreme home rulers set themselves to oppose the men chosen by the clergy was very bitter. Of course the bishops and clergy had to bear a good deal of popular odium. I heard on the best authority that at Roscommon when the Vicar General read from the altar a circular of Dr. Gillooly exhorting the people to have nothing to say to these extreme Politicians, a number of people walked out of the church. In Roscommon, Mayo and the city of Cork, the Parnellites were returned in spite of the Bps. and clergy." "It would be well perhaps," he then hinted broadly to Kirby, "to call attention to the want of union among our body in this matter of promoting Parnellism. It is useless for the Bishops of one district to oppose it, if it is encouraged in other places. On yesterday in all the parish churches of the diocese of Meath a collection was made by order of the Bishop in order to defray Mr. Parnell's election expenses for that county." "How can you persuade the people," Moran asked helplessly, "that Parnellism is wrong after that?"

Kirby already had good reason to know as he read Moran's letter that the bishops were not all of one mind about Parnell's recent electoral victory, for the intrepid bishop of Down and Connor had written him from Belfast several days before. "Ireland is erect," Dorrian announced triumphantly on April 14, "and the drones and lukewarm M.P.'s are set aside. Some bishops and priests are short-sighted in opposing the active policy. The people see their way and must have themselves rooted in the land. They are right and will succeed"(K). Dorrian also assured Kirby that there was nothing against religion in the agitation and that Parnell had said nothing against "equity and justice." Indeed, those bishops and priests who had opposed Parnell and his supporters at the polls had been chastened by their losses. Moran, for example, had attempted to mask what was in effect a political rout of the anti-Parnellite clergy by explaining to Kirby that the over-all result was really a Tory disaster and a Catholic victory. MacEvilly, however, who did not possess Moran's dialectical gifts, was more to the point in writing Kirby when Parnell chose to sit for Cork rather than Mayo or Meath where he had also been elected. "Think of Catholic Mayo," MacEvilly wrote, obviously aghast, on May 23, "returning a presbyterian minister to represent it, at the bidding of Mr. Parnell who wields such power."[10]

While Parnell's power was manifest in the country, what his real parliamentary strength would be in the new House of Commons was another question. When Gladstone, in forming his ministry, filled eight of the eleven Cabinet posts with Whigs, while the Radical wing of the Liberal party was virtually ignored, it was an ominous sign for the Parnellites. Further, though some sixty Irish members were returned as Home Rulers in 1880, Parnell could not count on more than twenty-four at the opening of Parliament. Of the rest, twenty-one were Irish Whigs, most of whom supported the government, while fourteen were of no definite affiliation. Most of this latter group of neutrals, however, and indeed two of the former, "were gradually drawn to the side which had enthusiastic popular support, good leadership, a coherent (though flexible) policy, and the probability of victory in the next general election."[11] What the relative weights among the factions really were became obvious when only forty-three members met in Dublin on May 17, to elect a sessional chairman. Twenty-three voted for Parnell and eighteen for William Shaw, who had succeeded at the death of Isaac Butt as chairman of the party in the last Parliament. Nominally, at least, Parnell commanded a Party of nearly sixty when Parliament opened, and Ireland awaited the pleasure of the House of Commons with calm expectation.

---

[10] K, May 23, 1880. See also the very touching and half-literate letter from Denis Riordan to his brother Michael, then a seminarian at the Irish College in Rome, testifying to the popular ascendancy of Parnell. OR, May 6 [1880]. ". . . I suppose you heard about the great Land Meeting that was held through the County this year protesting against Evictors and all that Mr. Parnell M.P. being the Leader, the case was so hard that some thousands of people used gang together and resist the Law against the Landlord wheare there was lots of police we have great hopes through the new Government (Liberal) of the Land Laws being changed. . . . Mr. Parnell was elected for Cork County, Co Meath and Co Mayo, there is no other man have such influence to the people as he." This letter was written in the part of the diocese of Limerick which borders on the diocese of Cloyne near the town of Charleville in County Cork.

[11] C. C. O'Brien, op. cit., p. 26.

Shortly after the general election, the executive of the Land League, which had been recently enlarged because of the rapid growth of the organization all over Ireland, called for a national convention on April 29, 1880 in Dublin.[12] A committee, meanwhile, was appointed by the executive to prepare a program for the consideration of the convention. The Programme presented to the delegates proposed the creation of a land commission for Ireland, pronounced in favor of compulsory sale where a tenant offered the landlord a sum equal to twenty years of the poor-law valuation of the holding, and demanded an organic reform in the law of real property.[13] The Programme further proposed, whether the sale was voluntary or compulsory, that the tenant woald be able to borrow the purchase price from the proposed land commission, out of funds provided by the Treasury, at the rate of five per cent per annum and repay the loan over a period of thirty-five years. "Time will be needed by the present House of Commons," it was pointed out in the preface of the Programme, "to inform itself as to the merits of a question which is only just commencing to be understood in Ireland and is scarcely understood at all in England."[14] The Programme then very sensibly suggested, "in view of the desperate condition of the country," that as an interim measure, a two-year moratorium on all evictions be declared. The delegates to the convention approved the Programme and authorized Parnell to press for the appropriate legislation in the new Parliament.

When the queen's speech was read at the opening of Parliament on May 20, 1880, no mention was made of Ireland at all. The Parnellites immediately moved an amendment to the address which was remarkable because it was so temperate. When William Shaw, spokesman for the Whig faction in the Home Rule party, supported the omission of Ireland in the queen's speech on the ground that the land question was too complicated for action in that session of Parliament, the amendment was withdrawn.[15] The Parnellites then introduced a bill designed to provide for the compensation of those tenants evicted for non-payment of rent. This maneuver resulted in the government's announcing on June 15 a meas-

---

12 Davitt, *op. cit.*, pp. 240-241.
13 *Ibid.*, pp. 242-243.
14 *Ibid.*, 241.
15 C. C. O'Brien, *op. cit.*, pp. 46-48.

ure of its own, and three days later a Compensation for Disturbances Bill was introduced. While Parnell was thus setting the political tone in the House of Commons, Archbishop Croke was setting the clerical, if not to say the episcopal, tone in Ireland. "There is no nation," the archbishop wrote in greeting to a meeting in his diocese in Emly on Sunday, May 30, 1880, "on the face of the globe that has suffered so much or so long as we have."[16] "There can be no sin," he maintained, "in striving to live and wishing to die in Ireland." "It is neither sin nor treason," he proclaimed courageously, "to say that where a man labors he has a right to be fed, and that it is cruel to punish a person for not paying a debt which nature has rendered it impossible for him to satisfy." While Croke was eloquently endowing the Irish people with a store of both hope and courage, he was also extremely politic in urging his clergy and laity to make a most generous contribution to the annual Peter's Pence.[17] Croke was in fact planning to visit Rome in company with six of his suffragan bishops in late October, and he wished to present the pope and Propaganda with some more tangible proof that the faith was still intact in Ireland than a mere verbal assurance. In opening two separate subscription lists—one for the clergy and the other for the laity—Croke gave his clergy heart and direction with a contribution of £100. When the clerical list was finally closed in September, it totaled £729, and the laity had not yet done their duty in a diocese whose annual average contribution was about £400.[18]

Needless to say, not all the Irish bishops were pleased with the tone being set by Croke with regard to the Land League. "Would it be possible," Moran asked Kirby on June 10, "to have some intimation from the Holy See as to what it considers expedient in the matter of the semi-communistic agitation

---

[16] *Freeman's Journal*, May 31, 1880, quoted in Davitt, *op. cit.*, p. 262. In the course of this letter, Croke also defended the leaders of the Land League for the cowardly terms of opprobrium with which they were labeled by their enemies. "We have borne so much," he wrote, "and borne it so meekly, that now when we are beginning to fret a little under our punishment, and cast ourselves on a small scale into the attitude of self-defense, persons are found to call us ugly names and words of ominous signification, borrowed from the vicious vocabulary of the Continent, are used to designate the efforts that are being made by well-meaning men throughout the country to prevent the Irish people from perishing at home or being drafted like cattle to climes beyond the sea."

[17] K, May 19, 1880, James Ryan.

[18] K, September 17, 1880, T. W. Croke.

that is now fermenting in many parts of the country"(K). "I think the matter must come on for consideration by the Bishops at their Maynooth meeting on the 22nd inst.," Moran further suggested, giving excellent example of why he was unpopular among his episcopal brethren and feared by the clergy, "and even an informal statement of the views of Propaganda would be very useful, and if sent to the Abp. of Dublin wd have great effect on the deliberations." Kirby obviously thought more was required than an informal statement from the Propaganda, for in the end it was the pope who wrote the archbishop of Armagh as the Primate of All Ireland and titular head of the Irish Church. The letter was read at the bishops' meeting, where, as McCabe explained to Kirby on June 28, the bishops "unanimously adopted an answer which was drawn up by the Bishop of Ossory, in which they thanked the Holy Father for his paternal care of his Irish children"(K). "But there was a general feeling," McCabe added, "that the dissensions amongst us were greatly exaggerated to the H. See: Indeed I think I may say that there are really no dissensions properly so called amongst us." "'Tis true that some of our body," McCabe further explained, indicating that Parnell's supporters among the bishops were still in a minority, "regarded Mr. Parnell with a favour that the majority of the Episcopate did not accord to him, but all this was unaccompanied with any breach of charity." McCabe concluded his letter by pointing out that the reading of the pope's letter had led to a discussion of the land question, which had resulted in the passing of a series of resolutions for publication.

Moran, who had also drafted the resolutions as well as the reply to the pope, wrote an expectant Kirby immediately after the meeting. "You will see," Moran explained on June 24, referring to the resolutions which he had enclosed, "that they are very strong in asserting our people's rights, but we endeavour to guide their agitation within the limits of justice and the teachings of religion"(K). The resolutions were, in fact, anything but strong. They were simply a tiresome rehash of the "rights and duties" of landlords and tenants. The crucial resolution was the fifth and last—not because it said anything, but rather because it said nothing.

> That we deem it our duty also to warn our devoted flocks not to allow themselves to be drawn by their sufferings or persecutions

to the employment of unjust or illegal remedies, and to be on
their guard against such principles and projects as are contrary
to religion and justice(K).

Obviously, what had happened at the meeting was that the
anti-Land League bishops, though still in a majority, were
unable to impose their views on their dissenting episcopal
brethren.[19]

Moran's penchant for interfering, which bordered on intrigue, was encouraged by Kirby, it seems, who wrote him
asking for more details about the bishops' meeting. After
explaining that twenty-two bishops in a hierarchy of twenty-
eight were present, Moran noted obligingly on July 19 that
there was something "quite abnormal about these annual or
bi-annual meetings which should be set aright by the authorities in Rome, as otherwise they will eventually do more
harm than good"(K). In the first place, he pointed out, the
bishops were not required to attend and those that pleased
simply stayed away. That should not be allowed, Moran argued, because it was impossible to secure "unity of action."
Secondly, the meetings were held without any canonical rule.
Some, for example, wore episcopal dress and some did not,
while everyone talked as much and as often as he liked and a
great deal of time was wasted. "What I would suggest is this,"
Moran advised, "That the sacred Congregation would write a
circular to the Bishops asking their views as to how these
annual meetings should be held and the matters to be treated
of. When they heard the opinions of all they can fix some
order of procedure." In his reply to this letter Kirby obviously
attempted to broaden the scale of Moran's proposed circular
from Propaganda to include something more substantial than
merely procedure. Moran, however, was too experienced a
Roman hand to be so easily drawn into what might in the end
prove a very awkward situation, given the present temper of
some of the bishops with regard to the land agitation. Instead,
he cautiously advised Kirby on August 4, that it might be more
expedient for the authorities to wait until November when a
number of the Irish bishops, including Croke, would be in
Rome. "The Cardinal Prefect," Moran deftly suggested,
"could then convene a meeting of the Bishops, to ask them for

---

[19] K, June 25, 1890, Patrick F. Moran; June 30, 1880, Patrick Dorrian.

any suggestions they might wish to make on our Irish affairs."

On August 3, however, the day before Moran wrote to Kirby, the House of Lords had rendered their Roman machinations largely academic by rejecting the Compensation for Disturbances Bill. The bill, which had passed the House of Commons on July 26, was designed to compensate those tenants who would be evicted in November when they were unable to pay their rents, thus not leaving them to face the coming winter absolutely destitute. While the bill was in progress, the country had remained relatively quiet, but when the Lords rejected it, agrarian outrage and crime began to increase alarmingly, and the constitutional leadership was hard-pressed to retain control of the renewed agitation. Parnell appears to have almost immediately realized that his control over the movement was threatened, for on August 5, in the House of Commons, he asked the chief secretary for Ireland a most significant parliamentary question.

> Whether in view of the rejection by the House of Lords of the Compensation for Disturbance Bill he proposes to employ the constabulary and military forces of the Queen for the purpose of assisting at the evictions of tenants who can be proved to be unable to pay their rents?[20]

"We shall protect," the chief secretary replied curtly, "the officers of the court of law in the execution of the law."[21] The next day, August 6, the Irish party met, only seventeen in number and nearly all Parnellites, and resolved to oppose the constabulary estimates and to place themselves at the disposal of the country at the end of the session. On August 10, John Dillon, who had accompanied Parnell on his American tour, and who had remained behind some months to help organize the American Land League, treated the House to a most violent harangue. Then, anticipating his colleagues' resolution, he returned to Ireland and at a Land League meeting in Kildare on Sunday, August 15, made "one of the most inflammatory speeches of the whole land campaign."[22]

The Irish bishops were scheduled to meet again at the end of August, and given the deteriorating state of the country,

---

[20] Quoted in C. C. O'Brien, *op. cit.*, p. 51.
[21] *Ibid.*
[22] *Ibid.*

and the opinions of some of their lordships, it was apparent the meeting would be a stormy one. The rising temper of those opposed to the Land League may be easily gauged from the remarks made to Kirby by the bishop of Ardagh, Bartholomew Woodlock, a few days after Dillon's outburst. "Some wicked and designing men," Woodlock complained on August 18, "are going about exciting our poor people, I know, to their own ruin. And what is worse I do not see how to stop the mischief which is being done by the propagation of these socialistic doctrines, and by the endeavours made in every direction to separate the people from the Clergy"(K). Kirby grew so alarmed that he wrote McCabe asking whether the country was indeed on the verge of revolution. McCabe replied on August 27, that the English papers were exaggerating everything, and that, though things were certainly not as he would wish them to be, there was "no fear of a general outbreak"(K). "I must tell you in great confidence," he added significantly, "that the letters and speeches of the A.B. of Cashel are doing great mischief." When the bishops did meet the following week at Maynooth, Croke prevented any action being taken on the part of the majority by absenting himself. Moreover, eight or ten other bishops also failed to attend. The bishops present, therefore, could do nothing about the crisis, and confined themselves to appointing a professor of theology for Maynooth, and issued a brief resolution on the education question.[23]

Soon after the bishops' abortive meeting, Parliament was prorogued for four months on September 7, and Parnellite M.P.'s immediately returned to Ireland to take the lead in the agitation. Parnell, however, coolly retired to his estate in Wicklow for ten days' shooting. When he finally did choose to speak at Ennis on Sunday, September 19, he boldly gave the agitation not only a lead but a direction. "When a man takes a farm from which another has been evicted," he announced amidst cries of "Shoot him!" and with eight priests on his platform,

you must show him on the roadside when you meet him, you must show him in the streets of the town, you must show him at the shop counter, you must show him in the fair and in the

---

[23] K, September 25, 1880, Patrick F. Moran.

market-place, and even in the house of worship, by leaving him
severely alone, by putting him into a moral Coventry, by isolat-
ing him from his kind as if he was a leper of old—you must show
him your detestation of the crime he has committed, and you
may depend upon it there will be no man so full of avarice, so
lost to shame, as to dare the public opinion of all right-thinking
men and to transgress your unwritten code of laws.[24]

By proposing an effective course of action in what soon came
to be known as boycotting, Parnell regained the initiative in
Ireland, and he and his supporters now proceeded to organize Land League branches in every part of the country in
order to resist the anticipated evictions during the coming
winter. While the harvest fortunately had been a very good
one, prices still continued low, and the farmers were deeply in
debt to their landlords for arrears in rent because of the
repeated failures over the past three years. The farmers,
therefore, were generally not expected to be able to pay both
their debts and the high half-yearly rents due in November. In
various parts of the country, the farmers had agreed not to
pay any more than what they considered to be a fair rent.
When the landlords threatened or attempted to evict, the
result was a rapid increase in agrarian outrages and boycotting in the affected areas. McCabe had become increasingly
alarmed by the outrages and the apparent indifference of the
Land League officials and their supporters to the intimidation
and violence. McCabe was particularly shocked by the brutal
murder of Lord Mountmorres in Galway in late September.
As he explained to Kirby on October 3,

from the language and action of the agents of the Land League
it is not much to be wondered at that an excited public should
express their wrongs by deeds of violence: in the harangues of
these agents when there is reference to the misdeeds of a landlord the exclamation "Shoot him," was sure to be heard: and
this never elicited a reproof from the speaker: and it has been
strongly commented on that the late cruel murder did not draw
forth a word of censure from the speakers of the Land League
who were certainly called on to repudiate all companionship
with its perpetration(K).

---

[24] R. Barry O'Brien, *op. cit.*, p. 186.

McCabe then concluded with an obvious reference to Croke, by remarking that it was very sad that some who were placed in a very high position were "giving the sanction of their names to very dangerous doctrines."

Kirby once again took the hint and wrote Croke on October 15, warning him that he was being complained of in Rome. "Once before you wrote me on this subject," replied Croke, who was on his way to Rome with the bishops of Limerick, Cloyne, and Ross, and writing from the Irish College in Paris on October 23, "and told me I was charged with the use of 'violent language'—the charge is now that I do not speak at all"(K). "God help us," he lamented in exasperation, "it is a curious world. After hard and anxious labours in Cashel for over five years doing the best I could, and not without success, for creed and country by way of recompense, I find myself in the *dock* and called on for my defense." "Tis a curious theory," Croke then remarked in a postscript, "that I approve of murders because I do not denounce them." "I have mentioned the prospect of your letter to my suffragans here," he added in deadly earnest in a second postscript, "and we are determined, one and all, to make a stand on the principles we have taken up. They are quite indignant at the charges made, or said to be made against us, or against me."

The tide, however, had actually turned with the murder of Lord Mountmorres in late September. The Land League's policy of tendering only a fair rent, and "boycotting" those who opposed them was proving very effective. Evictions fell, for example, from 3,447 in the third quarter of 1880 to 954 during the final three months of the year.[25] The landlords were obviously intimidated, and it was rapidly becoming a question of who was governing the country, the Land League or the government . By the end of October, however, the government had had enough and decided to take action. On November 2, they arrested Parnell, four parliamentary colleagues, and the key Land League officers on the charge that they conspired to prevent the payment of rent. The government realized the prosecutions, in the face of trial by jury, might not prove successful, but they acted on the assumption that it was better to do something than nothing. Even if the

---

[25] N. D. Palmer, *Irish Land League Crisis* (New Haven, 1940), p. 271; quoted also in C. C. O'Brien, *op. cit.*, p. 55, n. 2.

prosecutions should fail, the government felt that this would only prove that ordinary law was not enough in Ireland, and the House of Commons would then be more easily persuaded to a strong coercion measure, or even the suspension of *habeas corpus*, when it reconvened in early January of the new year. The arrests, however, instead of checking the activities of the Land League, only resulted in an intensification of the agitation.

Archbishop Croke, meanwhile, had finally arrived in Rome with his three suffragans. They seemed to have a calming effect on the pope and at Propaganda, for Kirby wrote as much to McCabe in early November. "I do not know what explanation Dr. Croke has made to the H.F.," McCabe replied on November 12, "but we are in a very bad state. I walked with a Bishop in the West of Ireland some time ago through his own Cathedral town on a Market day, and there was scarcely a man to put his hand to his hat: you know what that means in Ireland"(K). "But," he then added, "I fear the prosecutions commenced by the Government will do more mischief than good. Yet they could not stand by and see disorder triumphant." "Since writing the foregoing," McCabe noted hastily in a postscript, "I read a letter from the A.B. of Cashel sending £30, the subscription of himself and suffragans for Parnell's Defense Fund. The letter is addressed from the Minerva Hotel. This will be construed into an approval by the Holy See. Is this the meaning [?]" Four days later, without waiting for a reply from Kirby, McCabe reported that his worst fears were realized, as the subscription of Croke and his suffragans was being "distorted into a sort of Papal Sanction for the act"(K). "I look upon subscribing to the fund," McCabe explained, "as an endorsement of Mr. Parnell's policy which has brought the Country face to face with revolutionary and communistic doctrines." "I find it very hard," he further complained, "to keep some of the young priests in this Diocese quiet. And the action of the Bishops now in Rome certainly gives them a strong argument against my view of things."

Within a week McCabe had also set out for Rome to present his "view of things." At this point Moran dropped what can only be described as a veritable bombshell on Kirby. After explaining to Kirby on November 25, in what was a masterpiece of understatement, that given the opposing views of the archbishops of Dublin and Cashel, he would undoubtedly be "somewhat puzzled between them," Moran unexpectedly changed sides. "It seems to me," he declared, "that the agitation for remedying our land-laws, as it at present has taken hold of the country is quite constitutional & legitimate, & most national"(K). "On the other hand," he added, compensating somewhat for his new course, "it has to be watched with the greatest vigilance & care, for there is no doubt that the originators of the movement laid down very communistic principles, & themselves were many of them without any religion whatever." "These false principles, and these irreligious elements," Moran now assured Kirby, "have been thrust under by the national spirit, but of course they may again show themselves at any moment, & hence we cannot be too much on our guard to prevent our good people from being contaminated by irreligious principles, & to keep them in paths of justice & equity." Moran then reported that Parnell and his associates would be tried about the middle of December. "There is very little excitement in the country about the trials," he added significantly, "as the national agitation that is now spread is quite independent of these individuals and will continue all the same even though condemned."

Why indeed did Moran change his mind? In all his letters since the beginning of the agitation he had consistently, if discreetly, supported the position of the archbishop of Dublin. The reason for his unexpected conversion, of course, was simply that he now found himself in the same position that MacEvilly had found himself the year before. The Land League was determined to organize in his diocese with or without his permission, and with or without the participation of his clergy. Like MacEvilly, therefore, Moran reluctantly came to the conclusion that he must allow his priests to participate or forfeit their influence with the people. In fact, as he was writing to Kirby explaining his new position, he had already made arrangements for the following Sunday, November 28, for a number of meetings in his diocese to found branches of the Land League. Moran had obviously conferred with his clergy, for the meetings were scheduled for Kilkenny, which in effect was the bishop's parish, and for Mooncoin, one of the wealthiest and most respectable of the country parishes. The Kilkenny meeting, moreover, was held in front of the parish church of St. Canise, and was presided over by no less a personage than the dean of the diocese, and Moran's vicar general, Edward M'Donald with numerous other clergy on the platform. M'Donald spoke in "the warmest terms of approbation of the conduct of Mr. Parnell and his associates and at the same time counseled moderation and obedience to the existing laws of the Country."[26] When two policemen in uniform appeared to take notes of the meeting, considerable irritation was reported as demands for their expulsion were made by the crowd. The clergymen present, however, advised that they not be interfered with and they were allowed to remain. The meeting at Mooncoin was also chaired by a priest. When one of the speakers remarked that there "were bad landlords amongst them" and there were cries of "Down with them," the reverend chairman was indignant. "Put these men off the platform," he ordered, "There will be no cries of down with them where I am chairman. I am responsible for the maintenance of order. I will not have the Tory press of England putting me down as sanctioning assassination by sanctioning such cries."[27]

Almost as soon as he arrived in Rome, McCabe was asked by the authorities at Propaganda whether he thought the position of the Irish bishops would be strengthened by a papal condemnation of the Land League. When McCabe replied that he did not think so, the news was relayed almost immediately by Kirby to Croke, who had set out for Ireland shortly before McCabe had arrived in Rome. Croke replied on December 8, from Thurles, in a letter marked "private," that he was glad that McCabe had recommended a policy of non-intervention(K). "I think I know Ireland, Croke explained, "as well as any man in it, and I do not hesitate to say, that if the Pope were to say anthing that could be constructed into hostility to the present agitation in this country, the results would be most disastrous." "First and foremost," Croke declared, "even *his* words would not at this moment check the movement in any appreciable degree, and, secondly, it would be terrible to contemplate the feeling of estrangement which they would necessarily engender between our beloved Holy Father and his Irish children." "As regards Dr. McCabe's *opinion*," he further pointed out, "of the *leaders* of the Irish land agitation,

---

[26] *Freeman's Journal*, November 29, 1880.
[27] *Ibid.*

it is of small account one way or another, in as much as he knows nothing of them except from prejudiced and unfriendly sources." "I know them well and personally," Croke emphasized, "and unhesitatingly say, that they have no object in view except the amelioration of the country, first by procuring for it a radical change in the land laws, and finally repeal of the union, or its equivalent 'home rule'—" "I have had," Croke finally reported,

> a long and confidential interview with Parnell and Dillon since I came home, and they unequivocally agreed with me in thinking, 1. that all violence to persons or property is to be discountenanced and denounced; 2. that the law of the land, is under no circumstances to be violated; and 3. that the agitation is to be conducted on O'Connell's principle of passive resistance, and within the lines of the constitution(K).

When Kirby received this very sound and sensible letter from Croke, he made the mistake of writing by return on December 13, advising calmness and moderation in word and deed in the present crisis. Croke, who had obviously had enough of Kirby's pious platitudes, replied on December 19, with yet another of his characteristic and refreshing letters, which certainly must have taken Kirby's breath away as he read it.

> It would have been a terrible mistake if the Holy See had interfered with the land agitation, or land agitators in Ireland: and it certainly would have led to some strong talk and writing, if it had become known for *certain* that I was complained of in Rome in connection with it. Something, however, of the fact has been suspected, and I received several letters asking whether, or not, there was any foundation for the rumor. I cannot at all agree with you and I think I know the country pretty well, in saying, that our great element of strength in Ireland is "calmness and moderation in our acts and language." We have tried calmness and what is called *moderation* "ad nauseum" in our dealings with the government, only to be laughed at by them and despised; I predict, not now for the first time, that should the day ever come (and grave fears are entertained that it will) when faith will grow cold in Ireland, and when the masses of the people will fall away from the clergy, it will be because of the well-known want of sympathy with the people on the part of some of the priests and bishops, because of the pusilanimity

(you call it "moderation") and lack of pluck, on the part of more of them. Take the case of the bishop who is now said to be in high favor in Rome—Doctor Macabe. By his so-called pastoral, or rather because of a short sentence in it, he has got himself lauded to the skies by the Orange Press of Ireland and the Tory Press of England, besides having his picture circulated gratis in the White Hall Review—but I suppose, in his communications with Rome he did not tell you, that, for the first time in Irish history, an Irish bishop has been served with threatening notices that he would be shot, a fact which he mentioned to me with his own lips. It is a rare fact too, in Irish history that an Irish Bp. wrote against prisoners in the grasp of the government, and wrote so as to have his words quoted against them by the prosecutor of the crown. So far has the feeling against him gone in some places, that some of my most important priests refuse to subscribe, this year, to St. Patricks Training School, Drummcondra, because it happens to be within his Grace's jurisdiction.

I mention these facts to show, that we must go with the people, manifest our sympathy with the people, and do nothing by word or act that would lead folk to believe that we are *for England* and *against Ireland*.

The cry about *socialism* and all that was simply a ruse. The people around us are threatened with starvation and begging boxes are sent around for them in England and America, and, still, it appears, we must speak with becoming moderation, and play the part of policemen and peace-makers for the government.

It cannot, and will not be done. Enough of politics(K).

By the end of 1880 Parnell had created a genuine national grass-roots organization in the Land League. A bad harvest, a severe winter, a general election, and the continued irresponsibility of Parliament had allowed him to focus and then crystallize a deepening national consciousness. In their general misery and especially in their particular grievances astutely organized and politcially structured by Parnell, Irishmen rapidly became more acutely aware of how necessary it was to transcend their local and provincial horizons and think and act in national terms. The crucial figure in this process of nationalization as far as the Irish Church was concerned, of course, was Thomas William Croke. By early and unreservedly committing himself to the Land League and its leadership, the archbishop of Cashel prevented the alienation of the people from the clergy, and preserved to the Irish Church then and for the future its very considerable power and influence in Ireland. In so committing himself, Croke not only made it eventually possible for the bulk of the clergy to join the League, but he forestalled any action the majority of his brother bishops might have been inclined to take against the League. This veto invoked by Croke resulted in a stalemate which in the last analysis could only be overruled by Rome. That is why throughout 1880, he moved might and main against any Roman interference. Croke realized that the considerable pressure being exerted by the people and lower clergy on his more conservative episcopal colleagues made it only a matter of time before the majority among the bishops opposed to the League would crumble, and with people, priests and bishops united in a national phalanx any untoward action on the part of Rome could be also forestalled. What Croke did not realize, however, was that the Rome of Leo XIII was not the Rome of Pius IX.

III. Intrigue at Rome

November, 1880 - April, 1881

While it appeared in early December, 1880, that the Irish bishops who had visited Rome had successfully forestalled any effort to persuade the pope to condemn the Land League, the struggle in reality had only just begun. The British government, which was responsible for maintaining law and order in Ireland, naturally did not take kindly to the Parnellites either in Parliament or the country, nor did they appreciate the developing clerical support for the Land League. The difficulty was that the Liberal Cabinet, which had assumed office under Gladstone in April, 1880, was actually a house divided on what was a proper Irish policy. On the one hand the Whigs in the Cabinet wanted to take strong coercive measures, and, if necessary, to suspend even *habeas corpus*, to check the worst effects of the agitation. The Radicals on the other hand were for more conciliatory measures, particularly a more equitable solution to the land question, in order to come to grips with what they thought was the basic cause of the agitation. In Ireland the Liberal and Whig political connections were being threatened with electoral extinction by Parnell, and they naturally wanted to check his developing power base before they actually were politically liquidated. They appealed, therefore, to their Whig brethren in the Cabinet to take some immediate and effective action. Those Irish Whigs, moreover, who were Catholic, had an additional grievance. They were especially bitter about the lead Archbishop Croke had given the lower clergy as well as the "veto" he had imposed on the majority of his episcopal brethren who opposed the Land League. These Irish Catholic Whigs, therefore, were anxious that the pope should interfere by condemning the League, which would effectively deprive it of its developing clerical support.

Early in November, one of the most influential of these Irish Catholic Whigs, Lord Emly, wrote Earl Granville, foreign secretary in Gladstone's Cabinet, that Archbishop Croke, in company with the bishop of Limerick, George Butler, among others, had set out for Rome.[1] Emly then went on to complain that the Irish clergy were attending Land League meetings and that some of them were even making violent speeches. In order, therefore, to offset the effect of any plausible explanations that might be made by the Irish bishops to the pope, Emly suggested that Granville might ask the British ambassador in Paris to have a word with the papal nuncio there about the situation in Ireland. That situation, Emly continued, was now so serious that he did not see how the Government could avoid calling Parliament into special session and suspending *habeas corpus*. Every week's delay, he argued, only increased Parnell's power in the country and made the ultimate vindication of the law more difficult. Viscount Monck, another influential Irish Whig and mutual friend, Emly further confided to Granville, had visited with Gladstone the week before at Harwarden, and the prime minister's "back was up," and he "per-emptorily rejected every suggestion for strong measures of repression." "Still," Emly concluded, asking Granville to play the Whig card in the Cabinet, "he surely could not resist you, Hartington, Spencer, Kimberley and Forster."

Indeed Granville knew better than to attempt to override Gladstone when his "back was up." Emly, however, it appears, also wrote W. E. Forster, the chief secretary for Ireland, who was a good deal more naïve than Granville where Gladstone was concerned. Forster obviously acted on Emly's advice, for he wrote Granville several days later, on November 7, explaining that he had written Gladstone dropping a hint about the nuncio in Paris, but that Gladstone had replied that it was not only a Cabinet matter, but that he did not think it would prove effective, and that it would also antagonize Protestant opinion.[2] The chief secretary then somewhat ruefully noted that he wished he had made the suggestion to Granville first rather than to Gladstone, and pointed out that he thought that the

---

[1] Granville Papers(GR), 30/29/149, Great Britain, Public Record Office, London.
[2] GR, 30/29/117.

pope could do great good with a pronouncement just now, though he admitted that, if the government's action in the matter became public knowledge, the effect of the pope's interference would be much neutralized and certainly counterbalanced by some harm. "We can not," he warned Granville in conclusion, still echoing Emly, "put off the decision with regard to a special session for the suspension of the H.C. Act beyond the beginning of next week & I fear we shall be driven to suspend."

Granville was, indeed, as foreign secretary, in an extremely delicate position. Since there were no diplomatic relations between the British government and the Vatican, he had no secure channel of communication, and a leak might have severe political repercussions among liberal non-conformists. He obviously informed Emly of his predicament, for Emly wrote him again on November 17, explaining that he had already taken another tack.[3] He had decided that the safest way to reach the pope was to write through Cardinal Newman. He further advised Granville that it would be best not to take any more action until the Irish bishops in Rome had left. He again suggested, however, that probably the safest way for the government to communicate with the Vatican in the future was through the nuncio in Paris. Granville decided that the approach through the nuncio was too dangerous, and in forwarding Emly's letter to Forster, he asked the chief secretary to write Emly in that sense.[4] What Granville did not seem to realize was that the Holy See was even more interested than some of Her Majesty's ministers in establishing a more effective and secure means of communication between the two governments. The Propaganda was especially anxious at this juncture for closer Vatican-British relations because the Italian government was once again threatening to confiscate Propaganda's real property in Rome. Throughout 1880, English and Irish Roman Catholic bishops made various appeals to the British government to use its influence with the Italian government to prevent what amounted to, in their eyes at

---

[3] GR, 30/29/149.

[4] GR, 30/29/117. Forster to Granville, November 20, 1880.

least, robbery.[5] Granville did, in fact, soon after assuming office in May, 1880, instruct the British ambassador in Rome, Sir Augustus Paget, to have a private word with Count Maffei, Italian foreign minister, about the British government's interest in preserving the property of Propaganda.[6] Relations between the Vatican and the Italian government, however, continued to deteriorate and by the middle of 1880, the question of the confiscation of Propaganda's property was again critical. The disposition of the Vatican, therefore, to do all it could to maintain good relations with the British government increased as the pressure from the Italian government became greater. The Irish situation was an obvious embarrassment to the Vatican and, especially, to the Propaganda, which had the responsibility of administering Ireland.

The visit of Archbishop Croke and his suffragans to Rome only increased the tension, as the Vatican press, and particularly the influential *Aurora*, softened in its attitude towards the Irish agitation. When Croke had left Rome, however, the pope obviously had second thoughts, and began to attempt to redress the balance by assuring the British government of his good intentions. On November 24, 1880, an article, "The *Times* and the Holy See," appeared in the *Aurora*. "My Lord," Paget reported in an official dispatch from Rome to Granville that same day, "the 'Aurora' newspaper is said to be the organ frequently employed by the Vatican to give expression to the views and sentiments of Pope Leo XIII, upon important polit-

---

[5] F. O., 45/402. Sir Augustus Paget to the Marquess of Salisbury, February 21, 1880. See also letter enclosed from Herbert Vaughan, Roman Catholic bishop of Salford, to Paget, February 19, 1880. See also K, June 5, 1880, Bartholomew Woodlock, bishop of Ardagh, to Kirby. See also K, June 19, 1880, George Errington to Kirby. Woodlock enlisted the aid of Errington, who was his member of Parliament. Errington wrote Kirby for information and was prepared to raise the question in Parliament. A note on Foreign Office notepaper dated August 3, 1880, and initialed H.A.L. reads: "Propaganda. / This will not come on. Cardinal Manning has told Sir C. D. [ilke] that the matter was being arranged 'a l'amiable' & that Errington's motion wd do more harm than good." F. O., 45/402. See also Errington to Granville, August 30, 1880, GR, 30/29/149, and Granville's reply, September 1, 1880: "Thanks for yr. letter. I will see if anything can be done unofficially by our Embassy at Rome. But the matter is one of some delicacy."

[6] GR, 30/29/82. Telegram, May 31, 1880, Paget to Granville, marked "approve G." See also June 4, 1880, Paget to Granville, where Paget says he spoke to Count Maffei in sense explained in telegram of May 31, 1880.

ical questions."[7] Paget then went on to explain that "the bulk of the article is devoted to considerations upon the present state of Ireland and the attitude of the Catholic Bishops and Clergy in reference thereto, at the conclusion an account is given to what the writer supposes to have been the language, or at all events the sentiments, expressed by the Pope to some Irish Catholic Bishops who had recently come to Rome." "The paper has been sent to me," he concluded significantly, "with the Card of Signor Pietro Pacelli 'Redattore in Capo Del Giornale L'Aurora,' and I have the honour to enclose the article in question accompanied by a translation."

Even more significantly, two days later, on November 26, Paget reported to Granville that he had just received a visit from no less a personage than Edward Cardinal Howard, an Englishman long resident in Rome, and high in the councils of the pope.[8] The cardinal had called to assure Paget that the article which had appeared in the morning's *Aurora*, as well as that which had appeared several days before, were authentic representations of the pope's opinions on the Irish situation. Howard also added that, since he only recently had a conversation with the pope, he could further assure Paget that the language reported to have been used by His Holiness in his audience with the Irish bishops was in fact what he did say. The cardinal then requested that what he had just said be considered confidential as well as the fact that he had been the channel through which it had passed. Granville sent copies of this dispatch to the Queen, Gladstone, Forster, and Sir William Harcourt, the home secretary. In his note to Forster covering the dispatch, Granville remarked that, though he was not very favorable to seeking anything from the pope, perhaps they ought to respond now that the pope had taken the initiative.[9]

---

[7] F. O., 45/408. November 24, 1880. The *Aurora* article, November 24, 1880, said in part:

"The duties of the Episcopate are more difficult at this time in face of the secret societies which permeate Europe. The Head of the Church will ever protect His See from revolutionary measures. He will consort with the Irish Bishops in upholding the principles of the Church, through all elements of order, it is but a few days since the Irish Bishops come to pay homage to Leo XIII. Who can doubt that he spoke to them in terms of which the English Government would approve. / We are certain that the Church will use its influence in Ireland for the furtherance of peace and order and for strengthening in every way the bonds of amity between its people and their English brethren."

[8] *Ibid.*

[9] *Ibid.* No date on this note.

Granville was almost immediately presented with his means, for George Errington, an Irish Catholic Whig, and M.P. for Longford, wrote him on December 1, explaining that Sir Charles Dilke had suggested that he ask him for an interview. "I am going to Rome at the end of this week," Errington explained, "and some rather important private information I have just received from there, makes me hope I might be of some use."[10] "The Vatican," he pointed out to Granville,

> is placed in a very difficult position with regard to what I am sorry to say is a somewhat influential section of the Irish Catholic Clergy in respect to the unfortunate state of Ireland. These difficulties are already producing the most serious results in Ireland; and it is the intimate knowledge I have of the gravity of this, as well as my anxiety to facilitate the difficult task Her Majesty's Government have just now, that makes me feel keenly the importance of supporting at Rome that other section of the Irish Clergy who think that Religion at any cost should be on the side of order(GR).

This indeed was the opening Granville needed. Errington, though a Liberal M.P., was not a member of the government and his presence in Rome could be explained, as indeed it was a year later by Gladstone to Newman, as an independent Roman Catholic gentleman and a volunteer.[11] Moreover, he had asked for the interview in the name of Sir Charles Dilke, Granville's under secretary at the Foreign Office, and a leading English Radical. The Radicals, therefore, could not with very good grace, at least, complain about Errington's activities in Rome, especially after having helped to initiate them.

Errington's contact in Rome was an extremely influential and very well-connected Irish Benedictine, Bernard Smith. Smith, whose specialty appears to have been intrigue, had been resident in Rome for nearly fifty years, during which time he had served as the official agent for various Irish and American bishops, and for a number of years had even been Kirby's vice-rector in the Irish College. Smith was also in close contact with several Irish Catholic Whigs, among whom Errington appeared to be the most promising politically, and

---

[10] GR, 30/29/149. See also for an important and comprehensive discussion of the "Errington mission," C. J. Woods, "Ireland and Anglo-Papal Relations, 1880-1885," *Irish Historical Studies* **18** (March, 1972), 69: pp. 29-60.

[11] John Morley, *William Ewart Gladstone*, **2** (London, 1906): p. 303; quoted from letter of Gladstone to Newman, December 17, 1881.

with whom he had already been corresponding for a number of years. Before Errington had written Granville requesting an interview, he had, in fact, written Smith a long and interesting letter from London on November 21, giving an excellent example of how an intelligent and politically ambitious Irish Catholic Whig viewed the current Irish situation and Rome's role in that crisis.[12] After explaining that he expected to be in Rome shortly before Christmas even though the dreadful state of Irish affairs made everything so uncertain, Errington added,

> You can form no idea of the state of things in Ireland, and good Catholics are very much pained at the news from Rome, especially certain articles in the Aurora. / We cannot help feeling that the Communistic and unChristian policy of Dr. Croke has received some countenance in Rome. / At all events this is the impression made in Ireland, and the result will be deplorable. / Numbers of excellent & sensible priests have needed all the support of authority both from the Bishops & the Pope to enable them to resist being carried away in the revolutionary flood which has swept the country; now if that authority is any way weakened, if questions *really involving* (as we all know) xtreme doctrines as to society and property are *ever left open*, the position of the moderate clergy will become impossible, and the results will be actually very serious for the Country, but what I think worst, [sic] *shameful for the Church*. This must be the result of even a doubtful pronouncement in Rome, & it will strengthen the most *sinister* influence the Irish Church has ever known. I shall bring to Rome some curious documents to show you, such as placards in letters of blood in which Dr. Croke is quoted (with Voltaire & Rousseau) as justifying nonpayment of rent from St. Paul!!! Now however just this may be as a piece of casuistry, to quote it to ignorant excited people was certain to have and has had the most incendiary effect. / As for the nonsense in the Aurora article that the Land League repudiates illegitimate means, it is the merest piece of hypocrisy & humbug. / No man with *common honesty* enough to admit it, can doubt that the Land League is directly responsible for the present astounding state of Social anarchy & for the numerous outrages & innumerable breaches of the law which are occurring; and certainly Dr. Croke and his friends are also responsible though not so directly as the Land League. / I know your feelings & that is why I write to you so openly. / I hope I shall

---

[12] Smith Papers(S), Archives of St. Paul, Outside the Walls, Rome.

be in time to give any assistance I can to Dr. McCabe in Rome for he will I have no doubt have great (and I am told not so very honest) difficulties prepared for him to contend against(S).

In conclusion, Errington finally assured Smith that he would see both Lord Granville and Dilke before he left and that he hoped something substantial might not only be done about Ireland, but also about Propaganda's property.

In his interview with Granville, Errington reported that the Irish bishops recently in Rome had "made the Pope change his language, and that he now at least to them favour the agitation."[13] Forster, however, wrote Granville from Dublin on December 12, that he for one did not believe the Irish bishops had made the pope change his mind about Ireland, and further insisted that it was now all the more important to keep the pope up to his good intentions as they had been represented by Cardinal Howard.[14] Forster then enclosed three documents which he suggested should be forwarded to Paget to give to Howard. The first of these was Parnell's "moral coventry" speech at Ennis in September, in which he had recommended what was, in effect, a campaign of boycotting. The second document was Archbishop McCabe's Pastoral issued in October, in which he had warned his priests and people about the agitation, and which had been used by the government in its indictment of Parnell and his colleagues after their arrest. The third was the recent charge of Judge Fitzgerald at the Winter Assizes on the state of the country because of the activities of the Land League. Whatever was to be done, Forster advised Granville finally in a postscript, it should be done quickly.

The same day that Forster was thus writing Granville and urging him on, the bishop of Limerick, George Butler, who had just returned from Rome, wrote Kirby informing him that there was a rumor, perhaps not well founded, "that efforts are being made in Rome by the anti-Irish party to poison the minds of the Roman authorities against the popular movement here, and urge them to make some pronouncement favourable to the upper classes & against the people"(K). "If any attempt in this direction is being made," Butler requested, "I would beg you to give it the most earnest

---

[13] F. O., 45/408. This is a note on back of Paget's dispatch No. 536, which is initialed by Granville and intended for Forster.
[14] GR, 30/29/117.

& strenuous opposition. In my opinion—and I ought to know something about it—nothing could tend more to damage religion just now in this country than any pronouncement of Rome against the movement in which the people are engaged, fighting, I may say, for their lives." "I beg you therefore," he then implored Kirby again, "to be on the alert, and to leave nothing undone to hinder such pernicious Councils from being followed by the Holy See." The good bishop of Limerick would have been even more alarmed, if indeed that were possible, had he known the extent and more to which the rumors he had heard were true. Several days later, Moran also wrote Kirby warning him against the expediency of a papal condemnation. "The newspapers have been publishing accounts from Rome," Moran explained on December 15, "that the Holy Father was about to condemn the land-agitation. I trust the accounts have no foundation. It would be, I think, most injurious at the present moment for the Holy See to interfere in the matter. The whole country is in a wild state of ferment of which no one can have an accurate idea except those who are living in the midst of it." "When this ferment will have subsided," Moran prudently advised, "will be the time for the Bishops and the Holy See to speak authoritatively and definitively, marking out the lines between what is lawful and what is unlawful."

In Rome, meanwhile, Errington had been making his contacts and gathering information. "The Ecclesiastical Authorities," he finally reported to Granville in a long and important letter on December 16, "feel deeply the painful position in which they are placed with regard to Ireland."[15] The pope, Errington explained, was terribly annoyed at Croke for the statement the archbishop released to the press shortly after their audience. Not only was the pope distressed by Croke attributing to him words that he did not use, but also in exaggerating those that he did use, especially since they were in reply to statements by the Irish bishops which were entirely *ex parte*. In a word, the pope thought that Croke had taken advantage of him, and he desired to say or do something that would counteract the effect of the press release. Errington then pointed out that he had been urging as strongly as he could that publicly contradicting Croke, or even the sending of private instructions to the Irish bishops, was not sufficient,

[15] GR, 30/29/149.

and that "the gravity of the situation calls for some public authoritative expression." He had already had a long interview, Errington noted, with the secretary and ruling spirit of the Propaganda, Ignazio Masotti. "He takes my view very strongly," added Errington, "and has already spoken to the Pope about it; he has arranged that I am to have an Audience this week, & they are all anxious that I should put the case before the Holy Father as forcibly as possible." "That we shall succeed," he assured Granville, "in getting something done is, I think, now certain; whether we can get all I desire is however, I fear, very doubtful: still the strongest influences have been brought to bear, and I am hopeful."

Errington then turned to what at first would appear to be the logical *quid pro quo* for a papal condemnation of the Land League—the saving of Propaganda's property from confiscation by the Italian government through British influence. Errington had assured Monsignor Masotti, that as far as unofficial and friendly representations to the Italian government were concerned, Granville had already instructed Paget to do what was necessary. Masotti, however, complained that Paget had not acted up to the spirit in which Granville's instructions had been conceived. "This is only one of the reasons," Errington observed, finally coming to the point as to what Rome really expected in return for a condemnation of the League, "which make the Authorities here so anxious for a renewal of the relations previously existing between Her Majesty's Government and the Holy See." "I have told them," he added,

> that as far as I was aware the Government would consider it a very difficult thing now to renew the interrupted relations, however much the interruption might be regretted. On the other hand, I can see that to carry on relations via Paris through the Embassy & the Nuncio, would not be considered nearly so satisfactory as to deal directly with Rome; unless indeed on the expectation that relations however indirect—might lead later to something more direct(GR).

"One thing appears to me quite evident," Errington finally concluded his long letter "that the present unfortunate misunderstanding with regard to Ireland could never have occurred had there been any sort of English representative here."

Granville, meanwhile, had written Paget on December 14,

enclosing the three documents which had been forwarded to him by Forster, and adding that Her Majesty's government felt that the pope's friendly communication made through Cardinal Howard should be responded to with frankness on their part. Paget, who received the documents by special messenger on December 17, immediately called on Howard and offered to leave the documents with him for submission to the pope.[16] In the course of describing the first document, Parnell's speech at Ennis, Paget mentioned the archbishop of Cashel and the bishop of Limerick. "On the mention of the names of these two Prelates," Paget explained to Granville, "Cardinal Howard winced, and observed that 'Irishmen were such wrongheaded people,—it was so difficult to understand or control them—but he was sure the Pope regretted and disapproved the course they had taken.' " Paget then made a special point of assuring Granville that he had explained to Howard that Her Majesty's government had no favor to ask of His Holiness, but since he had taken the initiative, the government felt they would not be repaying His Holiness's confidence if they neglected to put the true facts of the case before him. The cardinal, Paget reported, agreed that there was no question of a favor involved, but "a question of church discipline and administration." "Howard spoke with evident sincerity," Paget then observed, "and I do not think he would have said as much as he did unless he knew that the Pope was distressed and disapproved the line some of the Clergy are taking, and that He was anxious to do what He could to correct them." Paget, like Errington, also concluded his long letter to Granville, significantly enough, by informing him "that the Irish question was being much discussed at the Vatican now, that although the Pope will not favor the agitation, He can hardly be expected to assist the English Govt. in putting it down, unless there should be a British Agent at the Vatican . . . ."

Several days after this account by Paget of his interview with Cardinal Howard, Errington reported to Granville on his private audience with the pope. "I found as I feared," Errington began on December 20, paying incidental tribute to the efforts being made by McCabe, who was still in Rome, and the other Irish Bishops, who were working through Kirby, "that the Pope was not fully alive to the serious state of affairs,

---

[16] GR, 30/29/182, Paget to Granville.

and that owing to the strong representations which have been made from certain quarters to him, he seems rather reluctant to take any very strong or public step, for fear of further complicating matters & doing more harm than good."[17] "I endeavoured as well as I could," Errington continued, "to impress on him how serious the case is becoming, especially as rightly or wrongly the Holy See itself has to a certain extent got compromised in it. He requested me to go up at once and talk over the matter fully with the Secretary of State, who will bring it before him tomorrow. I accordingly had a long conversation with Cardinal Jacobini, I was able to go fully with him into every branch of the question, & he is certainly quite alive as to its great importance. He will bring it before the Pope tomorrow, and he asked me to call on him again on Wednesday." "I had been asked yesterday," Errington further informed Granville, "to draw up a memorandum on the case, and accordingly I hastily put down a few observations on the leading points and had them lithographed last night, and at his request I left a copy with Cardinal Jacobini." "I enclose a copy of them herewith," explained Errington, "in order that your Lordship may see the line of argument used."[18] "I hope some good may be done," he concluded. "I am

---

[17] GR, 30/29/149.

[18] *Ibid.* (the author's translation): Jacobini, who had just been appointed papal secretary of state, had been nuncio at Vienna since 1874. Sir Henry Elliot, British Ambassador at Vienna, reported of Jacobini to Granville, on October 16, 1880 (F. O., 107/295), "He is a man of high intelligence, of moderate opinions, and likely always to exert his influence on the side of conciliation. / He has frequently spoken to me with a willing recognition of the position enjoyed by the Roman Catholics in England, saying that if they were treated in the same way in other countries they would have nothing to complain of." See also Elliot to Granville, October 27, 1880, from Budapest (F. O., 170/296): "Cardinal Jacobini, the Papal Pro-Nuncio, has been received in an audience of leave by the Emperor, and will proceed to Rome in a few days. / H. E. called upon me this afternoon to say goodbye, and I took the opportunity of saying that as he was understood to be about to hold a position of influence, I hoped that he wd exert it in endeavouring to induce the Roman Catholic Prelates of Ireland to pronounce themselves more energetically than some of them had done against the lawless spirit prevailing in certain parts of the country. / If they considered that these were grievances of which a part of their flocks had reason to complain it would of course be quite proper for them to strive to have them removed by legal means, but I was sure H. E. wd be the first to acknowledge it to be the duty of the Bishops publicly to stigmatize as it deserves the lawless terrorism which would disgrace any cause however good. / The Cardinal said that he fully concurred in these remarks and that on reaching Rome one of his first objects would be to inquire into the state of things in Ireland, with which he was at present very slightly acquainted. / He was perfectly aware that no wish to oppress the R. C. existed in England, and it was one of the duties of those in authority in the Church to strive for the observance of the law and for the maintenance of order."

pretty sure we shall get them to do something, but I am endeavouring that it should be done as promptly and efficiently as possible."

In his long memorandum in French on the state of Ireland, Errington argued that the Holy See must do something, pointing out in conclusion that public opinion in England was becoming exasperated. "If this sentiment continues," Errington wrote, "it will probably produce an anti-Catholic reaction which would have terrible results for religion." "It is also necessary," he argued, and Granville must have been amused,

> to consider the effect that this sentiment will produce on the conversions of Protestants, and how it would retard the movement of souls towards the true religion. But there are still other interests to consider. The British Empire extends over the whole world. In the Indies, in America, everywhere it finds itself in *rapport* with the Church and her works, and the interest of civilisation and of Religion require that the understanding between the two powers should also be as cordial as possible. Nothing would tend more to establish this understanding on a solid base, than the re-establishment of diplomatic relations between the Holy See and England. We are working with ardour to attain this goal, and we hope for the power to conquer the difficulties which stand in the way at the moment(GR).

"The occasion for advancing these projects," added Errington, blending the spiritual and the temporal, "would appear therefore almost providential; we are at a moment in which the Holy See would be able to clearly express her true sentiments, render at the same time a very great service to Catholicism and to the Church in Ireland, and win the good will of the English people and government." "But time presses," Errington urged in conclusion. "Anarchy advances day by day: the English Parliament ought to meet on January 6, and a word now would have an influence and an importance that later perhaps it would no longer have."

Finally, on Christmas Eve, Errington telegraphed Granville, "Communiqué Will Appear Tonight in Osservatore Condemning Land League."[19] The following insertion was carried by the *Osservatore* on Christmas Day:

> It is with real grief that we read daily the reports on affairs in

---

[19] GR, 30/29/149.

Ireland which become every day more serious. And the more distressing are these reports as the secular faith and Christian virtue of the Irish people inspire universally and deep and sincere sympathy. God grant, is the universal wish, that timely and careful measures on the part of the Government may put a stop to the deplorable conflict.

But in the heart of the strife it is the supreme duty of the clergy and of the Irish people to show that even in the defence of their legitimate interests, the sons of the Church separate themselves from the followers of the revolutionary movement, not forgetting the fundamental principle of the Catholic religion that the end does not justify means which are anarchical and reproved by conscience, the employment of which might even compromise the future of the country.[20]

What indeed was there to be said, except that Errington had moved mountains in the name of the British Empire and had produced a mouse.

The communiqué was, in fact, missed entirely by Paget, who wrote Granville two days after Christmas, explaining that it had just been called to his attention by Cardinal Howard, who had only seen it himself the day before. Though Howard was not authorized to say it, Paget reported to Granville, he did say the pope ordered the insertion in the *Osservatore*. "The present declaration contains, I presume," Paget commented, "the measure of interposition which has to be looked for from the Vatican in regard to the strife in Ireland."[21] "A direct injunction," Paget observed shrewdly,

addressed to the Bishops, conveying the Pope's disapproval of the part taken by some of them and of the Clergy in identifying themselves with the revolutionary movement, would have been, of course, far preferable as carrying more weight, but I own that from Cardinal Howard's language the other day, I was not very sanguine of so decided a course being pursued. I gathered indeed from Cardinal Howard this morning that one of the Bishops had distinctly said that some of the Clergy were so far compromised in the movement that it would be useless to try and stop them now(GR).

The communiqué in the *Osservatore*, Paget pointed out, "un-

---

[20] F. O., 45/408. December 27, 1880. This translation from the *Osservatore Romano* was quoted in this letter of Paget to Granville.
[21] GR, 30/29/182.

doubtedly contains the sentiments of reproval and disapprobation of which a very efficient use might be made by a well disposed Hierarchy in imparting directions to the lower Clergy,—and if the Pope should have given private instructions to the Bishops that it was his wish that it should be used for this purpose, its good effect would of course be increased." "Whether, however, the Pope has caused such an intimation to be made to them," Paget concluded, "I was unable to ascertain from Cardinal Howard who said, in short, he had now done all he could."

In Ireland the communiqué in the *Osservatore* seemed to have gone unnoticed. In asking Kirby to thank the Propaganda authorities very warmly for a monsignorship he had requested while in Rome for one of his priests, Croke remarked on December 30, "Individual pronouncements just now would do more harm than good"(K). "Dr. McCabe's Pastoral (so called)," Croke added, and referring to the prosecution of Parnell and the leaders of the Land League which had begun in Dublin on December 28, "was produced in open court yesterday, by the Attorney General as evidence *against* the accused. / This will have a very bad effect amongst our people." "The 'Daily News' and 'Telegraph,' through their Roman correspondents," Croke went on to complain to Kirby, "have issued most lying paragraphs against me, to the effect, that 'a high dignitary at Propaganda' had 'animadverted' (to correspondent) 'on me in most unmeasured terms for having falsified the words of the Pope.'" "I cannot, of course, believe," continued Croke, protesting a little too much, "that anyone at Propaganda could have made such a statement, and that the Pope was to fulminate some tremendous document against me in consequence. Lies are the order of the day." "The truth," he added more judiciously,

> is that I gave only substance of interview to *Doctor Vaughan of Salford,* that he put it into shape, called at Minerva to see me for my approval of it, but not finding me there, as I was at the Irish College, he read what he had written for Doctor Butler, and I believe, the other Bishops, and had it approved of as correct. This regarded the first interview. The second contained nothing worth mentioning, the Pope having simply said that he would wish to have his voice heard from time to time in Ireland and for Ireland, "en Irlande et pour Irlande"(K).

"No chance of a verdict *against* the accused," Croke remarked in a postscript. "There may be a disagreement—perhaps, acquittal. Latter not likely."

Several days later Croke wrote another of his remarkable letters. This letter, however, which had obviously been in his mind for some time, was not addressed to Kirby, but rather to the Cardinal Prefect of Propaganda.[22] "The pressures and arrears of business," Croke informed Cardinal Simeoni on January 2, 1881, "which had to be attended to on my return home, have prevented me from writing to you before now and I write now chiefly to make my acknowledgements to you, on my own part, and on the part of my suffragan Bishops, for the extreme kindness and courtesy with which you received and treated us during our sojourn in the Eternal City."[23] "Kindly accept then Eminence," Croke added politely, "this somewhat tardy (but sincere expression) of our united thankfulness and gratitude." "I write also," Croke observed further, coming to what was really on his mind,

> to explain a circumstance to which I understand, you referred more than once lately, the circumstance namely, of our having subscribed to the "Parnell Defense Fund," and written a letter, at the same time, in connection with it, dated from Rome. In the first place, then, it can hardly have escaped your Eminence's notice that the "Defense Fund" has nothing whatever to do with the *League*, that its object is simply to provide for the legal expenses of the trial, and that numbers have subscribed to it who are unfriendly to the *League*, and opposed to its aims and operations. Twelve of the Irish Bishops have in point of fact already publicly subscribed to the "Defense Fund"(K).

"As for the matter of having dated our letter from Rome," Croke further explained, "I have simply to say that we acted in doing so on the good old maxim that 'vis dat qui cito dao'; and the few lines that accompanied our subscription could have had no possible significance beyond exhibiting our sympathy with the cause of fair play and even handed justice. Our prompt action had an immense effect in procuring the need-

---

[22] See K. December 22, 1880, Croke to Kirby.
[23] Croke Papers(C), Archives of the Archdiocese of Cashel, Thurles. There is a microfilm copy of the Croke Papers on deposit in the National Library of Ireland, Dublin.

ful funds; and it was the anticipation of this result that caused us to write from Rome, rather than to defer doing so until our return to our respective Dioceses."

I know your Eminence is beset," Croke sympathized, "with all manner of correspondence in reference to the Irish land agitation." "I have no wish to increase your perplexity," he assured the Cardinal, "but will take leave, nevertheless, to call your attention to the following *facts*:

1. It is a fact, that the Irish as a nation are the worst fed, the worst clad, and the worst housed people in the world, the only people who have been periodically forced to beg for bread in Europe, America, and Australia, and to seek shelter, by hundreds of thousands, in foreign lands from the cruel exactions which they had to endure at home.

2. It is a fact, that the Irish are the most practically religious people in the world, devoted to the Holy See, devoted to their priests, regular recipients of the Sacraments of Penance and of the Blessed Sacrament, believing in divine Revelation, and a divinely constituted Church, and, such being the case, it is preposterous to suppose, that they could join, as a body, in any movement opposed to the principles of their faith or to the morality of the Gospel.

3. It is a fact, at the same time, that nine-tenths of the Irish people at home, and all the Irish race abroad, are enthusiastically in favour of the Irish land League and of the agitation to which it has given rise.

4. It is a fact, that the Junior Clergy of Ireland almost without exception are simply in favour of the *League* and of the changes that it contemplates.

5. It is a fact, that considerably more than half the Senior Clergy entertain the same views.

6. It is a fact, that every priest and Bishop in Ireland firmly believes that the land laws as at present regulating the relations between landlords and tenants, are most unjust, calculated to enslave the people and impoverish the Country, and that there exists, in most cases, no binding contracts whatever between landlord and tenant, owing to the important fact, that the latter has not possessed the freedom required for entering into a valid contract. The Revd. George MacCutchen, Protestant Rector of Kenmare, writing on this subject in yesterday's *Freeman*, says— "The fact is beyond all doubt, that the laws regulating the tenure of land in Ireland permit the people to be degraded into a position little raised above actual serfdom, where every *family*

relation may be harassed by the interference of estate rules; *where freedom of contract is unknown*; and the self respect of the great bulk of the community is degraded into craven fear of offending those who have the power to make or mar the tenants future."

7. It is a fact, that fewer acts of violence have been committed this year in Ireland than there were at any corresponding period of our history for the last 20 years.

8. It is a fact, that all the leaders of the land movement, whether lay or clerical, and notably Messrs. Parnell, Dillon and Davitt, have, over and over again, discouraged violence and denounced the agents of it, as being the enemies of Ireland and the tenants' cause, besides being guilty of weighty offenses against the law of God.

9. It is a fact, that the League has already done a vast deal of good for the Country at large, as well because it has made landlords lower their rents to an equitable level, as because it has extracted from the Government the promise of a good Land Bill next year.

10. It is a fact, that the leaders of the land agitation have never recommended the absolute non-payment of rent, but only the payment of excessive and exorbitant rents. On the contrary, they *insist* on the payment of a *fair* rent according to the Government valuation and the faithful discharge, likewise, of every just and honourable liability.

11. It is a fact, that, though Mr. Parnell is, unfortunately for himself, a Protestant, he is, nevertheless, a man of high honour and unimpeachable moral character. He has repeatedly denied the charge that he contemplates armed insurrection in this Country. He is neither a Fenian nor a Freemason; and his sole aim *I* believe to be to save his native land, and to emancipate an enslaved people by the means afforded him under the British Constitution(K).

"I will not weary your Eminence," Croke finally remarked considerately, "by a more lengthened statement." "I think I know Ireland and Ireland's agitators," he maintained unequivocally, "as well as any man of my race, and I do not hesitate to assure Yr. Eminence most solemnly, that I firmly believe in the truth of everything that I have herein set forth." "I believe, moreover," Croke affirmed in conclusion, "that the people will have a *peaceable* triumph over their oppressors, and that any interference on the part of the H. See just now in Irish affairs would be attended with the most ruinous results."

Before Croke's letter had time to reach Rome, however, the pope had already taken the action he had warned so strongly against. Suddenly, and unexpectedly, Paget telegraphed Granville confidentially from Rome on January 4, 1881: "The Pope has addressed today for immediate publication a Pontifical Letter to the Archbishop of Dublin of which the following is the substance. It must however be considered confidl. until published—"

He praises the Pastoral of the Archbishop, then after having recalled the firmness of the Faith of the Irish Catholics and expressed the desire of seeing their present condition improved, He exhorts them to do nothing which is contrary to the obedience due to the legitimate authorities.—He recalls that in past times in moments of commotion the Holy See did not fail to give exhortations in order that justice should not be thwarted by failure of moderation. In proof of which He recalls letters written by Gregory the 16th on the 12th of March 1839, and the 15th October 1844, and also the letter written by Himself, through Propaganda, on the 1st of June of last year, and the words addressed in last November to the Irish Bishops who had come to Rome. He expresses confidence in the equity, experience, and political sense of the English Govt., affirms that Ireland will more readily obtain what she desires if she remains within the limits of the law, and finally exhorts the Bishops to take measures in order that the Irish people in such a serious situation should not go beyond the limits of equity and justice.[24]

In his official dispatch covering this telegram the following day, January 5, Paget described to Granville how "Cardinal Howard called upon me yesterday afternoon, having written previously to ensure my being at home."[25] Howard had given him the text, Paget reported, which was in the cardinal secretary of state's own handwriting. Furthermore, Cardinal Jacobini had written it in Howard's presence and the pope had asked Howard personally to bring it to Paget for immediate communication to Her Majesty's government.

The timing of the pontifical letter was, indeed, one of the most interesting things about it. In urging the need for prompt action, Errington had stressed the point in his memorandum that Parliament would meet on January 6, and,

---

[24] F. O., 170/302.
[25] Ibid.

if something were to be done, it should be done before that date. Parliament did not meet, in fact, until January 7, and the pontifical letter was conveniently "announced" in the *Aurora* that same evening.[26] The pope had, undoubtedly, been impressed with Errington's argument that action on his part now would put Parliament in a more amicable state of mind regarding a consideration of diplomatic relations between Great Britain and the Holy See. Then too, the way in which the Pope decided to show his hand was revealing. In courteously taking the British government into his confidence with regard to Ireland, by giving advance notice of his intentions, he was encouraging like confidences.[27] The initiative taken by the pope was cordially responded to by the British government in the person of Paget. "I went to see Cardinal Howard yesterday," he wrote Granville on January 7, "and requested him to convey to the Pope 'The appreciation of H. M.'s Govt. of the interest manifested by His Holiness in the cause of peace and order in Ireland.' "[28] "It is quite evident," Paget then noticed, "at all events, from the facts of the Pope personally desiring Howard to bring the substance of the letter to me that His Holiness wished it to be understood as having been issued in consequence of the recent communications with H. M. Govt., and therefore He will no doubt be very much pleased with the message sent to Him through Howard yesterday."

---

[26] *Ibid.*, January 7, 1881. Telegram, Paget to Granville.

[27] There had, indeed, been a number of such "confidences." The affair of the property of Propaganda has already been mentioned. There was also a request, however, on the British side for the appointment of a British subject when the successor to the late vicar apostolic of Gibraltar should be chosen. Granville wrote Paget on November 13, 1880 (F. O., 170/296): "The Secretary of State for the Colonies has informed me that in a recent despatch from the Governor of Gibraltar, Lord Napier expressed his opinion that it is very essential to the interest of the Garrison and the good of the Roman Catholic population that Dr. Scandella's successor should be a British Subject. / If Your Excellency approves of the course, I request that you will communicate Lord Napier's wishes to Cardinal Howard, in order that His Eminence may make them known in the proper quarter. Lord Kimberley having stated that he would be glad if the object recommended by Lord Napier could be attained. Paget reported to Granville on December 4, 1880." (F. O., 45/408): "Cardinal Howard came to see me the day before yesterday. He could not, he said, then tell me anything more than that he had already mentioned the subject, that there was always a disposition at the Vatican to do anything agreeable for the British Government, and that when he was in a position to give me a decided answer on the present question he would return." Paget wrote Granville on December 18, 1880 (GR, 30/29/182), in part—Howard "had reason to believe that a name had been proposed which would give full satisfaction to H. M.'s Govt, but that he could not say more at present. He would let me know as soon as he could."

[28] GR, 30/29/182.

When Errington learned about the letter in Rome on January 4, he immediately set out for London to take his place at the opening of Parliament. The following day, Wednesday, he arrived in Paris where he had a long conversation with the British Ambassador, Lord Lyons, who professed himself in favor of an English representative in Rome and promised to write Granville to that effect. When Errington arrived in London on Thursday the first person he saw was Sir Charles Dilke, who confided that they had just received the text of the pope's letter, and that it was "quite as strong as could be expected." Finally on Saturday, the day after Parliament opened, Errington had a long interview with Granville, who asked Errington when he wrote to Cardinal Jacobini to tell him how obliged he and his colleagues were, and how much they appreciated the view the cardinal and the pope had taken. In reporting all this to Smith on Tuesday, January 11, Errington apologized for waiting more than a week before writing, but that he wanted to see what effect the papal letter had before he wrote(S). The letter, Errington explained, had only appeared the previous morning, Monday, and it was still too early, therefore, to say what its impact on the public was. What line the Irish clergy were likely to take on it, Errington confessed that he did not know, but he suspected that Croke would simply ignore the papal pronouncement. "As far as English representation in Rome," he assured Smith, and finally coming to the essential point, "I of course pressed the matter very strongly on Lord Granville and have done so on the other Ministers. Lord Granville is extraordinarily favourable, though he still points out difficulties: it appears to me however from various indications that we are almost certain to have the thing granted, & perhaps much sooner than any of us expects." "I was at Lady Granville's in the evening," Errington added, by way of example, "& the thing was spoken of as quite a natural subject of conversation, & Lady Herbert was even discussing with me who should be sent. We must not of course be premature in expecting this, for I know nothing certain, but I have the greatest hopes." "Pray tell all our friends," he begged Smith in conclusion, "Masotti and others, how pleased our people are with them."

What Granville and his colleagues must have realized was that the pope's letter was really only a very clever gambit in his effort to secure diplomatic relations with the British government. Errington's enthusiasm for diplomatic relations, and perhaps even seeing himself as the future English representative in Rome, could not have obscured the fact that the pope's letter was only an implied condemnation of the League. The crucial point of the letter was that while vaguely exhorting the Irish bishops to take what action might be necessary in the crisis to preserve equity and justice, it actually left the initiative in the hands of the bishops as a body. The burden was now on the Irish bishops, and the great question was what indeed would they do. Given the fact that the episcopal consensus had been and still was against any interference, whether from principle or expediency, the odds, of course, were that they would continue to do nothing. The pope would then have a series of options open to him, all of which he could use in furthering his project for diplomatic relations. He could, for example, either privately or publicly instruct the Irish bishops to take action through the Propaganda; or instead of exhorting the bishops he could himself publicly or privately instruct them to act; or he could alternately act himself and present them with an authoritative *fait accompli*. There was also the possibility, of course, that the pope would decide to do no more than he had already done. In any case, the next move in this elaborate diplomatic game initiated by the pope was up to the Irish bishops.

The reaction to the pope's letter among the Irish bishops was a mixture of caution and consternation. The archbishop of Dublin, who had the responsibility for publishing the letter, for example, took the unusual course of covering it with an explanatory letter of his own. Both letters were published on Monday, January 10, in the *Freeman's Journal*. "Lest there might be an attempt," McCabe explained to Kirby that very same day for the benefit of Rome, "made to show that the Holy Father took up his stand against the legitimate demands of the people, I wrote a few lines in which I explained the opinion of the Pope from the instruction given verbally to myself"(K). McCabe, of course, had forwarded copies of the pope's letter to all the Irish bishops immediately on receiving it. Moran, who replied on January 10, thanking McCabe for forwarding the letter, was cautious but contained in his brief note. "I have not as yet maturely considered it," he wrote, hedging a little, "but I fear that it will be construed as implying much more than what it says & that it will be a cause of joy to many who have but little love for Ireland."[29] Moran then concluded by remarking simply that it was well that the meeting of the bishops scheduled for a consideration of Gladstone's proposed Land Bill would be held so soon, for it would give them "an opportunity of taking collectively some common action in the present grave crisis of our people."

Several days later when Moran had more time to consider the implications of the pope's letter, he also wrote Kirby, but a good deal more candidly than he had written McCabe. While admitting politely on January 12, that the Pope's letter was in many respects a noble one, Moran pointed out that "it was written at the urgent importunity of those who have no love for Ireland"(K)."They expected," he added shrewdly, "that it would be much stronger & hence they are not at all satisfied with it. On the other hand the friends of Ireland & of the Holy See, must look on the letter as an implied censure of the present movement." "Such a censure on the movement," Moran declared, with surprising firmness, "so far as it regards the material condition of our people, neither the Bishops nor the faithful will accept." Moran then explained that the pope's letter would be considered, as a matter of course, by the bishops on January 25, their next scheduled meeting. What the reply of the bishops would be, Moran confessed that he did not know. "But," he continued, beginning to sound more and more like Croke, "I do not think that I misinterpret the opinions of the Bishops when I anticipate that they will declare their resolve that in political matters our Bishops & clergy shall be united with our people. Englishmen, even English Catholics, do not understand Irish feelings. They think we shd. unite with the Government against the people. We will I trust soon undeceive them in this." "There is," Moran then finally warned Kirby in conclusion, "a secret agitation going on at present about renewing diplomatic relations between the Holy See & England. However I trust that Providence will guard the Holy Father & not allow him to become a tool of English politicians."

Archbishop Croke's reaction to the pope's letter was dif-

---

[29] McCabe Papers(Mc), Archives of the Archdiocese of Dublin, Dublin.

ferent only in that he began on a contemptuous rather than a cautious note. "The Pope's 'manifesto,' " he wrote Kirby on January 15, "is a very 'milk and waterish' document. It cannot possibly do any good, and it is calculated to do a deal of mischief"(K). "I speak plainly to you," confided Croke, in a letter already marked "private," "but of course, I mean it only for yourself." "The Pope," he continued, "might as well have written recommending the observance of the 'ten commandments' by the Irish people as recommending them to do no injustice and keep within the law. The Bishops and priests have been *constantly* preaching of the observance of the latter recommendation as well as the former."

But, the Pope's pronouncement appears to imply, that, in the latter respect, we either have actually been wanting in our duty, or may possibly be so in future. In so far, then, in the first place, it is not satisfactory.

Secondly, it gives a sanction of the Pastoral of the Archbp. of Dublin which 999 out of every 1,000 Irishmen, all over the world, were unanimous in denouncing.

Thirdly, it insinuates, but does not openly say, that the agitation as was carried on is not to be approved of. With Doctor Macabe's commentary that is, in fact, openly stated.

Fourthly, it expresses confidence in the English Liberal government, the successor of Palmerston who plotted against the Holy See, and having for its actual chief, Gladstone, who wrote the bitterest invective, a few years ago, against Church and Pope.

Fifthly, it is known to have been issued, more to please English prejudice, than to benefit the Irish tenant.

Sixthly, it ignores the advice given to the Holy See by the Irish bishops, not to interfere in Irish politics, *just now*, and it practically prefers the advice of the enemies of Ireland who are ignorant of her needs and only anxious for her humiliation.

Other things, too, have been urged against it. On the other hand, it has not produced a favorable effect amongst *anti-leaguers* at home or abroad. The English papers have thoroughly and contemptuously ignored it—no paper in Ireland has referred to it except the Freeman and that in no laudatory terms.

The National Land League have determined not to say a word about it in one way or another; and so, as I said in the beginning, it can do no good and *may* do yet a deal of harm(K).

"However," Croke than added, "time will tell." "In my document to Propaganda, and to Card. Jacobini," he summed up, "I took care to state solemnly that, at present, the Pope should keep silent 'libera anima meum.' " "Still," he then complained, "we see the results." "The Bishops will do their duty," Croke firmly concluded, "—and their first duty is to stand by their people."

What indeed would be the reply of the bishops at their general meeting at Maynooth to the pope's letter to Archbishop McCabe? A large number in fact chose to solve the problem of tender conscience by boycotting the meeting. On January 26, the day after the meeting, Moran reported to Kirby that only fourteen bishops in a hierarchy of twenty-eight were present. "No Bishop," Moran remarked significantly, referring to Croke's archepiscopal jurisdiction, "was present from Munster, but the Abp. of Cashel wrote to have his name attached to any letter that would be forwarded to the Pope."[30] "The most important matter done at our meeting," continued Moran, "was to adopt a letter to His Holiness which was unanimously agreed to and which I think will please you. As soon as it can be copied it will be forwarded to you for presentation to the Holy Father." "The last sentence," Moran noted, "is one which will not please some English people. It states that several things have been published in the English Catholic and Protestant newspapers injurious to our clergy and our country, which were based solely on calumny and falsehood." "We pray His Holiness," he concluded solemnly, "to pay no attention to such reports, and in all matters connected with the Irish Church to listen solely to the Irish episcopate."

In deciding to do nothing, however, the Irish bishops had, in effect, as must have been anticipated by Rome, deferred to the pope. In fact, Kirby reported to McCabe immediately after the joint letter arrived, that Rome was pleased. Indeed, the pope might well be pleased, for the bishops' refusal to act, had by default left the initiative with him, and he could now

---

[30] K, January 26, 1881. See also Croke to Kirby, K, January 24, 1881. "This heavy blow," Croke wrote, referring to the death of a member of his household, "will prevent me from being, tomorrow, in Dublin, with the other Bishops, but I have written my views to Dr. McCabe, and otherwise submitted to any arrangements, or expression of opinion, which the assembled Prelates may make." "All is quiet here," Croke added, "You need have no fears about Parnell."

turn to the various options open to him in his pursuit of diplomatic relations with the British government. The price the pope had paid, however, in his new found freedom of action was considerable. He had not only pushed the more moderate of the bishops, such as Moran, into the Crokite camp, but he had increased the disunity among the bishops by now adding a papal and anti-papal dimension to a difference that simply had been defined in Land League and anti-Land League terms. In his reply to Kirby's letter reporting that Rome was pleased, McCabe attempted to put the best face possible on the recent boycotting of the bishops' meeting. "Owing to the inclemency of the weather," he explained discreetly on February 5, "some of the Bishops were not at the meeting, and as it would not have been easy to procure the signatures of those who were absent it was thought better instead of getting the signature of the Prelates present that I should sign it in the name of all"(K). Not all the bishops, however, were as discreet as the archbishop in writing to Rome about the poor attendance at the episcopal meeting. "I am sorry to say," wrote the Bishop of Ardagh, Bartholomew Woodlock, the same day as McCabe, "that Dr. Croke, whom, as you know, I esteem very much, and the other Bps. of Munster absented themselves from our meeting last week in Maynooth"(K). "No good can come from division at present," Woodlock then added, "— & much evil may come from even the appearance of disunion."

The problem of disunity among the Irish bishops was about to be solved, temporarily at least, by the startling news they were soon to receive from Rome. About the middle of February, Moran had finally set out on his long deferred trip to Rome. When he arrived in Rome, he was sent for on February 25, by the papal secretary of state, Cardinal Jacobini, and they had a long conversation well into the evening about Irish affairs. Moran was so disturbed that he immediately wrote McCabe the following day. "There is one matter about which he spoke to me," Moran reported, "which I think it right to communicate to you all at once. It is of the effort which is being made by the English Catholics to avail themselves of the present feeling in England in order to establish diplomatic relations between the Holy See & England"(Mc). "The Cardinal," Moran continued,

asked me my own opinion in the matter & though I told him I

felt very reluctant to give an opinion on a subject so intimately connected with the welfare of the whole Irish Church, without having the question examined by the whole Irish Episcopate, yet as he pressed me to state my views I told him that I considered that the direct communication between Ireland & Rome was essential for the well-being of our Irish Church & that neither our Bishops nor Clergy nor people wd. ever consent to have our Ecclesiastical affairs transacted through London(Mc).

"Of course," Moran explained, "if a Nunzio be sent to London it is through him that all our Ecclesiastical matters shd be transacted, & I need scarcely say that the Nunzio living in London wd naturally take up the spirit of the English Government & wd view matters altogether through an English atmosphere." "As far as I have been able to learn from enquiries which I have made at various sources here in Rome," Moran added, "the English Bishops here have called on Lord [sic] Paget about these Diplomatic Relations, & on the other hand are negotiating the matter with Lord Granville through his relative Lady Georgiana Fullerton." "I would ask you," Moran requested, "to bring the matter before the Bishops when they hold their Meeting on Mr. Gladstone's Land-scheme." "If any steps are to be taken," Moran warned, "they must be prompt, otherwise when the matter is settled it will be too late for us to interfere."

The pope had now obviously made his next move, and once again the question was what would the Irish bishops do. Almost as soon as he received Moran's letter of February 26, McCabe wrote a "private" circular letter on March 4, to all the Irish bishops.

My dear Lord,

I have received a letter from the Bishop of Ossory who is now in Rome in which he says that great influences are brought to bear on the Holy Father to induce him to establish a *Nunciature* at London.

If this arrangement be carried out I believe the business of the Irish Church must pass to Rome through the hands of the Nuncio.

If the Bishops of Ireland think this *inexpedient* the sooner their opinions are known in Rome the better.

The Bishop of Ossory remarks that there is no time to be lost.

I would not trouble your Lordship with this letter only that I
fear the Land Bill being postponed the Meeting of the Bishops
must be postponed also(Mc).

Never before, perhaps, in the history of the Irish Church
were the bishops so united about any one thing. In a hierarchy
of twenty-eight, twenty-four bishops objected to the establishment of a nunciature in London. The replies of three
bishops, Cork, Ardagh, and the coadjutor of Killaloe, if indeed they wrote, do not survive and one, Archbishop
MacHale's, was a simple acknowledgment by Thomas
MacHale of McCabe's circular letter(Mc). The range and
tenor of the bishops' objections varied greatly, but the replies
of the anti-Land League bishops were as fully condemnatory
as those who sympathized with the League. The foremost
among the anti-League bishops, after McCabe, Laurence Gillooly, the Bishop of Elphin, for example, thought the establishment of a nunciature in London "under any conditions
would be an unmixed evil."[31] The reaction of those who
sympathized with the League may well be imagined. "I would
strain every nerve," wrote Patrick Dorrian, the Bishop of
Down and Connor, to McCabe on March 6, "to resist an
intermediate Nunciature in London between Ireland and the
Apostolic See"(Mc). "I need not adduce reasons," he added
melodramatically, "Hunger and famine always welcome in
preference to hostility and cunning!" Even those who had
remained neutral for fear of either losing their hold on their
flocks or antagonizing Rome were shaken. Michael Logue, the
bishop of Raphoe, for example, thought the project would be
"ruinous." "The more fervent among the Irish people," he
wrote McCabe on March 9, "might still, no doubt, remain
good Catholics, and render true, though less cheerful, obedience to authority; but those who are already shakey [sic], and
they are becoming more numerous of late, would simply turn
against the Church the hatred which is now directed against
the Government"(Mc).
Though the Irish bishops were certainly agreed, the real
question was what they were going to do about the proposed
diplomatic relations. "The isolated action of *individual* prel-

[31] Mc, March 5, 1881. See also John MacEvilly, coadjutor to the archbishop of
Tuam to McCabe, Mc, March 6, 1881, for another example of an anti-Land League
bishop's reactions.

ates," wrote James Donnelly, the bishop of Clogher, to McCabe on March 5, expressing the episcopal consensus, "would not meet such a crisis"(Mc). "For all sakes, My dear Lord," he implored McCabe, "summon us together without a day's delay, that we may *conjointly* and strongly address the Holy See on the subject." The following day Croke wrote Kirby that the bishops were most anxious to know for certain whether there was an attempt "either by the English Government or by the English faction in Rome, to *induce the Pope to establish a nunciature in London*"(K). "If it were so," Croke explained, asking Kirby to send a telegram saying yes or no, "we would unanimously protest against it." McCabe, meanwhile, had also written Moran that same day, asking him to send a telegram if he should consider it urgent to hold an immediate meeting of the bishops. Moran did not send a telegram, as he explained to McCabe on March 10, because he thought that since the bishops were about to meet to discuss Gladstone's Land Bill, which he assumed was about to be introduced in the House of Commons, they could then do double duty without the inconvenience of two meetings(Mc). The Land Bill, however, was not forthcoming until April 7, and McCabe had sent out another circular letter on March 11, calling for a general meeting of the Irish bishops on March 15, in Dublin(Mc).

In his letter of March 10, Moran had explained to McCabe more fully the details of the proposal to establish diplomatic relations. "The Project," Moran began, "may be said to have two parts, one of which regards the sending of an English recognized agent to Rome, & the other regards the presence of a Roman agent in London"(Mc). "My own opinion," Moran commented, "is not worth much, but undoubtedly I think that the Holy See shd. pay no attention to any of the English agents or to the statements which they present. In Missionary countries the Bishops of each country are the best confidential advisers whom the Holy See can consult & whose advice will be most conscientiously given." "However," Moran added more realistically, "shd. the Pope consider that an English agent in Rome wd. be desirable I don't suppose that we could complain much of such a concession being made to the British Government."

"The second part of the project," Moran continued, and

providing the bishops with the necessary food for thought at their meeting, "is that which wd. prove detrimental or rather destructive to us." "It wd. be the more disastrous if as it is whispered the agent of the Holy See in London would be an English Prelate. It is supposed that the Govt. in London wd. not look with favour on an Italian & hence that it wd. be more expedient to appoint to that post one of the English Prelates." "If the Holy See were to decide on such a course," Moran advised, "it seems to me that one of two things shd. at least be accorded us, viz—either that our Irish Ecclesiastical affairs shd. be withdrawn from the jurisdiction and province of such an agent, or that a special agent for Irish matters shd. be granted to Ireland." "It will be difficult & morally impossible I fear," Moran noted, "to obtain either of these alternatives, and hence it only remains that we do our best to oppose directly this part of the project." "Since I last wrote to you," Moran further explained to McCabe, "I had a long audience with His Holiness. He was most kind. He was very desirous to receive accurate information about the political aims of the Land League & about our hopes for the future. He then introduced the matter of the Diplomatic Relations as one to which he looked forward as a source of many advantages for the Holy See & for the Church in England & in other countries." "I boldly said," declared Moran, "that if His Holiness sent an agent to London we never wd be content in Ireland unless we got an agent for ourselves in Ireland." " 'But would the English Government,' " Moran then reported the pope as asking, " 'look with jealousy on such an agent in Ireland?' " "I replied," Moran wrote, "that as his business wd solely regard the spiritual concerns of Ireland there wd be no grounds for such jealousy." "I have entered into these details," Moran concluded to McCabe, "as perhaps they may be of some use to you when considering the matter with the assembled Bishops."

How closely the Irish bishops hewed to Moran's line was evident from the letter which was attested to by the entire Irish hierarchy, except Archbishop MacHale, and addressed to Moran for presentation to the pope.

Dublin
March 15, 1881

Dear Monsignor,

We have heard with great alarm that rumours pointing to a change in the relations hitherto existing between the Holy See and the Irish Church are widely circulated in Rome. The report of these rumours has filled us with so much anxiety that at great inconvenience to ourselves and to our diocesans we have assembled in Dublin to take mutual counsel on a subject fraught with deepest importance to the Catholics of Ireland.

It is stated that powerful influences are being brought to bear on the Holy Father to induce him to accredit a Nuncio to the British Court, and that in future the business of the Irish Church with Rome must pass through his hands.

We need not here repeat a profession of our devotion to the chair of Peter. We need not here assure the Holy Father that we, like our glorious predecessors, are prepared to obey the Pastor of the fold in all things pertaining to His sublime office; though that obedience entailed on us the loss of all earthly goods even of life itself. We feel therefore assured that the expression of our well-considered judgement on a matter of vital importance to Ireland will not be misunderstood.

We have given the subject of the suggested change our most serious consideration, and we have formed our deliberate conclusion that to subject the affairs of the Irish Church to the care of a Nuncio resident in London would lead to the most disastrous results. It would weaken, if not destroy the filial confidence which has hitherto bound our people to the Holy See. It would fill this Country with alarm and would create in the minds of the Irish race distrust for the decisions and appointments coming to them through his hands from the Holy See.

We feel it unnecessary to mention here the causes which would give birth to these feelings in the minds of our people, but that they would spring up it cannot be doubted. We will content ourselves with pointing to the commotions caused in Ireland in the early part of this century when the question of the Veto was discussed. Sooner than tolerate the obnoxious innovations involved in that question the Catholics of Ireland were content for years to forego their just rights to the Emancipation of their religion.

Convinced that these rumours, if uncontradicted would cause dismay in the minds of all good Catholics in Ireland, we avail ourselves of your presence in Rome to lay our views respectfully at the feet of His Holiness, we will also ask you when presenting to His Holiness this respectful expression of our opinions to convey to Him the assurance of our veneration for His exalted station, and of our unbounded confidence in His wisdom and love for Ireland(K).

McCabe obviously telegraphed Moran the substance of the bishops' letter, for he wrote McCabe from Rome on March 18, "Owing to the determined attitude which was so opportunely & so promptly taken by our Irish Bishops, the projected Diplomatic representation in London has been quite exploded, & all the authorities here with whom I have conversed on the matter regard it as impracticable & impossible"(Mc). "Among those who view it in this light," Moran reported, referring to the influential prefect of Propaganda and secretary of state, "I may name Cardinals Simeoni & Jacobini." Three days later Moran again wrote McCabe to report that he had received the bishops' letter, and had applied for an audience to present it to the pope. He also explained again that he thought the project was "already exploded." "Indeed," he added, "the only hope such a project could have of succeeding, was its being carried on in secret. The moment it became known, every one saw through it, & even its original promoters (some of them at least) have become ashamed of it." "The Bishops' letter," he concluded confidently, "seems to me to be everything that could be desired, & I trust it will have the effect of setting the question at rest forever."

One of those "original promoters," referred to by Moran, who was obviously still not reconciled, wrote McCabe a "private & confidential" letter the day after Moran left Rome for Ireland. In fact, Herbert Vaughan, the bishop of Salford, who was in Rome with his colleague, the bishop of Clifton, on English church business, had been corresponding with McCabe for the better part of a month about the situation in Ireland. Moran, Vaughan reported to McCabe on March 28, "seems to have made a famous mess of the Nuncio business, which will not be forgotten in Rome for some time." "The Pope in speaking of diplomatic relations," he explained to McCabe, "spoke altogether in the abstract & without any reference to immediate action." The only practical point that had really been considered, Vaughan added, was the propriety of having a semi-official representative as in the days of Pius IX. "It would not be easy," he further informed McCabe, "to describe the annoyance felt here at what had happened & our friend of Ossory has the credit of it." Moran, moreover, had told him to his face, Vaughan complained, that he and the bishop of Clifton had the credit "of *promoting* the renewal of

diplomatic relations & of seeing Sir A. Paget on the subject."
Vaughan then protested that not only had neither he nor his
colleague seen Paget or anyone else on the subject but that
they both would be unwilling to see a nuncio in London.
"P.S.," Vaughan reminded McCabe, "I have put *Private &*
Confidential to this letter—I wd rather put it to *my name, which*
had better remain unknown: the details you can make any private
use of you please." Two weeks later, Vaughan again wrote
McCabe, reporting how the pope had really taken the Irish
bishops' recent letter. "The Holy Father," he explained on
April 12, "I know and have heard again yesterday has been
greatly pained by the resolution passed on the Nuncio business. It was considered bad even in form; being much too
direct and positive & besides having been unasked for," "I told
Card. Simeoni," Vaughan assured McCabe, "of your Grace's
assurance that whatever might be the conclusion the Holy
Father might arrive at in such a matter he can count on the
entire devotedness & loyalty of the Irish Episcopate. This he
will tell the Pope." "I hear our Bull," he finally concluded,
referring to the ecclesiastical business that had brought him to
Rome, "is in type: there has been strange intrigues to stop and
modify it—a portent of efforts: but thank God they were
foiled."

Who indeed is to be believed in this apparent web of intrigue? Was Moran or Vaughan telling the truth? Was the
pope really serious about establishing a nuncio in London? If
not, what did he hope to accomplish by floating so controversial a trial balloon? Though Vaughan was seldom a man ever
to be taken on his word alone, Moran was probably mistaken
in crediting him with promoting the nuncio affair. The bishop
of Salford was indeed too shrewd and knowledgeable about
English politics, lay and ecclesiastical, to have committed himself seriously at this stage to such a project. For, if the British
government had misgivings, in deference to Protestant public
opinion, about sending an English representative to Rome,
how could they have braved the proposal to establish a nuncio
in London? Vaughan must also have known that his primate,
Cardinal Manning, was not only opposed to a nuncio, but to
any form of diplomatic relations. Moreover, the great majority of the English bishops were probably of Manning's persua-
sion. Finally, and more conclusively, there is nothing in Granville's, Errington's or Paget's correspondence to indicate that

any such project was promoted by Vaughan or even proposed by Rome. This is not to say, however, it was not contemplated by Rome. Moran was too old and experienced a Roman hand to have misunderstood either the words or the intentions of Cardinal Jacobini when the Cardinal broached the subject to him in late February. Who was responsible, then, if the initiative came from Rome? Neither the secretary of state, nor the prefect of Propaganda, Cardinal Simeoni, according to Moran, were willing to admit they had ever taken the project seriously. Vaughan corroborated this when he wrote McCabe at the end of March explaining the imbroglio. Since Cardinal Jacobini, however, could hardly have introduced so important and controversial a subject, without having been authorized to do so, the responsibility must be assigned to the pope.

Why did the pope, then, introduce so controversial, and at this stage even irrelevant, a subject? The British government could not have agreed, the Irish and English hierarchies were opposed, and the Roman authorities, especially at the Propaganda, were not enthusiastic. The answer, in large part, appears to have had most to do with the kind of mind and character possessed by the pope. While Leo XIII had a very good mind, he appears to have also had a penchant, if not a weakness, for symmetry. He realized that a beginning had to be made by accepting an accredited English representative in Rome, but he logically looked forward to a complete diplomatic relationship, which would involve in the end an exchange of an English ambassador for a papal nuncio. On this level, therefore, Moran had simply overreacted to what amounted to a diplomatic projection on the part of the pope rather than any immediate project. But still why did the pope have the subject introduced at all? This question of timing had more to do with the character of the pope than the subtleties of his mind, for Leo was a curious mixture of cunning and rashness. By introducing the terrible prospect of a nuncio in London, the pope shrewdly acquired more leverage with the Irish and English bishops, not to mention British public opinion, in attempting to secure what he realized was more practicable—an accredited English representative in Rome.

Whatever benefit the pope thought he would secure, however, for the universal Church in these preliminary negotiations with the British government for reestablishing diploma-

tic relations, the result in Ireland for Roman power and influence was disastrous. The Irish clergy and people were not
simply opposed to a nuncio in London, but to any form of
British representation, official or unofficial, being accepted by
Rome because they felt that such representation would be
used against their best interests. While the Irish bishops had
formally protested against only one side of the papal proposal, that did not mean they liked the other aspect of that
proposal any better. What frightened them most, of course,
was that, if Rome continued to pursue such a policy in the face
of the rising national temper in Ireland, they would inevitably
be confronted with a situation in which their loyalty to their
people and their allegiance to the pope would be put in the
balance. The effect of the agrarian agitation during 1880 had
been to reduce the majority of the bishops opposed to the
Land League, and the efforts made at the end of the year to
secure a papal condemnation of the League had further impaired the effectiveness of the reduced majority. By the end
of January, 1881, with fourteen of the bishops absent in a
hierarchy of twenty-eight, and eight of them from the province of Cashel, it was obvious that the tide had certainly
begun to turn among the bishops as a body in favor of Croke's
policy, if indeed it had not already turned. When Rome then
introduced the question of diplomatic relations, the position
of those bishops opposed to the Land League became all but
untenable.

If Croke had been the crucial figure among the bishops in
helping the Irish Church to find its national focus during
1880, Moran was certainly the critical figure. Moran had
begun the year a decided opponent of the Land League and
its leadership, and had ended it by astutely trimming his
political sails to meet the dangers of the rising agrarian gales.
What made Moran the critical figure, however, was that the
issue at stake for him was not simply how to maintain the Irish
Church's influence with the people, and therefore its power,
but also how to preserve that ultramontane control which
Rome had enjoyed in the Irish Church during the ascendancy
of his late cousin, Cardinal Cullen. The cardinal had strug-
gled for thirty years to make his own and Rome's will effective
in the Irish Church, and the key to that effectiveness had been
in his ability to secure virtual unanimity in the episcopal body

as a body in all their public actions. He had succeeded to such an extent that by the time of his death an individual bishop publicly dissenting from a decision of the body, or taking a decision by himself which obviously concerned all would have amounted to a grave public scandal. The corollary to such unanimity was, of course, that Rome would accept the advice of the bishops when collectively offered. While the bishops, therefore, were divided on the merits of the Land League, they were unanimous on the inexpediency of condemning it. When the Pope's letter was published in early January, 1881, implicitly condemning the League, it was evident that Rome had acted contrary to the advice of the bishops, and Moran as an upholder of the ultramontane tradition in the Irish Church was obviously shocked. While the bishops might be divided on the issue of the League, for Rome to ignore their advice would only divide them further and weaken their respect for Rome's authority. Moran realized that the bishops must both check the disunion among themselves and strengthen their deteriorating position with regard to Rome. From Moran's point of view, therefore, the nuncio affair was the ideal issue, for the bishops could act decisively and unanimously, and in doing so prevent Rome's recent action from becoming a precedent by quickly asserting that in missionary countries such as Ireland, administered from Propaganda, the best confidential advisers Rome can have are the bishops. In immediately alerting the bishops, and in providing them with their course of action, therefore, Moran did as much as one man could to preserve for Rome its power and influence in Ireland, while attempting to retain for the Irish Church the loyalty and affection of the people.

IV. Coercion

December, 1880 - October, 1881

The situation in Ireland, meanwhile, was a curious mixture of hope and anxiety because Gladstone had promised the country both a remedy for its grievances and law and order. He proposed to introduce, therefore, a land bill and a coercion bill during the coming session of Parliament. Parnell, of course, was averse to any measure of coercion, but he did want a land bill that would, at least, soften the agitation if it did not settle it. Moreover, a good land bill would focus the attention of the tenant farmers on him and his party in action in Parliament rather than on his more advanced colleagues agitating on Land League platforms in the country. In early December, therefore, he attempted to have his trial for conspiracy postponed until the spring so that he might be in his place when Parliament convened in early January.[1] Since he and his co-conspirators, however, would not be obliged to attend the trial unless absolutely directed to do so by the court, Parnell astutely surmised that the government would not attempt to prevent him from being at the opening, on January 7, of Parliament.[2] When his jury was finally sworn in on December 28, Parnell and everyone else realized that, since eight of the twelve jurors were Roman Catholics, neither he nor his colleagues would be convicted, and there was even a possibility they would be acquitted. Parnell, therefore, would not only be in his place when Parliament convened to hear the queen's speech outlining the government's proposed measures for Ireland, but that since there was now no danger of his having to go to jail, he would be also able to focus the attention of the country politically in Parliament.

The Irish bishops were even more anxious than Parnell that the game should be played in Parliament and not in the

---

[1] Katherine O'Shea, *Charles Stewart Parnell* 1 (London, 1914): p. 163.
[2] *Ibid.*, pp. 169-170.

country. Their universal hope was that the next session of Parliament by producing a satisfactory land bill would save them from being ground out between the forces of law and order and a semi-revolutionary agrarian agitation. When John MacEvilly, for example, wrote Kirby from Tuam on December 18, he explained how worried he was about the agitation in his part of the country(K). "What I fear most," he confided to Kirby, "is that even after the Land Question is fairly settled, there lurks an Infidel Godless principle, which would do mischief." "At the same time," he added shrewdly, "I am convinced, if a fair measure of Tenant security were enacted, the *great majority* of the people would accept it, while no doubt, the leaders interested in the agitation would reject it." Only two days before, in fact, one of those "leaders," Michael Davitt, had written John Devoy, head of the *Clan na Gael* in New York, substantially confirming MacEvilly's worst fears.[3] "The landlords," Davitt explained on December 16, and referring to the chief secretary, "are scaring old Forster with stories of an intended Rising, importation of arms, etc., in order to have the League squelched. I am necessitated, therefore, to take a conservative stand in order to stave off coercion, for if the H.C. is suspended the whole movement would be crushed in a month and universal confusion would reign. These damned petty little outrages are magnified by the Tory organs, copied into the English Press and play the devil with us on outside public opinion." Davitt further reported that Gladstone's Land Bill was certain to provide free sale, fair rent, and fixity of tenure for the Irish tenant farmer. "This of course," he added, "will not be enough, but it will satisfy a great number inside the League, and be accepted by the Bishops and Priests almost to a man." "I anticipate a serious split in the League when the Government measure comes out," Davitt shrewdly prophesied, "and I only see one way in which to combat it and neutralise the evil it would work upon the country—that is, by calling a Convention. The Delegates that would come from the country would be certain to support the No Partnership platforms of the League against the compromise of the three F's." "If we could carry on this Movement for another year," he concluded confidently,

---

[3] William O'Brien and Desmond Ryan (eds.), *Devoy's Post Bag* **2** (Dublin, 1953): pp. 23-24.

"without being interfered with we could do almost anything we pleased in the country."

What view one took of the state of the country obviously depended not only on whether one was opposed to the League or not, but also whether one was partial to the tenants' or the landlords' cause. Davitt was undoubtedly right in arguing that the outrages were being magnified out of all proportion by the landlords and their friends. Still, from the landlords' point of view, aside from the outrages, the situation might indeed be termed revolutionary. The tenants were combining everywhere, and agreeing to pay no more than the valuation that had been made by the government in 1852 of their holdings under the supervision of the Chairman of the Irish Board of Works, Richard Griffith. In the thirty years since "Griffith's valuation," rents in Ireland had increased considerably, and the landlords were undoubtedly shocked by the proposition that they either accept the reduced rent offered or they would get none. Moreover, they were horrified to find that they had little real recourse, for if they proceeded to evict those tenants who refused to pay, they were faced with being "boycotted," and threatened with worse. One's view of the state of the country, however, also appears to have had a good deal to do with temperament. "We are in the midst," the ever sanguine archbishop of Armagh, Daniel McGettigan, reported to Kirby on December 17, "of very extraordinary events and exciting times in Ireland. Here in the North there is quiet. We don't feel the storm"(K). "Still," he concluded, "all classes and creeds are uniting in the Land Question because it comes home to every Farmer."

"I had settled," wrote Denis Riordan, one of those "Farmers," who was only half-literate, on January 1, 1881, from County Limerick, to his brother Michael who was studying for the priesthood at the Irish College in Rome, "with my Landlord before the agitation had become properly fruitful"(OR). "Very probably," he explained, "but for the action of Mr. Parnell half the people would be ejected from their Homes, and in spite of the power of Landlord or Government he have stoped Eviction and reduced the rents to Griffets valuation in many cases. Now for instance, my father who was paying £116-0-0, the[y] were obliged to take £56-0-0 it being the valuation." "There is a Land League," he continued, "in every parish in the County with the Priests in all most all cases at the head of it. The County is at present in great excitement as Mr. Parnell T D Sullivan & twelve others are being procuted by the Government but we have great hopes the jury will not find them guilty as the charges are innocent ones, because he want to put down tyrants." "I will not say any more on this subject," Denis concluded, "as I could not properly explain to you the good he has done for the Irish people and the terrible stroke he have given the Landlord class."

It seems, however, Michael Davitt was not the only one who understood that the Land Bill might destroy this ascendancy of the Land League. "It appears to me," wrote Laurence Gillooly, the astute and shrewd bishop of Elphin, to McCabe from Sligo on January 4, "that the introduction of Mr. Gladstone's Land Bill, if it turns out to be what is expected, will give us an opportunity of asserting our proper influence & authority in this Land Question—and of taking the tenant farmers of the Country from under the ruinous & tyrannical control of the L. League, which is already filling them with disgust & alarm"(Mc). "I should greatly wish for that purpose," he suggested, "that our Meeting should be held, if possible before the 25th—indeed the sooner the better, after the introduction of Mr G.'s Bill." "I have no doubt," he shrewdly pointed out to McCabe, "but the L. League will promptly & strenuously oppose any Bill no matter how just & favourable to the Tenant Class, which the Govmt will propose—and they will also I am sure use their organisation to pronounce a speedy condemnation on the Govmt proposals by the tenant farmers throughout the Country." "It would therefore be essential," he advised in conclusion, "that if we are to advise the acceptance of the Bill we should do so before the pronouncement & action of the League."

Gladstone, however, who was apparently caught between his warring Whig and Radical colleagues, upset Gillooly's proposed time table. He decided not only to introduce a coercion bill to appease the Whigs along with his land bill to placate the Radicals, but he decided to introduce the Coercion Bill before instead of simultaneously with the Land Bill. Gillooly wrote McCabe again on January 8, explaining that he now thought the bishops' meeting scheduled for January 25, would be time enough, if indeed not too soon, for a consideration of the Land Bill(Mc). "It appears to me," he added persistently, "that every effort should be made by the four Archbps or even by three of them to establish at our next meeting some principle of united action in reference to the Land League and land agitation." Parnell, however, who was determined to oppose any measure of coercion for Ireland, further upset the episcopal time table by continuing the debate on the queen's speech for eleven nights. When it finally ended on January 20, he crossed over to Dublin where he and his friends had the added safisfaction on January 23 of hearing their jury, after a trial of twenty days' duration, admit that they could not agree. He then immediately returned to London in order to be in his place in the House of Commons on January 24, when Forster introduced his coercion measure. Parnell took the lead in obstructing the bill, and the sitting on January 25 took some twenty-two hours. On January 31, a sitting began which lasted forty-one hours and was only brought to an end on February 2 by the unprecedented action of the Speaker, who proceeded to put the question from the chair. When the home secretary, Sir William Harcourt, announced to the House the following day that Michael Davitt had been arrested and sent to Portland prison for violating the conditions of his ticket-of-leave, or parole, Parnell immediately asked, "What conditions?" The home secretary gave no answer, and Gladstone then rose to move a closure resolution, when John Dillon interposed to ask the home secretary further questions about the arrest of Davitt, but the Speaker chose to recognize Gladstone. Dillon objected and was eventually suspended for disregarding the authority of the chair, and was called upon by the speaker to withdraw. He refused and was removed by the sergeant-at-arms. When Gladstone again rose to propose his closure resolution, Parnell coolly moved that "the right hon. member be no longer heard." The Speaker, amid scenes of indescribable excitement and confusion, refused to hear Parnell, who, however, insisted that his motion be put. Before it was all over, Parnell and some thirty-five Irish members had been suspended and ejected from the House.[4]

Parnell, however, had a new series of problems to face now that he and his colleagues had been ejected from the House.

[4] This paragraph is a composite account drawn from three main sources: R. Barry O'Brien, *The Life of Charles Stewart Parnell* (London, 1910), pp. 207-222; Michael Davitt, *The Fall of Feudalism in Ireland* (London, 1904), pp. 304-310; Conor Cruise O'Brien, *Parnell and His Party, 1880-1890* (Oxford, 1957), pp. 57-65.

Some of his more radical followers expected that he would fulfill the promise he made on January 16, that the first arrest under the proposed coercion measures would be the signal for a "no rent" campaign in Ireland.[5] Instead he crossed to Paris for a meeting of the executive of the Land League on February 13, where he and the other officers of the League made arrangements to carry on the work in spite of the arrest of Davitt and the imminent threat to themselves. John Dillon was appointed organiser in the place of Davitt, and Patrick Egan, one of the treasurers, was requested to remain in Paris in order to keep the funds forwarded from abroad out of the reach of the government. Parnell at this meeting of the executive also submitted a manifesto which rejected the revolutionary course of seceding from Parliament and proclaiming a strike against the rent in Ireland, and proposed instead the more constitutional alternative of "widening the area of agitation" by effecting an alliance between Irish nationalism and the English democracy.[6]

What had obviously irked Parnell was the large number of English Radicals who supported the government both in its coercion measures and closure resolution. "The Radicals of England," Parnell had warned on February 4, in London, the day after his expulsion from the House, "will yet discover the mistake they made in condoning the autocracy of the speaker of the House of Commons, and allowing liberty to be trampled on in her own temple."[7] "Sooner or later," he continued, prophesying accurately future party divisions along class and property lines, "a coalition of the Whig and Tory territorialists must be formed to make head against the English democracy, and they [the Radicals] will then find how fatal for their own freedom was the precedent of yesterday." In inaugurating his new policy of "widening the area of agitation," in order to bring the Radicals face to face with developing political realities, Parnell began with a gesture to the French democracy by visiting Victor Hugo and the "notorious Cummunard" Henri De Rochefort.[8] "Parnell's Paris expedition," wrote Cardinal Manning from London to the bishop of Salford,

---

[5] *Annual Register*, January 16, 1881, quoted in C. C. O'Brien, *op. cit.*, p. 60.

[6] C. C. O'Brien, *op.cit.*, p. 64.

[7] *Boston Globe*, February 5, 1881, quoted in Davitt, *op. cit.*, p. 304. This is a cable from Parnell to the American Land League.

[8] C. C. O'Brien, *op. cit.*, p. 64.

Herbert Vaughan, in Rome on February 18, "is a showing of cards which has damaged him and his works."[9] Some days later Archbishop McCabe in his Lenten instructions called the attention of his clergy and faithful to Parnell's new-found friends. "A calamity more terrible and humiliating," McCabe wrote apocalyptically on February 23, "than any that has yet befallen Ireland seems to threaten our people to-day. Allies for our country in her struggle for justice are sought from the ranks of impious infidels, who have plunged their own unhappy country into misery and who are sworn to destroy the foundations of all religions."[10]

The day after the archbishop's pastoral was published, Parnell protested that there was no political significance in his visits to the leaders of French radical opinion.[11] Indeed, when the bishop of Limerick, George Butler, wrote Kirby on March 1, he admitted that Parnell had been criticized for appealing to the "French infidel party"(K). He also pointed out, however, what had received a good deal less attention, that Parnell had not only visited Louis Veuillot, a prominent Catholic journalist, but the cardinal archbishop of Paris, who received him kindly.[12] The good bishop of Limerick, however, forgot to mention that Parnell also had the acute political foresight to visit the ultra-respectable, and very Catholic, former president of France, Marshal MacMahon.[13] The bishop of Elphin

---

[9] Shane Leslie, *Henry Edward Manning* (London, 1921), p. 383, quoted in C. C. O'Brien, *loc. cit.*

[10] *Freeman's Journal*, February 22, 1881; also quoted in C. C. O'Brien, *loc. cit.*

[11] C. C. O'Brien, *loc. cit.*

[12] See also letter of the cardinal archbishop of Paris to McCabe, dated March 9, 1881 (Mc), for an account of his interview with Parnell: "M. Parnell avec un autre député de l'Irlande est venu me faire une visite pour me remercier de l'intérêt qui j'avais toujour témoigné pour leur pays. Ils m'ont naturellement parlé de la crise qu'il traverse en le moment. Je leur ai recommandé avant tout d'éviter de donner à la cause Irlandaise le caractère d'une révolte contre les lois et contre l'autorité, et de s'en tenir rigoureusment aux conseils et à la discretion de leur évêques, qui ont reçu des instructions du Souverain Pontife."

[13] K, Feast of St. Patrick, 1881. "I received," McCabe wrote Kirby on March 17, "a few weeks ago a letter from His Eminence, the Archbishop of Paris, in which he gave me an account of his interview with Mr. Parnell. As the Land League was turning that interview into a political engine, I thought it due to the Cardinal to give his own account of it, which I have done in the Pastoral I sent to you. I did not mention the name of H. E. because I had no authority. The reference to the interview with Marshal MacMahon, I asked Fr. MacNamara [rector of the Irish College in Paris] to learn something about it, for the same reason as in the case of the Archbishop, and I give his words in the Pastoral also." McCabe's pastoral was read on Sunday, March 13, in all Dublin churches, but was published in part on Saturday, March 12, in the

was the first to congratulate McCabe on his condemnation of "Parnell's new alliance with the Infidel Communists of France—the sworn enemies of the Church"(Mc). Gillooly, who was boiling over with righteous indignation, further asked McCabe whether the bishops at their next meeting should not indeed take united action and deprive Parnell of his episcopal support. "Then," Gillooly maintained in conclusion, "there is the other very grave question of the organisation of a Female Land League which we should I think put down in the most determined way." The archbishop's pastoral also gave great pleasure, it seems, in Rome. "Allow me (if an Englishman may presume to do so!)," the bishop of Salford, Herbert Vaughan, wrote McCabe on March 1, from the English College in Rome, "to congratulate & thank you for your Pastoral (the Extract from it which we have already seen). It has given wide pleasure here"(Mc). "Your Grace," Vaughan added, "has taken up a grand position. You & the Pope have saved the Church from being misunderstood in her influence & probably from persecution. For this you have to suffer & hundreds of thousands will thank you." "Your Pastoral," he reassured McCabe in conclusion, "has given *great pleasure* at the Vatican. They have asked me to get the entire Pastoral."

The Coercion Bill, meanwhile, moved quickly along under the new rules of procedure inaugurated after Gladstone's closure resolution. Everyone assumed that Gladstone would produce his Land Bill as soon as the coercion measures became law, and the bishops once again had to consider what they would do when it was finally introduced. McCabe, therefore, circularized the bishops on February 14, reminding them that those who had met on January 25 had agreed to meet again when the Land Bill should be laid before Parliament, and asked the bishops whether they would be able to attend on short notice. Gillooly, who was determined to prevent the Land League from stealing the thunder of the bishops,

---

Freeman's Journal; the pertinent passage referred to by McCabe read: "Very Reverend dear Fathers, Set your faces against this dishonouring attempt, and do not tolerate in your sodalities the woman who so far disavows her birthright of modesty as to parade herself before the public gaze in a character so unworthy [of] a child of Mary. This attempt at degrading the women of Ireland comes very appropriately from men who have drawn the country into her present terribly deplorable condition, where deprived of the safeguards of the Constitution, her people may become the prey of perjured informers; men who have sent their agents to fawn on notorious infidels and revolutionists; and to escape the odium of their act, abuse the Christian politeness of a most venerable prelate and an illustrious soldier of France. . . ."

replied on February 16 that he thought "it would be a very grave mistake not to hold this Meeting—and I am therefore prepared at any inconvenience to attend it"(Mc). The bishop of Cloyne, John McCarthy, also thought, in writing the same day, the meeting should be convoked as soon as possible "as an unanimous pronouncement of the Bishops of Ireland in favour of a thorough & satisfactory settlement of the land question would I have no doubt have a most salutory effect on the Government, whilst it would shew our people, that we were not unmindful of or indifferent to their wrongs"(Mc).

Not all the bishops, however, were enthusiastic about a meeting. Patrick Duggan, the bishop of Clonfert, who was very partial to the Land League, for example, also explained on February 16, in a letter to McCabe marked "private," that, if the government should legislate half-heartedly, and not give a measure which the bishops could either support or condemn, it would be best, perhaps, not to meet(Mc). He complained that the government, by bringing in a coercion bill before the Land Bill, had "so complicated matters that I dread *interfering* between them and the people." Another strong supporter of the League, Thomas Nulty, the bishop of Meath, shrewdly advised McCabe on February 22 to wait for the Bill itself, because he remembered that Gladstone's introduction of the Land Bill of 1870 was magnificent, yet the bill itself was very disappointing(Mc). Nulty also reminded McCabe that by waiting for the actual Bill, the bishops would have time to see what the reaction of the press would be and would be then better able to gauge the temper of the country. Gladstone, however, was not to be hurried, and though the first and last of the Coercion measures were passed on February 28 and March 11, respectively, it was not until April 7 that he finally introduced his long awaited Land Bill.

The problem of trying to settle the date of the next episcopal meeting was quickly resolved by the rumors of negotiations between the British government and the Holy See about establishing diplomatic relations. Several days before the meeting scheduled by McCabe for March 15 to consider these rumors, however, he and the bishop of Ardagh issued pastorals condemning the Ladies' Land League.[14] The ladies had

---

[14] See *Freeman's Journal*, March 7 and March 12, respectively, for Woodlock's and McCabe's pastorals.

launched their organization early in February, under the presidency of Parnell's sister, Anna, at the suggestion of Michael Davitt, who thought it would prove a most useful auxiliary, both practically and propagandistically, especially if the government attempted to break up the Land League by mass arrests when the Coercion Bill should become law.[15] "The last form of the agitation," McCabe complained to Kirby on March 17, and two days after the episcopal meeting, "is the establishment of a *womans* League, and to carry out this, a *Monster* Meeting of women was to be held in the Rotunda"(K). "Thinking this very *Monstrous*," McCabe explained, obviously enjoying his pun, "I condemned the whole thing for which I have been well abused." "At our Meeting on Tuesday," he then confided, less lightheartedly, "some of their Lordships endeavored to pass a Resolution condemning Dr. Woodlock and myself for what we did in reference about the Ladies League but the Resolution was withdrawn."

The meeting was, in fact, much stormier than might have been suspected from Archbishop McCabe's account of it to Kirby. Rumors of a serious split among the Irish bishops, in any case, were freely circulating in Rome before Kirby received McCabe's St. Patrick's Day letter. "I have heard," the bishop of Salford wrote McCabe from Rome on March 20, "from the Editor of the Aurora, a certain Father Mori, an Italian adventurer from New York, that he had received information from Ireland to the effect that your Grace's Pastoral was all but brought under the notice of the Irish Bishops for condemnation by them the other day"(Mc). "This F. Mori," Vaughan went on to explain, "was the writer of certain articles in the Aurora while the Abp of Cashel was in Rome, & I suspect he is in communication with him or with other persons in authority in Ireland. I also know that he mentioned the above circumstances to Cardl. Jacobini." "I think it wise to give you this information" Vaughan explained, setting up his wedge, "for I do not know how many friends you may have here, or whether they will have told you of it—if they know it. An effort I know has been made to create the belief that you & the Bp of Ardagh are under Govt. influence—but it *has failed*. Your line has been strongly commended within my hearing here where you could most desire approval & support." "It

---

[15] Davitt, *op. cit.*, p. 299.

would be a useful thing," Vaughan concluded, finally driving his wedge, "were it possible to state how many of the Bishops think with your Grace—for an effort is made to shew that you stand alone. The Abp of Cashel appeals to numbers & majorities as though truth & prudence were determined by counting noses."

What actually happened at the meeting on March 15 more than justified the rumors that reached Rome. "With regard to the dissensions," John Power, the bishop of Waterford, wrote Kirby on March 29, two weeks after the event and still obviously angry, "which unhappily exist between some of the Irish prelates, and are so much to be deplored, I take this opportunity of conveying to you my impressions"(K). "You are aware," Power began his long letter, "that the recent pastoral letter of the Archbishop of Dublin was discussed at the meeting of the Irish prelates that took place some days since in the Catholic University.

> Several of the Prelates took offense at the severe and unmeasured language in which Dr. McCabe condemned and denounced certain proceedings and associations connected with the Land agitation now so general throughout the country. Those Prelates who differed with the Archbishop of Dublin in his views and who either sanctioned, or tolerated in their respective Dioceses the proceedings which he denounced, felt themselves placed in a most embarrassing position before their flocks and the public at large. In view of guarding against a recurrence of such a painful state of things, the Bishop of Limerick introduced the subject at the meeting of the Prelates, and submitted for their consideration a resolution to the effect, that on questions whereon the Prelates held different opinions, no Prelate should pronounce publicly on the merits or demerits of any such question, and furthermore that when the Prelates are divided in opinion the minority should be bound by the decision of the majority. . . .
>
> Some of the Bishops objected to the resolution on the grounds that notice of its introduction had not been given, whilst Dr. McCabe objected to it in toto, and declared that he would not bind himself by it, even though every Bishop in Ireland should agree to its terms, and added that in addressing his Clergy and flock, he would not be bound by any authority, but that of the Holy Father. That declaration put an end to all further discussion, and led to the results that followed. As long as the Archbishop of Dublin assumes to be dictator of the Irish

Church, and acts on the foregoing declaration, harmony among the Prelates cannot be expected. As regards the apprehensions expressed by some of the Faith of the people of Ireland being weakened, and their respect for the Clergy being diminished, by the present Land agitation, I do not share in these apprehensions. Within the memory of the present generation there was not a time when religious Sodalities were so numerous, and practical piety so general as at present. And so long as the people have the active sympathies of the Clergy, and their reasonable cooperation in seeking by constitutional means the removal of their manifold grievances, they will retain their hereditary love of religion, and will continue attached and amenable to their Clergy. The real danger would be if the Priests stood aloof from the people, and allowed them to get under the control of dangerous guides(K).

"As the Archbishop of Dublin has, I understand," Power concluded firmly and strongly, "brought the present occurrences under the notice of the Holy See, I shall feel obliged, by you taking an early opportunity of placing the foregoing views before the Propaganda."

The "occurrences" referred to by the bishop of Waterford are now as well known as this prelude to them is not. When McCabe condemned the rotunda meeting of the Ladies Land League in Dublin, one of the chief promoters of that meeting, Mrs. A. M. Sullivan, was gallantly defended by her husband in an open letter to Archbishop McCabe in the press. The result of this letter by Sullivan, the brother of a parliamentary colleague and supporter of Parnell, and a staunch Catholic, was the following remarkable letter from Archbishop Croke:

Cashel, March 16, 1881

Dear Mr. Sullivan,

I congratulate you very heartily on your timely and, under the peculiarly provoking circumstances, very temperate and withal touching letter that appears over your name in this day's *Freeman*.

I adopt, unreservedly, the sentiments you have so admirably expressed, and am delighted to find that some one of mark has at last stepped forward from the ranks of the laity to vindicate the character of the good Irish ladies who have become Land-Leaguers, and to challenge publicly the monstrous imputations cast upon them by the Archbishop of Dublin.

His grace will not be allowed in future, I apprehend, to use his
lance so freely as he has hitherto done, or to ventilate unques-
tioned the peculiar political theories which he is known to hold
in opposition to the cherished convictions of a great, and indeed
overwhelming, majority of the Irish priests and people.

It is a satisfaction, however, to feel that his grace's political
likings and dislikings, though possibly of some consequence
elsewhere, carry with them very little weight or significance,
except with a select few, in Ireland.

Your very faithful servant,
X T. W. Croke
Archbishop of Cashel[16]

Needless to say, this caustic and contemptuous public dis-
missal of one archbishop by another in a letter to a laymen
raised more than a few eyebrows in ecclesiastical circles, and
especially in Rome. "What I wish to call your attention to
now," Errington wrote Smith from the House of Commons
the next day, March 18, "is the painful letter in yesterday's
Irish papers (in this day's English Times) from Dr. Croke in
reply to Dr. McCabe's *admirable* pastoral about the 'ladies
Land League' "(S). "Dr. Croke's letter," Errington explained,
"appears to me positively scandalous, & things cannot remain
as they are. I hope you will use your influence to make the
truth known to Card. Jacobini, Msgr. Masotti, Cardinal Howard, and others." "It was suggested," Errington reported,

> that the laity should send an address of thanks and confidence
> to Dr. McCabe, but the danger of this is that a counter address
> much *more numerously* signed would in the present state of
> feeling be sent to Dr. Croke. It appears that the Holy See, must
> support Dr. McCabe, otherwise I apprehend the greatest dan-
> gers and scandals; the most effective step would be to make him
> a Cardinal; I hope this is not impossible(S).

"Depend upon it," Errington warned, "if something is not
done evil will come of it."

Croke's supporters, like the bishop of Waterford, stood by
him, and concentrated on the extreme provocation given by

---

[16] *Freeman's Journal*, March 17, 1881. For A. M. Sullivan's letter, dated March 14,
1881, see *Freeman's Journal*, March 16, 1881.

McCabe at the recent episcopal meeting.[17] Those who sympathized with McCabe, like John MacEvilly, felt "embarrassed in writing to express the heartfelt pain it gave me to read the letter of Dr. Croke in the Freeman"(Mc). Those bishops, like Patrick Duggan, the bishop of Clonfert, who were bound in principle or friendship to both men, were in a cruel dilemma. "The episodes in our current history," Dugan wrote McCabe, obviously bewildered, on March 22, "since we met, have pained and perplexed me, beyond expression"(Mc). "I hope very soon," he sadly concluded his letter marked "private," "to see your Grace—Until then I say no more, but to pray God to preserve us from trouble." The majority of the bishops, however, probably felt as did Daniel McGettigan, the archbishop of Armagh. "Every one," McGettigan wrote Kirby on March 30, "but the enemy of Religion deplores the unhappy publication which has lately appeared. No one ever imagined that the trifling differences of opinion regarding Political affairs would end so unseemly. However, the small storm will just be a *nine days wonder* and all will be over." "All are on the lookout," he concluded, unable to dwell on the dark side of things, "for the 7th April when the Prime Minister is to bring in the long expected Land Measure. If it be a thorough one, it will tranquilise the Island."

Kirby, meanwhile, had written Croke asking him for an explanation. "As regards my letter to the Freeman," Croke replied unrepentantly on March 28, "it did not appear a bit too soon"(K). "I am inundated with letters," he reported to Kirby, "from Bishops, priests, M. P.'s & c thanking me for putting a stop to the endless and offensive pronouncements of his Grace of Dublin." "When Bishops differ on a political point or policy," Croke then declared, "I hold to it that silence is the proper course to be pursued." "That," he pointed out to Kirby, "was embodied in the resolution proposed at our meeting which Dr. McCabe so contemptuously rejected." "If a Bishop," Croke added, "has special views, let him address them, if he likes, to his own flock by way of a circular; but he has no right to address them to the priests and people of Ireland generally, especially when he knows, that in doing so, he is

---

[17] See also K, March 31, 1881, for William Fitzgerald, bishop of Ross, who also wrote Kirby in favor of Croke for the benfit of Propaganda. Power's letter to Kirby, which has been already quoted, was dated March 28, 1881.

placing himself in opposition to the views of the majority, and likely to provoke '*to a breach of the peace.*' " "I am for neutrality in politics," Croke added for good measure, "rather than for speaking out, when to do so is to proclaim war." "There are my views," he declared pugnaciously, "I hope you will represent them at Propaganda, or elsewhere if necessary." "Dr. McCabe has intimated to me," Croke then reported, "that he has complained of me to Propaganda. So he can. He is the aggressor I am acting in self-defence." "Write," he commanded somewhat imperiously in conclusion, "on receipt of this as I wish to know how the land lies." " 'Elsewhere' in my letter," he added in a postscript, obviously responding to one of Kirby's criticisms of his letter to A. M. Sullivan, "means England and the English feeling in Rome."

Some days before Croke wrote this rather truculent reply to Kirby, Moran wrote McCabe a very sober letter from Rome. "I cannot say how pained I have felt at the letter of His Grace of Cashel of the 16th inst.," Moran explained on March 25, "& I beg to assure you of my sincerest sympathy in the anxiety & annoyance which it must have caused you"(Mc). "It has been the more painful to me," he continued, "as I happen to be from former times an old friend of the Archbishop of Cashel. Relying upon that friendship, I have written to him to-day admonishing him of the grave mistake which he has committed & asking him to offer you at once prompt amends." "I will pray you," Moran added, "to allow the matter to be set at rest. At the present moment it wd be particularly distressing to have such a question brought before the authorities here: it would give delight to all the enemies of our poor country & they are at present numberless in Rome: & it would afford some pretext for propping up those schemes which we are all so anxious to pull down." "Last evening," he confided, "Cardinal Simeoni spoke to me of this controversy & urged me to use my endeavours to have it amicably arranged. It wd be difficult for Rome to interfere in any way at the present moment without exciting strong political feeling in Ireland & I dare say they wd fear to irritate without being able to heal the wound which all must deplore." "I trust," Moran concluded, "that your Grace will not refuse me this request which nothing induces me to make but the deepest conviction that in our union at the present moment the most vital interests of the Irish Church are at stake."

Several days later, one of those enemies who according to Moran were numberless also wrote McCabe from Rome. "Cashel's attack," the bishop of Salford wrote McCabe in a letter marked "private & confidential" on March 28, "has produced the most painful impression"(Mc). "I may mention under all reserve," Vaughan confided, "that Bp. Moran has been commissioned to speak to him & to induce him to make a public amende to your Grace." "This looks to me," Vaughan confessed, "like asking 'the pot to correct the kettle,' but I hope more will be done, & that you will be made Delegate Apostolic, which would be the best reply to Cashel." Moran had also, of course, written Croke asking him to apologize to the archbishop of Dublin, and by the time he had arrived home he found that Croke had acted on his advice. Croke had forwarded the required apology to Moran with a covering letter asking him to send it to McCabe, and requesting him also to assure the Roman authorities the controversy was at an end. "When I was passing through Dublin," Moran explained to Kirby on April 8, "everyone to whom I spoke about the controversy laughed at the idea of the letter being withdrawn by the Abp. of Cashel, nevertheless heaven has secured this most desirable result"(K).

The archbishop of Cashel had, indeed, written another remarkable letter.

The Palace, Thurles
April 8, 1881

My dear Lord Archbishop,

Our mutual friend, the Bishop of Ossory, has been in communication with me for some time in reference to a certain letter addressed by me to A. M. Sullivan, and which appeared over my signature in the Freeman's Journal of the 17th of March.

His Lordship has given me good reason to think that the publication of that letter dealing, as it did, with portions of your Grace's pastoral, which should have been held, it appears to be a privileged pronouncement, was in so far a mistake, in as much as no member or members of a National Hierarchy has a right to question publicly, or even criticise (unless it be obviously absurd) the official advice or instructions formally given by a brother Bishop to his flock.

Of the privileged character of a Chief Pastor's address to the members of his flock I, of course, never had and could not have had, the slightest doubt.

But when committing to the press the few lines of commentary that have been complained of I viewed the actual situation in quite another light: and having regarded your Grace's latest "Pastoral," published as I assumed it to have been in quite an unauthorized and indeed fragmentary shape, as an unoffocial document addressed directly to be sure to the clergy and laity of the Diocese of Dublin, but indirectly at the same time to the Irish people at large, I believe it was competent for me to deal with such portions of it as referred to questions of Irish politics and were of universal application as regards this country, without transcending in any way my powers of legitimate criticism or trenching on the privileges or jurisdiction of the Archbiship of Dublin.

However as I have been given unmistakably to understand that in forming this estimate of the case I was technically wrong, I wish now to correct the mistake such as it was and hereby unequivocally withdraw the letter in question.

I desire only to add that this disagreeable episode shall not have the effect of lessening even in the minutest degree the feelings of respect and friendship which I have always entertained for Your Grace as an exalted and estimable Member of our National Hierarchy(Mc).

"I am glad to tell you," McCabe, who seemed either entirely or charitably to have missed the point that this was an apology in form rather than substance, wrote Kirby on April 14, "that, as far as I am concerned the late unpleasant occurrence is forgotten and forgiven"(K). "The Bishop of Ossory," he then explained to Kirby, "was commissioned to require from the Archbishop an apology. The apology was written, and with it, full authority to me to publish it if I liked. But as I know that its publication would only lead to a renewal of the scandal I kept it to myself so far as the Newspapers were concerned." "But as we gave Propaganda trouble," he continued considerately, "I thought it my duty that Cardinal Simeoni should know how the matter ended. So I wrote His Eminence on Sunday sending him Dr. Croke's letter to me; I pray earnestly that we may never again have a recurrence of this unpleasant affair." If McCabe had, indeed, especially after Moran's letter describing Rome's reluctance to interfere, expected that this apology would have been forced by Rome, if Croke did not volunteer it, he was certainly disabused of that idea in a letter from Vaughan a few days later.

The bishop of Salford had reported to McCabe on April 12, that he had had a long conversation with Cardinal Simeoni the previous evening, and he had given him the substance of what McCabe had written in his recent letters(Mc). While assuring McCabe that he had both the confidence of Propaganda and the Holy See, Vaughan explained that it would "take some time to come to the ultimate conclusion—for they are evidently anxious not to provoke a wider breach than that already created by Cashel." Vaughan also reported that Croke had been written to by the authorities and informed that his conduct was under consideration, but that he had not yet replied. "Would it be possible," Vaughan then smoothly suggested, "to call a meeting or a Synod of the four Provinces and in that to pass some resolutions or decrees under which the conduct of the Abp of Cashel in attacking a Pastoral by another Bishop should be *indirectly* condemned—at least by laying down the rule to be followed in future and the doctrine of the Church in regard to contracts and the obligations of justice and honesty should be set forth?" "Such a procedure," he significantly informed McCabe in conclusion, "approved as it would eventually be by the Holy See could probably receive a greater strength and a closer unity than a declaration of the Holy See which might be regarded as a public rebuke to the Episcopate in general." In a word, Rome felt she had gone far enough, for the present, in Irish affairs, and the archbishop of Dublin could expect little real immediate support in his quarrel with his brother of Cashel.

The archbishop of Cashel, in fact, appears to have quickly grasped the situation. He must, of course, have been prompted by Moran's plea for an apology, accompanied as it must have been by all the cogent reasons. But when he was notified by Rome that his conduct was under consideration, he must have also realized that Rome was serving notice that, if the Irish bishops could not keep their house in order, the duty must eventually devolve on Rome. In apologizing to McCabe, therefore, Croke had both forestalled Rome and effectively checked Vaughan's very clever suggestion that a meeting of the Irish bishops be called ostensibly to deal with his public

criticism of McCabe's pastoral, but which really would have
been called to condemn the Land League by upholding "the
doctrine of the Church in regard to contracts and the obligations of justice and honesty." That Croke was not only aware
of what was at stake, but also of the strength of his own
position as far as Rome and the bishops opposed to the Land
League were concerned, was made apparent in a long confidential letter to Kirby some days after his apology to McCabe.
"It is most extraordinary," he declared in high dudgeon on
April 13, "how easy it is to displease the Roman authorities,
especially when the displeasing word, or act, is applauded by
the *whole Irish race at home and abroad*. I have received up to the
present 207 resolutions of thanks passed by different bodies
in Ireland, and 170 letters thanking me for having checked
Dr. McCabe in his headlong course against a popular movement in this country"(K). "I have withdrawn my letter," Croke
then explained, and obviously unrepentant, "and acknowledged in writing to Dr. McCabe that I was *technically* wrong in
referring to his so-called pastoral or criticizing it publicly. For
the rest, we are as great friends as ever. I dined with him, on
Monday last." "It is contemplated," he reported further, "to
have all the priests in Munster make a declaration in my favor
as regards this matter next week. But I am taking steps to
effectively prevent it." "The vast majority of the bishops,"
Croke added most significantly, "are at my side. I am striving
to keep priests and public together and preserve the faith, and
instead of being commended for my efforts, which, thank
God, are acknowledged in Ireland to be successful, I am daily
assailed and threatened with pains and penalties from Rome."

"If Rome keeps interfering in Irish politics," he finally
warned Kirby, "or it gets publicly and generally known that
the Roman authorities side with those who have gone by word
and deed, *against* the public, Papal influence in Ireland will
fall as low as it is in France or Italy." "I'll tell you now,"
he confided,

one fact that speaks volumes. When the Pope's letter to Dr.
McCabe was published the National Party were terribly vexed
and a deputation came here to me asking how they were to treat
the document. I made them promise that no reference whatever
would be made to it, either in the Central League in Dublin,
or at meetings through the country. Otherwise hard things

would have been said and great indignation generated against the H. See. So, thank God, I have the power to keep things right(K).

"But, indeed," he again reminded Kirby, "it is very trying to my patience to be perpetually 'fired at,' not alone by the sworn enemies of our creed and country, but even by those in ecclesiastical places from which I should expect sympathy and support." "Land Bill is out," Croke then wrote in a hurried conclusion, "it is substantially good; but must be largely amended to be acceptable. Bishops meet after Easter to examine it thoroughly."

When Gladstone finally announced he would introduce his long-awaited Land Bill on Thursday, April 7, Laurence Gillooly, the bishop of Elphin, again wrote McCabe on March 23, urging him to convene an early meeting of the bishops. Gillooly suggested that the bishops' legal advisers could meet over the weekend, and that the bishops could then meet on Monday, April 11 "in order to give time for organising the action to be taken by the Clergy on the following Sunday(Mc). It would be in my opinion," Gillooly added, "a most advisable course to have Petitions on the Bill prepared for the signatures of the people on that day—the Petitions to express approval & thankfulness for what will be good in the Bill and to ask for the changes which we will consider necessary." Gillooly, it seems, was still determined to steal a march on the Land League. McCabe, however, was somewhat less anxious for another meeting, especially after the debacle of March 15, but he steeled himself and wrote Daniel McGettigan, the archbishop of Armagh, suggesting April 12, the Tuesday before Easter. McGettigan replied, on April 3, that Holy Week was a very inconvenient time for the bishops to meet without urgent cause and suggested that they meet after Easter(Mc). "By that time," he added significantly, "the measure will be thoroughly discussed by practical men of the Tenant Class who are excellent Judges of what is fair and suitable." Most of the bishops, in fact, felt as McGettigan did, in that they preferred the Land Bill to be discussed from the bottom up, rather than, as Gillooly, from the top down.

McCabe, however, failed to heed the sensible advice of the archbishop of Armagh and called for a meeting on the Tuesday, April 12, of Holy Week. When many of the Bishops signified that they would be unable to attend, McCabe was obliged to adjourn the meeting until April 26. The immediate reaction of the bishops to Gladstone's Land Bill was favorable, as was indeed the reaction of most moderate and sensible men. "So far as I have been able to understand it," Moran wrote Kirby, rather typically, the day after the bill was introduced, "it will be a great boon to the farmers, as it practically grants the three *F*'s, and in part at least guarantees the tenants' rights."[18] Moderate lay opinion was, perhaps, best represented by J. Cashel Hoey, who wrote Kirby from London on April 14, enclosing a copy of the bill. "I think it goes," he observed sensibly, "as far as it is possible for such a measure to go with any chance of passing Parliament(K). I doubt," Hoey explained to Kirby, "whether there ever was a Bill with the preparation of which so much pain was taken. I have reason to believe it was reprinted in 23 different forms. The subject is naturally very complicated, but in my judgment the provisions of the Bill cover the entire ground."

A week later, Moran reported to Kirby that, since the Land Bill had been very generally discussed at meetings, in the press, and at a two-day convention of the Land League in Dublin, the bishops could not complain, when they met on April 26, that they did not have enough information about the feelings of the people on the measure. "I do not know," Moran confessed on April 22, "what the opinion of the Prelates may be, but, so far, all moderate people including some of the leading agitators are for accepting the Bill as a whole, and trying to make some improvements in the committee on the third reading of the Bill in Parliament"(K). "The Bill then," Moran explained to Kirby, "proposes that five hundred thousand occupiers of land who have no leases should ipso facto acquire fixity of tenure, so that they become at once independent of the landlords' caprice, subject however to a

---

[18] K, April 8, 1881. The "Three F's"—Free Sale, Fair Rent, and Fixity of Tenure—are well described in Davitt, *op.cit.*, p. 324: "The act purported to give all yearly agricultural tenants (1) the right to sell their tenancies for the best price that could be got; (2) the right to have a fair rent fixed by the land courts at intervals of fifteen years; (3) security of tenure, inasmuch as that, so long as the rent was paid and the conditions of the tenancy observed, the tenant could not be evicted."

fair rent." "The main difficulty," noted Moran, coming to what would be the heart of the matter, "that can arise is to settle what is to be considered a fair rent. A new Court is to be formed independent of either landlord or tenant, to hold even the balance between both." "So far as my opinion goes," Moran concluded finally, "the Bill is a most useful one, and so far will greatly benefit our tenants: and with very few improvements will give to the tenant every security that can practically be desired."

Parnell, however, now found himself in a very difficult position. Though a majority in the country certainly supported the bill, a minority in his Parliamentary party, and a larger and more militant minority in the Land League, were hostile. The American Land League, moreover, which had sent large sums of money in support of the agitation, was also opposed. To mollify both right and left, therefore, Parnell shrewdly declared the bill was unsatisfactory as final solution, while admitting at the same time it was a great improvement over all previous measures. When the convention of some fifteen hundred Land League delegates met in Dublin on April 22, under the chairmanship of Parnell, the result was a resolution embodying the Parnellite position. The convention declared that only the abolition of landlordism could be considered as a final solution, but left the Parliamentary party at liberty to accept or reject the bill as they pleased. Parnell's position, which was awkward enough, had been made even more difficult by the action of John Dillon, who had assumed Michael Davitt's mantle in the Land League affairs. Dillon had returned to Ireland during the parliamentary recess for Easter, and denounced the Land Bill root and branch. At the Land League Convention, Dillon and his friends attempted to carry a condemnation of the bill in spite of the position taken by Parnell. Finally, when Parliament resumed sitting, Dillon chose to remain in Ireland to agitate against the bill, until he was arrested ultimately under the Coercion Act on May 2, for a most violent and inflammatory speech.[19]

The bishops, meanwhile, who had met on April 26 to consider the bill, issued a preamble and eighteen resolutions. In general they approved of the bill and added that the accep-

---

[19] For the substance of this paragraph, see Davitt, *op. cit.*, pp. 317-318, and C. C. O'Brien, *op. cit.*, pp. 65-66.

tance of their resolutions, in the amending stage, would render the bill entirely satisfactory from their point of view. The food for thought on the bill at the meeting was provided by a five-member episcopal committee, which included the archbishops of Dublin and Cashel, and the bishops of Elphin, Meath, and Raphoe. The committee itself had, in fact, asked Charles Russell, John O'Hagan, and The O'Connor Don, the best legal talent available on the subject of the law of real property in Ireland, to consult with and advise them. The meeting was a very full one, with twenty-one bishops present and several others sending their authorization to have their names attached to the resolutions. "The only point about which there was anything like serious disagreement," Moran reported to Kirby on April 28, "presented itself in the 18th Resolution. All the others with the Preamble were very fully discussed and a great many alterations were made in the scheme which the Committee had drafted, but all unanimously acquiesced in the alterations"(K). "In the last resolution (No. 18)," Moran explained, "the Committee had recommended the appointment of two Assessors *to be appointed by the Commission*, that is by the Court in Dublin. All our Bishops agreed that two Assessors were necessary as for the most part our people have no confidence in the barrister who acts as County-Court Judge." "I proposed as an amendment," Moran added, "to the Resolution which was drafted by the Committee that the two Assessors should be elected by the County-Electors, with of course the approval of the Bench." "We had a fierce battle about this," Moran confided, "but the amendment was carried by an overwhelming majority. This 18th Resolution in its present amended form has annoyed the Archbishop of Dublin beyond measure." McCabe, who wrote Kirby the next day, did not waste many words on the resolutions. "I hope," he commented tersely, "Mr. Gladstone will be able to carry his Bill. Even as it stands it would be a great blessing"(K).

When Dillon was arrested on May 2, Parnell again found himself politically embarrassed. In an effort to placate his clamoring left, Parnell moved at a meeting of the party on May 5, that they should protest Dillon's arrest by abstaining from voting on the second reading of the Land Bill. The bill was, in fact, certain to carry whether the Parnellites voted or not, and such a parliamentary move on Parnell's part was no more than a *beau geste*. How reluctant the party was to make even a gesture of hostility to the bill, however, was made amply clear when twelve of the thirty members present voted against the motion, and a grumbling number only voted for it because Parnell threatened to resign as chairman of the party if his motion was not sustained. When the *Freeman's Journal* condemned the party decision the next day, and Archbishop Croke pronounced against it the day after, Parnell issued an open letter to the archbishop explaining that not voting for the second reading was only a tactical demonstration, which could not endanger the bill. From early May then, until the bill passed its third reading in the Commons on July 29, and was submitted to the Lords for their consideration, Parnell and his party refrained from any gesture that might even imply hostility to the bill, and settled down to amend the bill in the interests and to the great advantage of the Irish tenant farmer.[20]

From the point of view of the situation in Ireland, however, Parnell's gesture on behalf of Dillon was not quite as empty as it seemed. The agitation in the country did not subside with the introduction of the Land Bill. The passage of the coercion measures in February had resulted in a sharp rise in evictions, which had actually increased with the introduction of the Land Bill. The landlords now realized that, since their tenants would soon have fixity of tenure under law, this was indeed their last chance to clear their estates and create viable economic holdings. The tenants were determined to resist evictions come what may, and the arbitrary arrests only convinced them that they had no real recourse under law. The result of these arbitrary arrests of the leaders of the agitation was that the temper of the people grew shorter and more ugly and, to keep the peace and to prevent bloodshed, some of the clergy, and especially the younger clergy, began to take up the places of the men arrested. "You will hear, ere this reaches you," John Bourke, the parish priest of Pallaskenry in County Limerick, wrote Kirby on May 22, "from the Irish Papers, that one of our Priests has been arrested under the late coercion act"(K). "It is very true indeed," Bourke continued, referring to Father Eugene Sheehy, a warm friend and supporter of John Dillon, "that the same Priest was very often very incauti-

---

[20] For the substance of this paragraph, see C. C. O'Brien, *op. cit.*, pp. 62-69.

ous in his public addresses to the people at some of our Land League meetings, and that you might infer from the boldness of his expressions that he seemed to court some such thing." "There is," he confided to Kirby, "a great deal of revolutionary doctrines [sic] inculcated, in some cases covertly, in many others almost openly, and I fear much that many of our Ecclesiastical Brethren may be classified amongst the latter. Unless the Priest goes with the hothead politicians, the Land-leaguers, in all their movements they will tell him they don't want him." "Some Land League Committees," he reported to Kirby in conclusion, "have got rid of their presidents, the Priests, because the Priests would not agree with their opinions, and woe to Ireland when that Communistic idea finds a footing in it."

The news from Tipperary was even more serious. "There is no doubt," James J. Ryan wrote Kirby in an undated letter from St. Patrick's College in Thurles in early June, "the situation is daily becoming graver. This is owing to the number of evictions, which are increasing every day, and to the action of the Government"(K). "The arrests of Dillon and Father Sheehy," Ryan pointed out, "cause the deepest indignation. The presence of large bodies of police, and military at the public meetings, has the effect of provoking the people to acts of violence. There is good reason to believe the Government is desirous of stirring up an *armed* resistance to this present system of evictions, that a most favourable occasion would be afforded of trampling the unhappy people." "The Government," he declared finally by way of example, "endeavoured to provoke a riot in our midst on the occasion of the sale of farms in town about ten days ago. The priests were there, and prevented a collision which, they say, was hoped for." The government did, indeed, recognize that the priests were the key to the maintenance of law and order. "The priests," wrote Earl Cowper, the lord lieutenant, in a minute to the Cabinet about this time, "still exercise an extraordinary influence over the people, as has been shown lately in the most marked manner by the power they possess of controlling and pacifying the most excited crowd, and to withdraw the priests from the movement would be an object for which a great deal of risk might be run."[21]

---

[21] Quoted in R. Barry O'Brien, *op.cit.*, p. 223.

Not all the bishops, however, were grateful for small mercies. McCabe, for example, felt that many of the clergy were going too far, and cited them to their bishops. "On yesterday," Moran reported to McCabe on June 8, "after our Diocesan Synod I sent for Rev. Mr. O'Halloran, to give him a little of my mind about his doings in Athy on Thursday last"(Mc). "He anticipated however," Moran explained, "my words by frankly acknowledging his fault as well as going to Athy on that day, as in the foolish speech which he made. I had intended to punish him severely, but as he seemed to fully realize his folly I have not taken any further steps." "I expect," Moran concluded, "that the whole incident will have a very salutory effect upon a few others who have been led a little astray by the political ferment of the present times." When McCabe wrote MacEvilly, the coadjutor to the archbishop of Tuam, about one of his priests, MacEvilly replied that he had sent for Father Waldron as the language imputed to him was inexcusable. "I know this Robert Henry," MacEvilly added in mitigation, referring to the landlord denounced by Father Waldron, "who lives about 2 miles from here to be the greatest tyrant and most cruel oppressor of the poor on Earth. He is a most intolerant bigot. The very sight of Priests puts him in a rage. He has ruthlessly depopulated the whole district."[22] While admitting this was no excuse for Father Waldron's language, MacEvilly explained to McCabe he was not quite sure what Waldron's reaction would be at their interview. "I found Fr. Corbett," he reported of another offending priest, "our *former* friend, very tractable. I would not be so sure of Fr. Waldron. However I shall do my best."

Croke, meanwhile, was doing his very best to keep his priests and people within the bounds of law and order by giving them a lead in terms of loyalty and affection rather than by resorting to authority and intimidation. As was his custom, he began the annual visitation of his archdiocese in May, and in every parish he attempted to moderate the anger and indignation of the people by preaching forebearance and charity. "You may have heard," James J. Ryan wrote Kirby in early June, "of the reception the dear Archbishop met with during his Visitation."

---

[22]Mc, July 8, 1881. See also letter of Bartholomew Woodlock, bishop of Ardagh, to McCabe, July 3, 1881, claiming that it was a case of mistaken identity for the priest cited by McCabe really was in the diocese of Kilmore.

The description given by the papers falls short of the reality. I went to see for myself and attended a couple of these demonstrations,—as I may call them. I never witnessed anything like the enthusiasm and at the same time the piety of the people. Last Tuesday he [Croke] held a Visitation in Clonaulty. About 6:30 P.M., according to his custom he left for the parish in which the Visitation was to be held the following day—Holy Cross. On arriving at the road he was met by three bands, a large number of cars, and quite a regiment of horsemen which accompanied us to Holy Cross. As we advanced the procession grew larger. The people came pouring out of every house on the way, and joined from the crossroads. As his carriage passed, they fell on their knees to receive the blessing. On entering their parish we were met by the people of Holy Cross accompanied by two bands, and an immense display of green banners. The Clonaulty folk having fallen back a little on quitting their own parish, the others took their places next to the Abp's carriage. You would be surprised, and pleased to see the order of the people, and the disciplined manner in which they moved. The horse was taken from the carriage, notwithstanding the Abp's opposition, and he was drawn by the people a distance of more than a mile, to the place of meeting,—the parish school. The procession which followed was over a mile in length. The Abp. addressed the people and then went to the Parish Priest's house.[23]

"My progress," Croke himself wrote Kirby on June 2, obviously still elated, the day after this visit, "through the Diocese on Visitation was the most extraordinary ever known in Ireland"(K). "I wish," Croke suggested significantly to Kirby, "you would call the attention of the authorities to my triumphal progress and the speeches I delivered everwhere as I went along."

Croke was, indeed, very conscious of the Irish cause in general, and himself in particular, being vulnerable in Rome, and especially at the Propaganda. "Apropos of Propaganda," he had written Kirby on May 7, complaining bitterly of Monsignor Masotti, the secretary, "I have heard from two priests who were lately in Rome, that Mgr. Masotti 'loses no opportunity of expressing his disregard for me' "(K). "If another authentic case of this," Croke threatened, "comes before me, I shall certainly remonstrate. I have never done anything to

[23] K, no date [early June, 1881].

displease him. Besides I recognize no one in Propaganda but the Cardinal, and I firmly believe in his goodness and sense of Justice." In reply to this letter, Kirby obviously remarked that some in Rome at least thought that Croke was allowing himself to be "led by the nose" by more unscrupulous men. "Little *they* know me," was Croke's comment, "who imagine I could be *'led by the nose'* by anybody living."[24] "I wish," he candidly confessed, "I were a little more flexible than I am."

During the summer, Croke prudently continued the attempt to mend his Roman fences, while also trying to correct the Irish image there. When the remains of Pius IX were removed from St. Peter's to St. Lorenzo outside the walls, on the evening of July 12, for permanent burial, the torchlight procession which wound its way through Rome caused a near riot.[25] Though the results had certainly more to do with insult than injury, it did provide the opportunity for Catholics the world over to express their indignation at the lack of respect for the remains of the late pope, and the weakness of the Italian government in handling the delicate affair. On Sunday, July 24, Croke took advantage of a visit by the mayor, aldermen, and corporation of the town of Clonmel, and some seven hundred members of the Confraternity of the Sacred Heart, to denounce the "fearful outrage in Rome." After describing the visit to Kirby that same evening, Croke added in a postscript, "I hope you all like what I said of the Roman affair"(K). Since Croke had to rush off to attend the funeral of the late bishop of Kerry in Killarney, he asked James J. Ryan to forward the newspaper accounts of his remarks to Kirby in Rome. "His Grace," Ryan concluded his note hurriedly on July 25, "who has just left for Kerry, desired me to let you have them *immediately*. You [will know] what to do with them"(K).

Surprisingly enough, towards the end of July, the Irish members of Parliament were persuaded to present an address to the pope commiserating with him in the insult offered to the remains of his predecessor. "It is however," Moran explained rather apologetically to Kirby on July 30, while enclosing a copy of the address, "only a poor expression of what our people feel in the matter"(K). The pope, however, was reported by Kirby to Croke, as being pleased with the

---

[24] K, June 2, 1881.
[25] F. O., 170/304, 170/305. See for respective dispatches of Paget to Granville, Nos. 297 and 307, dated July 13, 1881, and July 25, 1881, describing the affair.

address. Croke replied on August 10 that he was glad the pope was pleased, but confessed to Kirby that there had been great bungling and intriguing among the Irish members over the address. In this same letter, Croke also enclosed part of a letter from a "Roman Monsigneur," who was reported as knowing Propaganda well, written to an Irish priest. The letter was forwarded by the priest to Croke to warn him how he stood in the estimation of some in Rome. "I am fully determined," Croke declared, "to write the Pope personally complaining of this Mgr. Mazotti. I never saw him or spoke to him except in yr. presence, and I cannot understand what is the meaning, or cause, of this hostility." "I shall not," Croke concluded with a safer second thought, "write to Pope till I hear from you again."

McCabe, who had to interrupt his citing of priests to their bishops, to go on his annual retreat at Maynooth with his clergy, reported to Kirby, meanwhile, that the conduct of his own clergy, at least, was both edifying and satisfactory. "We *had one hundred and sixty priests* of the Diocese," he wrote Kirby on July 16, "and nothing could exceed the order, silence, and piety of this large assemblage. Thank God the priests of Dublin, whilst yielding to none of their brethren in love of country and of our people, have kept aloof from the angry turmoil while many young and well meaning clergymen have involved themselves and their order in disgrace"(K). "There are," continued McCabe, turning to the burning question of evictions, "many poor farmers who cannot pay their rents, but I am afraid that *very many* more have dishonestly availed themselves of the state of the country to avoid obligations that they are bound to meet and could meet." "For the eviction of such men," he concluded firmly, "and they are not by any means a few, I can feel no sympathy or compassion."

Less than a week later, McCabe again wrote Kirby, and while explaining that he was shocked by the way the Romans treated the remains of the late pope, he went on to report that wickedness was not the monopoly of either Romans or even some Irishmen. "Delegates," he informed Kirby on July 21, "from the Democratic Societies of England have appeared amongst us, and have received a welcome in quarters where their real mission ought to be known: I fear very much that the teaching of the Landleague agents has done a good deal to

prepare our people for the teaching of their men who are
infidels, but as yet with a mask"(K). "With all my respect for
Cardinal Manning," McCabe went on to complain, "I must say
that I think he has done very great mischief by giving his
approbation to the Landleague, and by applauding the A-B of
Cashel." This did not prevent McCabe, however, from taking
advantage of a letter written to him by Manning about the
Land Bill from London on July 22, to ask the cardinal for
information and his opinion of the Democratic League. "I will
send," Manning replied on July 27, from Birmingham, "full
information by tomorrows post from London."[26] "Meanwhile," he reported, "the Democratic League has a Committee
on which were the names of Bradlaugh, Victor Hugo, Parnell,
Helen Taylor & others. It is to be resisted by all means, & its
contact with the Land League & with Ireland can only be
disastrous to us." "The line you so wisely & boldly took," he
hinted broadly, "when Mr. Parnell went to Paris seems to me
all the more necessary now." When Manning forwarded the
promised information on July 30, McCabe could not resist
publishing another pastoral denouncing the Democratic
League and its works, before retiring for a brief rest to Harrogate in England on his doctor's orders.

"Poor man," wrote Michael Verdon of McCabe on August
10, to Kirby from Belfast, "he is not happy, he feels criticism
very much and he knows that he gets a larger share of abuse
than praise"(K). Verdon, who had served over two years as
Kirby's vice-rector, had only just returned to Ireland to raise
some badly needed funds for the Irish College in Rome. Since
he had not been in Ireland for some time, and since his
fund-raising mission took him to all parts of Ireland, Verdon
was the nearest thing to an independent witness that could be
had. Since he was also an intelligent, confident, and sensible
man, his testimony may be taken with a good deal less salt than
most. Verdon reported to Kirby on August 10, that

All the Priests & laymen whom I have met are unanimous in
saying that a certain amount of agitation was necessary, and that
it was perfectly fair and right to force landllords to reduce rents
by at least 20 per cent. Indeed outside the landlord classes there
is no pity for landlords & I have heard persons who are above all

---

[26] Mc, July 27, 1881. See also letter of July 30, 1881, from Manning to McCabe,
enclosing a letter of July 29, 1881, from Henry Bellingham, M. P., to a Mr. Beck [?].

interest in the agitation saying that the rents through the country have been scandalously high. Of course many tenants are now acting as rogues but, an example on the other hand, the Clonliffe tenants who had fair rents never asked for any reduction and paid in full. The Primate told me that religion was never in a more flourishing state in the country(K).

Some two weeks later, while reporting to Kirby on August 27, from Dublin, that he had collected some £736 and would have a £1,000 by the following week, Verdon again entered into a description of the situation in the country.

The weather is bad and there is now great alarm about the harvest. The agitation will continue, and all the bishops who have spoken to me on the subject are strongly in favour of the priests joining with the people and taking part in the meetings. Many priests and bishops told me that if the priests had been withdrawn from politics religion would have suffered a terrible blow in the Country. As far as I can make out Dr. McCabe & Dr. Gillooly are the only bishops in Ireland in favour of the abstention policy. Of course many deplore the unfortunate letter of Dr. Croke against Dr. McCabe—but with the exception of that—his policy meets with very general approval, and very many say his action has been most beneficial to religion in the Country(K).

In making his final report to Kirby, that he had collected £1,321 and expected more, before returning to Rome, Verdon also reported that the weather had taken a turn for the better, and, if it continued fair, the harvest in Ireland would yet be very good. He then turned his attention to the Land Bill, which had passed the Lords on August 22 and was now law. "Dr. Croke," Verdon pointed out to Kirby on September 1, "has done much to induce the people to give the new land bill a fair trial, and it is probable that those who give it a trial will soon retire from the land league"(K). "A good harvest," he concluded, "will help considerably to calm the agitation."

Indeed, what kind of a land bill might emerge as law prompted as acute an observer of the political scene as existed, Cardinal Manning, to write McCabe, before it had even left the House of Commons, about the action which might be taken to save the bill from being amended out of existence by the Lords. "I cannot resist the desire," Manning observed on

July 22, at his subtle best, "to write and ask your Grace
whether it does not appear to be prudent that the Bishops of
Ireland should meet, as soon as the Land Bill has left the
House of Commons, so as to anticipate any actions or expressions in the House of Lords"(Mc). "Such a declaration on their
part," Manning pointed out, coming to cases, "would do two
things. It would greatly quiet the 'pars senior' of the Irish
people, & it would greatly hinder the Lords from mutilating
the bill. Excuse my making this suggestion, but out of Ireland
it would not be easy to find any one with its welfare more at
heart." "If four or five of the Bishops with your Grace at their
head," Manning suggested in conclusion, "were to request the
Primate to invite the Episcopate to Maynooth, it would make a
mark upon the public opinions of both Ireland & England."
McCabe replied politely that he was grateful for Manning's
suggestion and that while it would give him great pleasure to
act on it, he was not quite sure that the bishops would be
unanimous about the bill as it was likely to come out of the
House of Commons.[27] Some of the bishops were so upset by
Gladstone having ignored their resolutions, he further
explained, that they felt they should abstain from any commendation of the bill.[28] In assuring the cardinal that this was
certainly not his point of view, McCabe added that he always
thought the 18th resolution very unfortunate because "it cast
a shadow over all the others." The result of this exchange,
however, was not the proposed meeting of the bishops, but
McCabe's pastoral denouncing the Democratic League.

The House of Lords, as Manning had predicted, then proceeded to mangle the Land Bill, but Gladstone refused to
accept their amendments, and the Lords reluctantly gave way.
The day after the Land Bill passed the Lords, Croke wrote
Manning a most reassuring letter. "I think the Land Bill," he
informed the cardinal on August 23, "will do a deal of good,
and I believe it will get a fair trial generally throughout the
country."[29] "There are a few, to be sure," Croke admitted,

[27] Quoted in Leslie, *op. cit.*, p. 383.
[28] McCabe was referring particularly to Patrick Duggan, the bishop of Clonfert,
who was very unhappy about the Bill and who wrote McCabe July 17, 1881, a very
strong letter indeed. Since the bishop of Clonfert seems to have been the only bishop
who complained of the bill, it is strongly open to question whether his letter was the
cause or the excuse for McCabe's reply to Manning about not convening a meeting of
the bishops.
[29] Leslie, *op. cit.*, p. 385.

"amongst what is known as 'the advanced party,' who do not look on it with favour. There are others who dislike the Government intensely that 'picked up' Michael Davitt and keeps such men as Father Sheehy in prison. This class is most numerous: so much so that I believe there will be no real peace in the country until the prison doors are thrown open." "I had a notion," Croke confessed, "of writing something to that effect to Mr. Gladstone. Of course, if I did anything of the kind, my communication would be quite private." "I fancy, however," Croke hinted to Manning, "that I shall leave him to gather his information from some other source." "There is nothing to be dreaded," Croke concluded finally, referring to Victor Hugo and the Democratic League, "I assure your Eminence, from what is called the 'French Alliance,' for the very valid reason that it is an alliance *in nubibus*; nor, indeed, from any other sinister influence, and I think I can safely say that the Irish people were never more reasonably religious than they are to-day, and as a rule so thoroughly devoted to their clergy."

Not all the Irish bishops, however, proved as optimistic as Croke. Michael Warren, the bishop of Ferns, for example, was more pessimistic. He informed Kirby on August 28, that much uncertainty prevailed with regard to the working of the Land Bill, though he thought that if it was given a fair trial it would effect immense good(K). "But the question is," Warren added significantly, "will it be allowed a fair trial."

> Success has thrown the people into the power of those who have & who are advocating the most advanced principles. And again these men not only assume to lead and guide the people, but they are being belauded by high authorities whose words have the greatest influence with the people. There is a Convention called by the leaders of the Land League to meet in Dublin about the middle of next month. It is to be composed of delegates of the various branches of the Land League, which have been very numerously formed in every County in Ireland. Those chosen, whether Priests or Laymen will be generally of the most advanced opinions, and the question of how the Land Law is to be treated will be decided by that body. I think it is a foregone conclusion that it will be condemned as insufficient & worthless and that—the advanced leaders will carry a resolution to make it so(K).

The bishop of Ferns, however, reckoned without Parnell, who, though caught between his right and left wings once again, proved himself to be as resourceful a politician as ever. On the right, his Parliamentary party, the press, the bishops, and the great majority of the clergy, as well as most of the tenant farmers, if they were left to themselves, were in favor of giving the Land Act a fair trial. On the left, the American Land League, and most of the leadership of the Irish Land League, were pressing Parnell to denounce the act. When the convention met on September 11-14, in Dublin, Parnell again produced the formula on which all could unite. He simply argued that the act should be tested. Only those cases selected by the League branches in each area should be submitted to the Land Courts for the determination of what was a fair rent. The advantage of such a course of action was patent to all, and especially the tenant farmers. In the first place, the Court calendars would not be glutted by a rush, and each decision, therefore, would set the local precedent with regard to what was a fair rent. In this way, and in the second place, the decisions of the Land Courts would be kept up to the mark by the intense anticipation, and the tenants would be enabled thereby to avoid time-consuming and costly legal procedures by coming to a satisfactory private settlement with their landlords, who would, undoubtedly, prove more tractable when they saw the handwriting on the wall in the form of the Land Court decision.

On the other hand, the local Land League branches would provide the machinery for the selective process, and build themselves into the Land Act by becoming a vital and necessary part in the working of the act, especially in its initial stages, while remaining, in the last analysis, the tenant's final court of appeal, if the decisions of the Land Courts, with regard to what was considered a fair rent, were not up to the mark. The government, naturally, had to wonder who, indeed, was to administer law in Ireland, the Land League or itself. When after the convention, however, Parnell stumped the country stressing the "hollowness of the Act," the government took him at his word, which was a mistake, and thought he was out to sabotage the administration of the act. Actually, Parnell was only attempting to placate his left wing and especially his American allies, with another of his tactical gestures of defiance. The bishops did what they could to redress the

balance by meeting on September 26 and issuing a manifesto
in which they described the act as a great benefit, while adding
that the gratitude of the country was due Mr. Gladstone for
it.[30]

Gladstone, however, not only misunderstood Parnell's tactics, but seriously misjudged the temper of the country. Early
in September he had been heartened by the defeat of a Parnellite in a by-election in North Tyrone by a Liberal. He took this
as an indication that Parnell was losing his grip in the country
and suggested to W. E. Forster, the chief secretary for Ireland,
the release of Father Sheehy might be the reasonable beginning of a reconciliation between the government and the Irish
people. Forster, who was by temperament less optimistic than
Gladstone, realistically pointed out that Tyrone was in Ulster,
and Ulster was not Connaught or Munster. After Parnell
spoke in Dublin on September 25, where he gave the impression that the Land Act would not do, Forster wrote Gladstone
the next day suggesting that Parnell be arrested. He also
intimated that Gladstone, in any case, would do great good in
the major policy speech he was planning to make in Leeds on
October 7, if he called Parnell to account. When Parnell then
stressed "the hollowness of the Act" on Sunday, October 2, in
Cork, and broadened the issue by raising the question of
legislative independence, Gladstone, indeed, had had
enough. At Leeds, therefore, he announced that "the resources of civilisation were not yet exhausted," and that they
would be used, if necessary, against the man "who stood
between the living and the dead, not like Aaron to stop the
plague, but to spread the plague."[31]

Two days later, on Sunday, October 9, in Wexford, Parnell
answered Gladstone's threat in a remarkable speech. "You
have gained something," Parnell told the people of Wexford,
"by your exertions during the last twelve months; but I am
here to-day to tell you that you have gained but a fraction of
that to which you are entitled."[32] "And the Irishman," he
counseled, "who thinks that he can now throw away his arms,
just as Grattan disbanded the volunteers in 1783, will find to
his sorrow and destruction when too late that he has placed

---

[30] *Freeman's Journal*, September 27, 1881.
[31] Quoted in R. Barry O'Brien, *op. cit.*, p. 237. For the substance of this paragraph,
see *ibid.*, pp. 235-237.
[32] *Ibid.*, pp. 238-240.

himself in the power of the perfidious and cruel and relentless
English enemy." "It is a good sign," Parnell continued, coming
to Gladstone, the particular English enemy, "that the mas-
querading Knight-errant, this pretending champion of the
rights of every other nation except those of the Irish nation,
should be obliged to throw off the mask today, and stand
revealed as the man who, by his own utterances, is prepared to
carry fire and sword into your homesteads, unless you humbly
abase yourselves before him and before the landlords of the
country." "The land of Ireland," Parnell then replied to those
critics who accused him of advocating confiscation and public
plunder, "has been confiscated three times over by the men
whose descendants Mr. Gladstone is supporting in the enjoy-
ment of the fruits of their plunder by his bayonets and his
buckshot, and when we are spoken to about plunder we are
entitled to ask who were the first and biggest plunderers."
"This doctrine of public plunder," Parnell announced soberly, "is only a question of degree." "I trust as a result of this
great movement," Parnell then finally concluded, with a parting shot at Gladstone's threat at Leeds, "we shall see that, just
as Gladstone by the Act of 1881 has eaten all his own words,
has departed from all his formerly declared principles, now
we shall see that these brave words of the English Prime
Minister will be scattered like chaff before the united and
advancing determination of the Irish people to regain for
themselves their lost land and their legislative independence."
Parnell had now raised the stake from "the Land of Ireland
for the People of Ireland," to Home Rule, and the next move
was Gladstone's.

The effect of this dialogue on the more conservative of the
bishops may be well imagined. Five days after Parnell's Cork
speech emphasizing "the hollowness of the Act," McCabe
wrote Kirby in despair. "We have got a fine Land Act," he
explained on October 4, "which will fix the people in the soil
without the danger of capricious rents or capricious
evictions—but we seem to be as far off from peace as ever: Mr.
Parnell and his friends are determined to keep the Country in
turmoil, and some, from whom better things might be expected, are helping him"(K). "The violence of the language &
conduct," McCabe complained, "of some priests through the
Country is bringing disgrace on us all, and there seems to be

no power Ecclesiastical or civil that they are afraid of."
"Boycotting," he concluded, "is in some parts becoming a
frightful tyranny, which well disposed men dare not oppose."

Several days after Parnell's Wexford speech raising the
stake to Home Rule, McCabe in writing Kirby was simply
aghast. "Our troubles are far from over," he assured Kirby on
October 12, "the leaders of the Land League do not mean to
stop at a reformation of the land laws: Their program is
unlimited, and wise men do not see whither we are drifting:
God grant that the whole thing will not end in a sea of
blood"(K). The following day, McCabe's staunchest supporter
among the bishops, and a man who did not panic easily, the
bishop of Elphin, wrote Kirby in the greatest alarm. "You will
have inferred," Gillooly reported from Sligo on October 13,
"from the N. Papers that Mr. Parnell & the Land League are
not satisfied with the New Land Act and are determined to
keep up their Agitation"(K). "I have just learned from a
telegram received in town," Gillooly concluded hurriedly,
"that Mr. Parnell was arrested this morning in Dublin. I dare
say several other arrests will follow—with what result it is hard
to say." "Pray earnestly for us," he begged of Kirby, "—we are
passing thru' perilous times."

V. Chaos

October, 1881 - January, 1883

"Politically," Parnell closed a hurried note to Mrs. O'Shea on October 13, as two detectives waited outside his door to take him away, "it is a fortunate thing for me that I have been arrested, as the movement is breaking fast, and all will be quiet in a few months, when I shall be released."[1] Protest meetings were immediately organized all over the country at which Parnell's lieutenants denounced the government in less than measured terms. For their pains, they were also arrested as "suspects" under the Coercion Act and joined Parnell in Dublin's Kilmainham Gaol. "The course pursued," Moran wrote Kirby on October 18, "by the violent members of the Land-League to deter farmers from making use of the excellent measure sanctioned a few months ago in Parliament and the arrest of Parnell and the other heads of the League during the past few days have thrown the people into a regular ferment that is hard to control. It is now we see what a blessing it was that the clergy had such a hold of the national movement and were so thoroughly united with their flocks. There is really no other power to moderate their ardor at present"(K). "The extorting of the Land-Bill," Moran remarked revealingly, "from a hostile Parliament has made our people realize the strength of a united peaceful national agitation." "We hope with God's blessing," he added most significantly, indicating that Parnell had made at least one important convert to Home Rule before he went to jail, "that the same will before many years secure for us our own Parliament."

That very day, October 18, the prisoners in Kilmainham issued their famous "No Rent Manifesto." "Fellow Countrymen!" they urgently announced,

The hour to try your souls and redeem your pledges has ar-

---

[1] Katherine O'Shea, *Charles Stewart Parnell* 1 (London, 1914): p. 207.

127

rived. The executive of the National Land League, forced to abandon the policy of testing the land act, feels bound to advise the tenant-farmers of Ireland from this forth to pay *no rents* under any circumstances to their landlords until the government relinquishes the existing system of terrorism and restores the constitutional rights of the people.[2]

The manifesto was signed by "Charles S. Parnell, President, Kilmainham Jail; A. J. Kettle, Hon. Sec., Kilmainham Jail; Michael Davitt, Hon. Sec., Portland Prison; Thomas Brennan, Hon. Sec., Kilmainham Jail; John Dillon, Head Organizer, Kilmainham Jail; Thomas Sexton, Head Organizer, Kilmainham Jail; Patrick Egan, Treasurer, Paris."[3] "Times are critical here," Croke wrote Kirby on October 20, "and, unfortunately, I am a bit struck down"(K). "The Prisoners at Kilmainham, headed by Parnell," Croke reported, "have issued a manifesto against paying *rent at all*. I issued another, yesterday, hot foot on the one of the day before, protesting against any such doctrine. I send you Freeman containing it." As Croke was writing Kirby from Thurles, W. E. Forster issued a proclamation in Dublin, in the name of the lord lieutenant, suppressing the Land League. "Now we hereby," the proclamation said in part, "warn all persons that the said association, styling itself the Irish National Land League, or by whatsoever other name it may be called or known, is an unlawful or criminal association, and that all meetings and assemblies to carry out or promote its designs or purposes are also unlawful and criminal, and will be prevented, and, if necessary, dispersed by force."[4]

Archbishop McCabe's immediate reaction to the no-rent manifesto was to sound out MacEvilly about calling a meeting of the bishops to deal with the crisis. MacEvilly, who replied from Galway on October 22, advised against a meeting, especially since Croke had just effectively checked the impact of the manifesto by his very timely declaration denouncing it(Mc). In the West, MacEvilly reported further, the people were very excited and there was nothing the bishops could say at the moment that would do any good. While MacEvilly also thought that the "wicked Manifesto" had revealed to those

---

[2] Michael Davitt, *The Fall of Feudalism in Ireland* (London, 1904), p. 335.
[3] *Ibid.*, p. 337.
[4] *Ibid.*, p. 338.

who were not willfully blind that there was much in the agitation that was simply Fenianism in disguise, he did maintain that the Land League agitation was chiefly responsible for the winning of the Land Act, and that it had been a wise policy for the clergy not to separate themselves from the people. "If they did," he insisted in conclusion, "I have no hesitation in saying, speaking for this part of the country, that the worst consequences would result, and our people irrevocably attached to godless, dishonest demagogues." McCabe could have taken little comfort in this letter, for MacEvilly was obviously the victim of having to choose between the lesser of two evils. If McCabe had been able to read the correspondence between Moran and Kirby, however, he would certainly have been even more upset than he was, for the bishop of Ossory was not only, like MacEvilly, now a declared supporter of the League, but he had also become a convert to Home Rule.

In the crisis, moreover, Moran seems to have almost developed a sense of humor. "Everything in Ireland," he reported ironically to Kirby on October 28, "is going on quite peaceably at present. A great number of persons have been arrested, & every day new arrests are being made"(K). "It seems," he continued in the same vein, "as if by a just retribution Mr. Gladstone is compelled to adopt the system of arbitrary arrests which he so violently condemned in the former Neopolitan Government. He now styles such measures 'the resources of civilisation.' " The chief danger, Moran observed more seriously, was that now that the Land League was suppressed, the people might be driven to join secret societies, but that he hoped the question of domestic legislation would be taken up throughout the country and act as an antidote to secret societies. "We suffer injustice," he explained to Kirby, "in so many ways & under so many heads that it is useless to hope for a remedy from a British Parliament. I anticipate that by a united national agitation, the Home Parliament would be carried in less than five years." "We intend of course," Moran concluded his startling letter, "to urge particularly the Education question on the Government, as it is a question that comes more properly within our sphere." By the time he went to jail, then, Parnell had not only successfully focused the national consciousness on the Land League agitation, but if Moran is an accurate example of what was happening, that consciousness was now beginning to crystallize around the idea of an Irish state. Moreover, in his concluding remark to Kirby about education, Moran was anticipating what indeed would become the Church's chief prerogative in the Irish state.

While all the bishops had certainly not moved as far to the left in the Irish political spectrum as Moran, they all, with the exception of McCabe and Gillooly, had gone at least as far as MacEvilly in allowing their priests to participate in the Land League. Now that the League had been suppressed, the bishops were afraid that the people would end up in secret combinations. The result was that a good many of the priests, and especially the younger clergy, stepped into the leadership breach created by the recent arrests, and at various public meetings throughout the country denounced the government for its coercion measures. In this way the clergy, with the tacit approval of many of the bishops, were able to retain their influence with the people and prevent bloodshed. Croke, who had been confined to his house and bed with sciatica since he issued his condemnation of the no-rent manifesto on October 19, does not appear to have appreciated the serious turn the crisis was taking. "Things," he reported to Kirby on November 7, "are quietening down here now. The 'no rent' cry is a failure"(K). "Had I not spoke so soon, and so emphatically," he maintained, "no power in Church or State could have checked it. 'Twas well I kept with the people, and that they trusted me." "Of course," he concluded philosophically, "I get a hard knock now and again, for not going ahead; but I don't mind that."

If Croke erred on the side of optimism, however, McCabe's state of mind can only be described as alarmist. He also wrote Kirby only two days after Croke, maintaining that "the *inner* circle of the Land League has thrown off the mask and the order 'No rent' has gone forth, and I regret to say with too much success"(K). "But calamity of calamities," he then added, "priests have preached and are yet preaching this Communistic doctrine: I believe Ireland's Faith was never exposed to greater danger: May God carry us through the Ordeal." McCabe concluded by explaining that he had attempted to tell the truth in another pastoral, and that he had been well abused for it. The truth, however, was not to be found in the extremes represented by Croke or McCabe, but in the mean. For the day after McCabe wrote Kirby, Moran also reported

that indeed in some districts the tenants had refused to pay
their rents, and in others they had appealed to the Land
Court, but in the great majority of cases they were trying to
arrange quietly and peaceably with their landlords(K). "As a
political engine," Moran shrewdly observed of the no-rent
manifesto,

> it is one that has much to be said in its favour, dealing, as it does
> with men whose only principle is their pockets. The landlords as
> a rule care very little for the rules of justice so long as they can
> extort an exorbitant rent. When their own weapons are turned
> against them they at once invoke the aid of the goddess of justice
> whom heretofore they despised(K).

McCabe, meanwhile, had embarked on a one-man crusade
to prevent that "calamity of calamities," priests preaching
communist doctrines, by citing the various reverend gentlemen to their bishops. Given the temper of the country, however, it was not always easy to deal with these self-appointed
tribunes of the people. "The conduct of this priest," the
bishop of Ferns complained, for example, in reply to McCabe,
"has given me much trouble and anxiety for some time."

> I had him repeatedly before me. I have admonished him,
> warned him, and removed him (he is not many months in his
> present mission), but all to no purpose. Many believe he is not
> in his right mind, at least in these matters. At the same time he is
> not wanting in cleverness and I cannot find anything serious as
> to the discharge of his purely religious duties. Nevertheless
> from various causes he has got great power over the masses of
> the people who are organized by the Land League, and whose
> organization was *long* exercised and perfected. However, I am
> informed his influence is on the wane, and probably may soon
> subside.[5]

"If I had a clear case, and if I suspended the Rev. Gentleman,"
Warren then explained, "I believe he would have at once
placed his mother in the workhouse and possibly he might

---

[5] Mc, November 1881; no day noted in this letter. For some more effective action,
see the replies of George Butler (Limerick), Hugh Conway (Killala), and James Ryan
(Coadjutor to Killaloe), respectively, in Mc, November 13, November 18, and
November 20, 1881. "I am convinced," Ryan replied to McCabe, "that the embryo
statesman had got a dose of Politics."

have gone into it himself for a short time. I believe he was anxious to be arrested and sent to prison." "I fully agree with the observation," Warren concluded somewhat lamely, "as to the injury that religious principles have sustained by the sayings and doings of some members of the clerical body."

By the middle of November it was becoming evident to one and all in Ireland that the worst was not over, and if the tide were not soon stemmed the result could only be anarchy. "My heart is broken," MacEvilly complained to Kirby on November 19, "by some wild young *Priests in Tuam.* God forgive those who encourage them. I have saved 3 of them from jail by dealing with the Government. Their language is *simply fierce*"(K). Episcopal authority, however, was not only apparently being threatened from within, but it was also being undermined from without, for Gillooly also reported to Kirby the same day as MacEvilly that secret societies were rapidly spreading, and great efforts were being made to prevent the people from being guided by the bishops in the crisis(K). The new watchwords, he complained, were "No Rent," "No Land Courts," and "The liberation of Ireland from English tyranny." He could not think, therefore, under the circumstances, of making his proposed visit to Rome, and that in any case he was then "engaged in establishing Land Committees in all our parishes—in order to induce the people to take advantage of the new Land Act, and to keep them out of illegal combinations."

Indeed, soon after the Land League was suppressed by the government, Gillooly had attempted to replace it with an organization patronized by him and run by his priests. He had submitted his proposed "Scheme for the Formation of Land Committees" to Thomas O'Hagan, but the former Irish lord chancellor refused to advise him on the merits of his proposal. In writing to McCabe on November 4, that O'Hagan had declined to offer an opinion, Gillooly explained that he was sending it to the printer in any case, and would forward a copy of the Scheme the following week to each of the bishops(Mc). He added that he hoped to have the Land Committees established in his diocese before he left for Rome. Since Gillooly's "Scheme" was only a slight modification of the recently outlawed Land League, it was small wonder that O'Hagan decided to have nothing to say to it. The fact that Gillooly's Scheme provided that the local clergy would be securely in control of the proposed Land Committees, did nothing in the way of recommending it either to the government or to some of the bishops, given the language and temper lately exhibited by some of the clergy. Moreover, by introducing the Scheme at all, Gillooly, who had made a point of standing completely aloof from the Land League, and forcing his clergy to do so, was now put in the position of admitting that some form of organization was necessary if the country was to be saved from anarchy.

The reason why, of course, there was so much dissatisfaction and ferment was that Parnell and Dillon's prophecies about the working of the Land Act were being fulfilled. The inability of the Land Court to handle the volume of cases in any reasonable time, and the unsatisfactory nature of the awards when finally made in fixing rents, were exasperating the tenants.[6] "There never was," wrote one exasperated bishop, Thomas Nulty, of Meath, to Kirby on December 4, "such a state of things in any Country as in this poor Country just now"(K). "The Govt has itself to blame for all:" he charged, "they wd take no advice and they thought to crush the spirit of the people by a overwhelming police and military force; but now they find all has failed, and that public opinion in England is now going fast against them." "The Land Commissioners," Nulty then reported, "are not giving satisfaction: some say they are cowed by the strictures passed on them by the Landlords' Press. In [any] case, they wont be able to carry the benefits of the Land Act home to the vast majority of the Tenants probably for the next ten years." "I think however," he concluded soberly, "they will have to adopt Parnell's principle for classifying the cases into classes of the *same kind* so that a *single* judgement will decide all the cases of a class. Then they will get on much better."

Since the legal resort proved so costly and time-consuming, and the popular resort, the Land League, had been suppressed, the tenants, as the bishops pointed out, began to enter into illegal and secret combinations to protect themselves.

[6] K, November 22, 1881. See Moran to Kirby, "The Land-Commissioners are busily pursuing their task, but it will be absolutely impossible for them to do justice to the tenants. The reduction of rents will of course do some good, but I fear the reductions will not be at all sufficient, or such as will enable the tenants to live comfortably on their holdings. In this part of the country our people are exceedingly peaceable and quiet; still we are all very determined to have a full measure of justice secured for the tenants.

Parnell, once again, found himself prophetically justified, for when he had been asked shortly before his arrest, who would replace him as leader, he had replied significantly, "Captain Moonlight."[7] Both the economic and political situations in Ireland continued to deteriorate during the rest of December and well into the New Year. Though the harvest had been bountiful, agricultural prices were still very depressed because of intense world competition. Many of the tenants, moreover, especially the smaller ones, were still deeply in debt because of the bad harvests of 1877-1879, and the continuing depression in agricultural prices prevented them from meeting their obligations. The reduction in rents granted by the Land Court was of little use to the small tenant because the sum was so marginal it would only be of real use as capital if he were free of debt. Many of the small tenants, who numbered some one hundred thousand, and were unable to muster their rent or their arrears in the winter of 1881-1882, were faced with eviction and emigration. These tenants were determined that they were not going to be cleared from their land, and they continued to offer the forces of property and the state a fierce resistance. If intimidation and boycotting did not serve to warn those who threatened their survival with "law and order," then murder and arson would have to do.[8]

Suddenly, after two years of intense discussion and argument about the agrarian agitation among themselves, the Irish bishops not only ceased writing to each other on the

---

[7] R. Barry O'Brien, *The Life of Charles Stewart Parnell* (London, 1910), p. 241.

[8] *Ibid.*, pp. 253-254: "The total number of agrarian outrages for the ten months—March to December, 1880—preceding the Coercion Act was 2,379. The total number for ten months—March to December, 1881—succeeding the Coercion Act, 3,821. When one classifies these outrages, the case appears even worse:

TEN MONTHS PRECEDING COERCION ACT

Homicides	*Firing at the Person*	*Firing into Dwellings*
7	21	62

TEN MONTHS SUCCEEDING COERCION ACT

Homicides	*Firing at the Person*	*Firing into Dwellings*
20	63	122

"In the first quarter of 1881, there was one murder; in the first quarter of 1882, there were six. The total number of cases of homicide and firing at the person, in the first quarter of 1881 was seven. In the first quarter of 1882, thirty-three."

subject, but they also stopped writing almost altogether to Kirby in Rome. All the Irish bishops were aware, and painfully aware, of the deteriorating situation in the country, and to chronicle to each other the portents of impending anarchy could have given them no joy; but there was still another and more depressing reason for the breakdown in communications. The British government had once again begun to intrigue at Rome to secure the aid of the pope in the good governance of Ireland. The Irish bishops, naturally, became more wary as they realized that their own position *vis-à-vis* the government and Rome was becoming more critical. If the pope again interposed his authority in favor of the government, the bishops and their clergy, given the state of the country and the temper of the people, would have a very difficult task, indeed, convincing their flocks that the Church was not forsaking them in their time of trial and in their hour of need.

The cause for Irish concern was that once again George Errington decided to visit Rome in late October. The only Irish bishop who broached the subject of Errington and English intrigue with Kirby was Moran, and, when he finally did write at the end of November, his letter was the last he wrote for more than three months. Moran complained on November 22, that there was a great deal of "noise" in the English newspapers about Errington's mission to Rome, and asked Kirby to note that Gladstone when questioned on the subject had denied that Errington had any official status(K). He hoped, therefore, the Propaganda would be very cautious in listening to any representations made by Errington about Irish affairs. What was really disturbing Moran, however, was the rumor that Errington was intriguing on behalf of the British government about the pending appointment to the vacant Irish bishopric of Kerry. "Such influence in the appointment of our Bishops," he warned Kirby, "would be disastrous, and there never was a time when it was more necessary to have vigilant and energetic Bishops in Ireland than at the present moment." What Moran and his brother bishops feared even more, of course, than the re-establishing of diplomatic relations, was that the government should secure any control over Irish episcopal appointments. For, while diplomatic relations might provide the government with an external control on their Church, which would certainly impair their credibility with the people, the prospect of the episcopal body being influenced by English nominees from within could only result in the complete collapse of their authority.

If Moran had known how well founded his suspicions were he would have been even more disturbed than he was. The government had, in fact, been negotiating with Rome about the appointment to Kerry for some three months. Their candidate for Kerry was the dean of the diocese, Andrew Higgins, who was reputed to be a determined opponent of the Land League. When Monsignor Masotti, the secretary of Propaganda, asked in late August whether he might communicate with the government on behalf of Cardinal Jacobini, the secretary of state, through H. G. MacDonell, the British chargé d'affaires in Rome, about the position of the Roman Catholic bishop of Gibralter, Granville agreed. Granville, however, prompted undoubtedly by Errington, decided to take advantage of the opening by suggesting to Rome that Dean Higgins would indeed be the appropriate candidate for the appointment to Kerry. When the chargé d'affaires, therefore, raised the question with Monsignor Masotti in their interview, Masotti assured him that Higgins would be the candidate selected, and went on to explain that the pope was very much concerned about the anomalous position of the bishop of Gibraltar.[9] His Holiness was under the impression that the government or someone high in authority at Gibraltar was opposed to the bishop. Since the bishop of Gibraltar was also selected, Masotti then cleverly pointed out, with the approval of the British government, something should be done to convince the Vatican that he had been fairly dealt with. Masotti immediately proceeded to clear what in effect was Granville's demand for a *quid pro quo* for Gibraltar in Kerry with Cardinal Jacobini and the pope, for the chargé d'affaires was able to reassure Granville only four days later on September 19 by telegram—"Private—Dean Higgins will be selected for the vacant Bishopric of Kerry."[10]

Well over a month later, however, the appointment of Dean Higgins to Kerry had still not been made, even though the government had arranged the difficulties between the governor and the bishop of Gibraltar. When Monsignor Masotti

[9] Gr, 30/29/182.
[10] F. O., 170/305.

visited Paget on October 29, he apologized for not being able to come before but explained that he had been suffering from a cold. In his report of the interview to Granville, Paget somewhat naively described Masotti "as a most affable and pleasant old gentleman," who was disposed to be communicative as well as obliging.[11] He not only expressed himself as pleased, Paget continued, with the outcome of the Gibraltar affair, but said that the Kerry appointment would certainly go to the candidate desired by the government. Masotti also spoke generally about Ireland and noted how much the pope regretted that some of the Irish clergy had identified themselves with those who had placed themsleves in an attitude of resistance to the law. In concluding the interview Masotti begged Paget not to scruple in sending for him whenever he might have occasion for his services. What was most interesting about Masotti's visit was what he did not say. In his report, for example, Paget noted that Masotti did not even allude to Errington's approaching visit. Masotti must have certainly known of Errington's approaching visit to Rome, for it had been the subject of very high level negotiations for more than two months. This was why the appointment to Kerry had not yet been announced, and why indeed it would not be made final for nearly two months more. The pope was waiting to see what real significance there was in Errington's second visit for the re-establishing of diplomatic relations, and the Kerry bishopric might prove a very useful piece in the great game yet to be played.

The arrangement of Errington's quasi-official position in Rome had already been some time in the making. Towards the end of August, Granville had written his Cabinet colleague, the Earl Spencer, who was by chance taking the waters of Aix-les-Bains, about the latest developments on the Roman front.[12] Granville, who had obviously just seen Cardinal Howard in England, reported to Spencer that Howard was also soon to be in Aix, and that he had, therefore, encouraged the cardinal to talk to him about relations with Rome. Granville explained that the government's line was that while they were unable to renew or promise to renew diplomatic relations with Rome, they were willing to allow their embassy in Rome to be

---

[11] GR, 30/29/182.
[12] GR, 30/29/142.

in communication with anyone the pope named, and that they were also willing, if Errington wanted to go to Rome unofficially, to give him a letter to show that they considered him trustworthy. The cardinal, Granville added, had maintained the proposal to communicate to the embassy was impossible, but the odd thing was that Monsignor Masotti on behalf of Cardinal Jacobini had only recently asked to do just that, and that he had agreed. Granville also pointed out in the course of his letter to Spencer, that there was one mode of communicating with Rome that he had not mentioned to the cardinal— that is through the British ambassador and papal nuncio in Paris.

Spencer was not able to reply, however, for nearly three weeks because Cardinal Howard was late in arriving at Aix. When he finally did see Howard, Spencer wrote Granville on September 15, explaining that he had gone over all the points mentioned by Granville in his recent letter, but that he did not think that he had elicited anything new.[13] Howard had again mentioned that it was impossible for Rome to confer with anyone belonging to an embassy accredited to the Italian government. When Spencer introduced the subject of communicating with Rome through the nuncio in Paris, Howard "did not appear to like it as well as the Errington method, which he evidently hoped would lead to more direct relations." Howard said he would, however, write at once to Rome, and when he received a reply he would write to Granville. When he did receive a reply from Rome, the cardinal chose to write Spencer instead of Granville.[14] After explaining on September 26 to Spencer that he had written Cardinal Jacobini going over the various modes proposed by the government for communicating with Rome, Howard reported that Jacobini had informed him that the pope had decided to accept the Errington mission as in all ways preferable to either the embassy at Rome or Paris.[15] Howard also explained that Car-

[13] *Ibid.*

[14] *Ibid.*

[15] For a copy of enclosure, see Balfour Papers(B), British Museum, Add. MS, 49690. See covering letter of Salisbury to Balfour, July 4, 1892, which explains why extracts of the Granville-Errington correspondence were forwarded by Salisbury, who was prime minister in 1892, to Balfour, who until recently had been chief secretary of Ireland and, lately, leader of the Conservative party in the House of Commons. "In view of Gladstone's speech at Glasgow I send you down a typical copy of the most important parts of the Errington correspondence. You have already seen it. I do not know whether you will think it worth using. . . ."

dinal Jacobini had already informed Granville through Errington of the pope's preference.

The eventual result of all these high level and complicated negotiations was that Errington finally set out for Rome in late October armed with Granville's promised letter of recommendation.[16] In his initial interview on October 31, with Cardinal Jacobini after his arrival, Errington read him Granville's letter, and the cardinal remarked that, as informal as the letter was, it was all that he had been led to expect, and he was pleased.[17] Errington then immediately introduced the real reason for his coming to Rome. He explained that Granville wanted him informed of the actual state of affairs in Ireland, for Granville felt that, if the true situation were known in Rome, the pope would realize that it was as much in the interest of religion as it was of the government that the actions of the Irish clergy should be controlled, and their influence used on the side of order. The government, however, Errington assured the cardinal, did not want to suggest what particular steps might be taken to effect this salutary end. In reply to this, Jacobini deftly turned the conversation away from Ireland, by expressing the hope that he might consider Errington's visit "as a step towards more complete representation later." Errington replied that Granville had explicitly told him that the present step was all the government could do, or had any intention of doing. He softened this somewhat by adding that what he thought they should aim at was to make the present step a success by showing some results. Granville was very pleased with Errington's report of his interview, and in complimenting Errington on his "great discretion," he added that his only regret was they had not taken advantage of his offer to go to Rome sooner.[18] Indeed, Granville might well be pleased, for Her Majesty's government had been committed to nothing, and the papal government was now in the position of having to make the first move if it hoped to effect anything in the way of diplomatic relations.

When Errington read Granville's letter to Jacobini, the cardinal had asked whether he might have a copy of the letter to show confidentially to the pope.[19] Why the cardinal made the

---

[16] B, 49690, October 3, 1881.
[17] *Ibid.*, Errington to Granville, October 31, 1881.
[18] *Ibid.*, November 7, 1881.
[19] F. O., 170/306, November 1881.

request, of course, was that all diplomatic representatives are supplied with credentials by their own government for presentation to the government to which they are accredited. What the cardinal was aiming at, therefore, was to transform a private representation on the part of an individual into an unofficial representation on the part of the British government. From Rome's point of view, then, taking formal notice of Errington's unofficial credentials was a very important step in their efforts to achieve fuller diplomatic relations. Errington, however, refused the cardinal's request, explaining that he had not been authorized to do so, but when the cardinal pressed him to ask Granville, he telegraphed in cypher through Paget and the embassy to Granville, relaying the request and remarking that such a course seemed imprudent to him. Granville, however, did not think so, and authorized Errington to give the cardinal a copy of the letter, which should be returned to him when the pope had seen it.[20] In asking that the copy of the letter be returned, Granville was anxious that no documentary evidence be left in the hands of the Romans because he had to protect himself on two fronts. At home he did not want to leave himself open in Parliament or in the press to the charge that he had in effect reestablished diplomatic relations with the Vatican, and on the international level he wanted to maintain the good relations that existed between his own government and the kingdom of Italy.

While Gladstone, therefore, was publicly explaining in a letter published in the press to the head of one of the Protestant associations, the unofficial nature of Errington's mission to Rome, Granville was privately explaining the situation to Count Menabrea, the Italian ambassador in London. Paget, while assuring Granville on November 24, in a long letter marked "private," that though no one connected with the Italian government had even alluded to Errington's mission, the king had, in fact, asked him about it.[21] "I thought it as well," Paget added significantly,

> that while making it perfectly clear that *Errington* had no sort of official Mission, to speak in a way so as not to exclude the

---

[20] *Ibid.*, November 4, 1881.
[21] GR, 30/29/182, November 24, 1881.

possibility of the idea of reestablishing diplomatic communications with the Vatican being some day entertained, and I feel
convinced, from the way in which this was received, that if such
a measure at any time be thought desirable, it certainly would
not be misunderstood by the King (GR).

"As far therefore," Paget then concluded, "as the diplomatic
and international side of the question is concerned, there
need be no apprehension of any difficulty arising. We should
in point of fact be only following in the wake of two other
non-Catholic Powers, Germany and Russia."

While Granville, Leo XIII, and Humbert I were amiably
playing the larger game of European diplomacy, Forster
was discovering that the smaller game of coercing the
Irish was growing both more difficult and disagreeable every
day. By the end of November the situation had become so
desperate for Forster that he also decided to enter a candidate
in the diplomatic arena. Thomas O'Hagan, a Catholic and
former Irish lord chancellor, who was about to visit Rome, was
enlisted by Forster in the interests of maintaining law and
order in Ireland. Forster asked O'Hagan to explain to the
Roman authorities how serious the situation was in Ireland
and provided him with the necessary proof in the form of
confidential police reports.[22] Errington naturally resented
O'Hagan's interference, and wrote Granville that the presence of another envoy was proving very awkward.[23] Since his
arrival in Rome, Errington had been working hard to have
McCabe's authority in the Irish Church strengthened. He had
suggested that McCabe be appointed apostolic delegate,
which would in effect make him an extension of the pope's
own person in the Irish Church.[24] The Roman authorities had
demurred, as well they might, from taking so extreme a step
because they were afraid that in the event of a confrontation
in the Irish Church there might be created a situation from
which there could be no drawing back, for if the delegate were

---

[22] GR, 30/29/117, Forster to Granville, November 29.
[23] B, 49690, November 23, 1881.
[24] GR, 30/29/117, Errington to Granville, November 2, 1881: "The Cardinal tells
me that they find serious difficulties about making the Archbishop of Dublin Papal
Delegate as suggested, so that he has reverted to the proposal I made last Christmas to
create him a Cardinal."

involved it was the Pope's authority itself that would be really at stake. Errington, therefore, had reverted to a suggestion that he had made the previous Christmas in Rome, and recommended that McCabe be made a cardinal. His efforts were now being undermined, Errington complained to Granville on November 24, because O'Hagan was saying that the government had already long ago decided not to maintain relations, much less send a representative, to the Vatican.

"This was certainly," Errington declared most revealingly,

> not my impression on coming. It would have been useless to come in such a case, and I cannot help asking myself whether I have been mistaken, or have overstated matters in saying, as I have most plainly and clearly, that you did not send me or even ask me to come, but only approved of my coming on my own account; that my coming was not and could not be taken as any engagement on your part to proceed farther, and that you had no present intention of doing so. But that your Lordship personally, and many leading men of both parties, regretted the breaking off of the old relations, and would be favourable to a renewal of such relations, were it not for the opposition and difficulties of popular feeling, the extent and weight of which it was not easy to ascertain(GR).

"The fair inference from this," Errington maintained further,

> was that my coming afforded a good opportunity for testing this feeling and these difficulties. That if this tentative step was satisfactory in its results, and proved the popular feeling to be not so dangerous as some people feared, there was no certainty, but a very reasonable ground for hoping and expecting that something more definite in the way of relations would, after a time, become possible, and be adopted(GR).

"Less than this," Errington argued, "would have left absolutely no locus standi for negotiation, but this, implying as it does, good will and a favourable disposition, is entirely inconsistent with Lord O'Hagan's theory of a preconceived determination to do nothing." "If Lord O'Hagan is right," Errington warned in conclusion, "very disagreeable results might follow. The Pope would feel deeply and reasonably hurt at being, as he might conceive, jockeyed out of a concession, and then thrown over."

Forster had also obviously received a letter from Errington complaining about O'Hagan, for he wrote Granville on November 29, explaining the situation, and remarking a little petulantly that as Irish secretary surely he had a right to ask a former colleague to exercise his good offices on behalf of the Irish government in Rome.[25] Forster then warned Granville in a postscript that he feared that he could not let the priests alone much longer no matter what the pope did. Several days later, Granville wrote Forster both to reassure and console him.[26] He explained that he saw nothing objectionable in his letter to O'Hagan, and added that Errington was going a little beyond his tether by very nearly promising diplomatic relations if the pope behaved well. He noted that he would have to write again to guard himself on that point, but that he did not want to do anything at present that would unnecessarily dampen Cardinal Jacobini's good will. Granville then consoled Forster by admitting the dilemma raised by the too violent priests was a difficult one in that while they could not allow them to go on the way they were going, to lock them up would only intensify the feeling in Ireland. In any case, Granville assured Forster in conclusion, "You have the full sympathy of everybody in England with you." Rome, however, had already decided to take limited action in Ireland by finally appointing Dean Higgins bishop of Kerry. The way in which the appointment was made, moreover, was designed to obligate the British government even farther, for Errington had telegraphed Granville on November 30, that Propaganda had selected Higgins as a person acceptable to the government, and that his name would be "submitted to the Pope unless you express desire to contrary."[27] The government, of course, made no objection, and Higgins was officially provided to the see of Kerry on December 18, by the pope.

This was indeed a great coup for the government, for Higgins was one of the few vigorous opponents of the Land League to be found among the clergy in Kerry. The relationship between agrarian disaffection and the ascendancy of Land League clergy and bishops was too obvious to ignore. The government accounted Kerry, West Cork, Limerick, and the district around Loughrea in Galway as the most trouble-

[25] GR, 30/29/117.
[26] *Ibid.*, December 2, 1881.
[27] F. O., 170/306.

some areas in Ireland.[28] The worst area in Limerick was that part where the bishop of Limerick, George Butler, and the archbishop of Cashel, both strong, if not to say enthusiastic supporters of the League, shared spiritual jurisdiction. The district around Loughrea was the responsibility of the bishop of Clonfert, Patrick Duggan, who was euphemistically referred to as an "advanced man" by the local patriots. Since part of West Cork was in the diocese of Kerry, a strong bishop there, from the government's point of view, would go a long way in killing two birds with one stone. Interestingly enough, it was from the date of the appointment of Dean Higgins to Kerry that the Irish bishops seemed to write each other either the most perfunctory notes, or not at all, and Kirby's correspondence with Ireland dwindled almost to nothing.

O'Hagan, meanwhile, had reported to Forster on December 7, that he had seen a good many people in Rome and had done what he could, but that he was sorry to say that things moved very slowly.[29] He did think, however, that McCabe would be invested with the rank of cardinal, and the influence that went with it would strengthen his position in the Irish Church. He also noted that, besides the project of an apostolic delegate, the suggestion of sending a papal envoy to Ireland to report first hand to the pope on what was happening, had been mooted, but the Roman authorities had again demurred because of the danger involved in accrediting an envoy who might not be well received. O'Hagan suggested that the best way to deal with refractory priests in the meantime was for Forster to write McCabe, who O'Hagan was sure would do all within his power to help. Before he had left for Rome, for example, O'Hagan explained, he had given McCabe the information about violent priests supplied him by Forster, and he was sure McCabe had acted upon that information. By the time Forster received this letter, however, rumors were circulating in Dublin that Daniel McGettigan, the archbishop of Armagh, would be made a cardinal rather than McCabe. In a panic Forster asked Granville to telegraph Errington explaining that a red hat for McGettigan would do no good.[30] Errington replied that there was no chance of McGettigan being made a cardinal and that he was still work-

[28] R. Barry O'Brien, *op. cit.*, p. 250.
[29] GR, 30/29/117, December 7, 1881.
[30] *Ibid.*

ing hard for McCabe.[31] "I fear these Machiavellian Italians," Forster complained to Granville that same day, "Pope Cardinals & all will be guided solely by what they hope they can get, & care little about religion or morality in Ireland."[32] Forster went on to explain that at Gladstone's request he had forwarded him the police reports on the priests, and the prime minister thought they should be brought before the pope and his advisers.[33]

To complicate matters even further, Gladstone meanwhile had decided to take action himself. "I will begin," he wrote Cardinal Newman on December 17, "with defining strictly the limits of this appeal. I ask you to read the enclosed papers; and to consider whether you will write anything to Rome upon them."[34] "I do not ask you to write," Gladstone explained, "nor tell me whether you wrote, nor to make any reply to this letter, beyond returning the enclosures in an envelope to me on Downing Street. Some members of the Roman Catholic priesthood in Ireland deliver certain sermons and otherwise express themselves in the way which my enclosures exhibit. I doubt whether if they were laymen we should not have settled their cases by putting them into gaol." "I need not describe the sentiments uttered," Gladstone added, "Your eminence will feel them and judge them as strongly as I do." "But now as to the Supreme Pontiff," Gladstone maintained, coming to the point, "you will hardly be surprised when I say that I regard him, if apprised of the facts, as responsible for the conduct of these priests. For I know perfectly well that he has the means of silencing them; and that, if any one of them were in public to dispute the decrees of the Council of 1870 as plainly as he has denounced law and order, he would be silenced."

Newman's reply was characteristic.[35] He was polite, cautious, relative, and didactic. He assured Gladstone that he would gladly find himself able to be of service. Since the pope, however, was only absolute in matters of theology, Newman explained he thought Gladstone overestimated the pope's power in political and social matters. While the pope might

[31] F. O., 170/306.
[32] GR, 30/29/117.
[33] F. O., 170/306, Gladstone to Forster, December 17, 1881.
[34] John Morley, *The Life of William Ewart Gladstone* 2 (London, 1906): pp. 302-303.
[35] *Ibid.*, p. 303.

anathematize those in Ireland, for example, who denied that
rebellion and robbery were sinful, his action in concrete matters was not direct, and was only effective in the long run. This
exercise of the pope's power, Newman added, was a matter of
great prudence, and depended on times and circumstances.
As to the intemperate language of priests, Newman thought
that this was surely more a matter for their local bishops than
the supreme authority. While Newman was thus patiently
making these subjective theological distinctions to Gladstone
about the pope's power and the expediency of its application,
Forster was faced with objective responsibility for a situation
in Ireland that bordered on the anarchic. When he met O'Hagan on December 26, after his return from Rome, Forster was
indignant to learn that the papal authorities were not likely to
do anything about the extravagances of some of the priests.[36]
O'Hagan still thought, however, that McCabe would be made
a cardinal, and Errington's letters to Forster at the end of
December were decidedly hopeful.

Early in January, the pope decided to take a giant step
towards making McCabe a cardinal, for Errington telegraphed Granville on Sunday, January 2, 1882:

> Cardinal Secretary wishes you to be informed privately that
> the Pope has just expressed his disposition to raise Dr. McCabe
> to the Cardinalate.
> The Cardinal considers this final but I press for stronger
> expression, and shall telegraph again Wednesday.
> It is important to sense the matter by an acknowledgement
> from you that I hope you will allow me to thank the Pope in your
> name for his decision, personally would be best, but please do
> not reply till you hear from me on Wednesday.
> Cardinal says the Pope used word *"disposition"* in order not to
> bind himself formally, but is really decided, still he fully recog-
> nizes desirability in view of hostile influences of guarding
> against possible change or hesitation.[37]

When Errington telegraphed him again on Wednesday,
Granville replied the next day by letter.[38] In asking Errington
to thank the pope for his disposition to promote McCabe,
Granville was indeed at his subtle and diplomatic best. "You

---

[36] GR, 30/29/117, Forster to Granville, December 27, 1881.
[37] F. O., 170/320, January 3, 1882.
[38] B, 49690, January 6, 1882.

are aware," he informed Errington guardedly,

> that H.M. Govt. have not asked his Holiness to perform any act, nor made any suggestions as to the course which he should pursue; but Mr. Gladstone, Mr. Forster, and I request you to convey to the Pope in suitable terms our appreciation of the motives which have determined the Pope to take a step which seems to us well calculated to justify the Pope's attachment to the interest of order and morality in Ireland(GR).

There were, of course, three important qualifications in Granville's letter. First, the government had not asked for or suggested anything. Second, the appreciation expressed, as had been advised by Errington, was personal rather than official, since it was not Her Majesty's government, but Granville and his most concerned colleagues who were thanking the pope. Third, and the most subtle qualification of all, they were not thanking the pope for his "disposition," but rather for the motives that inspired it.

When Forster heard the news, he immediately pressed Errington to have the pope confirm his disposition.[39] Why the pope insisted on waiting had undoubtedly to do with the fact that he did not want to proceed in an unusual way, and thereby make McCabe's appointment even more resented by the Irish clergy than it was bound to be. The pope, therefore, decided to make the announcement after he had made arrangements for a consistory at which a number of other cardinals besides McCabe would be elevated. Forster, however, stubbornly continued to press, and on January 21, he telegraphed Errington that in order to check the revival of the actions of the more violent clergy, and those bad effects which must inevitably follow from a month's delay, it was important to hurry the promotion of McCabe.[40] Errington had also reported to Forster that while he was anxious to return to London for the opening of Parliament in early February, that he did not think it was wise to leave Rome unattended in his absence, especially with McCabe's appointment not yet confirmed. He asked Forster, therefore, to arrange to have Monsignor Henry Neville, rector of the Catholic University of Ireland, and a confidant of McCabe's, to take his place in Rome. In explaining all this to Granville on January 22, For-

[39] GR, 30/29/117, January 6, 1882.
[40] Ibid.

ster was not enthusiastic about arranging for Neville to go to Rome.[41] He suggested instead that Errington be asked to stay in Rome until McCabe's promotion was settled, and added that there was an advantage in his not being in the House when the inevitable questions were asked about his visit to Rome.

The pope, however, was not to be hurried, and Errington had to remain in Rome. When Parliament did meet, notice was immediately given in both Houses of questions about Errington's mission to Rome. Gladstone and Sir Charles Dilke replied for the government in the Commons, and Granville, who replied in the Lords, reported to Errington on February 16, that nothing had really been said that could have injured his position in Rome.[42] Granville then explained to Errington that some information had come to him confidentially, which indicated that he had been indiscreet, and especially in his conversations with the ladies. He had been told, Granville noted, that the reports which had appeared recently in the press about his interviews in Rome with Cardinal Jacobini were the production of a lady who said she had received the information from him. Moreover, Sir Henry Drummond Wolf, a prominent conservative, who had asked one of the questions in the Commons, Granville added, told Dilke that "he had received the information about your being paid from the Secret Service Fund from a lady to whom you had said it." "Although I vote for women having medical degrees," Granville remarked good-humoredly in conclusion, "I have a horror of them in politics. Their indiscretion is great, and their imaginative powers wonderful."

Errington wrote Granville by return on February 23 that he had to confess to being indiscreet, but it was not because he was in the habit of talking too much to the ladies.[43] He had confided in Robert Stuart, the Roman correspondent of the London *Morning Post*, and his confidence had been betrayed. Errington was convinced that both leaks mentioned by Granville could be traced to the same source. In the course of this letter, furthermore, it became quite clear that Errington was not being paid by the government, though Granville had indeed offered to compensate him. After his apologies, Er-

---

[41] *Ibid.*, Forster to Granville, January 22, 1882.
[42] GR, 30/29/149.
[43] *Ibid.*

rington then turned to render a long account of the business that had brought him to Rome in the first place. Though he was wearied out with the pope's constant delays, Errington assured Granville that the events of the last few days had resulted in a change in the pope's attitude that was decidedly in their favor. The pope had had a long audience with the earl of Denbigh, a prominent English Catholic, and an old friend of the pope. Denbigh, who was also a Conservative in his politics, was very concerned about the situation in Ireland, and the Pope was reported much impressed with Denbigh's account of what was happening there. After hearing what Denbigh had to say, Jacobini told Errington that the pope had not only decided to make McCabe a cardinal, but to address another and this time a stronger letter to the Irish clergy. Before his audience with the pope, Errington had begged Denbigh to stress the urgency of promoting McCabe, and the importance of advancing it even by a single day.

> I had also asked him to ascertain how far the Pope was really well informed and conscious of the gravity of the Irish question, for I had my doubts how far some of the information I have been supplying had really reached him. Lord Denbigh's impression was that his knowledge was very superficial & that though he evidently considered himself well informed on Ireland was very ignorant on many facts. I mentioned this to the Cardinal next day, who assured me he did all he could to impress the Pope, but that the difficulties of doing so were often very great indeed. It is generally understood that the Pope's suspicious temper makes the position of his regular advisers very difficult. They sometimes cannot mention a particular subject to him for days together, & so it happens that a casual visitor's observation will often have more effect on some particular point than all they have been urging for a long time.
>
> I could see how delighted the Cardinal was by the good effect Lord Denbigh had produced.[44]

Lord Denbigh's recent visit, however, was not the only event likely to produce a change in the attitude of Rome towards Irish affairs. Some of the American bishops were obviously concerned about whether the American Land League was a proper organization for Catholics to belong to, and one in

---

[44] *Ibid.*

particular, Bernard J. McQuaid, the bishop of Rochester, had
recently written Rome asking for an opinion on the legitimacy
of the League.[45] Errington had strong hopes that Rome would
condemn the American Land League, which would not only
strengthen the position taken by McCabe and his supporters
with regard to the Irish Land League, but also demonstrate
that the pope was not merely acting solely in the interests of
England in these matters. In finally summing up for Granville,
Errington explained what he thought the long and short
term results of his Rome mission would be. In the short run he
hoped to get the pope, who was "very suspicious and vacillat-
ing," firmly committed "to a policy of repression by the promoting of Dr. McCabe, by the letter addressed probably
through the new cardinal to the Irish Church, by the action
against the Land League in America through the Bishops."
Once the pope had decided, it would be comparatively easy to
carry out the details, for they would be left almost entirely in
the hands of Cardinal Jacobini and the Propaganda. In the
long run, therefore, Errington concluded, and with very great
acuteness and insight, "the most serious difficulties with Ireland will at all events be staved off for many years, for it will be
a long time before any really great National Movement in Ireland could go on quite independently of the Clergy and by
that time the conditions of that Country may be greatly
changed."

In winding up his very long and interesting letter Errington
reported that he had told Jacobini that he would most likely
have to return home in the event the government might need
the support of all their friends in the House of Commons. The
cardinal had urged him to remain, and to return immediately
if indeed he must go. Errington explained that he could give
no guarantees, and the cardinal said that it would be well to see
the pope before he left. Errington had misgivings about a
farewell audience for he was afraid the pope would introduce
the awkward question of diplomatic relations, but he thought,
on the balance, given Denbigh's opinion that he was badly
informed, there might be a chance of saying something that
he had not yet heard. In finally concluding, Errington assured
Granville that everyone was pleased with his recent reply in

---

[45] *Ibid.* See for copy of Bishop of Rochester (U.S.A.) letter to Errington, dated
January 15, 1882.

the House of Lords to the questions about his own mission to Rome, and Cardinal Simeoni, the prefect of Propaganda, had particularly asked him to thank him and Lord Kimberley, the colonial secretary, for their good offices in the Gibraltar affair.[46]

The reaction of the Irish bishops and clergy to all of this has for the most part to be imagined since they considered silence to be the better part of discretion. There are, however, several instances of the Irish bishops being unable to contain themselves, and if their utterances are any indication of the general temper prevailing in the Irish Church, it must have been nothing less than fierce. "Have you read," demanded Patrick Duggan, bishop of Clonfert, of McCabe, the day before Christmas, "the address of the Bishop of Salford to the Catholic Club, Manchester, spoken a few evenings ago, on the 'Mission' of Mr. Errington to Rome?"(Mc). "It is quite clear," he declared, referring to Herbert Vaughan, "his Lordship speaks the views of the English episcopate, on that 'Mission,' whatever its purport may be." "Your Grace has opportunities—not given to others—," he told his old friend, "of knowing what is coming. Hence, I express my *presentiments* to you specially."

The "Diplomatic" relations, urged by the Bishop of Salford, with remarkable force, *may* cover and *probably will* cover more *now*, than similar "relations" in the past. It is more than probable, Mr. Errington's power will be more extensive. It is certain those "relations" will affect in a special manner, Irish Catholic affairs, more directly and vitally than at any former period. Otherwise, why not select an *English* Catholic to look after "Imperial" concerns. The whole force of English influence will be exerted to secure the support of ecclesiastical influence in and of what is called—*"law and order"* in Ireland. Now, here arises the crucial position for ecclesiastics of all grades in this country.

A crisis has come upon us, without parallel in our history. The long expected *conflict* of classes *has come*. It is folly to ignore or deny the fact. It is visible on every side. It is in the air. It is

---

[46] For Gibraltar, see GR, 30/29/182; Paget to Granville, February 15, 1882. Contents of dispatch of Lord Kimberley, the colonial secretary, of January 19, 1882, were communicated by Errington to Cardinal Jacobini and Monsignor Masotti. Paget reminded Errington that Kimberley's dispatch was confidential. See also B, 49690, Errington to Granville, December 27, 1881; Errington to Granville, telegram, January 21, 1882; Granville telegram to Errington, January 22, 1882.

everywhere. It is true our people are, in *one* sense, more Catholic than ever; but it is also evident, they are determined to put an end to the causes from which so many famines and miseries have proceeded. Nor will they brook opposition in this point from Ecclesiastics of *any* degree. It is quite clear, they will ignore or reject Ecclesiastical influence in any *former* sense of the word. This is patent.

In this state of things, if Mr. Errington's mission should eventuate in extracting from any Ecclesiastical source a condemnation of the resolve of the people, I shudder to think of the consequences. At this moment, I think Ecclesiastical influence *hangs in the balance*(Mc).

While the bishop of Clonfert's analysis was somewhat extravagant, this threat to Irish ecclesiastical home rule by English influence in Rome was viewed by even the most ultramontane and conservative of the Irish bishops as repugnant. Kirby in Rome was also obviously very unhappy about the ascendancy of English influence in Rome, for he wrote MacEvilly in late January complaining about it. MacEvilly replied on February 5, that he agreed, and that the English "ought to mind their own business"(K). "I can also tell you," warned MacEvilly, who had always been accounted an ardent ultramontane, "any attempt at giving them control over Irish Eccl affairs wd be [a] strain our people *wd not bear*."

Early in March, the pope finally confirmed his "disposition" to raise the archbishop of Dublin to the cardinalate. McCabe received his red hat at a general consistory, in company with four other cardinals, on March 30, in Rome. After more than a month of briefings and discussions with the Roman authorities and some communication with his brother bishops in Ireland, the new cardinal returned home well prepared and authorized to put the Irish ecclesiastical house in order. Soon after his return, he called a meeting of the Irish bishops for June 6, at which he would naturally preside. When the bishops had settled their appointed business, reportedly in a most cordial and harmonious way, the cardinal then turned his attention to the larger problems that now fell to his lot as a prince of the Church. "Cardinal McCabe," Spencer, who had replaced Earl Cowper as Irish viceroy in April, reported to Granville on June 11, 1882, "asked to see me last week. I

appointed an hour and he came to meet me at the Castle."[47]
"He said that since his first interview with me," Spencer continued, "he had received instructions from 'the Holy Father'
to see me and to say how anxious he was to be on good terms
with England." The pope, McCabe had explained to Spencer,
"was very anxious to have some means of official communication with England and without naming Mr. Errington pointed
at some such appointment at Rome as his." After reporting
what had passed the previous summer with Cardinal Howard
at Aix-les-Bains, Spencer pointed out that the strong Protestant feelings which existed in England made direct representation with Rome very difficult. McCabe readily admitted this,
and said the pope also understood the difficulty. Spencer then
explained that what Granville was most anxious about was
that the pope should receive accurate information about what
was happening in Ireland. McCabe agreed and added that the
pope received conflicting reports from bishops of equal
weight and influence, and he could not tell who was right.
Spencer concluded by promising McCabe that he would inform Granville of their conversation, and especially of "the
strong desire expressed by the pope to have an English agent
near him."

Granville apparently decided to do nothing about this gambit on behalf of diplomatic relations by the pope. Leo XIII,
however, was not to be so easily put off when he really wanted
something, and in late July, he again had Cardinal Howard
call on Granville in London. Howard, Granville reported to
Spencer on August 4, wanted to continue some form of diplomatic relations and what he would like most was to keep
Errington permanently on in Rome.[48] Granville raised the
usual difficulties, and told Howard that no one could be
expected to stay on in Rome unless the government had the
means to pay them. What Granville was alluding to, of course,
was that any compensation other than out of the Secret Service Fund would come under the scrutiny of Parliament when
the government annually presented its budget and estimates,
and the government would face very awkward questions year
in and year out about the anomalous position of their unofficial agent in Rome. Granville then suggested to Howard unofficially that perhaps the best way out of the apparent impasse

[47] GR, 30/29/142.
[48] *Ibid.*

might be if the ambassador in Rome always sent a member of his embassy to the pope, who was not accredited to the king of Italy.

What Granville really wanted to know from Spencer, however, was whether those who were responsible for governing Ireland thought that it was of great importance to keep up diplomatic relations of some kind with the Vatican. He explained to Spencer that his new chief secretary for Ireland, G. O. Trevelyan, who had replaced Forster in May, apparently did not attach much importance to keeping up contact with Rome. Granville confessed some surprise about Trevelyan's opinion for he felt that the attitude of the Irish clergy must have an important effect one way or the other. Granville concluded by pointing out again that the real difficulty was Protestant public opinion, and how it would affect "the Parliamentary, or rather the electioneering question." At this stage Granville certainly appeared to be in the mood for a form of diplomatic relations, but since Gladstone was hostile, he did not want it to appear that the project had originated with him. If the Irish government or, in reality, Spencer, who was now its driving force as lord lieutenant, would initiate proceedings and argue from necessity, perhaps Gladstone could be persuaded as to the need for diplomatic relations, as indeed he had been reluctantly persuaded to the need for Coercion the year before. Granville enclosed along with this broad hint to Spencer, a letter from Errington, which supported the contention that some effective means of communicating with the papal government was necessary because of the situation in Ireland.

Spencer obliged Granville by responding not with one but two letters from Dublin. One was obviously meant for Cabinet consumption, while the other was marked "Private," and for Granville's eye only. In his first letter of August 6, Spencer came immediately to the point after acknowledging that he had read Errington's letter and largely agreed with it.

I attach great importance to the influence of the R. Catholic Clergy & Bishops. In some places their influence has diminished but in others it is as powerful as ever. The worst districts are those where the Catholic Curates, sometimes but rarely Parish Priests, throw themselves actively into the arms of the disaffected. It is in those places that disorder is strongest

and cannot be put down. Directly any of the Clergy who have
unfortunately acted against the Law change their antics and
support the Government officials of the District a beneficial
change occurs. The best Resident Magistrates constantly go to
the Priests for support & help, & I often hear that such & such a
district has been free from boycotting or outrage because the R.
C. Clergy have actively opposed these systems of terror. I have
no doubt that Cardinal McCabe both before he got the Cardinal's Hat & since has had a marked influence for good. . . .

I believe it to be of great importance that the Pope shall be
kept properly informed of what is going on in Ireland. I do not
see how this can be done without someone at Rome, who will
keep him duly informed. The difficulty as you say is Parliamentary & Electioneering. It is a pity that the old arrangement has
been dropped of having an Attaché at Rome in communication
with the Papal Court, but could not someone be nominally
attached to the Embassy, who shd communicate with the Pope.
It is a pity that Errington is not in Diplomacy for he seems to
have done very well, but it would not I presume do to continue
him without an official position in Rome. There is a manifest
advantage in having an Irishman & an R. C. like Errington in
that position. You will know how best to carry this out, and I am
satisfied that it is of great importance to the Irish Government
to keep up friendly relations with the Pope, & to have him
thoroughly made acquainted with what is going on here. . . .[49]

"It will be a great pity," Spencer lamented again in conclusion,
"if we were now to lose the benefits of the friendly communications which have been established."

In his second letter of August 6, and marked "Private,"
Spencer reported to Granville that he had "done a good deal
sub rosa by means of a R. C. A. B. C. who knows the Cardinal
well, the Cardinal is very ready & desirous of getting information and he has I doubt not on several occasions quieted & in
some cases got rid of dangerous men."[50] Spencer then added
that though he had not had a chance of talking to his chief
secretary about this, he was sure that Trevelyan would agree
with what he had written. When Granville passed Errington's
letter on to Trevelyan for his comments, however, the chief
secretary replied non-committedly on August 7 that "I have
no time to comment on it; but it has impressed me very

---

[49] *Ibid.*
[50] *Ibid.*

much."[51] Why Trevelyan was being evasive, of course, was that he was counted a Radical, and many of the Radicals, unlike Sir Charles Dilke, were lukewarm, if not opposed, to enlisting the aid of Rome in dealing with Ireland. Granville's colleagues in the House of Lords were more enthusiastic.[52] "I have read these papers with great interest," the Whig Lord Selborne replied on August 7, "and I entirely agree with Lord Spencer." "So do I most fully," the Tory Lord Cadogan concurred in a note on Selborne's memorandum the same day.

Granville, however, does not appear to have followed up on his ground work because a letter from Spencer nearly a month later indicated the project had bogged down. "I do not know," Spencer confessed on August 31, "what more to say about the Pope & our Embassy at Rome. You know best how it should be done."[53] "All I should like to argue," he commented candidly, "is that by hook or by crook we have someone who will be able to keep the Papal Government correctly informed of what is passing in Ireland." Still Granville made no move, and the reasons were mainly two: First, Gladstone could not be persuaded that the "Parliamentary & Electioneering" question was not primary. In other words, neither Parliament nor the country would swallow "diplomatic relations" with Rome. Second, the situation in Ireland was steadily becoming less threatening and the necessity for the pope's aid was becoming less apparent. In November, however, there were a series of shocking murders in Galway, Meath, and the City of Dublin, and the bishop of Meath, Thomas Nulty, a strong supporter of the League and Parnell, was obviously complained of in Rome because he had not denounced murder in his diocese. "I am privately assured," Paget telegraphed Granville from Rome on December 11, "that the Pope has given instructions for a letter of reprimand to be drafted which is to be sent to the Bishop of Meath."[54] On December 16, Paget assured Granville in another telegram marked "private & confidential" that the letter to the bishop of Meath had been sent from the Propaganda.[55]

---

[51] Ibid.
[52] Ibid.
[53] Ibid.
[54] GR, 30/29/182. The occasion for the Roman letter to Nulty, however, was a meeting in Navan, which was one of the bishop's parishes, in late November, 1882, featuring Michael Davitt with Nulty's administrator and some thirty of his clergy in attendance. See Woods, op.cit., p. 43.
[55] Ibid.

On receiving the letter from Propaganda, the bishop of
Meath immediately wrote Kirby on December 20, that the
situation in Ireland was not understood in Rome(K). He
pointed out that the violence complained of in his diocese had
nothing to do with the land agitation, but rather with private
revenge, and that in Ireland, "except in the City of Dublin and
the Co. of Galway outrages have ceased everywhere."
"Throughout this diocese," he explained, indicating a curious
moral myopia, "all through we have had ["only" crossed out] 2
murders: one was a very bad young girl, who is believed—
although the matter is shrouded in mystery—to have been
murdered by her sister. . . . The other was a woman (named
Mrs. Smythe) and the bullet that killed her was undoubtedly
intended for her Brother in Law who sat beside her." According to this line of reasoning, it seems, Propaganda might have
had something to complain of if the "bad" young girl had only
been "good," and if the bullet that killed Mrs. Smythe had only
killed her brother-in-law. The real truth, of course, was that
Nulty, and with very good reason in Meath, did not like
landlords, had never liked them, and was supported in this by
the great majority of his clergy and people.

Before the bishop of Meath had even received his letter of
admonition from the Propaganda, Paget, who had previously
been most reserved in dealing with the Vatican, now began to
prove himself zealous in the good cause. On December 17, he
sent Granville another and much longer telegram, announcing, in effect, that Rome was only too anxious to please. The
"Ecclesiastic" referred to was undoubtedly Errington's contact, Bernard Smith, the Benedictine.

An Ecclesiastic in constant communication with the High Authorities of the Vatican, tells me as his personal opinion that if
the Irish Govt. should proceed against any ecclesiastic for illegal
acts, no question or difficulty would be raised by Rome. Could
any official document with reference to the illegal proceedings
of the Priesthood be sent me for communication to the Vatican
through my informant? He attaches importance to this, as at
present there are only newspaper reports to go upon. I have
strongly urged him to have letter of reprimand to Bp. of Meath
communicated to Cardinal McCabe with orders to publish it as
in the case of the Pope's letter to the Archbishop of Dublin and
he promises to speak at the Propaganda in this sense.[56]

_____
[56] *Ibid.*

Before Paget's suggestions could be acted upon in Dublin, London, or Rome, however, the whole issue of "diplomatic relations" was suddenly blown up by the unauthorized publication of an exchange of letters between Cardinals McCabe and Jacobini in the London *Standard*.

According to the *Standard*, McCabe had reported to the cardinal secretary of state from Dublin on December 20:

> Yesterday I had a long and confidential colloquy with Mr. _____, sent to me by the Viceroy of Ireland to treat upon diverse questions. In the course of the conversation he said to me the following words:—In consequence of the refusal of the Holy See to accept a Secretary of the Embassy accredited to the Italian Government, as being charged to treat with the Vatican, the English Government on the proposition of the Viceroy, is not adverse to send the Holy See a Minister with the same attributes as the Minister of Prussia. Could the Holy Father accede to this proposal without having a representative of his own in London? I allow the hope that such an arrangement might be very possible (*possibilissima*), but I require formal permission to speak in the name of the Holy See.[57]

The *Standard* reported Cardinal Jacobini as replying to this letter on December 24, from Rome:

> After having taken the necessary consultation with His Holiness, I believe I may amply authorise your Eminence to reply affirmatively to the question made and contained in your letter of the 20th inst. In case of the English Government deciding, as appears likely (literally, as appears, *come pare*), to nominate a Minister to the Holy See, the latter would only reserve to itself the power of indicating the modality of the attributes of the person to be nominated.[58]

A week before the publication of these letters, the *Standard* had, in fact, published a telegram from their Roman correspondent indicating that such negotiations were indeed taking place.[59] On reading the report in the *Standard*, the Rev. G. R. Badenoch, a Protestant clergyman, wrote Gladstone asking him whether the report had any substance. He received the

---

[57] GR, 30/29/142. Newspaper clipping, no date [*Standard* (London), January 3, 1883].

[58] *Ibid.*

[59] *Standard*, December 27, 1882. See also December 30, 1882.

following curt reply, dated January 1, 1883, from Gladstone's private secretary:

Sir,—I am directed by Mr. Gladstone to acknowledge the receipt of your letter of the 27th ult., and to say that he thinks your inquiry would be more regularly addressed to the Foreign Office. He is not aware, however, of any such intention on the part of Her Majesty's Government as that which you quote from the *Standard* newspaper.[60]

"In view of this, and of some other more or less direct denials," the *Standard* explained, "we think it right to print the following Despatches, copies of which have been placed in our hands by a gentleman who vouches to us for their authenticity."[61] Naturally, the consternation in Dublin and London was very great and was probably only exeeded by that in Rome. Spencer telegraphed Granville from Dublin on Monday evening, January 3, 1883, that—"Hill of 'Daily News' telegraphs as follows:

Standard publishes alleged [*sic*] despatches between McCabe and Jacobini as to negotiations with Viceroy for English Representative at Vatican. May we deny the fact of such negotiations?[62]

"What reply," Spencer asked desperately, "shall I give? I never had negotiations." Spencer followed up this telegram the next day with a long letter to Granville marked "private" in which he tried to explain all. "I had not seen the Article," he began, referring to the letters in the *Standard*, "when I telegraphed last night. I need not assure you that I never sent a message to McCabe about the question of an English representative at the Vatican."[63] "About the 20 Dec.," Spencer then explained, "Errington came to me, & I recollect his reference to the subject, & that he recited to me what had taken place, & that he wished the same arrangement would be made with England as with Germany. I replied in generalities, & listened rather than spoke." "There are only germs of truth," Spencer then noted, "in the supposed despatches." In

---

[60] *Ibid.*, January 3, 1883.
[61] *Ibid.*
[62] GR, 30/29/142, January 4, 1883.
[63] *Ibid.*

concluding his letter Spencer further assured Granville that there was in any case nothing in writing from him to McCabe about diplomatic relations.

What really happened, and who indeed is to be believed? In the first place the dispatches between McCabe and Jacobini are undoubtedly authentic.[64] The details are too intimate, the translation too awkward, and the time elapsed between the exchange of letters and their publication too short for them to be forgeries. Who then was telling the truth—Errington to McCabe or Spencer to Granville? It is unlikely that Errington would have lied to McCabe to his face, and inconceivable that Spencer would have lied to Granville on paper. Yet it is just as unlikely that Spencer was as reticent as claimed to have been with Errington, and it is also inconceivable that Errington was not more enthusiastic than he should have been, if indeed their letters are any indication of the former's willingness to talk, and the latter's tendency towards enthusiasm, in a course they were both deeply and personally interested in.

What must have been the consternation in Rome on seeing the patient negotiations of more than two years go for nought? During that period they had been investing heavily in British good will, and to have all their diplomatic assets lost in a moment, and lost moreover through a leak in their own apparatus, was only to have indignity heaped on injury. To win British favor, Rome had sent letters, rescripts, obliged in episcopal appointments, and created a cardinal before his time, and what was the result—an enraged British public opinion, and nothing to show for it. Moreover, Rome had paid a very heavy price in terms of Irish good will, as people, clergy, and bishops all became very wary and suspicious of Rome's good intentions. The British government, and Granville in particular, however, must have been most pleased to get out from under so heavy a burden of diplomatic obligations at so little cost. Since Ireland was now settling down to a constitutional rather than an agrarian agitation, the need for Rome's aid in governing Ireland was becoming less necessary.

---

[64] See *Standard*, January 5, 1883: "We have received the following telegram from Cardinal McCabe: —/ 'The statement in your Journal respecting the Despatches said to have passed between me and Cardinal Jacobini, concerning diplomatic relations between England and the Holy See, is utterly destitute of foundation." Note, that all that McCabe is denying is the statement made by the *Standard*, and is not in effect really referring to the dispatches.

The irony in all this, of course, was that Rome in helping to achieve peace in Ireland had removed the only reason why the British government was interested in establishing diplomatic relations with the Holy See.

By the end of 1882, the vast majority of the priests and bishops in the Irish Church had come to realize that they could expect little aid or comfort from either London or Rome in their efforts to meet the legitimate needs of their people. British coercion, for example, coming as it did from the hands of a Liberal government, emphasized the fact, for most Irishmen, how few Englishmen were really sympathetic. Even Mr. Gladstone's magnificent conciliatory effort in the Land Act of 1881 had only proved workable in Parnellite terms, and as such had given even the well-disposed among the Irish clergy serious cause for reflection on the nationalist proposition that legislating for Ireland from Westminster was constitutionally impractical. Moreover, Rome's attempts to re-establish diplomatic relations with London over and against the Irish bishops' unanimous and explicit advice had not only resulted in undermining the confidence of bishops and priests in Rome's good intentions, but had seriously embarrassed them in their efforts to prevent the Irish tenants and small farmers from resorting to outrage and secret combinations in order to redress their grievances. The combined result of London's intransigence and ineffectiveness, and Rome's intrigue and ineptness, was to deepen the growing conviction among Irishmen, ecclesiastical even more than lay, perhaps, that in the last analysis they had only themselves alone to depend upon.

VI. The Circular

February, 1882 - July, 1883

The crucial factor in the pacification of Ireland during 1882, however, was neither the British government's use of Coercion nor even its extra-constitutional efforts to govern through Rome, but rather Parnell's decision to give up the agrarian agitation. "When I was arrested," Parnell complained to Mrs. O'Shea on February 14, after he had been in Kilmainham for four months, "I did not think the movement would have lasted a month, but this wretched government have such a fashion of doing things by halves that it has managed to keep things going in several counties up till now."[1] Parnell had, at first, expected to be released by Christmas, and then by the opening of Parliament on February 7, but he still found himself in jail at the beginning of April, and the government, furthermore, gave no indication that it was willing to come to terms. When Parnell, therefore, was released on his parole on April 10, to attend the funeral of a nephew, he took advantage of the opportunity to open negotiations with Gladstone for a settlement.

What emerged from these negotiations has come to be called the "Kilmainham Compact." In brief, the government promised to legislate on the arrears question and admit leaseholders to the benefits of the Land Act, while agreeing also to drop Coercion.[2] Parnell, for his side, agreed to give up the agrarian agitation and "to cooperate cordially for the future with the liberal party in forwarding liberal principles and measures of general reform."[3] The bargain when finally

---

[1] Katherine O'Shea, *Charles Stewart Parnell* 1 (London, 1914): p. 226. February 14, 1882.

[2] How important the Arrears question was to any settlement may be easily gauged by the reaction of the archbishop of Tuam, whose diocese in the County Galway was accounted one of the worst troubled areas in Ireland. "If they," he wrote the bishop of Ardagh, on January 21, 1882, referring to the government, "attended to our recommendation in regard to Arrears, the inextricable & interminable compulsion now existing wd. be avoided. Arrears the people *wont* & *cant* pay." Mc, January 21, 1882.

[3] Quoted in Conor Cruise O'Brien, *Parnell and His Party, 1880-1890* (Oxford, 1957), p. 77.

162

struck resulted in the release, on May 2, of Parnell and his colleagues. W. E. Forster, the chief secretary for Ireland, resigned in protest and was succeeded by Lord Frederick Cavendish. The evening of the day Lord Frederick arrived in Dublin to take up his new post, he and his under-secretary, T. H. Burke, were murdered in the Phoenix Park by a gang of assassins armed with surgical knives. The savagery of the crime was only exceeded by its cowardliness and it struck deep in the Irish mind. "We hardly know what we are doing," wrote the archbishop of Tuam to Kirby on May 13, "since this atrocious murder in the Phoenix Park"(K). "I firmly believe," he charged, unable to endure the shame of their being Irish, "it is the work of foreigners. Some wicked English or American rowdies."

No one, perhaps, was more shocked or stunned than the seemingly imperturbable Parnell, who immediately offered his resignation to Gladstone. That consummate politician and statesman wisely refused to consider it because he undoubtedly realized that in Parnell, and in him alone, he had the key to the pacification of Ireland. Dropping coercion at this point, however, given the state of public opinion in Britain, was impossible. Gladstone quickly introduced a crimes bill in early May, which was stubbornly and resourcefully "obstructed" by the Parnellites. The other terms outlined in the "Kilmainham Compact," however, were fulfilled and they endured. When the crimes bill finally became law on July 12, Gladstone introduced an arrears bill, which also admitted leaseholders to the advantages of the Land Act. This comprehensive measure passed the Commons on July 21, and shortly thereafter became law. Parnell, on his side, broke the back of the agrarian agitation by dissolving the Ladies Land League, over the strenuous protests of his sister Anna and to the great disgust of Michael Davitt, by the simple expedient of cutting off its funds. The Parnellites also co-operated with the government to the extent, at least, that they caused little or no trouble in the House of Commons for the next three years and concentrated, instead, on building and perfecting their political machine in Ireland in preparation for the next general election.

Between the liquidation of the Ladies Land League by Parnell, in May, and his launching his new political machine, the Irish National League, in October, the country was without any formal political organization. By late August, however, there were obvious signs of those clouds no bigger than a man's hand. "There probably will be a good deal of controversy," Moran wrote Kirby on September 9, referring to the next general meeting of the bishops scheduled for October 3, "about some new schemes of agitation which have been set on foot during the past few weeks. No fewer than three new schemes have been started, one relating to the labourers, another to the evicted tenants, and the third to the payment of Members of Parliament"(K). "For my part," Moran concluded, "I have kept aloof from them all, but should anyone propose that they shd. be condemned, I think that the Bishops wd. not at all consent to such a course." When it became obvious that the harvest would be a failure because of the incessant rain, and that there would consequently be great distress during the winter, Parnell, in order to be able to contain and, therefore, to control any new agitation, launched the Irish National League in Dublin on October 17, 1882.

Parnell's policy was made plain by the constituent elements that went to make up the orgainzing committee of the new League. The committee included among its thirty members "five members of the Mansion House Committee for the Relief of Evicted Tenants, five members of the Labour and Industrial Union, five members of the Council of the Home Rule League, and fifteen other gentlemen."[4] The National League was, in fact, and continued to be throughout its existence, controlled by its organizing committee. Since the "fifteen other gentlemen" were all probably nominated by Parnell, it is more than obvious that the National League would not easily escape his guiding political genius. The other significant feature about the organizing committee, besides Parnell's paramountcy, was its composition. Twelve of the thirty members were M. P.'s, and seven more would eventually join their colleagues in Parliament. In other words, the committee was more political than agrarian in its instincts. Once again, Parnell, by shrewdly anticipating events, and giving a lead and direction, had prevented political power from falling into any hands other than his own.

During 1882 the Irish Church, within this political framework, attempted to work out its problems with Rome,

---

[4] Quoted in C. C. O'Brien, *op. cit.*, p. 128.

the British government, and the Irish people. Before he had received word that he would be made a cardinal, McCabe had called for a meeting of the bishops on March 22, to discuss primarily what should be done about the distribution of some 24 fellowships, worth *in toto* about £12,000 per year, which would be voted on by the Senate of the Royal University. These fellowships would, in fact, be distributed among the various colleges and universities that combined to make up that elaborate educational fiction, the Royal University, which in reality was only an examining and degree-granting body. The archbishop of Armagh, in accepting McCabe's invitation to attend the meeting, pointed out the bishops would also have to say something about the sad state of the country. "The tenant farmers," he reported on March 5, somewhat less optimistic than usual, "even in the North are demoralised with the decisions of the Land Commissioners, and many of them were on the point of withdrawing their *originating notices* from the courts, on account of the lame awards made by the Commissioners in most parts of the Country, and I have hopes that a firm and moderate expression of opinion as to the working of the Land Act, coming from the Prelates will do good, and remedy defects"(Mc).

Since the Senate of the Royal University would vote on the distribution of the fellowships on April 12, and since the country was in a deplorable state, with some 600 suspects in jail, the meeting could not be well postponed, even though McCabe could not attend. Before he left for Rome, however, McCabe explained to Bartholomew Woodlock, the bishop of Ardagh, that he would be satisfied with twelve of the twenty-four fellowships as being a fair Catholic share, especially if the lion's share of the remainder did not go to the Queen's Colleges in Belfast, Cork, and Galway. These colleges had proved to be the educational *bête noir* of nearly all the Irish bishops, since their foundation in 1846. For nearly forty years, episcopal fulmination after fulmination had been issued against them, but all to little avail. McCabe could hardly have expected, therefore, that his more relaxed policy would be either appreciated or understood by the great majority of the Irish bishops. Woodlock, in fact, wrote McCabe as much on March 16, when he pointed out that he did not think the bishops, or the country for that matter, would be satisfied with twelve fellowships, but he would do what he could at the episcopal meeting(Mc).

When the meeting was held on March 22, things went very much against McCabe's proposed "new departure." "A Resolution was adopted," Moran reported to McCabe on March 24, "against giving any fellowship to the Queen's College, and a subsidiary Resolution after a long debate was also carried to the effect that shd. Fellowships be granted to the Queen's College officials it wd. be a matter for consideration for Your Eminence & Dr. Woodlock whether you should continue your connection with the Senate"(Mc). Moran neglected to mention, however, that the bishops had also privately resolved to ask for two-thirds of the fellowships, instead of McCabe's proposed one-half. "No Resolutions on the state of the country were adopted," Moran then explained, "but a Committee of four Bishops was appointed to draw up such Resolutions in detail for our next Meeting." Woodlock also wrote McCabe that same day, enclosing a résumé of the proceedings. He further explained that it was Croke who moved the two resolutions and that "He had it all his own way"(Mc). "God grant," he exclaimed timidly, "we have not made a mistake, & that our action may not evoke opposition on the part of our lay Cath. Senators as well as that of the Queen's Colleges party."

When Woodlock then reported that the four bishops, referred to by Moran, appointed to draw up the resolutions to be presented at the next meeting on the state of the country, were Duggan, Nulty, Moran, and Gillooly, McCabe must have been very annoyed. Duggan and Nulty, of course, were notorious for their Land League sympathies and Moran, of late, was not accounted much better. "The Resolutions," Moran, in fact, explained to Kirby some ten days later, on April 3, "taken by the Bishops protesting against a single fellowship being given to the Queen's College Professors will be considered by the Cardinal as too strong, & Mgr. Neville will also be displeased at them"(K). Neville, who was the rector of the Catholic University and influential with McCabe in educational matters, had set out for Rome immediately after the bishops' resolutions were published. "The Bishops however," Moran continued, and obviously pleased, "were quite determined to strike a blow at the Queen's Colleges, and it was quite cheering to see how determined in the matter the great majority of the Bishops were." "We will get nothing," he then firmly concluded, "from those who oppose our education claims, unless we show our determination to fight them on every point."

Kirby obviously informed Croke that the new cardinal was very upset. "The extracts I enclose about the new Cardinal," Croke replied on April 14, in a short note marked "strictly private," "will give you an idea of the situation here in Ireland"(K). "Our 'resolutions' are sound," Croke added unabashed, "and as the Freeman's leader says, have created a sensation throughout the Island." McCabe, however, was not to be so easily put down, for on April 10, Cardinal Simeoni, prefect of Propaganda, forwarded to the archbishop of Armagh a letter which summarily quashed the resolutions. The bishops then had to eat some very humble pie indeed, when on April 18 the Senate of the Royal University awarded twelve of the twenty-four fellowships to those connected with the Queen's Colleges and only nine to the Catholic Associated Colleges. "You will have seen," Moran wrote Kirby the next day, April 19, "the letter which Cardl. Simeoni forwarded to the Primate in this matter. It is the result of Dean Neville's & Mr. Errington's negotiations with Cardinal Jacobini, & of course had Cardinal McCabe's approval"(K). "It will I fear," Moran maintained, "embitter very much the feelings of the Irish Episcopate, and can do no good." "All the Bishops," he reported in conclusion, "who met at Maynooth or in Dublin on Sunday or Monday, with the exception of Dr. Butler, lamented the sending of such a letter."

The Senate, moreover, added insult to injury, at least as far as Moran was concerned, by awarding five of the nine Catholic fellowships to English and Scottish converts. "This is a very poor installment," he wrote Kirby again several days later, on April 21, "of justice to Irish Catholics"(K). "It would be well," Moran then advised Kirby, "to tell them at Propaganda not to be too hasty in listening to the suggestions of Mr. Errington and Dean Neville." "The Rescript from Propaganda," he complained, ". . .will do an incalculable amount of mischief, not so much for the decision which it conveyed, as for the unpleasant fact that it set aside practically the resolutions of our body of Bishops without asking for an explanation of their resolutions or for the grounds on which they acted." "I had a very strong letter this morning," he concluded, and it would not be difficult to guess from whom, "from one of our leading Bishops strongly condemning the course pursued by Propaganda." Another of the leading bishops, John MacEvilly, was somewhat less forceful, but not less anxious when he wrote Kirby almost a month later. "*Entre nous*," he confided on May 13, "the letter from Propaganda about the University fellows has not pleased many. I take no part in such things, nor will I. Whatever is done by those above me, I take as directed by a higher wisdom"(K).

Some days before the rescript was sent from Propaganda, McCabe had written to a number of the Irish bishops, asking them what they thought needed to be done and what powers, if any, he should be invested with before he left Rome. Needless to say, the bishops to whom he wrote for advice were all, like himself, of one political color and had all, in their varying shades of gray, opposed the Land League. They included the archbishop of Tuam(MacEvilly), the bishops of Elphin (Gillooly), Ardagh (Woodlock), Cork (Delany), Kildare and Leighlin (Walshe), and the latter's coadjutor (Lynch). The weight of the resulting advice, the bishop of Elphin always excepted, was clearly against strong measures.[5] What emerged were really two suggestions—first, that some formal procedure be worked out for episcopal meetings with regard to rules, attendance, non-departure, and secrecy, and, second, that something be done about checking the younger clergy in their enthusiasm for political agitation.

In his letter of April 8, MacEvilly had also expressly advised McCabe to beware of anything like English influence in Irish ecclesiastical affairs, and suggested that perhaps the best way to avoid this was to have all Irish business at Rome come through himself as cardinal(Mc). McCabe then informed MacEvilly that the pope was determined on having an English agent in Rome, for MacEvilly replied somewhat insincerely, on May 4, that it was certainly strange that if the Holy Father really wanted an official agent that any opposition should be offered(Mc). What MacEvilly's real views actually were it is hard to say, for he wrote Kirby only a little more than a week later, on May 13, "There is one great evil ahead. It is this: the danger of giving the English Government any power over our Ecclesiastical affairs, or even the suspicion of such on the part

---

[5] Mc, April 7, 1882 (Gillooly); Holy Saturday, 1882 [April 8, 1882] (MacEvilly); Easter Sunday, 1882 [April 9, 1882] (Woodlock); April 9, 1882 (Delany); April 10, 1882 (Walshe); April 11, 1882 (Lynch).

of the people"(K). "Of course," he continued, "whatever the
H. Father does or wishes every good Catholic, every good
Priest will receive with the most filial submission. But the mass
of the people are now easily excited." "*Repression* of any kind
they won't stand, . . . they must be treated like children." "An
immense number of Priests," he warned, "(I don't say if any
Bishops, I am not among them) would hardly be brought to
have ["give" crossed out] cordial obedience."

In welcoming the cardinal home on May 17, and in reply to
his question as to whether an immediate meeting of the
bishops should be called on his arrival, Gillooly unexpectedly
advised caution(Mc). There was a rumor abroad, he
explained to McCabe, that he had returned from Rome with a
mandate to bend the bishops and clergy to English influence,
and that it would be wise, given the excitable state of public
opinion, to avoid all appearance of giving help or sympathy to
the opponents of the people. He then shrewdly suggested that
the bishops should meet ostensibly to consider educational
matters and that they could then discuss the problems relative
to the sad state of the country. Two of the other three bishops
canvassed by McCabe, McGettigan and Moran, were opposed
to an immediate meeting and the third, MacEvilly, was his
usual quaking self.[6] McGettigan and Moran suggested that it
would be wiser to wait for the next scheduled meeting of the
bishops on June 24, which was near enough at hand. Their
reasons were varied, but the real reason was that in calling an
extraordinary meeting so soon after the cardinal's return
would only give currency to the rumors already abroad.
Further, the bishops were not yet quite sure what powers or
instructions McCabe would return with and the bishops were
anxious to delay, if not avoid, any possible confrontation with
Rome in which the political interests of their people were
involved.

When McCabe arrived home, however, he found, besides
the letters of the bishops, a letter from the cardinal prefect of
Propaganda instructing him to call a meeting of the bishops
"*statim et quamprimum*."[7] McCabe immediately circulated the
Propaganda letter among the bishops, and after some further

---

[6] Mc, May 17, 1882 (Moran); May 17, 1882 (MacEvilly); May 20, 1882 (McGettigan).
[7] Mc, May 21, 1882, Moran to McCabe.

correspondence scheduled the required meeting. "A Meeting of our Bishops," Moran informed Kirby in a letter marked "private" on May 28, "has been summoned for the 6th of June, & an Instruction from Propaganda dated the 8th of May conveys the wishes of His Holiness that all the Bishops shd. attend & take part in the Meeting till its close"(K). "The only matters suggested by the Propaganda for consideration," Moran then explained, "are the old question about Priests interfering in politicks, & the new question about the lady land leaguers. The Cardinal Archbishop of Dublin further suggests the consideration of the Catholic University Jesuit College & the Royal University Fellowships." "However," Moran pointed out,

> there is another question which will arise & which will engage a warmer discussion than all the others. It is the relations between the Holy See and the Irish Church. We cannot conceal from ourselves that the English government is desirous to have its official agent accepted by Rome as the authentic exponent of the attitude of Irish Catholics, & so far as we can learn there are many in Rome anxious to meet the wishes of the English government & to allow to the British agent that authoritative position which he claims(K).

"This is a state of things which both clergy & people view with alarm," he concluded, "& at our next Meeting, it will be a burning question. *What are we to do under the circumstances?*"

What indeed could Kirby have replied? More than two years before, Moran had himself pointed out to McCabe there was little the Irish bishops could object to if the pope wished to have an official English agent in Rome, and that the really great danger to be avoided was the appointment of a papal nuncio to London. How then had circumstances so altered as to make the one proposal now seem as bad as the other in Moran's mind? In those two years a fundamental shift had taken place in the management of Irish ecclesiastical business in Rome, the culmination of which, it seems, was that Kirby had not been informed about the two recent rescripts sent by the cardinal prefect to the Irish bishops and that, perhaps for the first time in fifty years, he had not been privy to Irish business at the Propaganda.[8] This apparent and increasing

---

[8] K, May 28, 1882. "I wd. also ask you," Moran wrote, "were you made aware by Propaganda of the two Rescripts before they were sent to us. . . ."

willingness of Rome to meet British demands in Irish affairs had so taxed and exasperated the good will of the Irish people that no sensible or responsible Irish bishop or priest could view the situation with other than alarm. Under "the circumstances" what indeed could Kirby have advised except that patience, that prudence, and that pious trust in Providence that had been his *forte* in Rome now for over fifty years.

In one sense, at least, the bishops must have been greatly relieved when they received, through McCabe, the cardinal prefect's letter about the meeting. The wild rumors regarding the extensive powers McCabe had returned with from Rome were certainly not confirmed by the letter. The bishops must have also realized the program outlined by the cardinal prefect was practically that suggested by the bishops whose advice McCabe had sought, and the only new feature, as Moran had pointed out to Kirby, was the reference to the Ladies Land League, which was obviously McCabe's own particular contribution. Appearances to the contrary, therefore, the initiative about what was to be done had really remained in the hands of the bishops. Further, though the letter pointed out what was to be done, how it was to be done was left to the bishops to decide as a body.[9] The minds of the bishops must have been further calmed when McCabe in his letter covering that of the cardinal prefect, again raised the question about the expediency of an immediate meeting when the regular meeting was only a month away. When several of the bishops pointed out in reply that to defer the meeting would, they were afraid, put too liberal an interpretation on the "*quam-primum*" in the cardinal's letter, McCabe then called for an immediate meeting.[10] This was a further indication that McCabe had probably not returned with any more power than the eminence which naturally attached to his new dignity as cardinal, and even if he had been delegated apostolic powers in Rome, he was obviously not inclined to use them as yet.

One and all, the various accounts of the meeting agree that a great deal of useful business was done in an atmosphere of

---

[9] Mc, May 23, 1882: "It contains most salutory suggestions," commented the Land League bishop of Clonfert, Patrick Duggan, when McCabe forwarded him the cardinal prefect's letter, "—whilst requiring things to be done, we are left sufficient room for exercise by our discretion as the position of affairs require."

[10] Mc, May 21, 1882, F. J. MacCormack to McCabe; May 21, 1882, Moran to McCabe.

perfect harmony.[11] "It gives me great pleasure," MacEvilly summed up for Kirby on June 17, "to tell you, that having attended Episcopal meetings for the last 25 years, I never attended a meeting that gave me such pleasure as this"(K). "I never saw such cordial unanimity," he explained, obviously surprised, "the Cardl acted with admirable tact, [and] united all discordant elements. Everything was conducted in a most orderly way, much important business quietly transacted, and all terminated with a unanimous address presented to the Cardl by the Primate in an eloquent speech and seconded in a still more eloquent speech by the Abp. of Cashel."[12] It was Moran, however, who had supplied Kirby with the more useful details. Moran had reported on June 11 that the meeting,

---

[11] The address to the people issued by the bishops after their meeting and which appeared in the *Freeman's Journal* on June 11, 1882, was the result of an obvious compromise, but it was also obvious that the voice was the authentic voice of Croke, even if the hand was still the hand of McCabe. After reminding their flocks that the end does not justify unlawful or immoral means, and condemning all such means, the bishops admitted that it was also "true that on religious, as well as political grounds, it is the undisputable right of Irishmen to live on and by their own fertile soil, and to be free to employ the resources of their country for their own profit. It is, moreover, the admitted right, and often the duty, of those who suffer oppression either from individuals or from the State, to seek redress by every lawful means; and to help in obtaining such redress is a noble work of justice and charity. On those grounds it is that the object of our national movement has had the approval and blessing not only of your priests and bishops, but of the sovereign Pontiff himself; and has been applauded in our own and in foreign countries by all men of just and generous minds without distinction of race or creed." The bishops then specifically condemned refusing to pay just debts, preventing others from paying them, injuring one's neighbor in his person, right, or property, resisting forcibly the law and those charged with its administration, or inciting others to do so, forming secret societies, and above all "the hideous crime of murder." Still, it was Croke rather than McCabe who had the last word, because "Before concluding, we feel it our duty to declare, without in any sense meaning to excuse the crimes and offenses we have condemned, that in our belief they would never have occurred had not the people been driven to despair by evictions, and the prospect of evictions for the nonpayment of exorbitant rents; and furthermore, that the continuance of such evictions, justly designated by the Prime Minister of England as sentences of death, must be a fatal permanent provocation to crime, and that it is the duty of all friends of social order, and especially of the Government, to put an end to them as speedily as possible, and at any cost."

[12] MacEvilly also wrote in his letter of June 17, to Kirby that, "I was so glad the Abp. of Cashel took such a stand. Believe me, His Grace, whatever may be said of some things he did and wrote, in wh. [*sic*] was a great benefactor to our country and religion. The stand he took at a certain period in this terrible agitation and crisis through which we are passing had a great effect in keeping the people from passing away from the clergy as they were instigated to do by bad men. I wish His Grace's differences with [our] excellent Cardl had never existed. This I need not say, I could never approve. But he is a thorough Irishman, a thorough defender of the rights of the H. See under all circumstances. I write this because there is a rumour that His Grace is misrepresented in *some* quarters."

which had opened on June 6 and had lasted four days, was the largest in recent years with twenty-five of the twenty-seven bishops present, the absentees being incapacitated by permanent illness(K). McCabe presided, and the first day four committees were appointed to prepare reports in the chief matters submitted for the bishops' consideration. One archbishop presided at each committee, with one bishop acting as secretary, and all the bishops were distributed through the four committees. The first thing done, Moran explained further,

> was to fix an order of procedure to our General Meetings. It was agreed that one General Meeting would be held in October every year, in which all the Bps. should attend, and to which all should remain until the Meeting or the sessions were brought to a close. It was also resolved that Secrecy should be observed in regard to the details of the Meetings and nothing be published in the newspapers except what was intended for publication. . . . The whole order of procedure was discussed and approved of. It corresponds very much with the order followed in the Congregations in Rome. In regard to the Catholic University College we resolved to hand it over to the Abp. of Dublin that he might work it on his responsibility, allowing him all the Fellowships granted by the Senate of the new Royal University. An address to the people will appear in tomorrow morning's paper. Another *Confidential* address to the clergy was also adopted marking out the course to be pursued in political matters(K).

"I need not say," Moran finally assured Kirby in conclusion, "that we adopted all the suggestions of Propaganda."

This last, however, was something less that the whole truth, as events were soon to prove. The bishops had, in fact, effectively parried two of Propaganda's most interesting thrusts. "I was authorised by the Bishops," McCabe, in explaining the first, wrote Kirby on June 22, "to thank the Sacred Congregation for the offer of its good offices with the Government for the temporal interests of Ireland, and to express their willingness to give all information in their power to the Cardinal for that purpose should he require it."[13] The bishops were obvi-

---

[13] K, June 22, 1882. Mc, The "Copy of Resolution" is in folder labeled "Meeting of Bishops Dr. McCabe (1883-1884)"—"The Cardinal Archbishop is requested when replying to the letter of Propaganda, to thank the Sacred Congregation for their promise to use their good offices in asking the British Government to promote the interests of the Irish poor; and to express the readiness and even anxiety of the Bishops to give to the Propaganda all authentic information, when required, in reference to the Condition of the Country."

ously determined that their implicit right to be the primary source of that information on which Propaganda should act would not be easily preempted by any British agent, official or unofficial, in Rome. Propaganda's other suggestion about the Ladies Land League was handled somewhat less deftly, but even more firmly. "Outside the pastoral letter addressed to their flocks," the bishop of Waterford, John Power, had gently broken the news to Kirby on June 15, "the Prelates came to an understanding that in the existing circumstances of the country, it was more judicious to leave each Bishop act in his own Diocese according to his best judgement and discretion"(K). "Owing to the great provocation," he explained, stubbornly standing to the people, "given by Government officials in carrying out the policy of coercion, and the heartless cruelties of evicting landlords, the people are greatly exasperated, and require to be treated with judicious forebearance." "Should a different spirit be shown by ecclesiastical authorities," Power concluded significantly with a grim warning, "there would be danger that the people in those districts most disturbed would receive the admonitions of Bishops & Priests with indifference, and perhaps in a less respectful manner."

Within a month, however, the cordial mood created at the bishops' meeting had evaporated. Almost immediately after the meeting reports were circulating that the bihsops had discussed the Ladies Land League, and the rumor spread that they had, in fact, condemned the ladies. To check the rumors and allay suspicion in the country, Croke wrote an open letter to the *Freeman's Journal*, which appeared on July 10, explaining that the ladies had not been condemned by the bishops. The letter excited a good deal of comment, and Errington, in particular, was furious. He immediately wrote Smith on July 11, from London, maintaining that something must be done by Rome(S). He complained that Croke's "outrageous letter" was not only in defiance of the intentions of the instructions recently sent by Propaganda to the Irish bishops, but that the letter would seriously compromise the negotiations for diplomatic relations. Gladstone had told him only yesterday, Errington added, that he wanted to talk to him about Rome. What would he say after he read Croke's letter? Errington had already written Cardinal Jacobini urging him to do something to modify the evil effect of Croke's letter. He had suggested,

Errington alerted Smith, that the cardinal "should authorize me *privately through you* to publish a translation of the part of the letter from Propaganda, and also the Circular of the Bishops." He would of course, he further assured Smith, publish them anonymously and with prudence. If something were not done, Errington warned in conclusion, "I cannot answer for the consequences and what the Pope & Cardinal have been trying for & is so nearly attained will be lost."

Several days later, on July 14, Errington again wrote Smith reporting that Croke's letter had produced an even worse effect in government circles than he had at first supposed, and that if nothing were done, it would be regarded as "proving that the whole attempt to negotiate with Rome is a mistake, that Dr. Croke can with impunity publicly *slight* the orders of the Pope, who can therefore be of no use." Errington again urged Smith that he be given permission to publish the bishops' confidential letter to their clergy, as well as portions of Propaganda's recent letter to the bishops. The following day, however, the bishops' letter to the clergy appeared in the English Catholic weekly, the *Tablet*, which was owned and published by the bishop of Salford. When writing Smith again a week later, Errington explained that though he had had nothing to do whatever with the publication of the letter in the *Tablet*, he was very pleased that it had been published because it demonstrated the will and power of Rome in the Irish Church.[14] He then urged Smith to tell Jacobini that the recent crisis also indicated "the mischief Dr. Croke is doing, & ought to prove to the Pope that if he expects to get anything from the English Govt. with all their difficulties, he must not allow Dr. Croke to play fast and loose with his orders, & make a mockery of the whole affair."

The pope was indeed finally persuaded to take action, but only in his own oblique way. He decided to take occasion to admonish the Irish clergy in his reply to the recent letter addressed to him by McCabe in early June in the name of all the Irish bishops. The pope's letter, however, which was dated August 1, from St. Peter's, was published and commented on in the English newspapers before it had time to reach McCabe and be distributed by him to the Irish bishops. Not only did

[14] S, July 25, 1882. This letter is marked "Sunday," although Sunday was July 23, in 1882.

some of the Irish bishops resent this slight, but the letter itself could not have given most of them much comfort. "On the one hand," Leo XIII pointed out to the Irish bishops, "the pressure is still felt of grievous hardships; on the other perplexing agitation hurries many into turbulent courses, and men have not been wanting who stained themselves with atrocious murders, as if it were possible to find hope for national happiness in public disgrace and crime."[15] After complimenting the bishops on their combined pastoral address to the Irish people, in which they "reasonably recalled the divine precept to *seek first the Kingdom of God and His Justice*," and condemning once again secret societies, the pope then announced that all the bishops had "thought proper to decree concerning priests, especially the younger clergy, we judge right and suited to circumstances."

> In this way and by these means We believe that Ireland without any violence will attain that prosperity which She desires. For, as We signified to you on another occasion, We are confident that the statesmen who preside over the administration of public affairs will give satisfaction to the Irish when they demand what is just. This not only reason advises, but also their well known political prudence; since it cannot be doubted that the well-being of Ireland is connected with the tranquillity of the whole Empire.
>
> We meanwhile with this hope do not cease to help the Irish people with the authority of Our advice, and to offer to God Our prayers inspired by solicitude and love, that He would graciously look down upon a people so distinguished by many noble virtues, and calming the storm blessed them with the longed for peace and prosperity. In pledge of these Heavenly blessings, and in token of Our great affection, We lovingly impart in Our Lord to you, Beloved Son, and Venerable Brethren, to the clergy, and to the whole people, the Apostolic Benediction(K).

The effect of this letter, though weighted obviously in favor of diplomatic relations and against the agrarian agitation, was that it hardly pleased anyone.

Another result of all this, of course, was that Croke was once

---

[15] K, August 1, 1882. [Printed] "Letter of Our most Holy Father, Leo XIII, By Divine Providence Pope to Eduard McCabe Cardinal Priest of the Holy Roman Church of the Title of S. Sabina, Archbishop of Dublin and the other Bishops of Ireland."

again much complained of in Rome, and Kirby wrote MacEvilly that it might be wise to say something to him. "I was very sorry," MacEvilly commiserated on August 3, "our friend of Cashel wrote that letter"(K). "If I get an opportunity," he promised hesitantly, "I shall not omit speaking to him, but it must be done cautiously." Some weeks later, however, Kirby worked up enough courage to risk another exchange with Croke and wrote him directly. He obviously phrased his news cautiously and judiciously, for Croke did not lose his temper until almost the end of his letter. "The Roman authorities," Croke admitted on September 6, writing from Dieppe, "are quite a puzzle to me"(K). "Is it possible," he asked, "that they do not know what passed at the meeting of the Bishops in reference to the Ladies Land League?" "The Bishops were, I might say," he explained to Kirby, "unanimous (except the Cardinal and another) that it should not be condemned for three reasons which were given in writing by the Secretary, Dr. MacCormack."

One it will soon die out. Two if condemned it would acquire fresh vitality, and condemnation would give great offense to the people. Three whatever it might have been in its inception it is now a purely benevolent society in Ireland and does not deserve to be condemned. We were most anxious to have it understood that the L. L. League was not condemned by Bishops, but as we said, it would acquire new life, it being, as we knew on its last legs(K).

"Therefore," Croke continued, "when it was stated (falsely) in papers that it was condemned by the Bishops, I felt called upon to contradict it." "In point of fact," he then added, "according to our anticipations, the L. L. League in Ireland has since been dissolved." "I don't care a sham," Croke then declared, coming to the complaints being made about him in Rome, "who writes against me. I shall always steer the same course, be always with the people, protect them from their tyrants and slanderers, and [shall leave?] the defense of my character in so far to my countrymen all over the world." "I shall be prepared at all times," he concluded pugnaciously, "to defend myself."

The very day he wrote Kirby from Dieppe, Croke also replied to a complaint made to him by McCabe about Cashel priests attending political meetings in Dublin. "After having been in quest of me for many days," Croke responded amicably, "Yr. Eminences letter reached me here"(Mc). "I had no idea," he candidly explained, "that priests would be prevented from attending Meetings in Dublin; and I'm quite sure the other Bishops thought as I do. Our regulations were simply Diocesan. Each Bishop undertook for his own priests." "There will be no meeting of any consequence held in Dublin in connection with politics for some time," Croke then advised, "and I would, therefore, respectfully suggest that things should be allowed to remain as they are till next meeting of the Bishops." There was little McCabe could do except acquiesce in Croke's suggestion, since by the time he received this letter the meeting of the bishops was less than a month away. When the bishops met on October 3, they did, in fact, agree with Croke that each bishop was responsible for his own priests, and the cardinal submitted to the opinion of the other bishops.[16]

In reporting the details to Kirby on October 8, Moran noted that, like the previous meeting in June, there was a very full attendance and all business was done in an atmosphere of harmony and cordiality(K). The bishops, however, unlike the June meeting, chose to deal primarily with religious and educational matters, and leave politics alone. They withdrew the National Seminary of Maynooth from all connection with the Royal University; turned the Catholic University over to an episcopal committee, with the cardinal holding all property in trust; and they gave the Jesuits permission to open a college in connection with the Royal University. A new catechism was also adopted for all Ireland, since the various local ones, as Moran explained, only caused confusion now that the people had begun to travel about. The bishops further agreed to begin the complicated process for the canonization of Oliver Plunkett, and other sixteenth- and seventeenth-century Irish martyrs. Finally, the bishops resolved to send a deputation to the chief secretary for Ireland to urge "the long-promised Training schools for our National teachers." Moran also reported that, though there was some discussion of the political

[16] S, November 17,1882, McCabe to Smith: "The dinner to Mr. Parnell went off quietly: there were no Clerical Speakers at it. I wrote to Dr. Croke begging of him to keep J. Cantwell who is the Administrator of Thurles at home. His Grace acted very well on the occasion."

situation, no address on the subject would be made public, since all the bishops agreed that "great peace now prevails throughout the whole country & that the new schemes of agitation which have been suggested by Parnell & his associates have failed to receive the sympathy of our people." "The whole agitation," Moran summed up warily for Kirby, "is in fact at an end, at least for the present."

Moran was wary because he realized, as did anyone who had eyes to see, and especially mouths to feed, that the mood of the country was sullen rather than satisfied. The harvest had been a dismal failure, and as the bishop of Meath explained to Kirby on December 20, the "prospects of our poor Country for the coming winter is very gloomy indeed. The crops were up to a fair average, but the incessant rain during the Autumn months destroyed *every where* fully a *third* of them and in many places fully one half"(K). He had just received word, Moran explained, from a County Court Judge, Charles Kelly, who owned considerable property in County Galway, that in the district Kelly knew best some 400 out of 500 families of the small farming class would be on the brink of starvation during the coming winter. This proved, Moran maintained, not only that there had been a great need for land reform, but "what need there is still of remedying the most defective administration of the Land-Laws." "At the rate of the present adjustment of cases marked for trial," Moran concluded gloomily, "many of the farmers who are acknowledged to be unjustly treated by their landlords have no hope of their cases being considered by the Court till the beginning of the next century."

In the light of the mood and the condition of the country, therefore, it is easier to understand how Parnell's new Irish National League, founded in the middle of October, was firmly established within two months, and why the bishops silently acquiesced when their priests once again took a prominent part in promoting the new organization. Not everyone acquiesced, however, in the launching of the new movement in the country. "Last Sunday," Errington complained bitterly to Smith from Castle Forbes in County Longford on December 3, "the new agitation was inaugurated by a series of Meetings, attended I am sorry to say by numerous priests some of whom made the most inflammatory speeches. So serious is this that I send you the Freeman with the reports of the speeches in question. I have marked some strong passages"(S). He then asked Smith to bring the matter to the attention of Cardinal Jacobini, but explain that he did not press for any step to be taken at the moment, since he would soon be in Rome himself to tell all. Errington had, however, been pressing Lord Spencer. He wanted the government to mark its sense of the gravity of the situation by prosecuting the offending priests. "Pray ascertain *cautiously*," Errington asked Smith, marking this passage in his letter "*Strictly private*," "and let me know *as soon* as ever you can whether Rome would disapprove of Govt. prosecuting moderately *one* or two priests for their extreme & dangerous language as a warning." Smith did proceed cautiously, for it was not for some ten days after he received Errington's letter that he was able to visit Paget and explain that he did not think that Rome would raise any objection to the government proceeding against any priest for illegal acts.[17] This whole project of the government prosecuting offending clergy, however, which was only a ploy on Errington's part to further diplomatic relations by involving the British and papal governments in some kind of official communication with each other, was soon rendered irrelevant by the publication of the McCabe-Jacobini correspondence in early January, 1883. The publication of the correspondence, moreover, also resulted in the postponement of Errington's visit to Rome that winter.

Meanwhile, the subject of the conduct of the clergy had already been much discussed in Rome, and more than Errington or perhaps even Smith realized. Four Irish bishops had immediately set out for Rome after the episcopal meeting in early October to fulfill the Tridentine requirement of a visit *ad limina*, at least once in every five years, to report personally to the pope on the state of their dioceses. The bishops, MacEvilly and Gillooly, and Dorrian and MacCormack, had traveled in politically compatible pairs, and both points of view among the Irish bishops were, therefore, well represented on November 13, when they were jointly received by the pope in audience. Attended by Kirby, they all assured the pope that the country was improving and that the clergy were only seeking a constitutional redress for the grievances of their people. The pope, however, reflecting on the reports of

---

[17] GR, 30/29/182, December 17, 1882, Paget to Granville.

the recent performances of some of the younger Irish clergy, asked whether the fault was not perhaps to be found in their training at the National Seminary at Maynooth. The bishops protested, one and all, that certainly could not be the case, for the discipline at Maynooth was very strict, and the proportion of superiors to students to see that it was enforced was unusually high. In reporting all this to McCabe, on November 20, MacEvilly added that he had borrowed on a comment of his for the occasion by explaining to the pope that if indeed he did get to heaven he would have Maynooth to thank for it.[18] MacEvilly also reported that Gillooly, who was a Vincentian and had not been trained at Maynooth, defended it to the pope like an alumnus. Then someone, fortunately, mentioned St. Thomas Aquinas, and the conduct of the Irish clergy was quickly forgotten, as the pope became eloquent and diffuse on a subject that was obviously closer to his heart.

While outrage at crime did indeed appear to subside, as the bishops had reported to the pope, with the establishment of the National League by Parnell and his colleagues, the winter still proved to be a very hard one for the Irish people. Though the distress was general, it was particularly evident in the West as the people began to flee the country in increasing numbers. The suffering was alleviated to some degree by private charity as well as by the recent decisions made by the chief commissioners in the administration of the Land Act. The chief commissioners had been systematically upholding on appeal the awards made by the sub-commissioners in the Land Courts. These awards had been in general favorable to the tenants by reducing their rents some twenty per cent, and more, and the landlords were now less likely to try to reverse such awards by appealing. In spite of the charitable efforts made and the heartening decisions of the chief commissioners, however, the distress in the West deepened with the coming of winter. Soon after his return from Rome, Francis MacCormack, the bishop of Achonry, reported to Kirby on January 3, 1883, that in another month they would be faced with famine if the government did not take some effective means to prevent it(K). Later in the month, four of the west-

[18] Mc, November 20, 1882. See also Gillooly to McCabe, November 20, 1882, in which he reports significantly that though they had seen the cardinal prefect of Propaganda (Simeoni) twice, they had not yet seen the new secretary (Jacobini).

ern bishops, including MacEvilly and Gillooly, requested an interview with the lord lieutenant in order to secure some help for their people. Spencer obviously handled the bishops' delegation very badly, for both MacEvilly and Gillooly were very upset by the treatment they received. MacEvilly, for example, was very annoyed when he reported to Kirby on February 3, that Spencer had not even deigned as yet to reply to the bishops' urgent request for help.[19] And Gillooly was still obviously very bitter some six weeks later, on March 22, when he explained to Kirby that every week for the next four months, until the new potatoes were harvested, the suffering was bound to become more widespread and more intense(K). "The bishops of the Province and their Clergy," he added sadly, are doing what they can to procure relief. Pray for us, and for our dear afflicted people." "The only concern of the Govmt," he concluded grimly, "seems to be to drive them out of the Country." Spencer had, in fact, by mishandling MacEvilly and Gillooly in the crisis, gone a very long way in alienating two of the most conservative bishops in the Irish Church with respect to their confidence in the good intentions of the government.

In the midst of this depressing calm, McCabe suffered an almost fatal heart attack. "Cardinal dangerously ill today," his secretary, P. J. Tynan, telegraphed Kirby on February 10, "Very little hope"(K). For days, McCabe's life was in the balance. A Dominican nun, Sister Mary Clare Elliot, who was attending him, explained to Kirby on February 15, "If a bad attack again come on, it is likely to be fatal"(K). "If we could," she added, "only raise His Eminence from the thought he is to die now!" The cardinal had not, in fact, been well for some time. In only late December he had recovered from an attack of bronchitis, and the worry over the successive outrages, revelations at the trials, executions, and finally the new arrests in connection with the Phoenix Park murders in January, 1883, all must have had a depressing cumulative effect. When to all this is added the mortification of the publication of his correspondence with Cardinal Jacobini regarding the negotiations for diplomatic relations, his physical and psychological

---

[19] K, February 3, 1883. See also F. MacCormack, bishop of Achonry, to Kirby, January 7, 1883: "There are signs of extensive distress here in the West. Another month, and we shall have famine, unless the Government take steps to save the people."

collapse is more easily understood. Ten days after the initial attack, the cardinal seemed to be out of danger, for the bishop of Raphoe, Michael Logue, reported to Kirby on February 20 that the patient was actually much better than the medical reports indicated because the doctors were wary about being optimistic in the face of a possible relapse(K). McCabe continued to improve slowly and steadily and by the middle of April, Father Tynan reported to Kirby that the cardinal was successfully recuperating.[20] McCabe was not, however, able to resume business, and even then only in a modest way, for some two months more.

Rome was now, however, on the verge of disaster in Ireland. She could have cut her Irish losses by giving up the game of attempting to establish diplomatic relations after the publication of the McCabe-Jacobini correspondence in early January. She chose, however, not only to continue to play the game, but to play it with even less caution than had been her custom. The day before the news of McCabe's heart attack reached Rome, Cardinal Simeoni, prefect of Propaganda, wrote Croke complaining that several letters of a political nature recently sent by him to the press had given great scandal and urged him to cease all such pronouncements.[21] When, less than a month later, Croke's name again appeared in the public press, Cardinal Simeoni's reaction may be well imagined. The occasion of Croke's newest foray was the launching of the Parnell Testimonial Fund in early March. The fund was as much designed to put new life and energy into a depressed political movement as it was to rescue Parnell's Avondale estate, which he had mortgaged to the hilt in the national interest.

Foremost among the early contributors was the archbishop of Cashel with the large sum of £50 on St. Patrick's Day. Soon a goodly number of the priests and several of the bishops followed suit. Croke's action was naturally viewed by his enemies as less an attempt to help a financially embarrassed national leader as signifying his approval of the launching of a new agitation, and he was once again cited at Rome. Smith had

---

[20] K, April 17, 1883.
[21] C, February 9, 1883.

obviously informed Errington that Rome was very annoyed, and the authorities had at last decided to do something about the archbishop of Cashel. Errington replied on April 15, that this was very good news indeed because if Rome allowed Croke to get away with his latest foray in the press, the government would undoubtedly break everything off(S). Only the other day, for example, Errington noted, Lord Salisbury, the Conservative leader, had said that "evidently Dr. Croke was master in Ireland, and that the Pope with all his good will was powerless." Rome had, in fact, already decided what it was going to do about the archbishop of Cashel. Cardinal Simeoni had written Croke on April 14, advising him that the pope wished to speak to him about Irish affairs as soon as possible(C).

Croke, who could not have received Simeoni's letter before April 18 or 19, left Dublin on Monday evening, April 23, for Rome. He stayed over a day in London, undoubtedly to have a word with Cardinal Manning, and set out again for Rome on Wednesday evening. When Errington heard that Croke had left for Rome, he immediately wrote Smith from Dublin that he was also on his way. He asked Smith to alert "very privately," the new secretary of Propaganda, Domenico Jacobini, who had succeeded Monsignor Masotti the previous year, "*but tell nobody else.*"[22] Two days later, from London, he again wrote Smith that he was leaving that evening, and that, since Croke had only left the evening before, he would not be long behind him(S). Errington further assured Smith that he had had interesting and important communications with both Spencer and Granville, and the impression produced by summoning Croke was "*excellent* and fully understood." What Errington meant, of course, by "fully understood" was that Rome was anxious to prove its good intentions in Ireland in order to keep up negotiations for diplomatic relations. But Croke would fight hard in Rome, Errington warned Smith, "and if he is allowed to return to Ireland without some public act or expression *he will deny everything* and *go on as before*: he ought to

---

[22] Ignazio Masotti was promoted to the office of "Segretario al Vescovi e Regolari," and was succeeded by Domenico Jacobini, archbishop of Tyre, on March 30, 1882. Msgr. Jacobini should not be confused with his namesake, the cardinal secretary of state. Nicola Kowalsky, O.M.I., "Serie dei Cardinali Prefetti e dei Segretari Della Sacra Congregazione de Propaganda Fide," *Collectio Urbaniana*, Series III, Textus Ac Documenta, 4, p.28 [186].

be made to write a letter to his Clergy from Rome and submit it to the Propaganda." Errington then advised Smith to prepare Monsignor Jacobini for the need to do something effective, for if they did not do so, Croke would beat them after all.

Croke, who arrived in Rome on Sunday, April 29, spent only a few days, and not much is known about what actually transpired between the pope, the authorities and himself. He stayed with Kirby at the Irish College and as one seminarian reported to a friend in Ireland, "We saw very little of him, he did not dine in our company even *once*, and he departed again as suddenly as he came."[23] "Regarding the object of his visit," he then concluded, "wild rumors are afloat and nothing more." The tone of Croke's discussions with the pope and the Roman authorities may be easily surmised from his unusual taciturn mood, while the results of his interviews may be easily determined from what followed.[24] On leaving Rome in early May, however, Croke wisely decided not to return immediately to Ireland.[25] He undoubtedly suspected that some Roman fulmination would soon be produced with regard to the national movement, and concluded that it would be more prudent not to be in Ireland when the storm broke, especially since he would be expected to say something. The famous "Roman Circular," condemning the Parnell Testimonial Fund, therefore, was sent out from Propaganda while Croke was still *en route* to Ireland. The Circular was dated from Rome on May 11, and issued under the signatures of the prefect and secretary of Propaganda, and said in part:

Whatever may be the opinion formed as to Mr. Parnell himself and his objects, it is at all events proved that many of his followers have on many occasions adopted a line of conduct in open contradiction to the rules laid down by the Supreme Pontiff in his letter to the Cardinal Archbishop of Dublin, and contained in the instructions sent to the Irish Bishops by their Sacred Congregation, and unanimously accepted by them at their recent meeting, at Dublin. . . .

It is certainly not forbidden to contribute money for the relief

[23] OR, May, 1883, M. F. Cagney to Michael O'Riordan.

[24] See Michael Davitt, *The Fall of Feudalism in Ireland* (London, 1906), pp. 400-401, for an account of Croke's interview with the pope, given by Croke to Davitt soon after his return from Rome. Davitt's recollection of Croke's account would seem to be highly colored given the action taken by Rome after Croke's interview with the pope.

[25] Croke did not, in fact, return to Ireland until May 23. See *Freeman's Journal*, May 24, 1883.

of distress in Ireland; but at the same time the aforesaid Apostolic mandates absolutely condemn such collections as are got up in order to inflame popular passions, and to be used as the means for leading men into rebellion against the laws. Above all things, such collections should be avoided where it is plain that hatred and dissensions are aroused by them, that distinguished persons are loaded with insults, that never in any way are censures pronounced against the crimes and murders with which wicked men stain themselves; and especially when it is asserted that the measure of true patriotism is in proportion to the amount of money given or refused, so as to bring the people under the pressure of intimidation.

In these circumstances, it must be evident to your Lordship, that the collection called the *"Parnell Testimonial Fund"* cannot be approved by this Sacred Congregation; and consequently it cannot be tolerated that any ecclesiastic, much less a Bishop, should take any part whatever in recommending or promoting it.[26]

The impact of this document on public opinion in Ireland can hardly be described. The clergy were dismayed and the laity were outraged. One of Kirby's former students, for example, wrote him from Roscrea the day after the Circular appeared in the press.[27] "My Lord," the young priest informed Kirby, "it is rather difficult at present to give you any idea of the feelings of the Priests and people over the circular issued lately from Propaganda. They are feelings of *astonishment*, of *almost utter unbelief* that his Holiness would stoop so low as to condemn in particular the 'Parnell Testimonial,' and even of (I use the word expressly) *indignation.*" "I am greatly troubled," he confided further, "about the matter, they speak so severely of it. They say that the Pope must have been deceived by misrepresentations, that it will be the cause of disunion between Priests and people; and that it will do more to injure religion than centuries of persecution." "Some even say," he con-

---

[26] C, May 11, 1883.

[27] K, [May] 17, 1883, W. Rourke to Kirby. See also a letter of MacEvilly to Kirby, January 25, 1883, which gives an insight into the mood of some of the clergy with regard to Rome some four months before the Circular was issued. In complaining that his minor requests were not being attended to in Rome, MacEvilly explained, "I have been really ashamed of the Priests who had asked several privileges for which I applied. One or two of them said to me in a half reproachful manner, 'We collected over £1100 from a starving people and sent it to Rome through Your Grace, and we don't get in return the commonest privilege of even blessing Beads or scapulars to promote the devotion of the Mother of God among our people.' I, of course, checked them. But I must confess I felt it deeply."

cluded in evident wonder, "that, of course, they won't be bound by it. That is what they say. But I hope and pray that they turn out to be false prophets."

By the time Kirby had received this rather disturbing letter, however, Croke had finally arrived in Paris where he decided to make a public statement. The occasion for his remarks was the presenting of an address of welcome to him on May 21, at the Irish College where he was staying. The *Freeman's Journal* reported on May 22, that in acknowledging the compliment paid him, Croke replied with "a short, pithy speech." "I come back from Rome," Croke maintained, "as I went to Rome— unchangeable and unchanged." "They asserted," Croke further declared, challenging the current rumors in the press, "that I was received coldly at Rome, when the fact is I was never received more warmly in my life. I was not summoned to Rome *ad audiendum verbum*. I was rebuked neither by the Supreme Pontiff nor by any member of the College of Cardinals." "In my interview with Pope Leo," Croke noted in conclusion, "I simply explained the Irish question in all its varying phases, and my explanations were listened to with respect." When Croke was then asked what the results of his mission to Rome might be said to be, he was reported as indirectly hinting that "they might not be construed as at present very favourable to what his Lordship called 'the National cause of Ireland.'" He went on to ridicule the idea, however, that there was anything seriously damaging to the National League in the recent Circular, and added that he was personally as unshaken in his political beliefs as he had ever been. Croke then finally concluded his remarks by assuring those present that the "voice of the Vatican would always be heard by him, and its commands strictly carried out."

The response, in private at least, of even the most conservative of the Irish bishops, however, was a good deal more qualified than Croke's public statement about Rome and its commands. The bishop of Kerry, Andrew Higgins, whose appointment some eighteen months before the British government had done so much to secure, wrote Kirby, for example, about ten days after the Circular appeared, that it "seems to have greatly ruffled the public mind in Ireland if we are to take the language and notions of 'public men' as a measure of that mind." Higgins further explained, in his letter of May 26, that the fund had certainly been stimulated by the condemnation, and strange to say, the names of priests from different dioceses still appeared among the subscribers, though perhaps they were made before the Circular was received. "At all events," he maintained, "the fact looks awkward, and enables the promoters of the Fund to assume a tone, and to use language, they would otherwise hardly venture on: And it embarrasses those who mean to stand by the instructions of the Holy See." Higgins thought that the feeling roused by the Circular was not the result of any damage done the Parnell Testimonial Fund, but rather that Rome was treating the fund as part and parcel of the agitation. In a word, it was the agitation Rome was aiming at and not the fund. And though the leadership of the agitation was still suspect in his mind, Higgins admitted that the substantial grievances of the tenant farmers had been redressed. In fact, their position had been so much improved that they now set no limits to their hopes. "But," he added significantly, "as *their* interest is the great interest in our agricultural country, they raise the whole country with themselves." Peace was now, Higgins concluded, the one necessary and sufficient condition for prosperity.

In writing Kirby some days later on May 30, from the West of Ireland, Archbishop MacEvilly indicated, though discreetly, that he was not finding the clergy very tractable about the Circular.

> When priests now speak to me, my only answer is, "Rome has spoken, our duty is simple hearty obedience." I am sorry to say, however, that the great majority of the Priests have strong feelings; but our duty, as Bishops, is to keep them down, a thing which requires vigour with prudence. Right or wrong, the people are under the impression that it was owing to Parnell's action they have been rescued from the direst tyranny ever endured by a people from the Landlord class. I myself don't join in that view, but nothing could remove it from the minds of the Tenantry at large. . . .I myself can never pardon Parnell his putting in a worthless Presbyterian Minister to represent Catholic Mayo, and many other slights offered the Clergy not to speak of his alleged association with French reds and Atheists, and hence I can never be brought to honour him(K).

An English bishop had recently asked him, MacEvilly added, whether he thought that a pronouncement by the English and Irish bishops about the Circular would do any good. He had pointed out that it "would do *irreparable mischief* at this *moment* and especially if the English Bishops spoke." MacEvilly thought that the proper course was that each bishop should be responsible for enforcing the Circular in his own diocese because the pope's authority was not dependent on any epis-copal consensus. In taking this very sensible line, MacEvilly obviously hoped the whole matter would be allowed to drop, but he reckoned without either the Irish abroad or the laity at home.

The reaction of the Irish abroad, who always tended to be more radical than their brethren at home, may be easily gauged from the remarks of the bishop of Dunedin in New Zealand. "By the way," he wrote Kirby on June 4, "I regret exceeding that His Eminence sent the now famous circular to the Irish Bishops."[28] "Irish Catholics," he pointed out, "are loyal to the Holy See, but I assure you they know how to draw a distinction between what they owe to the Vicar of Christ, and to themselves and their country. It is a distinction they *were not* fond of making, and it is greatly to be regretted that the recent action of Propaganda has given occasion to them to make it now in a very marked manner." "I assure you, My Dear Lord," he solemnly informed Kirby, "that the general charges of neglect in denouncing crime in Ireland, and the personal assault on Mr. Parnell, have roused a very bitter feeling and tempted Irishmen to entertain unfilial sentiments, not against the Holy Father, but certain Roman officials who are charged with having permitted themselves to be misled and with hav-ing misrepresented such affairs to His Holiness." "It is al-together," he concluded candidly, "a deplorable business."

The outrage of the Irish abroad, however, was as nothing compared to the concentrated fury of the laity at home who felt they had been betrayed by Rome. The tone and temper of the articulate laity may be best gauged perhaps from the most Catholic of the nationalist journals, the *Nation*. "There is," it declared rather dramatically on May 19, "evil and disastrous news from Rome. Never since the priceless Treasure of the Faith was brought to our Irish shore has so terrible a stroke been dealt at religion in Ireland as it is our lot to chronicle today."[29] "The deadly intrigues of England," the article charged, "have triumphed at the Propaganda.The sword is

---

[28] K, June 4, 1883, Patrick Moran to Kirby. The bishop of Dunedin was only a namesake and no relation to Patrick F. Moran, the bishop of Ossory.

[29] *Nation* (Dublin), "The Roman Letter," May 19, 1883.

drawn on our faithful devoted prelates and priests. As we have through blood and fire held our Faith against England, so we shall at all human price hold our country against Rome. We will not desert our priests and prelates, they will not desert us." "A letter," it explained, "has been addressed by the Propaganda to our Irish prelates, in which the inconceivable outrage is offered to our country of mixing up crimes and disorders wholly abominable, and detested by all good Catholics and good citizens, with the justifiable and legitimate political warfare waged by the Irish people for the defence of their lives and the recovery of their just rights." "If Rome," the article concluded with a defiant warning, "will enter into an unholy alliance with England against us, then, trusting in the help of the good God, we shall stand for the national rights and liberties of Ireland against Rome and England."

In the following weeks the *Nation* continued the onslaught on Rome and its Circular by reviewing for its readers the celebrated struggle over the veto demanded by the British government in the appointment of Irish bishops as the *quid pro quo* for Catholic emancipation.[30] Needless to say, the story was retold to the greater disadvantage of England and Rome than ever. More serious, however, were a series of some twenty-three very pungent letters published by "An Irish Catholic Layman," in the *Nation* between May and November.[31] The series which began with a denunciation of the Circular, went on to denounce those "Castle Bishops," who had failed Ireland as publicists, patriots, and educators. The "Castle Bishops" designated by name were the late Cardinal Cullen and those who continued to follow in his wake, McCabe, MacEvilly, and Gillooly. McCabe, who was still recuperating, was very upset about all this early comment by the press and individuals on the Roman Circular. In his first letter to Kirby after his heart attack, acknowledging some Roman documents, on June 18, McCabe wrote:

Nothing could prove more clearly the bad effects of Modern Journalism and popular platform oratory than the insolent wickedness of some of the so called leaders of the country in

_____

[30] *Ibid.*, "The Veto," May 26, 1883. "The Veto and the Circular," June 2, 1883.
[31] *Letters of an Irish Catholic Layman, Being an Examination of the Present State of Irish Affairs in Relation to the Irish Church and the Holy See* (Dublin, 1883-1884). Reprinted from the *Nation*.

reference to the last letter from Propaganda. Mr. Healy who is going to present himself to the Catholic electors of Monaghan made himself conspicuous amongst his fellows by designating it "an Idiotic Circular" and I fear the Catholics of Monaghan will elect him. We may all well pray "God Save Ireland"(K).

When Kirby received this letter, he immediately wrote James Donnelly, the bishop of Clogher, in whose diocese the Monaghan election was to take place. In his reply on July 1, Donnelly informed Kirby that he had spoken to Healy even before he had received his letter from Rome. "I insisted," Donnelly explained, in his account of the interview with Healy, "that he must make a public *amende* or that I could have no relations with him. He said he had done so privately and that he intended to do it publicly after the election. I said he must do it *publicly* and *at once* or take the consequences. He consented; and on the day following, June 24th, at a large public meeting in the centre of the most Catholic district in the County, he did so." Though Donnelly had done his duty with regard to Healy, that he did not much relish such duty was made amply clear in the rest of his letter to Kirby. "After his making this perhaps important *amende*," Donnelly further explained, "I offered no further opposition to Mr. Healy's candidature. To oppose the almost unanimous (I might say *perfectly unanimous*) wish of my people might have serious consequences." "I wish there were some agency for making the Roman Authorities aware of the real state of affairs in Ireland," he then declared warmly, "and of the grinding oppression *still* exercised by a Government at the head of which stands Mr. Gladstone the enemy of Catholicity and the papacy and the friend and panegyrist of Garibaldi and every rebel and revolutionist in other lands." "I shall say no more," he abruptly concluded, "on this topic just now." "I hope and trust," he added grimly in a postscript, "that your Lordship will communicate the substance of the foregoing note to my ecclesiastical superiors in Rome."

Rome was obviously shaken by these reports, if received, of the reception of its Circular in Ireland, for Cardinal Simeoni wrote Moran about a month after its publication, asking him for his opinion. When Kirby wrote Moran that the cardinal was pleased with what he had written, he obviously also inquired what collective action the Bishops proposed to take with regard to the Circular. Moran replied on June 27, that the bishops would hold their general meeting in Dublin the following week, and one of the items on the agenda was the Circular(K). "I have not had any conversation," he explained, "with my brother Prelates on the matter. Indeed, everyone is rather disposed to observe silence about it, and when we are all called on to give our opinion, it is not at all easy to know what course to suggest." "So far as regards the dissensions among the Clergy," Moran added, giving a glimpse of what must have gone into his letter to Cardinal Simeoni, "and dealing of the Clergy with political matters, the Circular will do good."

> The delicate point is where it touches on the Parnell Testimonial. The Parnell Collection has gone on in every part of the country and will soon be £20,000. In fact, the Circular instead of injuring this Collection, gave a fresh impulse to many persons to contribute to it. This Collection being regarded as purely a political matter many are of opinion that the Propaganda stepped beyond its province by interfering in it and that the authorities there permitted themselves to be led astray by interested political advisors(K).

"However," Moran concluded more prudently and piously, "good will eventually come from the whole transaction and with the blessing of God, no harm will be done to the devoted faith of our good people."

The Irish bishops, as Moran pointed out to Kirby, certainly seemed disposed to observe silence with regard to the Circular. Kirby, however, who was not of like mind, had actually been indiscreet enough to write Croke on June 26, hinting that the Irish bishops should issue some joint pronouncement on the Irish Church and her problems at their next meeting(C). Croke, who does not appear to have replied, decided to avoid the problem of having to consider or comment on the Circular by simply not attending the meeting. Furthermore, when the bishops did meet in Dublin on July 4-5, ten other bishops besides Croke were also absent. In reporting the proceedings to Kirby on July 7, Moran tried to explain rather lamely that the summons for the meeting was not issued in proper time and many of the bishops were engaged in Diocesan work which could not be conveniently postponed(K). "On account of so many Prelates being absent," he concluded, "nothing was done in regard to the Circular. Indeed the matter was not even spoken of during our Meeting but I suppose it will come on at the stated Annual General Meeting in October." On October 3, however, less than a week before the episcopal meeting, an obviously embarrassed Moran wrote Kirby again(K). "No notice," he confessed "has been put in the *Agenda* list of any reply to the letters of His Holiness, but it is quite possible that such a matter of primary importance may be brought forward without any formal notice." When Moran did not write as he usually did immediately after the meeting, Kirby was forced to write asking what indeed had happened, and why had he not written. "I did not write you," Moran replied, somewhat testily, on October 27, "from our Dublin Meeting as I had nothing particular to write to you about. The most important business which engaged the attention of the General Meeting was the putting Catholic University College, Stephens Green, on a proper footing"(K).

In issuing the Circular, it is now easy to understand that Rome committed a blunder of the first magnitude. For well over two years Rome had been attempting to endow the archbishop of Dublin with the requisite authority necessary to effect its will in the Irish Church. That Rome, then, should have chosen the moment when their focus of power was incapacitated by illness to take precipitate action almost borders on the incomprehensible. Why Rome acted so, of course, is not explained simply by the fact that the authorities at Propaganda were finally exasperated by Croke and lost their tempers. This was the occasion rather than the cause. The real reason for the issuing of the Circular was that the pope and his advisers were finally stampeded by Errington and Smith at a critical moment in the interest of reestablishing diplomatic relations. Why they were stampeded, of course, was not simply that they had now lost their focus of power in McCabe, but that they felt the publication of the McCabe-Jacobini correspondence the previous December had seriously impaired their credibility with British public opinion. They hoped, therefore, by taking drastic action in Ireland, to repair the damage done to their image in December with the British public. From Rome's own point of view, the consequences, whatever may be said about the causes, were indeed very sad.

By her action, Rome had turned the uneasiness so often expressed by the Irish clergy, high and low, into a quiet estrangement if not, in fact, into a silent hostility.[32] Further, the suspicions and fears of the Irish people were galvanized by Rome's action into an outright and bitter defiance. Worst of all, Rome had defeated her own purpose by giving the British government a concrete example of the effective limits of Roman authority and power in Ireland.

---

[32] K, July 22, 1883, MacEvilly to Kirby. There is some evidence that some of the lower clergy went further than silent hostility. "In some Dioceses, scandalous latitude has been allowed to some priests in reference to the Circular. I don't understand why their Bishops did not compel them to retract and apologise. I have no such complaint to make. But I told my priests if any of them wrote certain letters, I would compel them to retract or suspend them. I have not been put to it."

Part II

THE CLERICAL-NATIONALIST ALLIANCE

VII. Rapprochement

May, 1883 - August, 1884

After the disastrous reception of its Circular in Ireland, Rome began the painful and necessary task of facing up to the realities of the situation created by her precipitate action. That the British government was not really interested in re-establishing diplomatic relations was now patent, and that the Irish Church was seriously alienated was undeniable. The problem for Rome, therefore, was how to disengage discreetly from the British government, while at the same time repair its power and influence in the Irish Church. That double process was largely effected through Rome's control over Irish episcopal appointments over the next two years. The process, in fact, was actually begun with the appointment of Thomas Carr as bishop of Galway towards the end of May, 1883.[1] In early January, the clergy of Galway, Kilmacduagh, and Kilfenora had commended the customary three names to Rome. Thomas Carr, vice-president of Maynooth, had received twelve votes, while Father Fahy, P. P. of Peterswell near Gort, and Father J. J. Carbery, a Dominican then living in Rome, both received four votes. When the names were submitted to the bishops of the province of Tuam, the bishops had "*unanimously* and *earnestly*" recommended Carr.[2] Nearly three months later, however, MacEvilly wrote Kirby that he and his suffragans were all anxious about their recommendation of Carr for Galway in their report to Propaganda. "The non-appointment of Dr. Carr," he explained on April 14, "will cause immense amazement, the more so, as his political views *have always* been *most moderate*, indeed more *conservative* than otherwise, and this the Card'l Apb of Dublin who knows him well would testify to"(K).

---

[1] Sir F. Maurice Powicke and E. B. Fryde (eds.), *Handbook of British Chronology* (London, 1961), p. 410. The official date of Carr's provision is June 5, 1883. See also K, MacEvilly to Kirby, May 30, 1883, thanking him for the early news of Carr's appointment.

[2] K. January 25, 1883, MacEvilly to Kirby.

Why Propaganda delayed in the appointment of Carr, of course, was because Errington and Smith were working hard to secure the appointment of Father Carbery, who not only had the advantage of living in Rome, but was liked and trusted by the authorities. Without good cause, however, Propaganda was obviously having difficulty in overriding the commendation of the majority of the clergy and the unanimous report of the bishops. By early April, in fact, Propaganda no longer seemed disposed to delay in the appointment of Carr, for Errington wrote Smith on April 15 that he was very sorry to hear that their plans had been upset with regard to the appointment to Galway. He pointed out that he was on his way to Dublin to see Spencer, but that he could now no longer tell the government that anybody they objected to would not be made a bishop. Spencer, however, does not appear to have either known very much about the proposed names for Galway, nor does he seem to have been as much concerned in the matter as Errington wanted it to appear. "Errington has been here," Spencer wrote Granville on April 20, from Dublin Castle,

> he was full of the Galway Bishopric & wanted to write to Rome to say that in conversation with me he found that I was strongly in favor of McCabe's Policy, & that I desired that his supporters should be made Bishops & he therefore urged with increased earnestness his support of Priest of the Regular Order instead of the Maynooth man. I said that though I cordially agreed in this view, I considered the question of the relations with Rome so delicate, that I did not like that I should be directly quoted in a matter of this sort without your knowledge, & I therefore suggested that before sending the letter you shall see it.[3]

Spencer went on to explain to Granville that a direct recommendation by the government for a bishopric was a far more serious matter than a general opinion expressed about such an appointment by a member of the government. Such an opinion, on which a recommendation by Errington could be based, might be forwarded to Rome if Granville approved. Spencer concluded, however, by pointing out he knew nothing about the candidates proposed for Galway.

Granville approved Spencer's suggestion, and Errington telegraphed Smith and wrote Monsignor Jacobini at Prop-

---

[3] GR, 30/29/142.

aganda. He explained to Smith in a letter on April 24, from Dublin, that his telegram had been submitted to both Granville and Spencer, and that he should inform Monsignor Jacobini confidentially that this gave it great weight. Jacobini, meanwhile, had written Errington that Rome had decided to take action against Croke, for Errington asked Smith on April 26, from London, to thank Jacobini for his most important letter, which "came at the right moment and has *been very much valued* here." Errington also expressed the hope that they would not decide Galway until he arrived. Propaganda did not, in fact, make its recommendation of Dr. Carr to the pope for Galway for nearly a month. By that time, however, not only the repercussions from the Circular had been heard in Rome, but more important, Errington's enthusiasm about the good intentions of the British government with regard to diplomatic relations was less appreciated by the pope and his advisers, especially since the government refused to allow Errington even to thank the pope for his recent good offices in Ireland. Errington, in fact, had made one desperate last effort by telegraphing Granville through Paget on May 22, from Rome:

> Following from E.—The Pope has been so anxious for some comment or expression from you about his letter, that I hope you will send me a few friendly words for him by telegraph. He is behaving admirably, and would be much pained at entire silence on your part.[4]

Granville wired unhelpfully in reply two days later, on May 24:

> Received telegram 22—; I purposely avoided sending any message respecting the censure. Undesirable that anything should be done to take away the character of spontaniety. I rightly expected that question would be asked in Parliament, but our sense of the importance of the step is great. Give nothing in writing on the subject.[5]

When the pope finally and formally "provided" Carr for Galway on June 5, Errington no longer had any real reason for remaining in Rome and returned to London to take up his

[4] B, 49690.
[5] *Ibid.*

parliamentary duties. The pope, however, must have been, to say the least, very upset by the way in which he had been snubbed by the British government. He had risked much by his late extraordinary action in Ireland, and had paid a very high price in Irish good will. For the next three years he would diligently pursue Rome's interest rather than Britain's interest in Ireland, therefore, and in his dealings with the British government, the pope would play the difficult game of diplomacy with ever greater skill and much cunning. The first task faced by the pope and his advisers, however, was how to restructure Roman power and influence in the Irish Church.

Shortly after the appointment to Galway was finally made, the pope and his advisers were presented with the opportunity to begin restructuring their power and influence. "For a considerable time," McCabe confidentially wrote Kirby on June 26, from Harrogate, where he was convalescing, "I felt that to be able to administer the Diocese as it should be administered I [would] require help." "The feeling of those whom I have consulted, and it is my own feeling also," he then explained, "is that I should humbly petition for that help through the Ministry of a Bishop *Auxiliary* such as I had the happiness of being to our late dear Cardinal. But of course this is a matter which the wisdom of the H. Father will determine." "Will you therefore at your convenience," McCabe asked Kirby, "speak to His Eminence Cardinal Simeoni on the matter, and let me know his instructions in this important business." "I don't know what form is to be adopted in the case of an auxiliary," McCabe concluded, "but if the nomination of the person is any way vested with me I think I have in my mind a good laborious priest who would give satisfaction and manage the Diocese." In less than a week and a half, rumors were abroad about the auxiliary for Dublin. In writing Kirby on July 7, explaining that McCabe was expected home about the end of the month, Moran added that he expected that an application for an auxiliary would be made by the cardinal at that time, and that he would probably select Canon Nicholas Walshe, parish priest of SS. Michael and John in Dublin.

When Kirby presented McCabe's petition, Cardinal Simeoni asked Kirby to write in his name to several of the Irish bishops, requesting them to present names for the Dublin post. "I have written today," Moran reported to Kirby on July 20, "to the Cardinal Prefect asking him to appoint the Rev. Nicholas Walshe to that important and highly responsible office"(K). After citing his reasons for recommending Walshe, Moran added that he did not like to nominate anyone else because he was not quite sure whether they would suit McCabe. But if Simeoni insisted, he was prepared to recommend Monsignor Edward Kennedy and Canon Nicholas Donnelly, both excellent Dublin priests. Kirby had also written MacEvilly, but the archbishop of Tuam was not very helpful. "I can hardly," MacEvilly explained on July 22, "see my way. I don't know the Dublin clergy well, and the appointment is one of great responsibility considering the state of Dublin and the dangerous times"(K). If he were pressed, MacEvilly added, there was one man he would point to, and that was William J. Walsh, the president of Maynooth. "For learning, zeal, industry, indefatigable vigilance," MacEvilly maintained, "he has no equal." But how Walsh's nomination would please McCabe, MacEvilly admitted that he did not know.

Cardinal McCabe, meanwhile, had returned to Dublin and was proceeding about the business of selecting a name to send on to Propaganda, blithely unaware that he had, in fact, opened a veritable Pandora's box by his petition for an auxiliary. "Since I wrote to you last," McCabe reported to Kirby on July 26, "I told the members of the Chapter that I was about to ask for an assistant and although it is a matter in which their formal votes could not be received, I asked them to help me by their *opinions*"(K). "These opinions," he explained rather innocently, "I have received, and, although the names of some of those mentioned belong to men who by their old age or from circumstances would not suit for the office we are speaking of, yet on the whole the opinion of the Chapter proves that the members are deeply interested in the matter and approve of my intention." The following day, Matthew Quinn, the bishop of Bathurst in Australia, and an old friend of Kirby's who was visiting in Ireland, reported that McCabe had indeed asked the members of his chapter to submit three names each. But since no one except the cardinal knew who was recommended, and since the cardinal, moreover, was not bound by the opinion of his chapter, it was difficult to say anything definitely, but it generally was believed that he would recommend Nicholas Walshe(K).

At this point, Rome upset all expectations. Some time in the last week in July or the first week in August, the pope was persuaded that the archbishop of Dublin should have a coadjutor, with the right of succession, rather than an auxiliary. Kirby broke the news gently to McCabe, for the cardinal replied on August 9, thanking him for his kind letter(K). McCabe explained that he had heard nothing on the matter from Cardinal Simeoni and he was therefore obliged to trouble Kirby again.

> I need not tell you that I will bow implicitly to the decision of His Holiness. Yet I feel obliged in duty to say a word in the matter before it is too late: I *am greatly concerned* about the future if the Coadjutor is to be appointed; and I believe my fears are those of the wiser part of the Clergy of the Diocese: Names are already freely mentioned for the list of three which I simply could not get on: All good men but between whom and me there could be no sympathy of·opinions(K).

"I imagined," he remarked a little petulantly in closing, "that the H.F. would have done for me what he did for His late Eminence." "However," he concluded piously, if not prudently, "as I have relieved my conscience by this letter I will leave the whole matter to God."

Few others, however, seemed willing to leave the whole matter to God. Moran reported to Kirby on August 14, from Kilkenny, that a priest from Dublin who had just passed through informed him that McCabe had received the news officially that he was to have a coadjutor rather than an auxiliary, but that the only delay in the holding of the necessary election in a *terna* was the absence of so many parish priests on vacation. Moran then further explained that there was a great deal of anxiety about the appointment because so much of the welfare of the Irish Church at home and abroad depended on it. He hoped that Propaganda would make the appointment without delay because there would undoubtedly "be any amount of intrigue on the part of English agents to influence the Holy See in its decision." He did not know what names would be forwarded by the Dublin clergy, Moran confessed somewhat ingenuously, but he had been told that some were determined to vote for Monsignor Henry Neville, the late rector of the Catholic University. He warned Kirby that the government would strain every nerve to secure Neville's appointment, but that he trusted the Propaganda would make no such recommendation. Moran then informed Kirby archly that there was also "great speculation as to the motives of Propaganda in altering its arrangement about granting an Auxiliary." He assured Kirby that he thought Propaganda acted wisely, and presumed even more ingenuously that the reason they did so was that they were being importuned by English agents about some name which they did not approve.

A few days after he had written to Kirby on August 19, McCabe wrote Cardinal Simeoni explaining that he would still prefer to have an auxiliary rather than a coadjutor, and that if the letter of the cardinal prefect, which he had been advised by Kirby as being on its way, arrived in the meantime, he would presume not to act on it until he heard from Simeoni again.[6] When McCabe did receive Simeoni's letter, therefore, he did not act on it. In waiting for Simeoni's reply, McCabe wrote Kirby again on August 25, attempting to clarify his stand against accepting a coadjutor(K). He had no objection in principle to a coadjutor, McCabe explained, "but it is quite possible a name or names may go to Rome against which I will be compelled to write *very strongly* to Propaganda. This will be most unpleasant work, but I must do it out of a sense of duty to myself and the Diocese: The parties whom I have in mind are holy and learned, but simply out of harmony with my views and opinions." "I have not the smallest ambition," McCabe maintained firmly in conclusion, "to occupy my present position which has been one of intense anxiety and in a contingency which may occur I would ask the H. See to allow me to retire and prepare myself for death which cannot be far from me." What McCabe meant by all this, of course, was that he was afraid that one of the names that would inevitably appear on the *terna* recommended by the Dublin clergy would be Moran's, and that neither he nor his clergy wanted him. Moreover, if indeed Rome insisted on appointing Moran as his coadjutor, McCabe was determined in that "contingency" to retire.

Early in September, however, McCabe's anxieties were finally laid to rest when he received a letter from Cardinal Simeoni explaining that in conformity with his expressed

---

[6] K, August 19, 1883. McCabe to Kirby.

wish, he was to have an auxiliary rather than a coadjutor, and would he please forward the appropriate name at his convenience. Some three weeks later a more relaxed and benign McCabe informed Kirby that he was preparing to forward a name to the pope that same day for consideration as his auxiliary(K). "As you may well imagine," he concluded pointedly, "this is a delicate work, and one requiring great caution; but I trust God will direct all things right." Kirby's position of trust at Rome had certainly not been much improved with either McCabe or the Dublin clergy by this imbroglio over an auxiliary or a coadjutor. If Kirby had any doubts about his stock in Dublin, however, he was soon disabused of them by the letter he received from his Vice Rector, Michael Verdon, who was again in Ireland attempting to raise money for the Irish College. "I am afraid," he complained to Kirby on September 22,

> that the whole business has been badly managed. It is very unfortunate that there was any talk at all about the election of a Coadjutor for it seems to have done a great deal of harm. It seems to have irritated the Authorities in Dublin very much—though they have it all their own way now—and to have made them more anti-Rome or at least anti-Irish College. It was plainly stated that the attempt at a Coadjutor was entirely your work in order to get in Dr. Moran—and there seems to be a corresponding feeling in certain quarters against Dr. Moran and ourselves. Indeed, some people seem to think the Irish College is the headquarters of intrigue against the existing authorities in Dublin(K).

"Though I was received in a very friendly manner at first," Verdon then concluded bitterly, "I did not receive the *slightest mark of attention* from the authorities in Dublin since the question was started, and a priest told me that certain persons were quite astonished that I did not resign my place in the Chapter as I was living in Rome—probably they thought I was over to vote."

When Kirby informed Moran that the name forwarded by McCabe was that of Canon Nicholas Donnelly, Moran replied that Rome need not have the slightest hesitation in sanctioning his appointment.[7] When the pope appointed Donnelly, McCabe wrote Kirby on October 14, that his new assistant, who

---

[7] K, October 3, 1883.

had served as his curate many years before, would indeed be a great consolation to him. The crucial question, of course, is why did Rome choose to opt for a coadjutor rather than an auxiliary for Dublin. There is no evidence, for example, to support Moran's contention that the British government was interfering either in the interest of Monsignor Neville or anyone else. All the circumstantial evidence, in fact, seems to point in the other direction, for Spencer and Granville's reluctance to interfere in the Galway appointment in April was certainly not indicative of a government still being diplomatically *engagé*.[8] Far more credible was the charge of intrigue on the part of Kirby in the interest of Moran. Still, the Propaganda authorities must have approved of Kirby's cautious efforts on behalf of Moran, for they were well aware, and especially Cardinal Simeoni, of his deep commitment to Moran's ecclesiastical prospects. Why Rome wanted a coadjutor, with the right of succession in Dublin, of course, was that it needed to stabilize in its own interest a rapidly deteriorating situation in Ireland.

If Roman influence in the Irish Church was to be maintained, an ultramontane archbishop of Dublin was absolutely necessary. Dublin was, for financial and geographical reasons, the center and focus of ecclesiastical power in Ireland. Now that Cardinal McCabe's end was threatening, Moran was, from Rome's point of view, the most attractive candidate for Dublin. The cardinal, however, and the largest and most influential part of his clergy, were determined in their opposition to Moran. The Dublin clergy, who had overwhelmingly rejected Moran less than five years before, encouraged the cardinal in favor of an auxiliary because they realized that, if there was an election, they could not prevent Moran's name from appearing on the *terna*, and that his appointment would be then a foregone conclusion. Once McCabe had firmly set his face against a coadjutor in favor of an auxiliary, Cardinal Simeoni

---

[8] Dilke Papers, British Museum, Add. MS, 43912, fol. 140. See note in Dilke's hand, dated February 27, 1883, "Errington wants to congratulate the Pope on 1st March. Fitzmaurice violently opposed." Edmund Fitzmaurice had just replaced Dilke, who had entered Cabinet as president of the Local Government Board, as undersecretary for foreign affairs. March 1 was the fifth anniversary of Leo XIII's succession as pope. See also Dilke's Memoirs, Add. MS, 43937, fol. 71: "On the 27th [February, 1883] Errington having applied for leave to offer congratulations to the Pope on the 1st of March in connection with some anniversary and on behalf of the British Govt, the matter was discussed, with the feeling that if it were to be allowed Mr. Gladstone would have much difficulty in explaining away the things which he had said about 'the Errington Mission.'"

was placed in a very difficult situation. To have forced a coadjutor on McCabe would have been an example of the rankest ingratitude on the part of Rome to the man who above all others had championed her cause in Ireland at great personal cost during the past five years, and further alienated the clergy who were coming to expect only the worst from Rome. The pope therefore decided to bide his time, and sanctioned the appointment of an auxiliary.   .

Moran, however, was shattered by this second rejection by the Dublin clergy and Rome. This frustration of what was his deepest personal ambition, to be archbishop of Dublin, was the reason why he consented within six months to leave Ireland for Australia and become the Archbishop of Sydney. When he learned that the bishops of the Province of New South Wales had presented his name to Rome for Sydney, along with those of William J. Walsh, president of Maynooth, and James Murray, bishop of Maitland, he wrote Kirby a most interesting and revealing letter.[9] "I will ask you," he wrote on December 6, "to take no part whatever in promoting that appointment. If the Propaganda asks me to go I will go, as I know that the Holy Father's will in the matter is God's will, and for my part I am quite indifferent as to the field of labor that may be assigned to me for the few years of pilgrimage that remain"(K). Walsh, however, who was second on the list for Sydney, was determined not to go. He was not only happy as president of Maynooth, but since he was the popular candidate among the Dublin clergy to succeed McCabe, the future was obviously brighter at home. Walsh also appears to have been much appreciated by McCabe, for the cardinal wrote him reassuringly on December 22, "I have heard of three names for Sydney— but I have heard of no others—yours, Dr. Moran's and Dr. Murray's. We could not afford to lose the President of Maynooth. I know nothing of Dr. Murray's episcopal life, but with his long experience of Australian life, it would seem to me that he would have the best claim."[10] "In *confidence*," McCabe

---

[9] K, October 2, 1883, James Murray to Kirby. Murray reported that the bishops of the Australian province of New South Wales had met on September 21, and chosen Moran, Walsh, and himself for the *terna* to be presented to Propaganda. Murray then explained that his name was included in the *terna* "solely with the view of excluding any Englishman in case neither Dr. Moran nor Dr. Walsh could be induced to come." Murray further informed Kirby that he was also writing to Cardinal Simeoni to make out a strong case for Moran.

[10] Patrick J. Walsh, *William J. Walsh, Archbishop of Dublin* (Dublin, 1928), p. 130.

concluded, and referring to Moran, "I think the owner of the second name would scarcely suit."

On January 7, 1884, Moran reported to McCabe that Cardinal Simeoni had written him asking him whether he would consent to go to Sydney(Mc). "I am, thanks be to God," Moran confessed, "wholly indifferent about the matter so far as my own sentiments are concerned. However, I fear that I have not strength enough for such a vast field of spiritual labour, and I dare say there is no other place where I could do less harm than in Ossory." Several days later McCabe wrote Walsh again reporting that Moran had written to him.[11] "I believe he is quite indifferent," McCabe observed dryly, "He says he fears he is not strong enough. But I dare say the interpretation of it all is that he will accept." When the official news of Moran's appointment to Sydney reached Ireland, McCabe politely wrote to congratulate the new archbishop. "I am most grateful for your very kind words," Moran replied on March 25, "It is to be sure a great change to pass from this very quiet Diocese to the vast world at the Antipodes"(Mc). "But He who sends me thither," he continued, still in a mood of deep resignation, "will not fail, I hope, to do His own work." "There is one very cheering feature," he concluded, perking up a little, "all the Bishops of the province almost without exception are old acquaintances, and I am sure I may rely on their prudent counsel and direction."

For some time, the venerable bishop of Cork, William Delany, had also been cautiously exploring the possibility of asking the pope for help in the management of his diocese. His heart's desire was to have his old friend and dean, Monsignor Henry Neville, former rector of the Catholic University, appointed as his coadjutor or auxiliary. He was worried, however, that the powerful enemies the monsignor had made of late among the Irish bishops by his open and avowed opposition to the Land League, and his support of Cardinal McCabe in the recent controversy over the fellowships in the Royal University, might be able to frustrate his appointment. Delany had, in fact, gone so far as to confide his fears to Cardinal Simeoni in the early fall of 1883, and had been reassured by the cardinal that

---

[11] *Ibid.*

the Propaganda "always consulted for the satisfaction of the *Coadjutus* in an application for a Coadjutor."[12] Reassured by Simeoni and heartened by McCabe's most recent experience in Dublin, Delany finally decided in October to make application.[13]

When it was announced early in January, 1884, that the voting for a coadjutor would take place later in the month, the problem for those opposed to Neville was to find a candidate strong enough to make a respectable showing on the *terna*. The technique adopted by the Cork priests was worthy of the traditional lore about Cork men. "You must be doubtless aware already," T. Murray, P. P., Drimoleague, County Cork, studiously wrote Kirby on January 7, "that the Bishop of Cork has received authority from His Holiness Leo XIII to assemble his priests to elect a Coadjutor Bishop for the diocese"(K). "A large body of the Parish Priests of the diocese," Murray went on to point out, "are conscientiously considering the claims and qualifications of the priest submitted as fit for this high and holy dignity and amongst them is Father O'Callaghan, the Prior of the Dominican Order, at present and for sometime past resident in Rome." "You may consider this application rather strange on the part of a total stranger," he continued, after asking Kirby for his opinion of Father O'Callaghan, "but my Lord I have been always hearing of your piety and devotedness to the cause of religion and the church, so that I don't know any better authority to apply to when there is a question of promoting the interest of peace and religion."

Kirby's reply to Murray, on January 11, was, in its way, a classic example of ecclesiastical rhetoric:

> Your esteemed letter has just come to hand, in wh. you are pleased to solicit that I wd. give you my opn as to the fitns of the Reverend F. O'Calln Dominican, for the office of Coadjutor Bishop of Cork. Although deeply conscious of the little value that my poor opn can have, I dare not refuse to give it to you, such as it is, with the humble confidence that the Divine Lord by his heavenly light may supply all its defects and guide you and your brethrn to select one for the most important dignity in question best adapted for the requirements of your diocese.

---

[12] S, Easter Sunday, 1884, Neville to Errington. This long letter is a most detailed history of the whole Cork affair.

[13] K, October 31, 1883, Delany to Kirby.

I have known the Reverend Father O'C. since his arrival in
Rome and have had many opportunities of studying his character, and the favorable impression which his first appearance
made on me went on increasing by every subsequent interview
with him. My sincere and candid opinion of him is, that he is a
pious and learned and prudent man, sincerely devoted to religion and the salvation of souls, and at the same time humble and
unassuming in his bearing and deportment and that to a degree
as to conciliate the respect and confidence of all who approach
him. It is my conviction that should the Clergy of your Diocese
succeed in obtaining him from the Holy See as their Coadjutor
Bishop they will not only never repent of their choice, but will
have the merit and consolation of having given a pastor to their
Diocese according to God's own heart and an additional bulwark
and ornament to the Irish Hierarchy.

The matter of the nomination of a subject who is to be one day
Bishop of your Diocese is a matter of the most grave importance,
not only for the peculiar circumstances to which you allude, but
also for the general importance of Cork itself, the second city in
Ireland, and of its Diocese and of the influence which it must
necessarily have on the general interests of religion in the entire
nation. May our Divine Lord in His Holy Spirit guide you Reverend Sir and your venerable colleagues to make in their wisdom such a selection in this weighty business as will be conducive
to the great object they have in view—God's Glory in the salvation
of souls and the advantage and decorum of their Diocese and of
the entire Church of Ireland(K).

Why was Kirby so imprudent as to write this unprecedented
open letter to the Cork clergy, recommending Father O'Callaghan? Simply because Moran had also written Kirby about
Cork the same day as Father Murray had. "The election for a
Coadjutor in Cork," Moran advised Kirby on January 7, "is to
take place in about a fortnight. That appointment will be a most
important one for the welfare of the Irish Church all through
the South"(K). "The city of Cork is increasing in wealth & importance every day," he explained, and alluding to the unfitness of Monsignor Neville, "& being a thoroughly Catholic city
should be sound on all the questions of Education &c that may
& must arise." "As you happen to be in Rome," Moran concluded artfully, "& are so well acquainted with the Southern
folk you will be able to give the authorities at Propaganda valuable help towards appointing a zealous energetic & devoted
man."

Errington, who had left Rome the previous June after Carr's appointment to Galway, had returned again in November, but his reception by the authorities had been very cool. He had, in fact, accomplished very little, when he had to return to London at the end of January 1884, for the opening of the parliamentary session. In apologizing to Smith on January 31, for having to leave Rome so suddenly, he explained that he had just heard that Neville and O'Callaghan had received an equal number of votes on the Cork *terna*(S). Errington then predicted that the majority of the bishops would undoubtedly favor O'Callaghan in their report to Propaganda, "but Monsgr Jacobini thinks Neville will win." Neville and O'Callaghan had, in fact, each received twelve votes of the thirty-three cast, while three others had received two votes, with three more receiving one each. The voting as Neville explained later to Errington had resulted in the very senior clergy voting for him and the younger parish priests voting for O'Callaghan. Eight of the ten canons in the Cork chapter, he reported, and four of the senior Parish Priests had voted for him. Indeed he would have been *dignissimus*, except that one canon, who was one of his strongest supporters, but who was in delicate health, was prevented from attending by the unusual severity of the weather. The one canon who voted for O'Callaghan, Neville added, did so because "he says the Kirby letter made him do it. He was also told that Fr. O'C. was the Pope's confessor. His curate who controls him is Fr. O'C's first cousin." Neville concluded his analysis of the voting for Errington by noting that, in effect, all the parish priests who voted for O'Callaghan were "professed Land Leaguers."

Some ten days after the voting, the bishops of the Province met in Thurles, under the presidency of the archbishop of Cashel, to report to the Propaganda on the *terna* commended by the Cork clergy. Of the ten bishops of the province, eight attended in person, and two, Killaloe and Waterford, were represented by proxies, which were held by Croke. "The result," Croke summed up for Kirby on February 8, the day after the meeting, "was that *Seven* voted for Father O'Callaghan and *three* for Dean Neville. The Seven were Cashel, Killaloe, Waterford, Coadjutor of Killaloe, Kerry, Ross and Kilfenora. The *three* were Cork, Cloyne and Limerick, the last stating that he voted for Dr. Delany, *not wishing to oppose him*." After complimenting Kirby on his letter to the Cork clergy as admirable and most opportune, Croke maintained that Neville was simply detested in Cork, and if Delany had not presided at the election of the *terna*, the Dean "would not have got *two* votes." As it was, Croke argued a little perversely, twenty-one out of thirty-one parish priests voted against Neville, and his other two votes were the result of proxies cast by canons' curates. "O'Callaghan," he declared in conclusion, "will be a great blessing to Cork, distracted as it is, by rival ecclesiastical and other factions. The old regime must die out."

After the election of the Cork *terna*, however, all the various factions opposed to Neville appeared to close their ranks behind O'Callaghan, as Kirby rapidly became their focus, if not indeed their principal agent. "God of Heaven," wrote an anonymous Cork nun to Kirby on January 30, "pity the Curate who would presume to differ from Monsignor Neville on any subject political, civil or religious. He is a one-eyed man—has but one view on every subject—that view is his own. He grasps at a conclusion without any idea of how—time, circumstances, or surroundings can alter or vary facts"(K). "Though Dean Neville is clever," wrote another of Kirby's correspondents on February 17, "exceedingly clever, as is well known, and though he has been our Bishop's confidential advisor, almost from the Commencement of his long episcopate, the great body of the Priests have never considered him a desirable person to be appointed Bishop of this Diocese"(K). "In devising & applying a remedy," this Cork P. P. shrewdly added, "to counter act, as far as may now be possible, the evils arising from a Godless College, & two model schools, which are in full operation in this diocese, it would be a great advantage for our future Bishop to be in no way connected with or responsible for the policy of the time past."

Croke was obviously very anxious about the Cork coadjutorship, for besides writing Kirby regularly at this time, he also wrote to his old friend the bishop of Bathurst, who had returned to Rome from Ireland for the winter, and who was staying with Kirby in the Irish College. In enlisting Matthew Quinn in the good fight, Croke was at his buoyant and bumptuous best. "It would be a national calamity," he confided to Quinn on March 6, after marking his letter "private," and underlining it three times, "if Neville were appointed. He is a desperate West Briton, a Castle hack, and, probably the most unpopular man in Ireland. O'Callaghan is a Cork man born, a good man, an humble man, and *no party* man—just the sort of head or boss cleric, *now* required in Cork"(K). Dr. Delany, Croke continued, "cannot live more than a year. He is 80— heavy from good feeding, and infirm from old age. He goes, of course, for his protégé the Dean—because he (the Dean) understands him (Dr. D) well, and O'Callaghan would not." "This would do something and mean something," he maintained, a little callously, "if Dr. D. were to live for the next score years, but as he must 'step out' soon, the question of understanding or not understanding between himself and his assistant dwindles into nothing." "What about Sydney?" Croke asked, turning to Moran's pending appointment. "Will it ever be settled?" "If there was question of making a Pope," he added irreverently, "there could not be more fuss or more moonshine." "Read mine to *Lita*," he commanded good naturedly, returning to his subject and referring to Kirby, "in re N__ and ponder thereon. There is more where that came from. Large *Stock on hands*. WRITE."

Several days after Croke had written Quinn, Moran again wrote Kirby about the Cork appointment. He complained on March 9, that Catholic city though it was, Cork had become estranged from the rest of the Irish Church because of its patronage of the Queen's College located there(K). He then proceeded to give Kirby a biographical sketch of Dean Neville, who after Delany, he thought was most responsible for the lamentable state of affairs in Cork. "The great defect of Dr. Neville," declared Moran, "is that he has no firmness and the people have no confidence in him."

> He has hitherto failed in everything. When Professor of Theology in Maynooth he spent a great deal of his time running into Dublin to dine with official people. He was appointed Rector of the Catholic University by a mere ruse, after a great part of the Bishops had left the Meeting understanding that the matter was deferred till next day. Everything failed in his hands at the Catholic University, although he spent immense sums of money, and we were at length obliged, though in as polite a way as we could, to get rid of him. The Govt. appointed him on the Senate of the new Royal University and he has given no satisfaction to the Cardinal and the other Bishops in this post (K).

"Some persons," Moran then warned Kirby, "have been circulating the report that it is only the ultra-Nationalists that are opposed to him." "That is quite a mistake," Moran declared flatly. "Every sensible man in Ireland is opposed to him because they regard him as quite unfit for that important diocese." "I had no intention of writing thus about Cork," he apologized in conclusion, "but you will excuse me for I have no thought in doing so save to preserve the faith of our people."

The buoyancy and determination of the anti-Neville coalition, and particularly of Croke, by the middle of March, had been very much the result of a developing *rapprochement* between the Irish Church and Rome. After the disaster of the Circular the previous year, Rome had begun the double process of disengaging diplomatically from the British government and restructuring its power and influence in Ireland. Since the British government had little need for relations with Rome now that law and order had been restored in Ireland, the process of disengagement did not, for the moment, pose a serious problem. Cardinal McCabe's refusal, however, to accept a coadjutor seriously frustrated Rome's attempt to restructure its own power and influence in Ireland. What to do about Ireland, therefore, was very much in the minds of the pope and the Roman authorities when Cardinal Manning visited Rome in late October and November of 1883. Manning, whose influence at Rome when he arrived was minimal, has left an interesting account in a long memorandum of the dramatic transformation that took place with regard to his power in the Church in the English-speaking world.

Manning made his memorandum immediately on leaving Rome in Florence, his first stop on his way home. "I went to Rome," he explained on December 4, 1883, "with no anticipation of satisfaction."[14]

An absence of four years and the industrious misrepresentations of many people, had, as I know, created strong prejudice against me. I am told that it was intentional that I was not consulted about Ireland, or our Government, and that the Bishops were invited to write severally on the Oxford question. For the last two years I have been silent; and I did not look for what has hap-

[14] E. S. Purcell, *Life of Cardinal Manning* 2 (London, 1896): pp. 577-579.

pened. Whether the Holy Father had any perception of this I do not know; but if he had he could not have done more to undo it. He desired me to come every Wednesday, so that in five weeks I had six audiences of more than one hour each. There is no subject on which he did not speak or allow me to speak.... We spoke fully of the "Letter on History" to the three Cardinals, on the religious state of England, three times; on the relations with Russia, Austria, Berlin, France very fully; on the two notes of his own Pontificate, the intellectual, and the diplomatic; and most fully on Ireland and on our Government.[15]

"I do not think," Manning added, "I could have had a more complete admission into the knowledge which for the last two years seemed to be withheld.... And all that I cared to know I have come to know."

The greater part of Manning's memorandum concerned Ireland in general and the "Errington Mission" in particular. Errington, who had arrived in Rome while Manning was still there, was the subject of a conversation on November 28, between Manning and the cardinal secretary of state in the pope's *ante-camera*. Manning had noted that Errington had visited the Propaganda and the cardinal secretary himself. The cardinal secretary had explained that Errington no longer visited him ("non è venuto più"). Manning then told Cardinal Jacobini that, while Errington represented the English government, he did not represent Ireland, and suggested that the Irish bishops should be called to Rome in groups as had been done with the Americans. Jacobini replied that Manning should suggest this to the pope, and when he did the pope said he thought this was an *Ottima idea*. The reasons Manning adduced for such a procedure were that it would allow for a full representation of the views of the Irish bishops, Ireland would take it as a sign of Rome's confidence, and it would be acceptable to the English government. The pope then agreed, "and he has since spoke of it fully with the Council Secretary and Msgr. Jacobini, and again with me, and said they would do it in this next spring."

This admission of Manning into the confidence of the pope was to have enormous consequences for the affairs of the Irish Church. Rome was soon to find in Manning that focus for its power and influence that it had been looking for in vain in Cardinal McCabe. Why the Irish bishops acquiesced in and even

[15] *Ibid.*

welcomed this new and novel arrangement was not simply because they found in the cardinal a vigorous and skillful defender of their cause in Rome, but because he understood as
well as they did themselves what that cause was all about. He
understood, for example, that the Church in England, and in
the English-speaking world, was fundamentally and essentially
Irish, and for Rome to continue to antagonize Irish opinion at
home and abroad was simply folly. Further, the cardinal was as
bitterly opposed, and for his own reasons, as were the Irish
bishops to the establishment of diplomatic relations between
Rome and London. Finally, there was no practical question of a
public nature that was closer to either the cardinal's or the Irish
bishops' hearts than the education question. Both the cardinal
and the bishops came to realize very soon that in the growing
strength of the Irish party they might soon have the means of
achieving their heart's desire.

Errington, meanwhile, who had arrived in Rome about the
middle of November, had written Granville attempting to explain how seriously the situation in Rome had deteriorated
from their point of view.[16] Ever since his departure the previous June the pro-Irish party had been exploiting the pope's
anxieties and fears about Ireland. Lately, moreover, they had
been powerfully and successfully seconded by Cardinal Manning. Manning had been saying in the strongest terms that the
pope's action with regard to Ireland had been a series of blun-
ders from beginning to end, that to please England, and de-
luded by false information, he had compromised his own authority and influence in the Irish Church, and that he had been,
in the most humiliating way, constantly disowned and re-
pudiated in and out of Parliament by the British government.
Cardinal Manning had even been reported as having said that
Archbishop Croke was the truest patriot Ireland has had since
Daniel O'Connell. What the pope really found irritating, Errington explained, was that, after having incurred so much
abuse and annoyance in rendering the British government so
great a service in Ireland, he received not even so much as a sign
of sympathy or gratitude. As one friendly and shrewd cardinal
had pointed out to him recently, Errington added, " 'When a
man has fought for you and got wounded in your service, the
least he can expect is that you should call and enquire how he is,

and show him some sympathy and gratitude.' "

In any case, what Manning was attempting to do now, Errington warned, was to persuade the pope to write a complimentary letter to Croke. He confessed that he could hardly bring himself to believe that the pope, no matter how annoyed he was, could take so disastrous a step. Still, he alerted Granville, he was afraid that such action was far from impossible, and that in fact other minor measures might also soon be taken by Rome to reverse their former policy. It was, therefore, necessary to reassure the pope, and the service that would be most helpful at the moment was effective British support for Rome in their quarrel with the Portuguese government over ecclesiastical jurisdiction in Goa.[17] The Propaganda, Errington assured Granville, was now very anxious about the situation in Goa, and the pope had been long concerned about it. After receiving Errington's long report from Rome, Granville wrote both Spencer and Gladstone, attempting to keep his diplomatic lines clear with them as well as open with Rome through Errington. In writing to Spencer in Dublin on November 24, Granville explained that at their recent Cabinet meeting, Gladstone had expressed some concern over whether indeed Errington being in Rome was worth the clamor that would be raised when Parliament met in February.[18] Granville asked Spencer whether indeed he had been justified in telling Gladstone that Spencer, as head of the Irish government, attached great importance to what Errington was doing in Rome. Spencer obviously responded that he did, and Gladstone was persuaded to acquiesce in Errington's plea for a small diplomatic morsel for the pope, since Granville telegraphed Errington through Paget on December 4, "H. M. Govt will support at Lisbon any initiative taken by the Nuncio respecting Goa."[19]

Errington, however, evidently gained very little diplomatic ground even after Manning had left Rome. This was made amply clear to Granville, at least, in a long and revealing letter by

[17] *Ibid.* See Errington to Granville, January 31, 1882: "Your Lordship may remember my mentioning the Portuguese religious Protectorates in India and elsewhere, a subject which might afford a good occasion some day, if necessary, for negotiation. I have been working up all the particulars of the Goa question from the original documents here, and I find it most curious and interesting."

[18] Agatha Ramm (ed.), *The Political Correspondence of Mr. Gladstone and Lord Granville 1876-1888* **2** (Oxford, 1962): pp. 115-116. See November 27, 1883, Granville to Spencer.

[19] B, 49690.

John Savile Lumley, who had just replaced Paget as the British ambassador at the Italian court. "I have seen Errington several times," Lumley reported to Granville on January 4, 1884, "& find him all you described him to be clever, discreet, full of information and a very pleasant companion."[20]

> From what he tells me his position at the Vatican is very different to what it was last year; the Irish Party have been actively undermining his work & Cardinal Manning has done much mischief & either directly or indirectly has succeeded in producing a great change in the feelings of the Pope towards England.[21] Several pious Fenians, Irish priests, acting no doubt from conscientious motives advocate everything short of murder which could embarrass H. M.'s Government & have been endeavouring to obtain from the Pope a reversal of his letter to Bishop Croke.[22] They have represented to his Holiness that he has been used as a cats paw & that while his action has been injurious to the cause of the Papacy he has obtained nothing in return for it & the compensation he had hoped for in the shape of the establishment in some form or other of diplomatic relations with England is as far removed from the reign of probability as ever. Having failed to obtain a reversal of the Pope's advice to the Irish Bishops, these pious Fenians have urged the Pope at all events to send off a letter by Cardinal Manning approving the zeal & general conduct of the Bishop [Croke] which might be made use of in support of the Irish movement, but this the Pope has declined to do.[23]

Lumley then observed that the pope was so very irritable that it was difficult to bring Irish matters before him, and Errington had not, in fact, been able to see the pope as yet. Since the possibility of diplomatic relations, "which was the bait that had been dangled before the Pope's eyes," had lost its efficacy, Lumley candidly pointed out, some other inducement was now necessary if the pope's assistance might be required in Ireland. He then suggested to Granville, as Errington had, that the Goa affair might provide a suitable inducement.

---

[20] GR, 30/29/182.

[21] See also C, February 29, 1884, Croke to Manning (copy), thanking the cardinal for his good offices in Rome.

[22] A mistaken reference, most likely, to the Parnell Circular, which was sent to all the Irish bishops, but which in the popular mind, at least, was meant for Croke, especially since it was issued almost immediately after his return from Rome.

[23] GR, 30/29/182.

That same day Errington also wrote Granville, but his letter was naturally a good deal more optimistic, if somewhat less objective, than Lumley's in his analysis of the situation.[24] He reported that the pope's irritation had subsided a good deal since Manning had left Rome, and that he was now on the friendliest terms again with the authorities at the Vatican and the Propaganda, though he admitted they appeared to be reluctant to do anything about the behavior of the Irish clergy except what might be absolutely necessary. One very disagreeable thing had occurred, Errington then alerted Granville, but he was doing his very best to have it mitigated in some way. A priest of the diocese of Kerry was in Rome attempting to persuade the pope to give his blessing to a church he was building as a memorial to Daniel O'Connell. The pope had not only warmly approved the project, but he had deputed Croke to perform the ceremony of laying the foundation stone. Errington further explained that he had remonstrated with the authorities as to the seriousness of such a step and suggested that instead of Croke, the bishop of Kerry was the proper person to represent the pope in the matter. Both Cardinal Jacobini and Monsignor Jacobini had promised, he assured Granville in conclusion, that they would urge the pope to reconsider and make the substitution.

While he was thus strenuously attempting to prevent what, in effect, would be a public demonstration of Croke's restoration to favor in Rome, Errington received yet another hammer blow. On January 11, Granville warned him by telegram that the secretary of the Protestant Association had written Gladstone asking whether the report recently published in the London *Standard*, that Errington had been directed to resume negotiations in Rome by the government, was correct, and if it was correct, what was the nature of the negotiations.[25] The answer that would be given, Granville added, was that he did not know of anything to warrant such a report and that if what was implied by negotiations meant a resumption of diplomatic relations, no such negotiations were in progress. He further assured Errington that Spencer attached very great importance indeed to his work in Rome. In thanking Granville that same day for his telegram, which he would use to smooth by

---

[24] B, 49690, January 4, 1884.
[25] *Ibid.*

anticipation the inevitable trouble such an announcement would cause in Rome, Errington hoped that the reply to the secretary of the Protestant Association would be as cautiously worded as possible.[26] When Errington, however, visited Cardinal Jacobini a few days later to prepare him for the worst, he did not find the cardinal in a very conciliatory mood, for Jacobini said that "it was impossible for him not to remark that the subject was a painful one, that there was a certain consideration due and supposed to be observed in the dealings of Governments with each other, and that these repeated disavowals seemed quite inconsistent with such considerations."[27] Errington refused to admit such an observation. He told the cardinal that Granville had risked a great deal politically in order to avoid appearing unfriendly to Rome, and now that the attack involved perhaps the stability of the ministry itself, the foreign secretary could not be expected to go as far in public as he was disposed to go in private.

Cardinal Jacobini's remarks in his conversation with Errington, however, were only a portent of things to come. Several days after their interview, the Pope finally decided not only to bless the cornerstone of the proposed memorial church to O'Connell, brought to Rome by Timothy Canon Brosnan, but to select the archbishop of Cashel to lay that cornerstone.[28] This was indeed a disaster for Errington, and when he was forced to leave Rome at the end of January for parliamentary duties in London, the prospects for any kind of relationship between the British government and the Vatican were very dim indeed. On the other hand, the position of Croke was transformed, by the announcement that he had been, in effect, rehabilitated at Rome. After what had amounted to his public censure by Rome in May, 1883, with the Parnell Circular, Croke had withdrawn from the national scene and devoted himself to his diocesan work. His correspondence had, in fact, dwindled almost to nothing until it revived with the coming of the Cork affair and the developing *rapprochement* with Rome. When Kirby's vice rector, Michael Verdon, had visited him in July, 1883, to ask him for a diocesan collection for the Irish College in Rome, he refused. "You will see by the enclosed," Croke then wrote Kirby, explaining his refusal, "that I have

---

[26] *Ibid.*
[27] *Ibid.*
[28] F. O., 45/499, January 18, 1884, Lumley to Granville.

done a good thing for our own Diocesan College of Thurles. I have just established Burses in perpetuum to the tune of £400 p. an."[29] "However," he relented, "I promised to give Dr. Verdon £100 more—*in all £300*—from *myself* when I can manage to have it." "P.S." he added tartly, "Those who are so ready to complain of me in Rome will not be in a hurry to bring the *enclosed* under the notice of the Roman Authorities." "But," he consoled himself, "I am equally indifferent to their praise or censure." Croke continued in his sullen mood (as indeed did the Irish people, and the great majority of the bishops and clergy), until he received news of the pope's public mark of esteem in selecting him to lay the cornerstone of Canon Brosnan's church in January, 1884.[30]

Croke's opportunity to respond to the pope's gesture came rather unexpectedly and in a way that was not entirely welcome. Towards the end of February, Kirby had written that the Italian government was once again threatening Propaganda's property by instituting legal proceedings in the Court of Cassation, and asked Croke to do something about rousing Irish public opinion against what in his mind amounted to outright confiscation. "Public meetings," Croke hastened to reply on February 29, after explaining how deeply he felt the blow, "are quite out of the question. The people, still smarting under the irritation caused by the Circular of last May, would not attend, and could not be got to manifest any sympathy with the Roman authorities."[31] Croke, however, was wise and politic enough not to allow the opportunity to pass. He suggested that Cardinal McCabe might draw up a petition, have it signed by the Irish bishops, and present it to the queen or prime minister, asking

---

[29] K, July 25, 1884. The enclosure announced the establishment of twenty-five burses (ten at £20, ten at £15, five at £5) for St. Patrick's College, Thurles, for the benefit of the foreign missions. Preference was to be given to native-born subjects of the archdiocese of Cashel and Emly, and were to be available on September 3, 1883 This foundation by Croke, it might be noted, involved a capital outlay of about £10,000. See also C, October 3, 1884, for a list of sums of money given away by Croke out of his personal resources for charitable, national, or diocesan purposes, amounting to   7,999-10-0.

[30] K, February 8, 1884.

[31] K, February 27, 1884. See also K, December 18, 1883, Thomas Nulty, bishop of Meath, to Kirby: "A most extraordinary change has taken place in the feelings of the people here. People who would I believe shed their blood for the Church willingly; would I think abandon it if they believed it interfered with them in asserting their political rights. It would astonish you to see the arrogant defiance with which they contribute to the Parnell funds; notwithstanding the Pope's Circular."

the government to interfere. He also suggested more practically that the Irish bishops should make an annual fixed contribution to Propaganda and, in proving that he was prepared to do more than talk, Croke started things off munificently by sending Cardinal Simeoni £100 and promising to send a like sum every St. Patrick's day of his life.

Kirby had also written the other three Irish archbishops about the threat to Propaganda's property and received a good deal less satisfaction than he had received from Croke. The Cardinal replied, on March 3, that he would, of course, do what he could, "But I fear it will be very hard to induce Mr. Gladstone to move:" McCabe explained pessimistically, referring to the event which in his mind had led to the collapse of Gladstone's first ministry in 1874, "He has never forgiven and I think *never* will forgive the Bishops of Ireland for breaking up his Government on his University Bill"(K). Croke, meanwhile, was his usual bustling and energetic self, and wrote Kirby again two days after McCabe, that the cardinal did not seem to approve of a petition, but might move to ask the bishops to subscribe to Propaganda. Croke also reported that he had written to the bishop of Waterford who had promised to send Cardinal Simeoni £50. "We have Mass in Cathedral at 6-½ OC," he closed buoyantly, "for labouring men and servants, and the Congregation is something astonishing. Mass(2d) daily at 8—/ Glory be to the Faith"(K). The archbishop of Armagh also expressed his sorrow to Kirby on March 18, about the threat to Propaganda's property, and noted that Gladstone's reply to Errington in the House of Commons about it seemed to indicate that nothing would be done(K). "There is nothing so useful," continued McGettigan rather surprisingly, "as a little noise and agitation for we know that the Ministers are *squeezable*."

This rising aggressive mood among the bishops with regard to the government was even more evident in the archbishop of Tuam's reply to Kirby some days before McGettigan had written. Though he was by temperament naturally an optimist, MacEvilly confessed on March 13, he had no confidence in the government where the interests of Catholicity were concerned(K). "Indeed," he added significantly, "I will say with truth, all we get from them is simply thro' fear or a feeling of self-interest or preservation." He then suggested more practically that if the Irish members of Parliament could be persuaded to raise the question in the House of Commons, and back it up with their votes, the government might be brought to the action about Propaganda's property. He would himself write to those members who might be of use in the matter, and assured Kirby that he and his colleagues could, of course, be counted on to join "in any movement that may be set on foot."

Croke, meanwhile, who had already gone into action, wrote Kirby again on March 13, that matters were progressing very favorably with regard to the Propaganda affair(K). The Irish bishops, he reported, would soon send a short letter to the pope protesting against the spoliation of the Propaganda's property and promising that bishops, priests, and laity would not be found wanting if Propaganda should require financial help. Both the bishop of Killaloe and his coadjutor, Croke noted, had already promised to send Propaganda a subscription, while the bishop of Ross was in the process of writing Cardinal Simeoni. Cloyne, Croke thought, would do something, while Kerry had not as yet said anything. "Limerick," he explained, winding up the review of his suffragans, "will sign protests, but does not appear disposed to advance Cash." "But of course he would do so at once," Croke added reassuringly, "if I put it to him— which I did not wish to do." "Say in your next," he then suggested amiably in conclusion, enclosing a sprig of shamrock for St. Patrick's day, "what your private opinion is as to the result of the Cork affair."

On his return to London, meanwhile, Errington had been attempting to move mountains on Neville's behalf with regard to the Cork appointment. He reassured Smith on February 15, from London, that both Granville and the ministry were friendly and most anxious to keep up communications with Rome(S). He also maintained, somewhat unrealistically, that since so much progress had been already made, he had little doubt that if only the Pope would be patient "we are on the high way to complete success." The pressing matter, Errington explained, was the Cork appointment, and if Rome passed over Neville, he feared that his mission would be ended. Errington then crossed over to Dublin where he had interviews with Spencer, McCabe, and Nicholas Donnelly, the cardinal's new auxiliary. After these conversations, he informed Smith on February 26, he was now "more convinced than ever of the great importance of getting Dean Neville for Cork"(S). He was again on his way to Rome, and assured

Smith that the government was most favorably disposed, and that he would bring, moreover, excellent assurances on various important matters, alluding undoubtedly to Goa, but that this only made him all the more anxious about the Cork affair. When he arrived in Rome in early March, however, Errington did not find the Cork affair very promising. In reporting to Granville on March 12, for example, he preferred to dwell on the probabilities rather than the actualities of Rome's good intentions with regard to Ireland.[32] As hard evidence of those good intentions, Errington could only adduce a conversation with Cardinal Simeoni the previous evening, who told him that Propaganda had written strongly to the Bishop of Meath, Thomas Nulty, about the violent language of one of his priests at a meeting of Michael Davitt's in his diocese several months before.

In order to bolster Neville's sagging cause in the face of both London and Rome's indifference, therefore, Errington had Smith write Delany, who was an old acquaintance, while he wrote Neville for more information. Two of the charges against Neville, Smith explained to Delany, were that he was at once too west British and also not Roman enough. Delany promised on March 14 that in refutation of the respective charges he would forward Neville's reply to Gladstone's celebrated brochure, *Vaticanism*, and an article of more recent vintage in the *Dublin Review* in which the Dean was sharply critical of the early Gallican tendencies of Maynooth.[33] In his letter to Neville, Errington asked him to have Delany write the Propaganda authorities again, stressing particularly the motives of the bishops who voted for O'Callaghan. In assuring Errington, on March 25, that he would certainly do so, Neville also revealed that he had only recently learned himself of the voting of the bishops. "Some of the Bishops," he confided to Errington, "arrived at Thurles the day before the voting. Ryan, Carr, Fitzgerald, & Higgins. At dinner the Archbishop spoke against my appointment. He urged two reasons. The first was that I was not a pious man. The second was that my appointment would perpetuate dissension in the Diocese of Cork. He gave the first as his own opinion. He proved the second by dwelling on the opposition of so many as twelve of

---

[32] B, 49690.

[33] S, March 14, 1884. The article appeared in October, 1879, and was entitled, "Theology, Past and Present at Maynooth."

the pp.'s to my views. . . ." "Dr. Higgins gave way," he explained, referring to the bishop of Kerry, "and the Archbishop slapped him on the back and called for another bottle of Champagne." "Dr. Ryan," Neville added, referring to the coadjutor of Killaloe, "got a mandate from his principle Dr. *Flannery* to go with the Archbishop." "I have all this," Neville reassured Errington in conclusion, and undoubtedly referring to Ryan, "from one who was *present*."

While Errington and Smith were thus industriously attempting to mobilize what information they could on Neville's behalf, they suffered another severe and unexpected shock. In the middle of March, the pope finally decided to act on Manning's advice about summoning a representative number of Irish bishops to Rome, and called a conference for the following September. This decision was a very serious setback for Errington and his friends. For years the Irish bishops had been constantly maintaining that the best means Rome had for determining the real needs of the Irish Church was in them, and certainly not in any agency provided by the British government. Now that the pope had recognized their claim, in his own interesting way, Errington's diplomatic future, to say the least, was not very promising. By early April, moreover, the Roman authorities were well aware that one of Errington's chief props, Cardinal McCabe, was simply dragging his feet over the threat to Propaganda's property. They must have also become aware, in spite of Errington's assurances, his other prop, the British government, was not using its good offices as promised in the interests of Propaganda with the Italian government.[34] Lumley, for example, had reported to Granville on April 3 that he had reason to believe that he was the only foreign representative in Rome that had received instruction to intercede with the Italian government on behalf of Propaganda.[35] He therefore had done nothing, because he did not believe it was the intention of Her Majesty's government to take action when those governments accredited to the Papal Court had not yet interfered.

---

[34] B, 49690. See Granville to Errington, March 28, 1884: "I bear in mind that while you would probably not be sorry if you could help Propaganda, our real object is to make the Vatican believe you are friendly to them, and so secure their good-will in Irish and other matters. It is not always easy to reconcile the two objects for it often happens that the conduct most likely to impress the Pope in our favour is not always the most likely to advance the real interests of Propaganda."

[35] F. O., 45/520.

How narrow the possibility of Neville being appointed to Cork had become was inadvertently revealed when Errington again reported on April 10 to Granville.[36] He had been advised at Propaganda, Errington confided, to induce Delany to write directly to the pope about securing Neville as his coadjutor. The difficulty in the way, he explained, was that since the majority of bishops of the province had voted for O'Callaghan, Propaganda was reluctant to pronounce against Croke and his friends, who were still smarting under the reprimand conveyed the previous May in the Parnell Circular. What Errington was actually saying, of course, was that Propaganda, given the procedure involved as well as the circumstances, now felt constrained to recommend O'Callaghan to the pope, and the only way out was for the pope to be persuaded to take the appointment into his own hands by an appeal from Delany. What made matters even worse at this stage for Errington was that Cardinal McCabe did not seem inclined to interfere actively on Neville's behalf at Rome. Errington, however, with Smith's assiduous help, doggedly continued to attempt to strengthen Neville's failing cause at Rome. Smith, for example, again wrote Delany asking him to write Cardinal Simeoni expounding on the motives of the bishops who voted for O'Callaghan, while Errington wrote Neville asking him what kind of letter Delany had written to the pope.

Neville replied on Easter Sunday, April 13, that Delany had written the pope a very strong letter indeed. Delany had ascribed the voting of the majority of the bishops to the " 'Machinationes ab intract ab extra et *oppositionem* apictum A. Episcopi Cassiliensis.' " He declared that O'Callaghan was a " 'vi missionario provisus inexpectus' "—that his appointment would give a triumph to a faction most dangerous to religion and would encourage a spirit of insubordination which owing to the political agitation had taken possession of so many of the young clergy and still prevailed amongst them. Delany had wound up his letter to the pope, Neville added, "by *supplicating* the Holy Father to permit him to spend what remains of life to him, in *peace* and to leave to his *Diocese* at his death a *successor* in whom he can *have confidence*." When Delany received Smith's letter Neville continued, he immediately

---

[36] B, 49690.

wrote Cardinal Simeoni explaining how the seven votes were gotten for O'Callaghan. Neville then reviewed for Errington why each of the bishops' votes were cast for O'Callaghan, and explained that he was about to go to Dublin. He promised Errington to acquaint McCabe with the substance of his last letter, for the cardinal "appears to be too confident about Dr. Delany's wishes being carried out." Delany's letter to the pope apparently had the effect of causing the decision about Cork to be adjourned, though the pope did not go so far as to reserve it to himself. As Errington explained to Granville on April 24, just before he set out for London to take up his parliamentary duties after the Easter recess, he had done all that was possible about Cork.[37] He did, however, express the hope that government would in the interest of Irish ecclesiastical matters "go as far as possible in support of the Pope's action in India about Goa."

All that could be done now by the supporters of Neville and O'Callaghan was simply to wait, and naturally rumors were the order of the day. Moran, who had been in Rome since Easter, and who had returned to Ireland in the middle of May to wind up his affairs before taking up his duties in the antipodes, was very pessimistic. "It was rumoured in Dublin yesterday," he reported to Kirby on May 20, "that Msgr. Neville has been appd to the See of Cork. I would regret this appointment very much, but from my observation of events in Rome, I fear that the report may be true"(K). Kirby was also very uneasy, for on June 6, he wrote Matthew Quinn, the bishop of Bathurst, who had also returned recently to Ireland from Rome, to send on any information he could get about the Cork affair. The *Freeman's Journal* of that morning, Quinn replied by return on June 10, said news had been received by telegram from Rome in Cork that O'Callaghan had been appointed, though "this does not tally with the account you give, yet the telegraph being later information may account for this fact." All speculation, however, was swiftly brought to an end when the pope appointed O'Callaghan coadjutor to the bishop of Cork on Friday, June 13, 1884.

Delany, who had begun a letter to Smith on that Friday, and did not close it until he had heard from O'Callaghan by letter some days later, provided a moving and pathetic account of

---

[37] B, 49690.

the impact of the news on him(S). Delany explained telegrams had arrived in Cork on Saturday evening, June 14, announcing the news, and one from O'Callaghan to him had announced that the Feast of SS. Peter and Paul was fixed for his consecration in Rome. "The newspapers," Delany complained, "have desseminated the intelligence whilst I have received no reply from Headquarters to all my statements & petitions."

A heavier blow could scarcely be inflicted on me, altho my physical labour might be hereby somewhat diminished. Fatigue is far less painful than anxiety of mind, and anxieties are constantly turning up in a large population such as that of Cork. They require experience in affairs, knowledge of the character of the people, extensive information, & solid natural abilities. All these I would have found [in] the Dean, who understands me so well & who would have contributed more than anyone else could do to the peace of mind and tranquility of feeling [of] an old man who wished to end his few remaining years or months in preparing for the land where no man returns. The future affords only gloomy prospects. God's will be done(S).

Croke, needless to say, was as delighted as Delany was disappointed. "I got your telegram announcing Dr. O'Callaghan's appointment," Croke responded immediately to Kirby on Friday, June 13, "and can safely say I rarely received more agreeable news"(K). "It has filled the Irish heart," he testified freely, "with hope and gratitude." In this exuberant mood induced by the good news, Croke then picked up on some remarks in a recent letter of Kirby's, which allowed him the opportunity of defending and discussing his favorite subject, and revealing at the same time in an insightful way the able and interesting man that he was.

Dr. Quinn has just left me. He has been here for the last few days. He is well.

You are anxious that I should write a Pastoral on Freemasonry, and think, moreover, that the B. Virgin will be hard on me for not publishing her praises more than, as you appear to believe, I do.

Now, as regards *pastorals*, my opinion is very clear and very precise, just as my practice is very well known and approved of.

I look upon *long* pastorals issued as they mostly are by a select few of the Irish Bishops, at the approach of Lent, and occasionally at other times throughout the year, as so much waste paper, inasmuch as they are rarely read by anybody, or, if read by a few, scarcely ever heeded in practice. This is my experience of them. They are written *for Rome*, and not *for Ireland*. So, I have never written, and, very likely, never will write and issue, any such lengthy document. I *preach* a great deal. Almost every month of my life, I issue a short circular to the clergy on some one practical subject or another. This month, I am on the collection of Peter's pence; and I think I shall be able to prove to you when I reach Rome that when I speak to my people on that, or any other subject, they hear me attentively, and do my bidding with pleasure, even though I do not address very long Pastorals to them enforcing and explaining my views.

So far as regards Pastorals *in general*, and my dealings with them.

Now, as regards the Pope's Encyclical on Freemasonry it has been read and commented on throughout this diocese: but I can assure you, at the same time, that if I were to address a letter to the people of Cashel and Emly on that subject, I would be reputed by them to have literally taken leave of my senses, inasmuch as there is not a single Catholic Freemason throughout the length and breadth of this ample territory, nor, as far as I can learn, in all *Munster*, except, perhaps, one or two at most, in the City of Cork.

Furthermore, since I came to Cashel, now fully nine years ago, I have never had to deal with a single case of *Fenianism* here, but one, and that one exists no longer.

On receipt of the documents forwarded by you to me from Rome, some of the Bishops have written to me saying, that it would be utter insanity for us to publish anything about Freemasonry as our people know absolutely nothing of it, and our writing, or pronouncements, under the circumstances, could be productive of mischief alone.

So far for Pastorals and Freemasonry—let me now give you some idea of what work I go through, in order to show that I am not idle, and that our Blessed Lady cannot think so badly of me as you seem to suppose.

I commenced my Visitation, this year, early in May. I closed my work on Tuesday last. During that time I confirmed over *4,000* children and about *300* adults. Every one of those 4,000

children I examined closely in the Catechism myself. I entered
the Church each day at eleven O'c. a.m. and left it at four p.m. I
spoke fully three hours each day, to enormous congregations,
and I never left a single day pass that I did not exhort the people
to be devout to the B. Virgin, to provide themselves with beads,
and to say the Rosary regularly all the days of their life.

The enclosed scraps will tell you how I was received through
the Diocese, as also of our proceedings here on Corpus Xsti. Dr.
Quinn says he never saw anything like our ceremonies and
procession in any part of the globe. Let me continue a few
details of work—

After tomorrow, Sunday 15th, I hold an ordination here. On
Wednesday next, 18th, I shall be engaged in a religious ceremony in the Archdeacon's parish of Fethard. The week after
that I shall hold my Conferences. On the 26th I lay the foundation stone of a new Church in Tipperary and make a speech
stirring up the people to subscribe to it. On Monday 1st of July I
go to meeting of Bishops in Maynooth. On Sunday 6th of July, I
open a new Church near city of Limerick, and preach the
dedication sermon. On Monday the 7th July I hold my Diocesan
Synod, and go on retreat with the parish priests. On Monday
15th retreat for curates, at which I *occasionally* assist. August X
I preach the dedication sermon of the new Church of the Holy
Trappists at Roscrea. On Sunday 17th I open a new Church
near Nenagh—and so on—today to say nothing of conducting
alone without a secretary, a correspondence such as no other
man in Ireland has to meet. So now let me ask you whether you
do not think that work enough without writing worthless Pastorals? I had no idea of entering into these details. However,
there is no harm done: and I do not often trouble you with long
Epistles. I am fairly well, but tired.

I went to Kilkenny, on Tuesday last, with Dr. Quinn to visit
the Archbishop of Sydney. He is quite well, and leaves old
Ireland on July the 3rd for his distant home. God guide and
guard him.

Farewell. Ever affectionately yours,

T. W. Croke(K)

Kirby had also written Cardinal McCabe not only giving
him early news, but obviously making some pious reflections
on the Cork appointment. "I am sure the Holy Ghost guided

the Pope," McCabe curtly reassured Kirby on June 16, "but some very sensible people fear that the result will encourage the young insubordinate priests of Ireland in their disregard for authority"(K). That same day Errington also wrote Smith from London after a flying trip to Dublin. He reported that the Cork appointment was very unfortunate, and that it was producing a great sensation. It was patently the most serious blow for the party of order, and a very great triumph for Croke and his friends. Cardinal McCabe, Errington explained, was much shaken. So much so indeed that he talked of not going to Rome in September with the other Irish bishops as it would now appear to be useless. Errington was also afraid the Cork affair would produce the very worst effect on the government, and result in a breaking off of all negotiations. He asked Smith, therefore, to warn all their friends, for he expected that he would shortly have to break the news directly to them. Errington, however, who was not only tenacious but a natural optimist, then proceeded to work out a new intrigue about three other Irish episcopal appointments, which had occurred while the Cork affair was in progress, and which were still pending. The advanced nationalist bishop of Clonfert, Patrick Duggan, had been persuaded by Rome that he should have a coadjutor with the right of succession, while the bishop of Ferns, Michael Warren, had died unexpectedly on April 22, and the see of Ossory was now vacant, with Moran's translation to Sydney. In writing to Smith, Errington recommended John Healy, professor of theology at Maynooth, and third name with only two votes on the *terna* as coadjutor for Clonfert, while noting that though all the names on the *terna* for Ferns were good, all the names for Ossory were very bad.

The Ossory case had indeed turned out to be a very troublesome one for Rome. Moran explained to Kirby on April 8, that the election for the *terna* for Ossory would take place on April 24, when he expected to be in Rome, and that the cardinal would preside(K). McCabe wrote Kirby on April 23, reporting that he was on his way to Kilkenny to preside, and that he would keep the letter open to tell him the result of the voting. He also noted that they had sustained a very great loss in the death of the bishop of Ferns the day before. The result of the voting was that Michael Murphy, vice president of

Carlow College, and a native of the diocese of Ossory, was named *dignissimus* with eighteen votes, while Edward McDonald, dean of Ossory, was *dignior* with fourteen votes, and Thomas Canon Hennessy, parish priest of Inistogue, was *dignus* with three votes. When Moran heard the news by telegram, he wrote McCabe from the Irish College in Rome on April 26, assuring him that the clergy could not have made a better choice than Father Murphy. "He has been," Moran noted, "Professor of Theology for about eighteen years, & his merits as a Theologian are indeed known throughout all Ireland. He is an excellent preacher and writes well. During his vacation time he has proven himself most zealous in giving missions & engaging in spiritual work almost beyond his strength. It will lessen a good deal my regret at leaving Ossory, if this energetic & zealous Priest be appointed to watch over the See." "Neither of the other two names," Moran declared firmly, "that is, Dr. MacDonald and Canon Hennessy, can be thought of for the present vacancy."

The bishops of the province of Dublin met on May 5 to discuss the relative merits of the *terna* commended by the Ossory clergy and made their report to the Propaganda. Since some further information, however, had come to their attention about Father Murphy, the bishops decided to defer their decision until Moran should return from Rome when they could consult with him. The problem, Moran reported very discreetly to Kirby on May 20, from Kilkenny, was "a family difficulty which has come to light, & which might render his episcopate unpleasant in this city." After Moran had investigated the matter the bishops consulted again and forwarded their report to Rome. In writing Kirby about a month later, on June 22, Matthew Quinn reported that he had just met Father Murphy by accident and thought that he was a very superior man. Quinn also reported that Moran thought that it was a pity that Murphy was not likely to be appointed through no fault of his own. "The young man," Quinn added, "through whom the mischief came to his sister has married her and the matter appears to be very little known." By this time, however, the Propaganda had not only set aside the Ossory *terna* on the basis of the bishop's report, but had written McCabe asking him to nominate of himself a new *terna*.[38]

---

[38] K, June 16, 1884, McCabe to Kirby. See also S, July 31, 1884, Delany to Smith, for the retrospective details.

When in addition to the setting aside of the Ossory *terna*, John Healy, who had been a weak third as *dignus* on the *terna* for a coadjutor to the advanced nationalist bishop of Clonfert, was appointed on June 26, and the first name on the *terna* for Ferns, James Browne, was appointed on July 8, it was only natural perhaps that Errington should assume that his influence at Rome was not yet entirely eclipsed.[39] He had, in fact, written Smith on June 30, after learning that the Ossory nomination had virtually been placed in McCabe's hands and that Healy had been appointed, initiating yet another complicated intrigue. After his usual warnings to Smith about how much damage had been done to their hopes for diplomatic relations by the Cork appointment, Errington explained that the rumors current in Dublin had Nicholas Donnelly, McCabe's auxiliary, being translated to Ossory and Bartholomew Woodlock, the bishop of Ardagh, replacing Donnelly as McCabe's coadjutor. The effect of moving Donnelly, Errington warned, was that it might ultimately make room in Dublin for the president of Maynooth, William J. Walsh, who was a most dangerous man. If Walsh were ever appointed archbishop of Dublin, Errington feared that "the Irish Church would be entirely in the hands of Dr. Croke." The real problem was that there was such a dearth of good men for the cardinal to choose from. "Would there be any use, Errington hinted finally in conclusion, "suggesting Dr. *Neville for Ossory*; that would repair some of the mischief at Cork? Pray think of this."

When Smith received Errington's letter in early July, he immediately wrote to Delany asking him to write McCabe suggesting that the cardinal should write to Rome recommending Neville for Ossory. The cardinal, however had already reported to Rome about Ossory before he received Delany's letter. "I hear Cardinal McCabe," Errington broke the news to Smith on July 9, "has (very foolishly) I think suggested that Dr. O'Callaghan should be sent to Ossory so as to make room for Neville at Cork; but this is flying in the face of the Pope's decision: & my plan is much better & the Pope might be induced to adopt it." Errington had pointed out earlier in this letter that he had also written to both cardinal

---

[39] Thomas Brett, *Life of the Most Reverend Dr. Patrick Duggan, Bishop of Clonfert* (Dublin, 1921), p. 168. See *Handbook of British Chronology*, pp. 403, 408, respectively, for dates of provision for Ferns and Clonfert.

and Monsignor Jacobini about his plan. Smith, naturally, was very annoyed when he read Errington's letter, and he immediately wrote Delany complaining that his lordship should have acted with greater dispatch. He also pressed Delany once more to have the cardinal write another letter to Rome recommending to Neville for Ossory. "I did not lose an hour," reported Delany to Smith on July 22, "in communicating your idea about Dean Neville & Ossory to Cardinal McCabe"(S). Delany, who evidently preferred the cardinal's original proposal, then went on to explain to Smith that his eminence had just written him to say that since he had already recommended the translation of O'Callaghan to Ossory, he was reluctant to complicate matters with another proposal. "I have complied," Delany assured Smith in conclusion, "with your desire of destroying your letters, altho I should have greatly wished to preserve them, as records of important matters & memorials of a valued friendship."

Early in August, rumor was current in Ireland that Kirby's vice rector in the Irish College, Michael Verdon, would succeed his cousin in the see of Ossory.[40] Kirby, however, wrote Croke in the middle of August that Verdon would remain at the College.[41] Smith, meanwhile, was still attempting to persuade McCabe through Delany to write to Rome recommending Neville for Ossory. Delany, who had been vacationing at Harrogate in England with McCabe, explained on August 10, after returning to Cork, that he had immediately done as Smith had suggested. The cardinal, however, who approved of Smith's suggestion, did not want to write Rome again unless he was asked to do so because he did not wish to appear obtrusive. Delany then hinted that perhaps the best course would be for Smith to introduce the subject at the Propaganda, and then the authorities could write McCabe again asking him for his opinion. In a word, after reflecting on Smith's proposal, Delany was not interested in having Neville anywhere but in Cork. He would have preferred Neville as his coadjutor, but having done his best and failed, it would have to be as his dean and vicar general. The crucial issue for Delany was the preservation of his own peace of mind and not Errington and Smith's conception of what the Irish Church,

---

[40] K, August 2, 1884, McCabe to Kirby, See also K, August 2, 1884, J. P. Leahy, bishop of Dromore, to Kirby.

[41] K. See Croke's reply to Kirby, August 25, 1884.

or even the Roman Church *vis-à-vis* the British government, needed at this critical moment in its history. Delany had early decided, in fact, that he would make things as uncomfortable for O'Callaghan as he could and thereby induce his coadjutor, perhaps, to ask Rome to release him from an unbearable situation. Delany was determined to make no provision for him out of diocesan funds or places at his disposal. He was further determined that his coadjutor would have no real authority in his diocese as long as he was alive. When O'Callaghan finally arrived in Cork to take up his duties, he accepted Delany's hospitality for a month and then took up residence with his sister who lived in Cork. "The key to all the difficulty," O'Callaghan explained to Kirby on October 15, some two months after his arrival in Cork, after referring to the fact that no provision for him had yet been made, "seems to me to be that the whole administration of the diocese is practically in the hands of Monsignor Neville who naturally feels hurt at my appointment. I mention these things not complaining but to inform you of the real state of affairs"(K). Some three months later, Delany, who was to live nearly two years more, made his last reference to his coadjutor in his correspondence with Smith. "Dr. O'Callaghan," he noted in a postscript on January 5, 1885, "accepted my hospitality for a month & then left me. No provision has turned up here as yet." "Is there any chance," Delany concluded, referring to the recent death of the coadjutor to the archbishop of Port of Spain, "of his promotion to Trinidad which is a Dominican Mission?"[42]

----

[42] The appointment to Ossory was finally made in the third week in September (K, September 25, 1884, W. Kelly, M.S.S., to Kirby), though the official provision was not made until October 22, 1884 (*Handbook of British Chronology*, p. 405). The new bishop, Abraham Brownrigg, had been superior of the House of Missions in Enniscorthy, a community in especial favor with Kirby and whose each succeeding Superior had been raised to the episcopal dignity. In fact, when the bishop of Ferns, Michael Warren, had died on April 22, Moran noted in his letter of April 26, to McCabe that with "the exception of Fr. Brownrigg I know of no one that can fill his place." When the original *terna* was set aside by Propaganda for Ossory in the second week of June, and McCabe was asked for his suggestions, it appears he asked Moran for his advice, for Moran replied, on June 25, "I will not refer to the important matters about which you wished to have my opinion until I have the pleasure of seeing you on Saturday." Circumstantially, there is little doubt that Moran suggested Brownrigg to McCabe, and the cardinal probably included his name along with the suggestion of translating O'Callaghan to Ossory in recommending a new *terna* to Propaganda. "I was at Dr. Brownrigg's consecration," Croke reported to Kirby on December 18, 1884, "Everything passed off admirably. He appears to be a good and a sensible man."

VIII. Reconciliation

March, 1884 - March, 1885

The developing rapprochement between the Irish Church and Rome, which had culminated in the appointment of O'Callaghan to Cork, had also the effect of contributing to the political reconciliation of the Irish Church and the Irish people. While the second process naturally lagged initially a good deal behind the first, by the end of 1884 the Irish bishops had made their peace with the Irish Parliamentary party as well as with Rome. The framework for this reconciliation was based on the adequate grain and plenteous potato harvest of 1883. The security thus given to the poor that they would not starve and to the small farmers that they could pay their rent resulted in the restoration of that peace and quiet on which law and order were dependent in Ireland.[1] The winter of 1883-1884 passed quietly enough and the bishops, obviously relieved, were anxious that nothing should be done to upset what they still felt to be an uneasy calm. This was why, for example, the bishops did not respond with all the enthusiasm that might have been expected of them, in March, 1884, to the pope's proposal for a conference of the bishops in Rome in September on Irish affairs.

The cardinal prefect's letter, which had announced the pope's latest move on the diplomatic chessboard, was sent to Cardinal McCabe about the middle of March. Simeoni asked McCabe to determine and then select an efficient and representative group of Irish bishops. He also asked McCabe for suggestions as to what subjects needed to be discussed. While a

---

[1] K, October 7, 1883, F. J. MacCormack, bishop of Achonry, to Kirby, writing from Ballaghdereen, County Mayo: "We are blessed this year with an abundant harvest; and the condition of our poor Country is promising well. The tenants will be able & willing to meet the just demands of landlords on the reduced scale of rents. The country is almost entirely free from agrarian outrages, and peace is being rapidly restored in the war of classes." See also K, September 24, 1883, J. Walshe, bishop of Kildare and Leighlin, to Kirby from Carlow; and K, October 8, 1883, Michael Warren, bishop of Ferns, from Enniscorthy, to Kirby.

good deal of the initiative was thus left in McCabe's hands, he immediately proceeded to dissipate it by asking a large number of his colleagues what they thought about the points raised in the cardinal prefect's letter. He also asked them, gratuitously, it would appear from their replies, whether they thought the proposed conference would result in any good. While most of his episcopal colleagues replied politely that they thought the conference would result in great good, several actually pointed out that since the pope himself had called the conference the question was really irrelevant.[2] As to the first point in Simeoni's letter to McCabe about the number of bishops, the consensus was reflected in the reply of the bishop of Achonry. "I observe," F. J. MacCormack noted on March 21, "that the Holy See is very desirous of having the different opinions of the Bishops represented"(Mc). "To carry," he added, "the wish of the Holy See into effect it might be desirable to have eight Suffragans with the four Archbishops." A consensus among the bishops about the proposed agenda, however, was a good deal more difficult to reach. Those bishops who did undertake to make suggestions to McCabe were either so vague or parochial as to be downright evasive. "As regard the subjects for consultation," Moran, for example, replied on March 20, "I have not anything very special to suggest"(Mc). "I suppose," he quibbled, "that the education of the Clergy will be treated of, and uniformity of discipline in the various Dioceses." "The manner in which the Holidays are kept," he concluded innocuously, "give me some trouble at times. I don't know of anything else at this moment that wd be worth mentioning." While most of the bishops consulted by McCabe evidently preferred to keep their own counsel as to the substantive issues, which were patently political and diplomatic, several were very candid with McCabe.

"I can hardly suggest at this moment," the intrepid and advanced nationalist bishop of Meath, Thomas Nulty, replied on March 22, "any subject for discussion at that Conference"(Mc). Religion, he pointed out to McCabe, was never in a more flourishing condition in the country, and the bishops were all of one mind about the important question of education.

---

[2] Mc, March 20, 1884, E. Butler, bishop of Limerick, to McCabe, and March 22, 1884, Thomas Nulty, bishop of Meath, to McCabe.

On politics, of course, we differ very widely, but if I wd venture
to offer a suggestion, it wd be that politics ought not to be
discussed at all at this Conference. In the present excited and
dangerous state of popular feeling, not merely at home but far
more among our Countrymen abroad, there is hardly any pronouncement that could be made on that subject that wd not be
interpreted into a hostile declaration against what are called
"National Politics." I am afraid that such a pronouncement wd
be disregarded. It seems to me that anything like popular indifference or disregard to any pronouncement sanctioned by the
Holy See is most injurious to the reverence and respect in which
the authority of Holy See has been always held by the Irish
Race(Mc).

"The veneration and reverence in which the authority of the
Holy See is held is of course," Nulty pointed out grimly, "the
mainstay of Religion: *both* must rise or go down together." "It
appears to me too," Nulty finally noted, and concluding his
non-recommendations for an agenda, "that the 'Communis
Sensus' of the Irish Episcopate discountenances the policy of
having an 'Apostolic Nuncio' accredited to the Court of St.
James."

If Nulty's reply to his questions gave McCabe some cause for
concern, the letter of the bishop of Kerry, Andrew Higgins,
must have left the cardinal in a state of shock. Higgins, whose
appointment the British government had been so anxious to
secure only a few years before, and who was presumably in
agreement with McCabe on political matters, was at least candid if nothing else in his fantastic sixteen-page reply. "I am far
from thinking," he bluntly told the cardinal on March 26, "the
Conventus will do good: I'm not sure it won't do harm"(Mc).
Higgins then argued that the reception of the Parnell Circular
in the country conclusively proved that the agitation had cut
its channel too deeply, and was now running too strongly to
hope that any effort from any quarter could change its direction or moderate its flow. He also pointed out that, now that
the reign of outrage seemed to be over, he did not think it wise
to attempt to suppress the popular spirit. The people had not
only learned their power, Higgins maintained, but their
power would soon be greatly increased when the government
passed the proposed reform in the franchise, which would
give the small tenant farmers and rural workers in Ireland the

vote. Furthermore, any effort to check the agitation would not be supported by the clergy who would "*at best* only *not oppose*." Even in the matter of the Parnell testimonial "they were sullen if obedient." It was hardly wise, therefore, to strain their reverence for the Holy See by insisting on courses which they had made up their minds not to support. "In a word," Higgins summed up, "as a means of influencing the agitation, I believe the Conventus will be powerless."

As far as the agenda for the proposed meeting in Rome was concerned, Higgins explained that the only practical question the bishops could touch without burning their fingers was the Education question, if even that was safe. He then shrewdly noted that it seemed to him the government was very much at present in the hands of the Irish party, both in Parliament and in the country. "And illumined as the Government conscience & that of the governing classes generally is by the light of the blaze their folly has kindled in our poor country, this time past," he added bitterly, "it is to be hoped even their blindness will see the intrinsic merits of the Catholic Education case as made by a body of representatives who can make things very hot for them, in and out of Parliament." What Higgins was saying, in effect, to McCabe was that the bishops as a body could achieve very little because all real power had now been focused in the Irish party by Parnell. If the bishops wanted anything done, therefore, they must come to some understanding with Parnell and his party. If indeed Nulty, or Dorrian, or Duggan, or even Croke himself had suggested this to McCabe, the cardinal would hardly have been surprised. But when the suggestion came from one of the most politically conservative members of his hierarchy, it could only be taken as a portent of doom for the position taken and argued by the cardinal and his supporters over the last four years.

A number of rather interesting points also emerge on reflection, however, from Cardinal McCabe's correspondence with the Irish bishops. Implicit, for example, in the pope's decision to call a conference was notice that the cardinal had failed to effect Rome's will in the Irish Church, and other means would now have to be explored. That is why McCabe was driven to ask his really irrelevant and even irreverent question about the good that might be expected from an act of the pope himself. That is also why the bishops, in general, avoided coming to terms on the substantive issues raised by

the agenda, and why Nulty and Higgins, in particular, were so
adamant about leaving well enough alone. The bishops must
have certainly wondered whether they were really being called
to Rome for a conference or for a lecture on the late and
still latent agitation. What indeed would their position be, if,
after they were representatively summoned to Rome, instead,
as Croke had been individually the year before, and then had
to face their enraged people with another Parnell Circular, or
worse? Small wonder the Irish bishops preferred to advise
Rome collectively from the precincts of Maynooth or Dublin,
rather than hazard their representative advice in the shadow
of the Propaganda or the Vatican.

Curiously enough, it was Rome which gave the initial, even
if unintentional, impetus to what would finally result in the
formal reconciliation between the Irish Church and the Irish
party. Rome had been grievously disappointed by its failure to
command any effective action, as indeed it had some three
years before, on the part of the British government with
regard to the threat to Propaganda's property by the Italian
government. Rome could hardly be blamed for thinking that
the only material difference in the situation was the order that
now prevailed in Ireland as against the disorder then. Rome
was also dissatisfied, it appears, with the patent ineffectiveness
of Cardinal McCabe and most of the Irish bishops in the
matter. "By the direction of Cardinal Simeoni," McCabe wrote
on June 16, in reply to a letter of Kirby's which had given early
news of O'Callaghan's appointment, "the Bishops will at their
approaching Meeting, address a letter to Mr. Gladstone"(K).
"No one," he added in this reply of June 16, 1884, "expects
any good from it."[3] "Some fear," he concluded feebly, "the
letter may do harm. But of course our duty is to obey authority."

At their Maynooth meeting early in July the bishops duly
drew up the required petition and presented it to Mr.
Gladstone. "We all knew what it would be," MacEvilly reported bitterly to Kirby on July 13, after Gladstone had replied, "but as Propaganda Authorities wished it, we of course
applied to the Government. But rely on it, they will never give

. [3] For at least one other who agreed with McCabe, see Mc, March 25, 1884,
MacEvilly to McCabe: "I am glad our views regarding the useless application to
authorities nemo tenetin inutile coincide."

Catholics or Ireland anything they can refuse"(K). "I am not as you are aware," he assured Kirby, "a violent Politician. But I feel very strongly the injustice practiced towards us."[4] Anticipating Gladstone's unsatisfactory reply, the bishops at their meeting had also adroitly drawn up a reserve resolution, which they forwarded on July 21 to all the Irish M.P.'s. The resolution proposed by Nulty and seconded by Logue read:

> That we request the Irish Members of Parliament, of all political parties, to use their influence with Her Majesty's Government in support of the letter which we have addressed to *Mr. Gladstone*, requesting him to take all effective steps in his power to prevent the threatened spoliation of the property of the Propaganda, in which so many of Her Majesty's subjects have a deep interest.[5]

"Your Lordship is doubtless aware," Matthew Quinn reported to Kirby from Harrogate on August 2, "of the vigorous remonstrance made by the Irish Bishops to Mr. Gladstone"(K). "Seeing however," Quinn then explained, "that Mr. Glad. could not do much their Lordships placed the matter in the hands of the Irish Parliamentary Party in the House. They have promised their most energetic support, and Mr. Parnell called on Card. Manning to obtain all information possible about it and telegraphed to Dr. Gilooley [sic] to telegraph to the Secretary of Propaganda and get accurate information of the amount of ecclesiastical property British and Irish funded in Propa." Quinn's misunderstanding of the fact that the Irish bishops had requested *all* the Irish members and not just the Parnellite members, was most interesting and highly significant. Parnell had obviously, once again, successfully seized the political initiative. For over a year he had been carefully cultivating a reconciliation between the Church and the party by a series of astute political moves. The bishops and clergy, in general, did not, of course, immediately perceive

---

[4] The particular cause of MacEvilly's general indignation at this time was the fact the chief secretary for Ireland, G. O. Trevelyan, had just informed him that there were no funds available to build an industrial school in Connemara. "The truth is," MacEvilly explained to Kirby in this same letter, "Trevelian [sic] & Co. are covert proselytizers and they will not do anything to stop proselytism. I cant trust myself to expose them as it might bring help to the Tories."

[5] Mc. See printed circular letter, July 21, 1884, covering the resolution and signed by Woodlock and Logue as honourable secretaries.

the Parnellite tactic, let alone appreciate that astute politician's strategy.

Parnell had begun his campaign the previous August by reassuring the clergy, who had in the main recently stood to him and against Rome on the Circular, that there was no doubt about his being sound in the education question. When the subject of voting money for prizes for the Queen's Colleges was introduced in the House, Parnell virtually made a one-man stand against voting any money for such purposes to those institutions. Some six months after the event, and in lamenting the fact that nothing was being done about providing university education for Catholics, that very shrewd and intelligent clerical politician, William J. Walsh, the president of Maynooth, wrote McCabe explaining what was as well as what was not happening. "So far as I know," Walsh pointed out to the Cardinal on February 12, 1884, "Parnell was not spoken to, or communicated with at all. I carefully avoided meeting him. Yet with his usual skill, he seized the opportunity, and in the absence of everyone else (except Col. Colthurst) made a Parnellite stand against the Queen's Colleges"(Mc). "This is the sort of thing," Walsh warned the cardinal, "that is throwing the whole country into the hands of him and his followers."

Parnell's "stand" on the education question was actually only a part of a broader and more comprehensive attempt to conciliate that segment of the clergy who might still have some misgivings about his earlier radical beginnings and associations in Irish politics. If the Irish clergy disliked and distrusted any group in the House of Commons more than the Tories, it was the English Radicals led by Joseph Chamberlain and Sir Charles Dilke. No one was more explicit about this than Laurence Gillooly, the bishop of Elphin, and the "strong man" on the Episcopal Education Committee now that Moran had been translated to Sydney. "In my episcopal life," he informed McCabe in late March, 1884, "no Government scheme has ever caused me so much uneasiness as the Education Bill."[6] "The dangers are in the future," he warned, "but I believe in the near future, when Mr. Chamberlain & Co. will succeed Mr. Gladstone at the head of affairs—and will have a thoroughly secularist House of Commons not only to support

---

[6] Mc, Wednesday Morn, 1884 [March 26?].

but to lead them in their Godless educational measures." "The dangers are so clear to me," he emphasized to McCabe, who considered him an alarmist, "that I really cannot understand how any one with his eyes open to the school war that has been raging in the world around us, can fail to see that the enemy is on our own borders—and will not fail to cross them, if not instantly & bravely repelled."

Those bishops and priests who agreed with Gillooly about the future dangers of godless education must have certainly been reassured by the mounting Parnellite attack on the English Radicals during 1884. In February, the House of Commons had once again voted against allowing the English Radical, Charles Bradlaugh, to take his seat for Northampton because as an avowed atheist he refused to do more than affirm the necessary oath.[7] From an Irish Catholic point of view, the most significant thing about Bradlaugh's rejection was the solid Parnellite phalanx of forty-three votes against him. Since it was obvious by March that the new franchise would result in Parnell's being returned with a following of well over eighty after the next general election, it must have been increasingly apparent to the Irish Bishops and priests that their best guarantee against the triumph of secular education in a new Parliament was to make their peace with the Irish party. Parnell, meanwhile, shrewdly continued to improve his image as far as the more conservative of the Irish clergy were concerned. In April, for example, Parnell went out of his way to denounce Davitt's radical ideas about land-nationalization as both delusive and divisive. Further, in July, the Parnellite *United Ireland* maintained that "a sense of meanness is the nearest approach to shame of which the liberty-loving English radical is capable," and during the summer Parnellite speakers made it a point to sneer at Radicals.[8]

The stock of the party in clerical circles had also been enhanced indirectly by a series of scandals involving a number of Dublin Castle officials in a homosexual ring which was uncovered in early July. "The iniquitous revelations," Quinn reported to Kirby at the end of August, "made concerning the

---

[7] Conor Cruise O'Brien, *Parnell and His Party, 1880-1890* (Oxford, 1957), p. 89. See also, for a more general discussion, W. C. Arnstein, "Parnell and the Bradlaugh Case," *Irish Historical Studies* **13** (March, 1951), No. 51.

[8] *Ibid.*, p. 88, quoting *United Ireland*, July 19, 1884.

Castle officials have made a profound sensation in Ireland. This together with the quiet businesslike work of the national party has gone far to unite all parties with them. It would amaze you to hear some of the persons who opposed them most vehemently denying that they ever disbelieved in them."[9] "Everything," he assured Kirby, "looks bright for Ireland at present. The material prosperity corresponds with the political. The summer has been very fine and there are prospects of a very good harvest." "There appears to be one drawback," Quinn then concluded significantly, "viz., that the Government will not correct any abuse till they are absolutely forced to do it." In keeping with Quinn's observation, the Parnellites in early September began to harass the government because of its refusal to consider the threat to Propaganda's property. On September 5, for example, F. H. O'Donnell made a motion as the House was sitting as Committee of Supply that the vote for diplomatic services should be reduced by an amount equal to the salary of Her Majesty's ambassador at Rome.[10] He also suggested that the papers concerning the question of Propaganda should be laid before Parliament.

The archbishop of Cashel, meanwhile, was taking good care to cultivate and develop his own late reconciliation with Rome. "Kindly get the enclosed short address translated into Italian," Croke requested Kirby, on August 25, "and published in one of the Roman clerical Journals—the 'Osservatore' for instance"(K). "It is not meant," he added good-humoredly, "to be a 'set-off' against the numerous heresies discovered by your inquisitorial eye in my Roscrea Sermon, but simply as a proof that I am not forgetting the financial claims of the Holy Father

---

[9] See also K, August 16, 1884, W. Maziere Brady to Kirby, from Lucerne: "We met, since we left Rome, Capt. *Talbot*, late Chief Commissioner of Police in Dublin, who has enlightened me considerably about the misdoings in Dublin Castle. He is a Catholic. . . ." For this whole and rather disagreeable exposé, see *United Ireland*, July 5, 12, and 19, 1884.

[10] Hansard, *Parliamentary Debates*, Third Series, **291**, Cols. 1634-1640. See also F. O., 170/347, September 10, 1884, Lumley to Granville from Rome, for a very indignant reaction on the part of Lumley. It would seem, if Lumley was correct, that Propaganda's property was actually augmented rather than confiscated by the action of the Italian government in converting Propaganda's real property into Italian government bonds, and any claim that Propaganda had lost by the conversion was, at the least, misleading, if not dishonest, and that insisting that the matter be raised in the House of Commons could only embarrass the Vatican and those bishops who had petitioned the government and who had been misinformed as far as the facts were concerned. The whole matter was in fact soon allowed to drop.

on the Church of Cashel." "The Collection when completed," he assured Kirby, "will be a great success, and I expect, P. G. to be able to hand his Holiness something like 50,000 lire [£2,000] as a result." "When in Rome in '80," Croke reminded Kirby, "I gave him 70,000 lire [£2,800], so that within 4 years, Cashel will have contributed 120,000 to the Peter's pence fund." Croke then asked whether indeed the rumors current in the press about the Irish bishops' visit to Rome being postponed indefinitely were true. The visit had indeed been postponed, but not indefinitely, for the Propaganda authorities had rescheduled it for September of 1885.[11] Why the visit had been put off for a year probably had most to do with McCabe's correspondence with the Irish bishops about an agenda for the meeting. Undoubtedly, McCabe wrote Cardinal Simeoni that the consensus of the bishops as a body was against a meeting because of the unsettling effect it might have on the country, and Rome appears to have agreed.

When the Irish bishops assembled, therefore, for their annual general meeting in Maynooth in early October, no one expected they would disturb the mood of quiet confidence and calm expectation that pervaded the country. The meeting, however, produced a political uproar. Besides the usual string of resolutions on the education question, an additional resolution was proposed by the archbishop of Cashel and seconded by the bishop of Meath to the effect.

> That we call upon the Irish parliamentary party to bring the above resolutions under the notice of the House of Commons, and to urge generally upon the government the hitherto unsatisfied claims of Catholic Ireland in all branches of the educational question.[12]

Some of the criticism of what amounted, in some minds at least, to shaking hands with the devil, and a devil moreover, who had been publicly condemned by Rome only the year before, was very embarrassing to the defenders of the new alliance. One of the first to applaud the new departure of the Irish bishops was Herbert Vaughan, the bishop of Salford,

---

[11] K, November 20, 1884, McGettigan to Kirby. See this letter for the archbishop of Armagh's retrospective remarks.

[12] Quoted in C. C. O'Brien, *op. cit.*, pp. 89-90, from *Freeman's Journal*, October 2, 1884.

who owned and published the English Catholic weekly, the *Tablet*. Vaughan, who appears to have been as politically flexible as he was ecclesiastically astute, appreciated very quickly, of course, that there was a new wind blowing from Rome, which had resulted in Cardinal Manning returning to London in high favor. One of Kirby's former students, for example, wrote him justifying the Bishops' new policy by an appeal to the *Tablet*. "Our Bishops," James Hasson explained on October 12, from Derry, "have, as the general cry goes, put themselves into the hands of Parnell, but, really, as the *Tablet* well says, no other course was open to them if they wanted their resolutions to be effective"(K). At least one of those bishops felt obliged to defend his conduct to Kirby several weeks later. "Some parties," MacEvilly reported on October 26, "affect to be scandalized at the Irish bishops at the Synod placing the Education question in the hands of the Irish Party"(K). "But the fact is," he maintained, "many of the Bishops, who, like myself, never joined the Irish Party, feel that there is no other possible way of gaining our rights from a Government that will give Catholics nothing from love." Both MacEvilly among the bishops and Hasson among the second order of clergy had been opposed to Parnell, his party, and the agitation over the last four years. They were, in fact, representative of those clergy who were the mainstay of the position taken by McCabe as against Croke in the Irish Church. Slowly but surely they had grudgingly to give way to circumstance, and in approving the new clerical-nationalist alliance as necessary, they had finally signified that Croke had at least been prudent if not right, and that Parnell had won.

In spite of the furor raised pro and con by this unexpected reconciliation of the bishops to the Irish party, this apparently revolutionary and, to some, unholy step was really the result of Parnell's foresight in creating a viable political alternative for the clergy. Parnell's end and aim was political power. No one understood better than he did that no power base in Ireland could be consolidated unless the clergy, high and low, were committed to it. Since his release, therefore, from Kilmainham some two and a half years before, he had been assiduously cultivating a new image which was political and constitutional rather than agrarian and revolutionary. There was, perhaps, no more remarkable an example of the success of his strategy than the political conversion in the summer of

1884 of Cardinal McCabe's old friend and dean of the arch-diocese of Dublin, Walter M. Lee. Dean Lee was one of Cardinal McCabe's three vicars general as well as one of the most respected and influential of his priests. "We have been contending here," he wrote Kirby on the occasion of his Gold-en Jubilee as a priest, "for six or eight months against an overwhelming Orange ascendancy: the so called liberal Irish Executive has deceived and betrayed us."[13] "I told our Whig Lord Chancellor," Lee explained, referring to Edward Sulli-van, "that treatment such as we have received is calculated to convince Priests and people that Ireland's only hope is now centered in the Constitutional efforts of Mr. Parnell and the Irish party—last July I sent him [Sullivan] a letter with this conclusion." "The Bishops at their last Meeting," Lee then concluded with obvious satisfaction, "seem to have endorsed this opinion." In a word, McCabe had not only lost control of his majority among the bishops, but he obviously no longer had even the confidence of those who were closest to him in politico-religious matters. The significance, moreover, of the cardinal being over-ridden by the body of bishops in the making of policy for the Irish Church was very great. For, a precedent had now been established in which basic policy was to be determined by the body of the bishops without either reference to the hierarchical structure of the Irish Church, or, more importantly, without even previous consultation with Rome.

The new alliance between the Irish party and the Irish Church, naturally, raised some very serious problems for both the British government and the Roman Church. The gov-ernment in its effort to govern in Ireland would now find it impossible to drive its customary wedge in nationalist ranks because it had been deprived by the alliance of its only effec-tive moral hammer. For Rome, the essential problem was still how to maintain its own power and influence in the Irish Church, and this was only further complicated by the alliance. At first, there was an almost instinctive drawing together again of the British government and the Roman Church vis-à-vis their own problems in Ireland. Errington, who had been in partial eclipse since O'Callaghan's appointment in

---

[13] K, October, 1884 [no day].

June and his failure to secure a place for Neville on the episcopal bench, suddenly again became a *persona grata* at Rome. Prior to Errington's rehabilitation, however, there occurred a useful and interesting illustration of one of the first principles in diplomacy—that one never firmly closes a diplomatic door. About the middle of August, with British-Vatican relations at their lowest point since his elevation, Leo XIII sent as a present, through his secretary of state, the complete works of St. Thomas Acquinas to Queen Victoria. In returning the compliment at the beginning of September through her foreign secretary, the queen discreetly opted for her own *More Leaves* rather than *The Life of the Prince Consort*, which contained references to papal aggression.[14]

In any case, about the middle of October both Monsignor and Cardinal Jacobini had written Errington asking him to use his good offices with the British government in effecting an accommodation respectively in Goa and Malta. "In replying to both of them," Errington alerted Smith on October 21, "I felt obliged to state plainly the very serious effect which recent decisions of the Irish Bishops at their Meeting has had & is likely farther to have." "It is triumphantly accepted by the Nationalist papers," he added, "as a formal adhesion of the Catholic Church to their cause, & is universally stated & believed to have been done with the Pope's express approval. The effect in England is simply deplorable." He had assured both Spencer and Granville, Errington added, that he felt certain the pope had not authorized an action so evidently hostile to England, but that the public and the press had put their own interpretation on it, arguing that the Irish bishops would never have dared to reverse themselves in so flagrant a manner if they had not the approval of Rome. "Pray write to me," an evidently bewildered Errington begged in conclusion, "what you hear & think of this and what you advise; I own I am much puzzled on how to act."

Smith, however, was apparently as puzzled as Errington, for he did not reply for some three weeks, at least, and Errington in the meanwhile had written Cardinal Jacobini asking him for an explanation. Cardinal Jacobini had replied to his complaints, Errington again alerted Smith on November

---

[14] Agatha Ramm (ed.), *The Political Correspondence of Mr. Gladstone and Lord Granville 1876-1888* **2** (Oxford, 1962): p. 235.

2, noting that he had spoken to the Pope, and that "the Pope had desired him to state *formally* that the Bishops' action was taken without his *knowledge or approval*." While this pleased Granville and Spencer, Errington explained, they pointed out that it was universally believed that the bishops' action had the pope's approval, and that the pope's denial should be made public. He had written Cardinal Jacobini again asking him to have the denial inserted in the *Osservatore*. Errington then asked Smith to speak also to the Roman correspondent of the *Tablet* about the denial because that paper he was sorry to say "has veered round and is now writing in a *Parnellite sense*, and the Parnellite papers instead of being grateful are ridiculing & abusing the Tablet for its change of front." In concluding his letter Errington returned to the well-worn subject of diplomatic relations by pointing out once again that both Granville and the government were very friendly and well disposed.

> Lord Granville is also quite willing I should return to Rome at Xmas, *if the Pope desires it*: but recent events have thrown some doubt on this, and I am placed in a delicate position. What do you think: It would be unfortunate to break off relations just now; pray have a talk about this with Card. Jacobini & let me know.
>
> I can only say that it was never more important to have some one at Rome: that Lord Granville is most friendly, that the prospect (for dip. relations) is to *my mind* most promising as soon as new elections are over, & that therefore any coldness or rupture now would be a misfortune(K).

In his reply to this letter, Smith evidently not only assured Errington that he would be most welcome in Rome, but that Cardinal Jacobini had agreed that the pope's denial that he had been consulted by the Irish bishops before their late action at Maynooth, should be published. After waiting about a week for the promised contradiction to be published, an anxious Errington wrote Smith again on November 22, asking him to enquire into the reason for the delay. The day before Errington wrote to Smith, however, the British ambassador in Rome had already reported to Granville why the contradiction had not appeared. The matter had indeed been brought to the attention of Cardinal Jacobini, who had indeed agreed that a contradiction "ought to appear in the Vatican press."[15]

---

[15] F. O., 45/500.

"Some days having elapsed," Lumley went on to explain in his dispatch to Granville "without the appearance in any clerical paper of the proposed contradiction, the subject was again mentioned to Cardinal Jacobini, who said he had forgotten the circumstance and that as some time had eleapsed since the fact occurred, it would perhaps be wiser not to notice it." The cardinal secretary of state, if not indeed the pope, had not only some very wise, but some very diplomatic second thoughts about the late action of the Irish bishops. A contradiction now would only alienate the Irish bishops at a stroke and upset the patient attempt of Rome to restructure its power and influence in the Irish Church. Further, both the pope and the cardinal must have realized that the late British anxiety to please was undoubtedly a direct result of the Irish bishops' action, and that Rome had acquired by that action a very valuable *quid pro quo* in any renewal of the game of diplomatic relations.

Still, the fact that the Irish bishops had stolen a march and presented them with a *fait accompli* could not have been very pleasing to the Roman authorities. The conference of Irish bishops in Rome, which had originally been called for September and then postponed for a year, was now, significantly, rescheduled for the end of January and the beginning of February. The meeting would be presided over by Cardinal Simeoni who had prepared an agenda which would include matters primarily having to do with Church discipline, but which would not preclude, significantly, the discussion of Irish political questions.[16] Originally, the cardinal archbishop, his auxiliary, the other three archbishops, and two suffragans from each of the four Provinces were chosen to go to Rome, or thirteen in all of a hierarchy of thirty-two.[17] Cardinal McCabe then raised the number to sixteen by requesting Cardinal Simeoni to add the bishops of Raphoe and Galway and the coadjutor of Clonfert as supernumeraries since they had just held teaching chairs in theology in Maynooth. When McCabe was obliged to ask for a leave of absence from the Conference called for January on the grounds of poor health, the delegation was reduced to fifteen.

The immediate reaction of the Irish bishops to this unex-

---

[16] *Ibid.*
[17] K, December 10, 1884, Croke to Kirby.

pected summons to Rome was evidently one of consternation. A number of them wrote the archbishop of Armagh, Daniel McGettigan, who as primate would head the delegation in the absence of Cardinal McCabe, and persuaded him to consult Kirby as to the best means of explaining their general reluctance to go to Rome in January. "Some of the Prelates," McGettigan wrote Kirby on November 20, enclosing some £600 in Peter's Pence, "who are to be on the deputation to Rome have written to express humbly and earnestly their wish that the Holy Father should be implored to postpone the Conference of the Irish Bishops till the Autumn of 1885 as your Lordship's first notification led them to believe would be the time"(K). "Most of the Prelates," he began his woeful catalog, "are beyond the middle age. January is the dreariest of the winter months: they will have to face cholera raging in Paris & smouldering in Italy: they will have to cross two Seas and travel by rail some 1500 miles at a season when they would wish to be at home." "Could your Lordship," McGettigan pleaded, "advise what the Prelates should do? And if a petion [sic] to His Holiness would be listened to for exemption at present?" Kirby pleaded McGettigan's brief before the pope, and it was decided early in December that the visit scheduled for January should be fixed instead for Easter. The Irish bishops, needless to say, all breathed a collective sigh of relief.[18]

"I write you this line," Croke wrote Kirby benevolently, on December 18, "to wish you a happy Christmas, and to thank you, as I do most sincerely, for your kind offices with the Holy Father in reference to our visit to Rome"(K). "Everything now, looks well thank God," he continued good-naturedly, "April will be a nice month for travelling, and we may reasonably hope our sojourn in Rome will not be protracted beyond the middle of May." "I desire greatly," Croke then came to his point, "to take with me as Secretary the very Revd Dr. Walsh, president of Maynooth, in the hope that he may be permitted to be present at our deliberations at Propaganda, and to assist us afterwards in putting our views in shape for presentation to the presiding Cardinals." "Could you ascertain," Croke asked, "whether a Secretary would be allowed to be present during

---

[18] See K, December 10, 1884, McCabe to Kirby; December 17, 1884, Mac Evilly to Kirby; December 23, 1884, McGettigan to Kirby.

our discussions?" "I believe," he added, citing his precedent, "Dr. Corcoran had that privilege, when the American Bishops were doing their business in Rome."

Errington, meanwhile, had been making his preparations to visit Rome during the parliamentary Christmas recess. Soon after Parliament adjourned, therefore, in the first week in December, he crossed over to Dublin to see both McCabe and Spencer. "In my visit to Ireland," he reported to Smith from Paris on Christmas Day on his way to Rome, "I saw Dr. Donnelly, Card. McCabe & others. The Cardinal *is going to* Rome he tells me at Easter; this is good; he is much better"(S). "He is quite alive," Errington further assured Smith, "to the importance of the Bishops' recent action; he says it is neither more nor less than a vote of confidence in Parnell & his party." "Dr. Donnelly gives me an extraordinary account," he concluded gravely, and referring to the recent consecration of Abraham Brownrigg as bishop of Ossory in Kilkenny, "of Dr. Croke's great advance in popularity, power, & position; his visit to Kilkenny was one long scene of triumph." After his visit to Dublin, Errington had returned to London where he had a final interview with Granville before his departure for Rome. Several days after their interview, Granville decided to put his very strong feelings about the Irish bishops' recent provocative action in effecting an alliance with the Irish party on paper in order to strengthen Errington's diplomatic hand in Rome. He reminded Errington, therefore, on December 23, that Lord Spencer was not only "painfully surprised" at the action of the bishops, but that the Irish viceroy was convinced "that any support given by the Roman Catholic Hierarchy to those who systematically attack the Judges of the Land, and the whole administration of justice cannot be agreeable to the Holy See."[19] "The object of this party," Granville declared of himself, "is the Separation of Ireland from Great Britain. There is a unanimous feeling here that this shall never be."

Some three weeks later on January 15, Errington reported to Granville from Rome that he had already spoken to Cardinal Jacobini and asked him to express formally to the pope Lord Spencer's deep concern about the action of the bishops.[20]

---

[19] B, 49690.
[20] *Ibid.*

The cardinal assured Errington that he would speak to the pope, and that he hoped, moreover, the pope would allow him to write a private letter to Cardinal McCabe, the substance of which would be divulged, disavowing knowledge or approval of the bishops' action. In any case, Errington reassured Granville that Cardinal Jacobini had authorized him to say that the government's representations would be carefully borne in mind when the bishops visited Rome at Easter. That very morning, Errington then explained, the cardinal had told him that he had laid his representations before the pope, and that His Holiness agreed that the visit of the bishops at Easter would afford a fitting opportunity to deal with their present attitude, but that he had not been able to persuade the pope to listen to his suggestion of a letter to McCabe. Errington further noted that he expressed his disappointment over this, but the cardinal had pointed out that the pope "was somewhat cold on the subject," and that this "was perhaps due to the Pope's disappointment that England has not shown more courage in renewing relations with him."

Errington then proceeded to explain to Granville that he needed some tangible demonstrations of British good will towards the Vatican if he were ever to gain any ground in Rome with regard to Irish affairs, and that the current situations in both Goa and Malta were excellent opportunities.[21] He asked Granville, therefore, to support the Vatican in its quarrel with Lisbon over the control of the jurisdiction of the archbishop of Goa in ecclesiastical matters. In Malta, the governor, Sir John Lintorn Simmons, had objected to the appointment of a coadjutor with the right of succession to the ailing bishop of Malta because the proposed coadjutor was not an Englishman. Cardinal Jacobini had assured Errington that

---

[21] For the initiation of this question, see Errington to Granville, November 18, and especially November 23, 1884 (ibid.): "I have read the papers as you were so good as to send me about Malta. The subject is not new to me. I have been kept fully informed from various sources, and have had more than one conversation about it at Rome during the last three years. When I spoke to the Cardinal Secretary about Malta three years ago, we discussed exactly the proposal now made by Sir Lintorn Simmons, that a Papal delegate should be sent to put things in order, and to this the Cardinal was quite willing to agree. This year, just after I left Rome, Mr. Hutchinson wrote to me at length on this subject; but it was too late. Had he written sooner, I have little doubt I could have arranged the matter. It is most important that no one should suspect at Malta that the Governor tried to get Rome to interfere. I do not agree with Sir Lintorn Simmons' suggestion that the proposed delegate should be an English ecclesiastic. An Italian would be more free and far more able to deal vigourously."

the Vatican would be willing to forego appointing with the right to succeed, thus leaving the succession to a future settlement, but that they wanted to appoint a Maltese, Monsignor Buhagiar, as the bishop of Malta's ecclesiastical administrator in the meantime. The government decided to override Simmons's objection, and Granville telegraphed Errington on January 31, that there was no objection now to the appointment of Monsignor Buhagiar.[22] In thanking Granville on February 12 for his good offices in the Malta affair, Errington continued to press for an accommodation about Goa.[23] "This long protracted Goa difficulty," he advised Granville, "has been a grief and a sorrow to successive Popes, and that is why a word from you would now be so highly valued."

The unexpected death of Cardinal McCabe the day before, however, had suddenly transformed the whole diplomatic situation. The cardinal had died early on Wednesday morning, February 11, after a brief illness, and after having received all the sacraments. The British government was now faced with a critical and immediate crisis in Ireland whose · final resolution rested entirely with the pope. Not only had the pope been placed in an excellent bargaining position vis-à-vis the British government with regard to diplomatic relations by the recent action of the Irish bishops, but he was now involved with a possible quid pro quo, which did not depend in the last analysis on the consent of the Irish Church or the Irish people—the appointment of an archbishop. When Spencer learned of the cardinal's death he immediately informed Granville that much would depend on who succeeded McCabe, and asked Granville to allow Errington to say in the proper quarter how deeply the government deplored his death.[24] "He not only stoutly supported the cause of Law & order," Spencer eulogized briefly, "in the face of Popular opposition but he was always most friendly & moderate in all his views. I had the most friendly relations with him." "I think," he concluded, in a less nostalgic vein, "this might be politic."

The news of Cardinal McCabe's death reached Rome late Wednesday evening, and Errington wrote Granville the fol-

---

[22] GR, 30/29/149.
[23] B, 49690.
[24] GR, 30/29/142.

lowing day. He explained that the news was particularly serious because he feared that the president of Maynooth, William J. Walsh, "a violent and dangerous man," who would be vigorously supported by Croke and his friends, was likely to succeed as archbishop of Dublin.[25] He asked Granville, therefore, to be allowed to urge on the pope as strongly as possible that the government had "a right to wish and expect that as important a post as the See of Dublin should be occupied by a man of loyal and moderate views." In order to improve his bargaining position Errington suggested that the new administrator to the bishop of Malta, Monsignor Buhagiar, as a courtesy might be transported to his new post in a British gunboat, and further recommended that Granville make some concession about Goa. Late in the day, after a visit to the Propaganda, and a conversation with its secretary, Monsignor Jacobini, Errington wrote Granville again. He explained that Jacobini also feared that Walsh was the strongest and most likely candidate to succeed McCabe.[26] Errington added that he took it for granted that Spencer would be opposed to Walsh, but he would like to know for certain what his views were. In conclusion, Errington warned Granville that Michael Davitt, who was on his way to Australia, was now in Rome, and he was reported to have brought strong letters of recommendation from both Croke and Manning.

In Dublin, meanwhile, the main concern after the death of the cardinal was the election of a vicar capitular, who would be responsible for administrating the diocese until the new archbishop was appointed by the pope. When the cathedral chapter, consisting of some twenty canons, met on Friday, February 13, to elect the vicar capitular, therefore, the speculation about who would be selected was as anxious as it was intense. How the canons would vote was likely to be a conservative preview of the voting that would take place a month later when the Dublin clergy met to commend the customary three names to Rome for their see. The vote of the canons did indeed prove to be highly significant. The president of Maynooth, William J. Walsh, received twelve votes, while the auxiliary bishop of Dublin, Nicholas Donnelly, received only four. The other votes were divided between the dean of the

---

[25] B, 49690.
[26] Ibid.

diocese, Walter M. Lee, who received three, and one of the
vicars general, Edward Kennedy, who received one. Walsh's
vice president at Maynooth, Robert Browne, immediately
telegraphed the good news to Croke, who instantly wrote
Walsh that no news had ever reached him that pleased him
more.[27] "All day," Croke confided, "I was brooding over this
Dublin affair; but was quite sure that the old fogies would go
in for Donnelly. The tables are turned completely. I'll say no
more now." Walsh replied briefly the following day, "A
thousand thanks. Awkward as the proceeding is for me, it has
one good side to it at all events. The 'Pale' is out of fashion."

Naturally, Spencer was almost as much upset by Walsh's
triumph as Croke was pleased. In reporting the results of the
voting to Granville on February 19, Spencer noted that what
was most disturbing was that all the canons who voted for
Walsh had been appointed by Cardinals Cullen and McCabe,
and that they were not presumably, therefore, radical in their
politics.[28] In further illustrating his point about this basic
change in political front, if not in heart, on the part of the
senior Dublin clergy, and independently echoing Walsh's remark about the Pale now being out of fashion, Spencer
explained that

> The Queen sent a message to express her regret at the death of
> the Cardinal which Bishop Donnelly received with much plea-
> sure & conveyed to the meeting. He said that it will be for the
> Vicar Capitular to write to me to express to the Queen their
> thanks for her message. / Upon his saying this there was a
> murmur throughout the assembly & it was pronounced as an
> impossible thing to do. / It was finally agreed that the Bishop
> should convey by word of mouth to me the acknowledgement.[29]

What this episode proved, Spencer maintained, was that "if
even if these Seniors of the Church are loyal they are afraid of
committing the expression of their loyalty in the form of a
Resolution." "These proceedings of the Chapter," he concluded finally, "are considered by the best R. C. Laymen in
Ireland as very grave, & they are much alarmed at the attitude

---

[27] Walsh Papers(W), Archives of the Archdiocese of Dublin, February 13, 1885.
Browne was Walsh's vice president at Maynooth.
[28] GR, 30/29/149.
[29] *Ibid.*

which the Church is adopting."

That same day, Croke wrote Kirby a long and interesting letter about what was happening and what had been happening in Dublin. "We have buried," Croke reported on February 19, "the poor Cardinal. He made a hard fight of it. But, indeed, I think, after his late attacks he was in no way fit to encounter any serious sickness"(K). "The great question now," Croke quickly came to the point, "is as to his successor, Dr. Walsh of Maynooth, now Vicar Capitular will have the vast majority of the Dublin Clergy to vote for him. It is thought he will have seven-eighths of the pastors on his side. He had 12 Canons out of 20 supporting him for the Vicar Capitularship." "Dr. Walsh, as you know," Croke then added persuasively, "is President of Maynooth, a young, active, zealous, earnest, and wonderfully gifted man." " In politics," "Croke continued, a good deal less candidly, "he is, I think, neutral." "So I dare say," he commented in his own picturesque way, "he will, as the Yankees say,'walk the plank.' " "Abbot Smith and Errington," Croke then warned Kirby, "are already at work."

> About six weeks ago, the former wrote to Cardinal McCabe to say that he ought to have Dr. Donnelly appointed Coadjutor, at once, with a right of succession; that this would be very pleasing to Mr. Errington and strengthen his hand greatly in Rome, and that he (Smith) had reason to know that the thing would be sanctioned by the Holy See. On this the late Cardinal called three of his Vicars to him—namely Lee, Kennedy, and Walsh[e] and consulted them as to what he should do under the circumstances. They advised him not to make such a move. Therefore he (the Card.) wrote to Smith to say that his Vicars did not approve of his taking the step suggested, but that he would write to Cardinal Simeoni to ask his opinion. . . . Smith, at once, wired, or wrote, to Cardinal McCabe praying him *not* to mention the matter to Card. Simeoni, as it was quite *unofficial*, and a proprio motu of his own aided by his friend Errington(K).

"This is all quite certain," Croke assured Kirby. "I have it from the Vicars whom the late Cardinal consulted on the matter, and it shows you what a 'boyo' Smith is." "Drop me a line," Croke suggested, "as soon as you have anything to communicate." "Has Davitt called on you?" he asked in conclusion. "He is a very good Catholic, and a most sincere upright man. It

would be a great blessing if he could get to see the Pope, as he
has something *special* to say to him."

Davitt had indeed been recommended the month before to
Kirby's consideration in Rome by the nationalist bishop of
Achonry, F. J. MacCormack, as well as by Croke.[30] In late
January, therefore, Davitt had stopped over in Rome on his
way to the antipodes in order to secure an audience with the
pope. Before leaving London, Davitt had confided to W. T.
Stead, the editor of the influential *Pall Mall Gazette*, the substance of the something special he proposed to say to the pope
if granted an interview. Stead later reported Davitt as saying:

> Ireland is to-day the great propagandist of the Catholic Faith.
> Irish bishops and priests rule the Catholic Church throughout
> the English-speaking world. Irish emigrants have taken the
> seeds of the faith into England, Scotland, Wales, America,
> Canada, South Africa, Australia. This missionary work has
> never been recognised at the centre of the Christian world.
> Ireland's enemies have been more than once on the point of
> poisoning your ear against the most devoted of Catholic na-
> tions, simply because you have never commanded *your faithful
> Irish people to send you an accredited representative to reside in Rome*,
> and to advise you from time to time regarding Irish political or
> social movements, and their real bearing on religion and mor-
> als.[31]

"Guard against the possibility of this," Stead quoted Davitt as
proposing to advise the pope in conclusion, "therefore, by
asking the Irish Bishops to send, on behalf of the Irish
Catholic race, an accredited representative to reside near
Your Person in Rome, and give him the dignity of a Cardinal
in compliment to the race which to-day is making the Church
truly universal."

On February 8, three days before the death of Cardinal
McCabe, the Roman correspondent of the London *Times* reported that "it would interest Mr. Davitt's friends to hear of
the distinction with which he was received in Rome."[32] The *St.
James's Gazette* of the same date, however, was even more
explicit. "It will interest other people," the correspondent in

---

[30] K, January 2, 1885.

[31] Patrick J. Walsh, *William J. Walsh, Archbishop of Dublin* (Dublin, 1928), p. 141;
cited as *Walsh*.

[32] *Ibid.*

the *Gazette* reported, "besides the elect who call themselves Michael Davitt's friends to hear that the 'Mission' of Mr. Errington also appears to have been futile here."[33] "The Papal Court," the *Gazette's* correspondent explained, "was to have been gained over to help us in our Irish troubles, and here is one of the chief movers in these troubles ostentatiously welcomed and patronised by great personages at the Vatican."

By the end of January, Errington's bargaining power, and the influence dependent upon it, had certainly been reduced to an all time low. His intrinsic importance both to the British government and to the Vatican, paradoxically enough, only appears to have increased. Errington had been arguing from weakness for some time past that in the great game of diplomatic chess the surrender of such British pawns as Malta, Goa, and the protection of the Propaganda's property, would encourage the pope to do something about that Irish castle recently erected in the form of the clerical-nationalist alliance, which if not taken before the next election would result in the annihilation of the Liberal party in Ireland. When the death of Cardinal McCabe placed a very valuable bishopric as well as a castle in the pope's offering, His Holiness might well be pardoned for wondering whether a bishop and a castle were not worth a queen in the form of diplomatic relations. Since Errington had become the symbol of that important piece to the pope on the great board, he was still therefore important, even if only parenthetically so, in terms of deferred hope. Even in the small matter of offering pawns, however, Errington was frustrated, as some of Granville's Cabinet colleagues did not seem either to appreciate the importance or to understand the complexity of the great game being played.

In writing to Granville on February 12, for example, Errington had recommended that, besides transporting Monsignor Buhagiar to Malta in a British gunboat, the government should in effect support the Vatican in its quarrel with Portugal over the question of ecclesiastical jurisdiction in Goa. Granville circulated Errington's suggestions to Gladstone and the Cabinet members who were concerned.[34] The first lord of the admiralty, Lord Northbrook, offered no objection to transporting Monsignor Buhagiar to Malta, and Northbrook

---

[33] *Ibid.*

[34] GR, 30/29/149. No date on Memorandum (probably February 16 or 17, 1885).

only wondered good-naturedly on February 18, whether the Colonial Office would pay for the prelate's entertainment.[35] The secretary for India, Lord Kimberley, however, proved a good deal less amenable to Errington's suggestion about Goa.[36] Obviously oblivious of the complications created by McCabe's recent demise, Kimberley declared that the object was "by a sidewind to get us to support the Pope in this quarrel between the Vatican & Portugal, and recommend that the Government not interfere." Granville, who seldom ever met a refusal head on, obviously sent his old friend, the Marquess of Ripon, late viceroy of India, and a very prominent and important Roman Catholic convert, who had just returned home, to speak to Kimberley. Several days later on February 20, a more tractable but still stubborn Kimberley wrote Granville again explaining that he had just seen Ripon, and now thought "we may safely go so far as to say that it appears to us that the proposal of Portugal would be no improvement on the present arrangements but would probably tend to greater inconveniences."[37] While this was obviously an improvement over his initial reaction, it was still a good deal less than what Errington thought was necessary. When Granville received Kimberley's initial negative reply, he obviously informed Errington by telegram of the objections raised by the Indian secretary. Errington was sorely disappointed, and did not hide his hurt in writing Granville by return. He explained on February 21, that he felt they "had lost an occasion, perhaps unique, of winning over the Propaganda, and at this moment, most critical for Ireland and for the Irish Church."[38] Cardinal Simeoni, the prefect, was in particular, "bitterly mortified and disappointed." The worst of it was that the cardinal had "more to do with Ireland than anyone, and I really believe that if we had now obliged him in this serious affair, for the Holy See, we might have made almost what terms we pleased about the Archbishopric of Dublin."

The Cabinet, however, may perhaps be pardoned for being more preoccupied at this time with the prospects of the government's survival than with relatively unimportant matters like Dublin, Rome, or Goa. On February 6, news had reached

---

[35] *Ibid.*
[36] *Ibid.*
[37] *Ibid.*
[38] B, 49690.

London that Khartoum had fallen and that the celebrated General Gordon was dead. Since a new parliamentary session was just about to begin and since the opposition would undoubtedly introduce a censure motion condemning the government, there was great anxiety about the ability of the government to weather the attack, especially in the face of a really outraged public opinion. The government whips, therefore, were exceedingly active and Errington had to return to London from Rome for the expected crucial division. After a full-dress debate, the censure motion was put on February 28 and the concern and anxiety of the Cabinet and the whips were fully justified as the government scraped through with a bare majority of fourteen votes.

While in London, Errington not only arranged for the transportation of Monsignor Buhagiar to Malta, but, more importantly, he finally succeeded in persuading Granville and the government to accept the views and wishes of the Vatican with regard to Goa. In reporting to Smith on March 6, Errington explained that he had already informed Cardinal Jacobini and Simeoni of the good news, but urged Smith to talk to them about it, *"and make the most of it,"* with regard to Ireland(S). He planned, in fact, to leave the next evening, Saturday, for Dublin, and would be, therefore, on the spot the following Tuesday, March 10, when the Dublin clergy finally voted their *terna*. "The more we look," Errington concluded significantly, "the less we can find anyone in Ireland fit to be Archbishop of Dublin; poor Dr. Donnelly is quite crushed by the attack made on him in the Chapter." Errington was naturally a good deal more candid with his old friend and confidant than he was in his letter to Cardinal Jacobini.[39] After reassuring the cardinal about Goa, explaining that he would return to Rome about March 15, and pointing out how seriously the British government would take the appointment of an archbishop "in accord with a political party hostile not only to the actual regime in Ireland, but one who attacks the function most essential to all administration such as justice and the repression of crime, and thus undermines the existence even

---

[39] GR, 30/29/149, March 5, 1885. This letter is a copy and is in French. It is also marked "confidentielle" and there is a covering letter of March 11, from Errington to Sanderson, a Foreign Office official, written from Dublin, explaining that "Lord Granville desired me to send you [a] copy of a letter which, after being submitted to him, I sent last week to Rome."

of all Government"; Errington then suggested somewhat insincerely that Donnelly "would be an admirable Archbishop whose prudence and wisdom everyone would acknowledge." "It is to be regretted," Errington finally observed, coming to what was really on his mind, and daring the incredible, "that Msgr. Moran is no longer in Ireland. He was the only one among the Irish Prelates fortified with the true Roman traditions, and in spite of a difficult moment three years ago, he has since displayed a rare prudence and firmness that would be very valuable to us at this moment in Ireland." "I know," he then added very shrewdly, and referring to the pope and Cardinal Simeoni, "that there is much affection and esteem for him in Rome, as much indeed as in the Irish College." Errington concluded by asking Jacobini to bring his observations about Goa and Ireland to the attention of the pope and Cardinal Simeoni. What Errington hoped to do, of course, by suggesting Moran to the pope for Dublin was to block the appointment of Walsh. Moreover, the introduction of Moran's name would split the Irish nationalist interest in Rome because Kirby could be expected to throw his considerable influence to his old friend and protégé come what may. In any deadlock that might result in a contest between Walsh and Moran, Donnelly might actually emerge as an acceptable compromise candidate between Dublin and Rome. In a word, Errington's suggestion was more than clever, it was brilliant.

In Dublin, meanwhile, Spencer was desperately trying to find a way to block Walsh's appointment. He had just been in London for the opening of Parliament where the question of re-establishing some form of diplomatic relations with Rome was discussed at a Cabinet meeting. No conclusion had obviously been come to for Spencer wrote Granville from Dublin on February 26, explaining that he had not been convinced by the arguments of either Derby or Kimberley, the colonial and Indian secretaries, respectively.[40] He also expressed the hope that Granville would be able to manage something about Rome. "A Secretary," Spencer suggested, "belonging to the Embassy but dealing directly with you & the Propaganda will surely meet the Pope's view." Earlier in this letter Spencer had reported that he had seen Ripon, but the former Indian viceroy had explained that he did not plan to visit Rome.

[40] GR, 30/29/142.

Ripon had promised, however, to ask the Duke of Norfolk, the premier English Catholic peer, whether he would make a representation on behalf of the Irish Roman Catholic laity to the pope about the appointment to Dublin. In fact, one of those "West British" Roman Catholic laymen, and Liberal M.P. for Kerry, Sir Rowland Blennerhasset, wrote Spencer a long letter several days later, providing the Irish viceroy with a good deal of food for thought if not for action.[41] "It seems probable," Blennerhasset began realistically, "that Dr. Walsh will be appointed Archbishop of Dublin." "If the Government desires to hinder this appointment," he added helpfully, "would you allow me to point out the only way it now appears possible to do so?"

> Someone thoroughly well acquainted with the methods and mechanisms of the Curia should be sent to Rome on a secret mission. His instructions should be to try and secure the nomination of a candidate selected by the government. The envoy should not be suspected at Rome of being there for the purpose of forwarding the views of the British government. He should not allow his right hand to know what his left hand does, and the secret of his mission should be known in England to those only to whom it is absolutely necessary to confide it.
>
> I venture further to recommend a person who possesses the qualities necessary to success. Mr. White, Her Majesty's Minister at Bucharest, is, as of course you know, one of the very ablest of our diplomatic servants. He is besides an instructed Catholic. He understands the habits and ways of the Curia. He is personally acquainted with the Pope. His presence in Rome might easily be accounted for by a desire to visit the city, and his intercourse with ecclesiastical authorities by the interest he has long taken in questions bearing on the reunion of some religious communities in the Balkan peninsula with Western Christendom, and in the disciplinary arrangements of those fragments of the Eastern Church in communion with Rome.[42]

In concluding his letter Blennerhasset noted that he had shown it to his good friend Lord Acton, the celebrated English Liberal Catholic, and stepson of Granville, who agreed with all he said. Spencer forwarded Blennerhasset's letter to Granville remarking that it seemed "worthy of consideration in addition

---

[41] *Ibid.*, March 1, 1885.
[42] *Ibid.*

to anything you may do through Errington."[43]

As the fateful Tuesday, March 10, of the Dublin election approached, the pressure on Walsh naturally also became very great. A week after his selection by the cathedral chapter as vicar capitular, Walsh had written Croke explaining how the voting of the clergy was likely to go. "I have been told," he reported on February 21, "that of the 64 votes about 40, or possibly 44, will go for me—the rest to D[onnelly], who will be second, and to Tynan who will be third. The suggestion of your Grace being voted for in the letter to the Irish Nation will probably lead to a certain number voting so."[44] "I wish," Walsh confessed, "we could transfer the 40. It is the only way I see out of the difficulty, so far as I am concerned." A week later Walsh's nervousness had only increased. "Speaking to your Grace," he again confessed to Croke on February 28, "as I would speak to *no one* else, I must say that I am so thoroughly satisfied as to my unfitness for the place in Dublin, I have not had two hours unbroken sleep since the election to the V. Cap'ship. I twice went to Dublin fully determined to lithograph a letter to the P.P.'s and Canons which would infallibly save me from getting even one vote on Tuesday week." "My sole difficulty in the way of doing this," Walsh explained, referring to Donnelly's "West British" leanings, "is the political side of the case." "I feel that no one," he lamented, "was ever placed in such an awkward plight." Earlier in this letter, Walsh had thrown out the suggestion, independently of Davitt, that the most useful service he could perform for the Irish Church was not as archbishop of Dublin, but as its official representative in Rome.

Croke had, meanwhile, written to both Davitt and Kirby in Rome. When he received their replies, both of February 26, he immediately forwarded them to Walsh for his comments. Kirby's curt reply to Croke's long letter of February 19 (in which Croke had eulogized Walsh and warned Kirby of Smith's intrigues) was ominous in its studied and pious abstractions about how he hoped the next archbishop of Dub-

---

[43] *Ibid.*

[44] C, February 21, 1885; also quoted in *Walsh*, p. 160. In this biography, Father P. J. Walsh has sometimes taken extraordinary liberties in quoting the documents. His emendations in some instances have been made in the interests of greater clarification, but over-all they certainly modify the tone as well as the materiality of the documents quoted.

lin would be a religious man(C). That Croke had written Kirby because he was very concerned about where the unofficial representative of the Irish Church in Rome stood was made evident by Walsh's comments on Kirby's reply. "Dr. Kirby," Walsh observed, in returning the letters of both Roman correspondents to Croke on March 3, "would no doubt have a leaning towards DY but I doubt if he can have a very strong one. He must know that when the Cardinal was last in Rome D. was thoroughly in with the faction and had in fact a good deal to do with bringing the Cardinal away from the Irish College to the 'Palazzo Strozzi' "(C). "Then I think he knows from Don Giorgio Dillon," Walsh added, referring to an Irish priest long resident in Rome, "that I am a very strong advocate for backing up that College to an extent that has never yet been done." "Naturally," Walsh explained, "he will be reserved. He burned his fingers by his outspokenness in the Cork case." "I think then," Walsh advised in conclusion about Kirby, "it would be unwise to deal with him as an opponent."

In his letter to Croke, Davitt had suggested that the vote of the Dublin clergy should be organized, and the resulting nationalist majority should then be so arranged that strong nationalists would be placed first and second on the *terna* and thus reduce Donnelly to the third place on the list. Davitt further suggested that Rome be advised to ask the Irish bishops abroad to consult about Dublin. In commenting to Croke about Davitt's suggestions, Walsh noted that while the first might be good in the abstract it was not really practical. "There is no organising power," he explained, "or next to none, in Dublin. Then, it is a very scattered, struggling sort of diocese, and the city priests form a body very much cut off in sympathy and in every way from those of the country, and the country, like Caesar's Gaul, divisa est in partes tres, the northern parishes, those of Wicklow, and those of Kildare." As to Davitt's suggestion about arranging the vote, Walsh pointed out that he was not at all sure that there was voting power to spare. "Plainly," he argued, "it would not be safe to split up *40* with the risk of a concentration of the bulk of those that remain. Besides, finally, I believe it will have greater weight in Rome to find a strong preponderance of votes in favour of an *individual*, than to have them amounting to a strong preponderance only when regarded as given on the Nationalist *side*."

The Nationalist character of the proceeding is the difficulty. It may be got over by the strong vote, backed up as this will be by the recommendations of practically *any* episcopal authority in Ireland to whom the matter may be referred for consultation. But if the vote went out, mainly as a Nationalist vote, and divided between two people our friend having *nearly* as many votes as one of them, I do not think there would be at all so much difficulty in setting it aside, and taking up the man recommended by the faction as *persona grata*, and supported by a respectable number of votes from the priests(C).

"And I don't at all like," Walsh observed, leaving aside the question of expediency for a moment, "the idea of wire-pulling in such a matter." Finally, Walsh thought that Davitt's last suggestion about having Rome consult the Irish bishops abroad a good one. Walsh suggested to Croke that letters from the archbishops of Philadelphia, Chicago, and Toronto, the bishops of Maitland and Goulbourn in Australia, Dunedin in New Zealand, and Cape Town in South Africa might be of great use.

In what was becoming a daily news letter, Walsh wrote Croke again the following day, on March 4, because he had overlooked one or two points in his long letter of the day before. In advising Croke how the four bishops of the province were likely to report to Propaganda on the *terna* commended by the clergy, Walsh noted that the bishops of Kildare and Ossory would probably favor him since they had been most friendly in writing to congratulate him on his election as vicar capitular. The coadjutor to Kildare, however, was likely to set up a lamentation about his being needed at Maynooth, but since, if he were passed over for Dublin by Rome, the mark of disapproval would be so great that he could not hope to continue as president, the coadjutor should be persuaded to consider the *terna* purely on its merits. As far as the bishop of Ferns was concerned, Walsh confessed that he knew nothing definite, but suspected that he had fallen into the hands of his old friend, the "West British" coadjutor to the bishop of Clonfert, James Healy. "I heard yesterday," Walsh reported finally, in conclusion, "that *many* of the country P.P.'s whose only idea of the Archbishop is that of a functionary who comes around for confirmations etc., simply took it for granted that D. was to [be] the Bishop. The vote of the Chapter opened their eyes. They now take quite the opposite view."

Two days later on March 6, however, and after a visit to Dublin, Walsh again wrote Croke, but in a more apprehensive vein. "The status quo," he reported, "is now represented as being rather notably changed"(C). The latest rumor was that the bishop of Ardagh, Bartholomew Woodlock, would now receive some votes, and reduce his own total. Moreover, it was also reported that a coalition had been effected between Donnelly's friends and those who had been supporters of the cardinal's policy with regard to politics. The combined results of the defection and the coalition would be to reduce Walsh's forty to the thirties, and bring up Donnelly's twelve to about twenty. "However things stand in reality," Walsh surmised glumly, "there is no doubt that an effect will be produced by the mere circulation of this new story. The following day, Saturday, March 7, Walsh wrote Croke again, "It is not easy to see," he confided, "what I should do with my vote on Tuesday. Of course I will take your Grace's advice and keep my mind to myself." "At first I assumed," he explained, "there would be an absolute concentration, i.e. *for* me and against me, as there was last time in Dr. McCabe's case. Then I would, as a matter of course, vote for your Grace, which would put you on the list." "Now that the votes not given for me may be more or less scattered," Walsh confessed, "I should not like to do this. Giving a vote to bring a Bishop on the list is one thing: giving it merely to throw it away is another." "*Omnibus pensates*," Walsh then declared, "I incline to think I ought to vote for Tynan. I regard him as certainly *fit* for the post, which, in the circumstances, is more than I could say for D. Then it may be of advantage to help Tynan's chances of being on the list, in preference to Ardagh who may possibly run him close." "The problem, however," Walsh concluded in this, his last letter to Croke before the election, "is a difficult one."

IX. Climax

March, 1885 - June, 1885

The voting which took place on March 10 was a most resounding vote of confidence in Walsh by the Dublin clergy.[1] Of the sixty-three votes cast, Walsh received forty-six, while Donnelly received only twelve and Tynan rounded out the *terna* with three. The other two votes were given to Bartholomew Woodlock, the bishop of Ardagh. The Dublin clergy had indeed confirmed even more emphatically the vote of their chapter. The large vote for Walsh, however, was also a very severe comment on Donnelly. While Smith's intrigue, some three months earlier, had undoubtedly resulted in Donnelly's losing a good many votes, the most influential of the Dublin clergy had, even before that sad episode took place, very serious reservations about Donnelly's capacities and abilities. "My rule through life," the venerable dean of Dublin, Walter M. Lee, explained to Kirby on March 2, "has been to mind my own business and leave others[s] to mind theirs"(K). "There may however," he qualified himself, "be an occasion on which I should do more than give a secret and a silent vote; it is important that the Holy Father on whom the responsibility of the appointment ultimately rests should be fully informed of the state of the case." "I have been urged," Lee continued, "as one of the oldest officiating priests of this diocese, Dean of the Cathedral Chapter, and Vic. General of the late Archbishop to write your Lordship fully and frankly on this subject: I hesitate to do so until I get your opinion and advice." "I may observe," Lee added cautiously, confirming what Kirby had already heard some weeks before from Croke, "that a few months before the death of Cardl McCabe an intrigue was on foot in Rome to secure the succession in this diocese for one who in the judgement of the late Archbishop and two of his Vicars whom he consulted, is by no means up to

---

[1] *Walsh*, p. 164.

267

the mark for the administration of this diocese." Cardl
McCabe was very indignant," Lee reported, "and put [a] stop
to this intrigue, at least for the moment, by answering the
letter of one of the prime movers, deprecating their proceedings and adding that he would write to Cardinal Simeoni on
the subject." "Cardinal McCabe," Lee concluded, "received a
letter by return of post begging of him not to write to Cardl
Simeoni as his Emce knew nothing of their proceedings."

The real significance of this letter from Lee to Kirby was not
so much, perhaps, that it gave the Dublin clergy the opportunity of raising a cry of righteous indignation against the intrigue of interested parties in Rome, but that it also gave them
their conscientious opportunity to explain why Donnelly was
not fit to be archbishop of Dublin. The campaign launched by
Lee, in his sounding out of Kirby, was followed up with a set
piece addressed to Lee from another of the vicars general,
Monsignor Edward Kennedy. "As the Holy See," Kennedy
formally wrote Lee on March 8, "will shortly be engaged in
appointing a successor to our lamented Cardinal: I think 'tis
our *conscientious duty*, to make known those particulars—with
which we are acquainted—connected with the appointment of
the Most Reverend Dr. Donnelly as assistant Bishop to the late
Cardinal"(K).

> We had remarked his preference for a selection of another of
> our Canons: (and I'm aware that there was a second, whose
> appointment he'd prefer). 'Twas solely at your and my rep-
> resentation that he decided on the selection of Most Rev. Dr.
> Donnelly... Indeed his first manifestation was in favour of the
> Bishop of Ardagh, and who appeared disposed to acquiesce,
> but afterwards refused. I asked him to select then, the President
> of Maynooth College. He said that he could not be spared from
> Maynooth: that he could not afford to give him 400 p. an. (the
> amt. I presume of the President's salary), but "that he (Dr. W.)
> was sure to come to the front." Some time after Dr. Donnelly's
> Consecration, on the occasion of one of those alarming attacks
> of illness from which the poor Cardinal suffered: I remarked to
> him how well Dr. Donnelly was getting on: "Yes, he replied, "but
> he has no depth."

"I think 'twas in last Nov. or Dec.," Kennedy added, coming
finally to the question of Roman intrigue, "that the dear
Cardinal spoke to us, and told us in confidence of the letter he

had just received from Rome, and of the reply he was about to send in answer to it." Abbot Smith had written he noted "to say that 'twas arranged in Rome, if the late Archbishop had an election for *a successor* and that if the Mt. Rev. Dr. Donnelly received *only a* few votes, he would be appointed *cum jure successionis.*" "A rather cool way," Kennedy commented, "to dispose of an Archdiocese in Ireland." "You and I," Kennedy then concluded, "can never forget the indignation of the poor Cardinal when speaking on this matter. Nor have we been suprised [*sic*], at the disgust manifested on every side when the facts were known."

When Kirby received Dean Lee's letter on March 5, he immediately wrote by return that he would be pleased to receive the facts in the Dublin case, for Lee wrote him again on March 16, and enclosed Kennedy's letter to him. "Monsig. Kennedy," Lee explained, "is one of the most experienced and zealous priests of this diocese: he was a fellow student of our late lamented Cardinal his fellow curate for 14 years in Clontarf and deservedly the most intimate and trusted friend of our late Archbishop."

> The nomination of M. R. Dr. Donnelly by Cardl McCabe as his assistant Bishop is calculated to leave the uninitiated to con-clude, that his Emce judged him qualified to be his successor in this diocese and as I am to some extent responsible for that appointment, I think it right to say that I recommended his appointment, for special reasons, and not because I thought him qualified to succeed as Archbishop of this diocese or even contemplated such a contingency, as I hoped that our beloved Cardinal had many years of valuable labour before him. The late Cardinal was by no means predisposed in favour of Dr. Donnelly—he hesitated for a long time and I believe he was ultimately influenced by my opinion and that of Monsigr Ken-nedy. Hence undue importance should not be attached to the fact that Dr. Donnelly was selected to be assistant Bishop to our late Archbishop(K).

"The large majority in favour of Dr. Walsh," Lee further informed Kirby, turning to the more positive side of the case, "is to be ascribed to a conviction on the part of the clergy that this diocese, especially at the present time, requires a Bishop of exceptional ability joined to a life of exemplary virtue: such is the opinion formed of Dr. Walsh in and out of this diocese,"

"I need not tell you," Lee added, "that we are loyal to the Crown, neither do we object to the Irish Executive as such, our real struggle is with the Masonic Sect which has its stronghold in Dublin Castle." "Dr. Walsh," he then emphasized in conclusion, "is an experienced and prudent administrator, he has materially improved the discipline of Maynooth College and he is at the same time respected and receives a willing obedience from the Community."

A month later, on April 16, Monsignor Kennedy wrote Kirby that he had made an error in his letter to Dean Lee of March 8, which he would like to correct. He had said then that Smith had been requested by the cardinal prefect to write McCabe, but the fact was that it was the secretary of propaganda, Monsignor Jacobini, who had been mentioned by Smith. "You can see this remarkable letter," Kennedy informed Kirby, referring to MacEvilly, who, along with Croke and five other Irish bishops, was on his way to Rome for the long-scheduled Easter visit, "which I have forwarded to his Grace the Archbishop of Tuam"(K). "You have heard, and truly," Kennedy assured Kirby, "that tis only per accident that Dr. Donnelly was appointed assistant Bishop." "There can be no doubt," he then maintained, "but that the votes given for Dr. Donnelly, were because he was assistant Bishop and regarded as the poor *Cardinal's choice*." It is amusing to read Walsh's comments to Croke about the vicars general in the light of this correspondence. "The ex V.G.'s," Walsh had written Croke on March 3, "who, of course, are thoroughly committed to the work, simply *assume* in all our transactions, that we have really entered on a permanent arrangement, though for form's sake we must act as if it were only a temporary one"(C). "But they are," he concluded naïvely, "in their way simple minded men, knowing nothing of intrigues."

Distinguishing intrigue from conscientious action is, perhaps, just as difficult in secular as it is in ecclesiastical politics. In any case, the government was just as assiduous on their side in attempting to block Walsh's appointment as the Dublin clergy were with regard to Donnelly. The day after Walsh's election as *dignissimus*, Granville wrote Spencer asking what he thought of sending Blennerhassett to Rome on a secret mission . Spencer replied the following day, March 12, that he thought Blennerhassett too much of the same calibre as Errington, and that Blennerhassett's suggestion about

White, the British minister plenipotentiary at Bucharest, would be better.[2] The next day, March 13, Granville informed Spencer by telegram that he was to see the duke of Norfolk the next day and did Spencer have anything he would like him to tell the duke.[3] "After seeing him," Granville concluded amusingly, "I can better judge as to black and white." "I have nothing to add," Spencer replied by letter the same day, and missing Granville's pun, "but the enclosed is curious & as I can rely pretty surely on the sources of information, it shows what kind of a man the Dignissimus of Dublin is."[4] "Pigott," Spencer noted, referring to one of his sources, "was the Editor of the Semi Fenian extreme Nationalist organ the Irishman." "Father Healy," he added, referring to a strong supporter of Donnelly, and the Parish Priest of Little Bray, "is a highly respected R. C. clergyman."[5] What was most significant, Spencer explained further, was the way in which the extremists all united behind Walsh. This proved, he argued, that Walsh was "much bound up with them." The enclosure sent on by Spencer, however, was more damaging than his argument of guilt by association.

As to this [,] Pigott wrote me a letter w. I have sent to Errington that the candidate used to write violent articles for the Irishman, and Father Healy has been with me today to say that it was at his [Walsh's] special advice that Parnell issued the No Rent Manifesto and that W. has very lately written for United Ireland.[6]

After his conversation with the duke of Norfolk, Granville evidently had some second thoughts about sending White on a secret mission to Rome. The real difficulty, however, was the effect this would have on Errington, who was too well placed to be able to keep White's mission a secret from him.[7] Further, Granville had to face up to the fact that if he alienated Er-

---

[2] GR, 30/29/142.
[3] Ibid.
[4] Ibid.
[5] Father James Healy was the parish priest of Little Bray, and an opponent of Walsh. See Memories of Father Healy of Little Bray (London, 1904), pp. 280 ff.
[6] GR, 30/29/142. Memorandum not dated, on Castle notepaper, not signed, and not in Spencer's hand. See also Campbell-Bannerman Papers, British Museum, Add. MSS, 41228, Campbell-Bannerman to Spencer, March 17, 1885, House of Commons: "He [Errington] is much exercised about a story of Walsh writing for the Irishman some time ago."
[7] Ibid.

rington now, he would be without a really effective agent in Rome in an increasingly critical situation.

A month later, Granville was still obviously attempting to gather some hard information for Errington which would prove damaging to Walsh at Rome, and solicited Spencer in the matter. Spencer responded as best he could by forwarding on April 13, a letter from Lord Emly, which he maintained was representative of what the respectable Roman Catholic laity really thought about the proposed appointment of Walsh.[8] In his own covering letter, however, Spencer was not much help. He had obviously been unable to uncover anything beyond innuendo that would compromise Walsh. In the main Spencer complained that Walsh was too much in league with the nationalist politicians, and that he did not demonstrate a sufficient loyalty to the crown in dealing with its representatives. The politicians with whom Walsh was too closely allied he charged had "held up the Viceroy to execration if he carries out the Law, they have no respect for the Crown or Law & Order. They have done everything they can to prevent the firm administration of just Laws." In adducing Walsh's lack of loyalty to the crown, Spencer noted that, when the queen had visited Ireland some twenty-five years before, in 1849, the archbishop of Dublin and the bishops had greeted her personally and presented her with a loyal address. When the prince of Wales had visited Dublin a few days before, on the other hand, not one Roman Catholic clergyman appeared at the Royal Levee. Moreover, Walsh demonstrated his disrespect for the queen by replying informally through Donnelly to her telegram expressing her regret to the cathedral chapter at the death of McCabe. Spencer finally concluded by pointing out, somewhat lamely, that there was "a very strong feeling among lay R. Catholics that Dr. Walsh will not be a proper man to succeed Dr. McCabe, & certainly I have this impression myself." "I cannot find more facts," he apologized in a postscript, "than these for you."

Walsh and his friends, meanwhile, were doing their best to counteract this specious and systematic slandering of his good name at Rome. No one, perhaps, was more enthusiastic or ardent in the effort to secure a nationalist archbishop for Dublin than Michael Davitt as he relayed the latest Roman

---

[8] *Ibid.*

news to Croke. "Two priests from All Hallows," he reported to
Croke on March 7, "had a private audience of His Holiness
yesterday, being introduced by Dr. Kirby"(C). "They report to
me the following," Davitt continued:

The Pope asked if they were "Americans."
"No Irlandesi" was the reply.
"Ah," turning eagerly to Dr. K. he then asked,
"Do you know *Walsh* personally?
"Yes" was the reply.
"Where was he born? was the next question.
"In the diocese of Dublin."
"Is he learned?"
Dr. K. spoke superlatively of Dr. W's accomplishments.
"Is he *sano in doctrina* [*sic*]?" was next asked.
Affirmatively answered.
"Un bravo?" was again asked?
"Un bravo" replied Dr. K.
"He has the support of the priests of his diocese?" was the final
remark of the Pope.
"And the public sentiment of the whole country also" was Dr.
Kirby's rejoinder(C).

"The good Padre Glynn," Davitt went on to reassure Croke,
referring to an Irish Augustinian resident for some time in
Rome, "is of opinion that this conversation is most important
and clearly indicates the selection that will be made by the
Holy Father." "The English faction, however," he warned
Croke in conclusion, "still proclaim that Dr. Donnelly or *Dean
Neville* will be *the choice*."

Croke forwarded this rather naïve and optimistic letter to
Walsh, who returned it, significantly enough, without any
comment. The pope's interview with Kirby and the All Hallows priests was more important, of course, for what it told
about Kirby rather than the pope. By March 6, Kirby had
evidently decided, for he had received and replied to Dean
Lee's letter of March 2, about Smith's intrigue, to come out in
favor of Walsh. As far as Croke and Walsh were concerned,
this was a most useful and reassuring piece of information. In
his long letter of March 14, returning Davitt's, Walsh also
reassured Croke about the report the Dublin suffragans
would soon make to Rome on the recent commendation of the
Dublin clergy. "I doubt," Walsh explained, "if there is much,

or any, document-producing power among them, especially in Latin. But there can now be no doubt as to their *intentions* in the matter. They will be unanimous and strongly so"(C). At the end of this letter, Walsh reassured Croke again in a different, and perhaps more interesting, kind of way. "All letters," he concluded briefly, *"burned* when read."

In this atmosphere of secrecy, maneuver, and intrigue, rumor was naturally the order of the day. When Donnelly, for example, who had written Cardinal Simeoni simply to find out whether he was still to go to Rome with the other bishops after Easter, received an affirmative reply from the cardinal prefect, the rumor was all over Dublin in a few hours and telegraphed to the London papers that he had been immediately summoned to Rome and that the appointment to Dublin had, in fact, been made. The rumor broke in the newspapers on Friday morning, March 20, and Croke telegraphed Walsh in a panic to find out whether it was so. "I heard the report," Walsh replied Friday evening, "for the first time yesterday evening"(C). "My informant," Walsh explained, "added that he believed it had been started for a purpose i.e. to entrap the weekly papers into violent articles, which would go a great way to influence the Roman people, putting them back from what would look like yielding to dictation."

> I believe the report came simply from a mistaken notion of what had occurred.
> The enclosed is a copy from Simeoni to D. I had from D. yesterday morning on his return from England where he had been preaching an engagement of 3 months' standing in Manchester.
> The document is a curious one. "Vescovo Aussiliare di Dublino" is a new ecclesiastical position, rather an undefined one.
> The report circulated yesterday in Dublin was that the summons was most urgent, so that D. was to start yesterday evening(C).

"Another rumor," Walsh then reported, "is that the Government have made overtures to the Pope on the basis of mutual concessions—D's appointment to be the quid pro quo for the granting of a Charter & endowment to the Catholic University." "Probably," Walsh conjectured, "the Nation will fall into this trap next week." "Could it be ascertained," Walsh suggested, "from what source the report to-day referred to reached the editor?" "I am inclined to think," he ventured in conclusion, referring to Father Healy, "the P. P. of Little Bray has had something to do with it."

The following day, March 21, Walsh wrote Kirby, explaining what had happened, in an attempt to soften by anticipation the worst that might happen. "The incident," Walsh concluded, after his explanation, "is a little inconvenient, as a great many of our laity feel very strongly on the whole question; and they may now, as they are likely to believe the report, lose control over themselves, and begin to say and do very inconvenient things."[9] Walsh in fact had anticipated a very serious danger, for a few days after his letter to Kirby, Davitt wrote Croke that rumors about the chapter's reception of the queen's message of condolence on the death of Cardinal McCabe, among other things, were having an adverse effect in Rome. Davitt also explained that the editor of *United Ireland*, William O'Brien, would have to be more careful, or the result would be another "Pale" archbishop. "Abbot Smyth, of the Benedictines—" Davitt further reported, "recently promoted by the Pope—has hinted to some of my friends here the likelihood of 'someone from abroad being recalled,' in connection with the vacant Cardinalate of Ireland. This is supposed to refer to Dr. Moran of Sydney."[10]

Errington, however, who had returned to Rome during the parliamentary Easter recess, had something more substantial and important to report to Granville than rumor. The pope, he explained on March 26, had taken the most unusual step of withdrawing the Dublin appointment from Propaganda, and reserved it entirely to himself.[11] The election of the Dublin *terna*, moreover, had not only been referred to the bishops of the Province for their customary report, but it had also been referred to the three other Irish archbishops, and the result had been a unanimous vote of confidence in Walsh. While the situation was thus very precarious, Errington noted, he was very hopeful that he would be able to prevent the appoint-

[9] K, March 21, 1885. See also J. Hasson, St. Columb's College, Derry, to Kirby, March 29, 1885: "There is great speculation about Dublin. In fact the Holy See is left no liberty in the matter. The 'Papers' think it comes within their province to pronounce on the matter and intimate strongly the consequences that would arise from passing over Dr. Walsh."

[10] C, March, 1885, Monday [March 23].

[11] B, 49690.

ment. Both Cardinals Jacobini and Simeoni, he assured Granville, were fully alive to the dangers of appointing Walsh, and the duke of Norfolk had recently written a fine letter to Cardinal Howard on the same theme, which the cardinal had translated and given to the pope himself. Two weeks later, on April 9, Errington again wrote Granville to assure him that everything was being done to convince the authorities of the danger of appointing Walsh, as well as to inform the pope, which was now more difficult since he had taken the matter into his own hands and resented any intrusion on what he considered to be his prerogative.[12]

Walsh, meanwhile, had been discreetly doing his best to prevent nationalist politicians and journalists from treading on the papal prerogative and thereby upsetting the apple cart. "Kavanagh of Kildare," he informed Croke on March 31, referring to the influential former president of Carlow College, and prominent nationalist priest,

> writes this morning. He went to Dublin yesterday and saw T. D. Sullivan, Clancy, Harrington, and Keatinge (the Irish Catholic Layman). He gave them his views on the situation and they have promised to keep quiet in the Nation and also to abstain from holding out temptations to the Dublin priests to appear on Land [sic] League platforms, as they have been doing, by holding their Sunday Meetings through the County Dublin so regularly for the last 4 or 5 weeks.(C)

"For myself," Walsh, who was beginning to show the wear and tear of rumor and counter-rumor, concluded, "every day makes me more and more anxious that the whole affair should be dealt with as soon as possible, and that some way may be found of dealing with it that will make it unnecessary to disturb me from where I am." Though Walsh, by energetically protesting and explaining, tried to scotch the various rumors, innuendoes, and half-truths, they seemed to be gaining an even greater currency and an ever widening circulation.

"My main object in writing now," Walsh wrote Kirby on April 21, "is to send the enclosed. It is from the *New York Herald* of April 8th"(K). "This sort of thing," he explained, referring to the delegation of Irish bishops who were on their way to Rome, "would be of invaluable service if the Bishops

---

[12] *Ibid.*

decide on making a stand against what Parnell would call the 'underground' party in Rome." "Here is a plain statement," he pointed out, "published in the leading New York paper, and thus sent with the utmost possible publicity all over the States, in which the appointment to an important Arch-brishopric is represented as a matter of 'facio ut facias,' the *quid pro quo* being specifically mentioned." "As to the absurd statement," Walsh protested to Kirby, "regarding the Queen's telegram, it is right that the exact state of facts should be known," "They are," he then systematically laid them out, "as follows:"

1. The Queen never sent me a telegram in her life: if she had done so, I should of course have answered it in a becoming way.

2. After the Cardinal's death, the Dublin papers circulated a statement that Lord Spencer wrote a letter of sympathy to Dr. Donnelly, enclosing a telegram, to the same effect, from the Queen.

3. Lord Spencer did in fact write such a letter. But he enclosed no telegram.

4. At the meeting of the Chapter, when I was elected Vicar, Dr. Donnelly told us exactly what had occurred, adding that he had gone (very properly) in person to thank Lord Spencer for his letter. Lord Spencer then *told* him he had the Queen's commands, conveyed by telegram, to express her sympathy &c.

5. Many thought the matter should rest here. But I saw the necessity of making an acknowledgement of this and in concert with Dr. Donnelly and the Dean arranged a plan, which was then proposed to the Chapter, and unanimously sanctioned— that Dr. Donnelly, through whom the message had been verbally conveyed, should again go to Lord Spencer, and in our name, as representing the Clergy, express our thanks to the Queen for her kind message. As there was no written or telegraphed communication before us, we had no other way of dealing with the matter.[13]

What had made the question of his supposed want of respect for the queen even more embarrassing was the recent visit of the prince and princess of Wales to Ireland. Walsh and Croke had indeed taken up the general nationalist line with

[13] See also K, Dean Lee to Kirby, telegram, April 29, 1885: "Please contradict in my name as Dean of Chapter unfounded statements of Vicar Capitular's discourtesy to Queen." See also K, Walsh's letter to Kirby, May 18, 1885, attempting to answer to the charge that he was wanting in loyalty since he did not attend vice-regal levees at Dublin Castle.

regard to the royal visitors and carefully avoided any contact. A week before the royal visitors were to arrive in Dublin, for example, Walsh wrote Croke, who would be passing through on his way to Rome, inviting him to spend a few days at Maynooth before he left for the eternal city with the other bishops. "Maynooth," Walsh explained good-humoredly on March 31, "will be a quieter place for you for headquarters than Dublin during the visit of their Royal Highnesses unless you care to figure as the centerpiece of some counter demonstrations!"(C). By the time the royal visitors left Dublin for Cork, however, the nationalist line had hardened, and they were greeted by angry demonstrators everywhere. Those who were hardy enough to pay their respects to the royal pair, moreover, were roundly abused in the nationalist press. "For my part," as the bishop of Cork explained to Smith on June 9,

> I endeavour to keep aloof from the contests that spring up amongst Catholics & our political friends. Yet, I have been abused & belied in so called Catholic Journals, because I went to pay my respects to the Prince of Wales, heir apparent to the English Throne, & that visit was for the purpose of paying honor alone to whom honor is due & that at a Catholic Convent, which the Prince wished to inspect(S).

"It remains for me," he concluded sadly, but most significantly, "to keep perfectly quiet."

Archbishops Croke and MacEvilly, with five of their episcopal brethren, meanwhile, had set out on their long-delayed visit to Rome. When they broke their journey in London, they stayed, naturally enough, with Cardinal Manning. The immediate concerns of the Irish bishops were rather obvious. They were anxious about both the appointment to Dublin and their approaching visit to Rome. Manning, however, was much more concerned about whether their views on Home Rule included the establishment of a parliament in Dublin. Several months before his conversations with the Irish bishops, Manning had, in fact, written the pope that it was his conviction that a parliament in Dublin would eventually lead to separation and this was not in the interest of either Irish Catholics or the Church in the empire. Manning then added in this letter of February 17 that he hoped this was the opinion of the Irish bishops as well, because, while he had no doubts as to their views on separation, he feared that there might be differences between them and himself with regard to a parliament in Dublin.[14] "For myself Holy Father," Manning had explained, "allow me to say that a Parliament in Dublin and separation are one and the same." "Ireland," Manning then concluded emphatically, "is not a colony like Canada, but an integral and vital part of our own country, as is often said, of the Mother Country."

Manning's uneasiness about what the views of the Irish bishops were with regard to Home Rule and the establishing of a parliament in Dublin was the result most likely of a long letter from Croke to the bishop of Salford in late January. Vaughan had asked Croke to write an article on Home Rule for the April issue of the *Dublin Review* of which he was the owner and publisher. In refusing, Croke explained on January 24, that he was not only busy preparing the required *Relatio Status* of his diocese, which he would be obliged to present on his visit to Rome after Easter, but also "because I am quite astray, moreover, as to the meaning of 'home rule' in the mouths of most of the men who speake or prate about it."[15]

I am not a *Separatist* to begin with, but quite the opposite, for however anxious I may be in the abstract to see our country free and unfettered mistress of its own destiny, and an honoured unit amongst the Nations, I should greatly fear, that as that result could never be achieved if at all except by the French or American influence, or by both, we would lose in religion and morality what we may gain in worldly wealth and opulance, and that as soon as England would be in a position to do so, she would either by intrigue or open violence, success [*sic* succeed] in swamping and strangling us once more—So I am no separatist(C).

"My main ambition," Croke then confessed, "is for the settlement of the land and education questions, on such a basis as would lift up our people personally both socially and intellectually without being I honestly confess very much concerned if the [illegible] dominant classes amongst us, should substan-

---

[14] Manning Papers(M), Archives of St. Mary of the Angels, Bayswater Road, London. Manning to Leo XIII, February 17, 1885 (copy, in Italian). Also quoted in English translation in Shane Leslie, *Henry Edward Manning* (London, 1921), pp. 402-403. I have preferred my own translation of the Italian to Leslie's.

[15] C, January 24, 1885. This letter is rather a rough draft than a copy.

tially suffer by the result." "And if I go in [at] all for a Native parliament," he concluded significantly, "it is on the clear understanding that the parliament should be as supreme for Ireland, as the British House of Commons is now for Gt. Britain, in all that concerns Ireland exclusively, while of course imperial questions should be subject entirely to the operation of the Imperial legislature."

The crucial question for Manning, of course, was, did Croke seriously contemplate a "native parliament." "Mgr. Croke," Manning reported to the pope on April 12, immediately after his interview with the Irish bishops, "asserted in the most explicit terms his own conviction that the union between England and Ireland ought to be inviolably maintained; and that the whole Irish Episcopate is unanimous in the same judgement."[16] "In my last," Manning continued, reminding the pope of his letter of February 17, "I quoted Mr. Davitt, an advanced Nationalist—that a Parliament in Ireland would present two dangers to the Church, the one, a more formidable political interference on the part of the Irish anti-Catholic party, and the other, the elimination from the Imperial Parliament of all the Catholic representatives." "Mgr. Croke," Manning then noted, indicating also who was the dominant figure among the Irish bishops, "fully accepted this judgement of Mr. Davitt, and adds a third very powerful argument, that his Parliament would have two Houses, and that the great majority in the House of Lords would be composed of persons most hostile to the progress of the Catholic Church in Ireland." "Two such Houses," Manning pointed out to the pope, "would be in open war and between the Irish Parliament and the Imperial Parliament opposition would be inevitable, and a source of extraordinary dangers."

"Mgr. Croke's complete agreement," Manning summed up for the pope, "with my humble opinions, recently expressed to Your Holiness, has greatly comforted me." "The exclusion of a Parliament," Manning explained, entering a crucial qualification, "does not at all in itself exclude the system of administration, or local government (*regime domestico*) that is called 'Home Rule,' and I am certain that Ireland will shortly receive

---

[16] M, April 12, 1885. See also Leslie, *op. cit.*, pp. 403-404. Leslie has deleted a portion of this letter without acknowledging the fact. I have again preferred my own translation.

from the Imperial Parliament the same freedom and control
over the internal administration that Scotland and England
possess." " I believe," he then added tactfully and shrewdly,
especially since the Irish bishops were on their way to Rome,
"that under the paternal guidance and authority of Your
Holiness, the Irish Episcopate will come to understand sound
principles of unity in word and action." "Once such unity of
the Episcopate is secured," Manning concluded, with his usual
emphasis on clerical power, "the Irish people will have a sure
and sound guidance in these days of social and political agitation." Since the Irish bishops', and especially Croke's, conception of Home Rule proved to be so essentially modest, and
since Manning was easily persuaded that Walsh was indeed
the best candidate for Dublin, the London conversations
marked the beginning of a real, effective, and enduring, if
informal, alliance between the cardinal and the Irish hierarchy. By virtue of this *entente* which ended only with the
cardinal's death in early 1892, Manning acquired some very
real political influence through the Irish party at Westminster, while the Irish bishops gained the cardinal's much-needed
and valuable support at the Vatican. Shortly after the Irish
bishops left London for Rome, therefore, the cardinal decided that it was time to go into action.

On Wednesday, April 22, he wrote his close friend of several years, Sir Charles Dilke, who was now in the Cabinet as
President of the Local Government Board, that he had some
important information for him.[17] The following afternoon
Dilke had a long interview with Manning, which he immediately reported in a secret memorandum to Gladstone,
Spencer, and Chamberlain.[18] In his memo Dilke explained
that he was not only aware of the recent stopover of the Irish
bishops in London, but that Manning had been largely responsible for the pope having called them to Rome, and that
the cardinal, moreover, "bitterly resented Errington's visits to
Rome."

This was all I knew on the subject till today when Manning
suddenly proposed to me to bring about peace & good will in
Ireland on the basis of Chamberlain's Local Gov't & Central

---

[17] Dilke Papers, British Museum, Add. MS, 43896.
[18] *Ibid.*, 43887.

Board Scheme, of which he had heard from the Irish Bishops. Manning has got a pledge from the R. C. Bishops, including even Archbishop Croke who has become frightened of the extreme Nationalists, & from Davitt, to denounce Separation. He has got from the Bishops, including Croke, a declaration against an Irish Parliament, provided they obtain the Local Govt. Central Board. I suggested that he should see Chamberlain at once & learn secretly the details of his proposals. I shall suggest that Manning be encouraged to let the Pope have Chamberlain's scheme.[19]

Chamberlain, with Gladstone's approval, visited Manning the next day, Friday, April 24, when the cardinal asked him to put his proposals on Irish local government on paper. In forwarding his proposals the following day, Chamberlain explained they were presented "as my personal responsibility alone, but if I have reason to believe that they would command the support of the most influential representatives of Irish opinion I should be prepared to press them on the consideration of my colleagues and to take any steps to secure their adoption."[20] What Manning was after, of course, was an *entente* with Chamberlain and Dilke that he would push their local government proposals with the Irish bishops and Parnell, if they would prevent their Cabinet colleagues from attempting to block Walsh's appointment at Rome. Dilke, for example, had also seen Manning on Friday, April 24, and advised Spencer, who was in London, that Manning wanted Walsh and was very angry at Errington's interference.[21] Spencer admitted there was much in what Manning said about interference, but that the cardinal was wrong in his estimate of Walsh.[22] By Sunday, however, Manning decided to put in writing what he had said in his interview with Dilke on Friday about the Dublin appointment. "My first and chief anxiety," he confessed on April 26, to Dilke, "is that the Government shall in no way either officiously through Errington or any other, attempt to influence the election."[23] "Already the belief to this effect," he warned, "has been expressed in the Irish papers. Two effects would at once follow, the Archbishop would become 'suspect'"

---

[19] *Ibid.*
[20] *Ibid.*
[21] *Ibid.*, 43891.
[22] *Ibid.*
[23] *Ibid.*, 43896.

and his influence for good would be paralysed. And next, the
influence of Rome in the Direction I desire as much as you
would be dangerously lessened." "So much in general," Manning concluded, turning then to particulars, "Next for the
three names before the Holy See."

> They are all good and safe in every sense. Any one of them may
> be confided in as holding the opinions and principles of the
> seven Bishops who were here the other day. But there is one of
> them beyond compare the ablest namely Dr. Walsh, President
> of Maynooth. He has been tried in governing that vast College
> and has been found very able and successful. He has great
> weight in Ireland, and as the Bishops unanimously assured me,
> he would unite the whole Episcopate; for they all confide in
> him. I have an impression that efforts have been made to
> represent Dr. Walsh as Nationalist. He is not more so than I am:
> and whether that is excessive or obstructive you may judge.[24]

"That you may better know," Manning then advised Dilke,
"how far my judgement may be taken, I will here add that I
had a special and unusual share in the selection and nomination of the late Cardinal Archbishop. And I believe you know
me too well to need that I should say more." "I put 'Private' on
this letter," Manning concluded, "but you may use it as you see
fit."

In spite of Dilke's complaints to Spencer, however, both
Granville and Spencer continued to support Errington's efforts to block Walsh's appointment. At a Cabinet meeting,
therefore, in the week of April 26, Chamberlain and Dilke
obviously raised the question and received the support of the
majority of their colleagues against any such interference.
Granville, therefore, was obliged to remind Errington on May
1, that he presumed that Errington would be ready to confirm
his instructions that while he was at liberty to give information,
he was not authorized to speak in favor of any candidate at
Rome.[25] It soon became obvious, however, that despite the
efforts of Manning and his new allies, Errington still had the
tacit support of Granville and Spencer. Chamberlain's *liaison*
on Irish affairs, William O'Shea, for example, informed Man-

[24] *Ibid.*
[25] B, 49690.

ning on May 4, that Dilke and Chamberlain had both been snubbed by Granville, who had assured them that Errington was not supporting Donnelly as a candidate for Dublin.[26] This did not mean, O'Shea pointed out, that Errington was not vehemently opposing Walsh. O'Shea further reported that, in an interview that very day with Spencer, Gladstone had failed to persuade the Irish viceroy to accept Chamberlain's proposals for Irish local self-government.

Manning, meanwhile, had been doing his best to fulfill his part of the bargain with Chamberlain and Dilke. He had an interview with Parnell on Tuesday, April 28, which he reported in conversation to Dilke, who immediately passed it on to Chamberlain. Parnell, it appears, was naturally very guarded in his acceptance of Chamberlain's proposals, which he regarded as neither sufficient nor final. Manning, however, did take his qualified acceptance as a sign, at least, that he would not oppose the proposals if introduced as Cabinet measure. In writing Chamberlain on Monday after the Tuesday of his interview with Parnell, the cardinal was perhaps more reassuring than he should have been in the light of Parnell's qualifications.[27] He assured Chamberlain flatly on May 4 that the interview "was satisfactory, and as the Irish Bishops are of the same mind, two conditions of acceptance for the scheme appear to be secure."[28] "I wish I was as sure," he confided in conclusion, referring to Chamberlain's Cabinet colleagues, "of the third nearer home first at least in the order of time." Five days later, on Saturday, May 9, the Cabinet rejected Chamberlain's local government proposals for Ireland, with all the commoners except Hartington voting for,

---

[26] Leslie, op. cit., pp. 389-390.

[27] Dilke Papers, op. cit., 43887.

[28] Leslie, op. cit., pp. 409-410; see for Manning to Chamberlain, June 23, 1886, a year after the event: "Six of the Irish Bishops came to me on their way to Rome. I did not produce the copy of your scheme, but I stated the objections of Michael Davitt to a Parliament. They seemed to accept any real power of self-government which should be effectual and not evasive. This seemed to me to be equivalent to your scheme. After this I saw Mr. Parnell. He was less satisfied: and I understood him to accept the scheme, but not as sufficient or final. His acceptance was very guarded, and I did not take it as more than not opposing it. More than this I could not say; and our interview was under conditions of such reserve that I should not feel justified in making it public. I think that I am now justified in saying this to you because it will show that the words I wrote to you were not written without sufficient grounds. To the best of my memory, Mr. Parnell desired that his interview at this house should not be known—at least publicly. I believe I made it known to you and to Sir Charles Dilke. You were both in the Cabinet, and I regarded it as a privileged communication."

and all the peers except Granville voting against. "Within six years, if it pleases God to spare their lives," Gladstone remarked prophetically to Dilke, as they were leaving the meeting, "they will be repenting in ashes."

Manning, meanwhile, had not forgotten the Irish bishops in Rome. "Let me hear of our affairs in Rome," he wrote Croke on May 1, "for the Newspapers make me especially anxious about Dublin. And let me know whether I can be of any use"(C). "I have received your Eminence's note," Croke replied by return of post on May 5, "and thank you sincerely for it, and still more for the communication which you so kindly sent about me to the Pope. His Holiness spoke to me on the matter and seemed pleased to know, that your Eminence entertained a favorable opinion of the turbulent Archbishop of Cashel"(M). "There is no news about Dublin," he added, "but there are various *reports*. One is that Dr. Moran will be recalled and appointed to Dublin." "It is *absolutely certain*," he assured the cardinal, "*that the government has made this proposal to the Pope*. I do not, and can not believe that it will be accepted by his Holiness." "Dr. Moran," he continued, "is doing well, I hear, where he is and is wanted there. Perhaps, he may not do so well in Ireland, where he certainly *is no favourite*." "Anyhow," Croke emphasized, "the setting aside of Dr. Walsh, *for anyone*, would raise such a storm in Ireland and in the United States, that his Holiness should be solemnly warned against doing so." "Your Eminence alone," Croke advised in conclusion, "can give such warning: *and I earnestly ask you* to give it."

Early in the second week in May, the rumors about Moran having been recalled were current in Dublin. Walsh immediately wrote Croke asking him what the real state of affairs was in Rome. "I got your two letters yesterday," Croke replied on Sunday, May 17, "and was so busy, in one way or another, that I had not time to drop you a line in reply. But, Dr. Carr undertook to do so for me; and did so I'm sure"(W). "You know just as much," he reassured Walsh at once, "about the Dublin appointment as we do here—the utmost secrecy is observed by all the authorities." "There are various rumours," he reported, "all of which are reflected in the Dublin and other papers: but there is nothing reliable. It will surprise me greatly if it should turn out that the Pope is for *M*. I cannot believe it—Needless to give reasons." "Still, on the other hand," he qualified himself immediately, "it is pretty confidently stated here, that letters bearing on the Sydney Synod to be held in September, and which should have been forwarded to *M*. have by orders of Simeoni, been detained at Propaganda." "That, if true," Croke surmised, "and I believe it is true, would go to show, that there is *question*, to say the least of it, of *M's* appointment." "The moment anything tangible transpires," Croke assured Walsh, "you shall know of it from me by wire."

"Conferences in Propaganda," Croke then turned to the business of their Roman visit, "close on Saturday. We were not brought out here I'm sure for these conferences, but as I always thought, for a lecture on politics from the Pope." "He has taken Tuam and Elphin," Croke then added most significantly, referring to MacEvilly and Gillooly,"into his confidence, and asked them to present him with an address setting forth the political requirements of the people and the views of the Irish Bishops. Gillooly has drawn up his address and it is to be read and presented on this day week, I believe, at our parting audience." "I cannot trust myself," Croke confided to Walsh, "to commit to writing what I think of the people here, and of the mode of doing business in the *'Eternal City.'* " "We are treated like children," he complained, "and we deserve it—that's all I'll say." "I do not know," Croke candidly confessed, "how we will face the country, if you are not appointed— or what we can say for the Pope." "'Tis a question really," he maintained, "of high principle." "Is the man of the people," Croke asked characteristically and rhetorically, "backed by priests and Bishops, to be put aside, for the nominee of the Government—and is Irish feeling to be sacrificed to expediency, and to the desire which the Pope obviously has of conciliating England?" "No Irish Ecclesiastic," he asserted, clearly referring to himself, "is esteemed here except he is *moderate* and *flexible*, and *conciliatory*. Sal Verbum." "I do not," he concluded with a flicker of hope, "despair yet." "P.S.," he added, referring to McGettingan, "The Primate wrote yesterday, to Dr. K. to say, that he thought you an excellent priest, and that you were voted for by a large majority of the Dublin Clergy!!" "I could make no use of it," Croke sourly complained, "—He is an ould woman."

This long, angry, contemptuous, and essentially despairing letter raises some very interesting questions, not all of which are simply explained by referring them to Croke's mercurial temperament. Why did Croke, for example, delegate a reply to Walsh rather than answer immediately himself, especially if he knew he would write the following day? More important, why did the pope choose to ignore Croke, especially after his initial cordial audience as reported to Manning? Why Croke could not bring himself to write Walsh immediately was because he had a very troubled, if not indeed, a very guilty conscience. By his lack of tact and prudence, to say nothing of moderation, flexibility, or conciliation, he had by alienating the pope at this critical moment, further compromised an already very delicate situation. In later accounting for why the pope had become annoyed with him, Croke explained to Kirby, on July 15, "I have solid reason for knowing that Mgr. Machi with whom I had a rather bitter controversy, on the day of my private audience with the Pope, reported what I had said, to His Holiness, thereby causing him (the Pope) to overlook me and send for Dr. MacEvilly and Dr. Gillooly instead"(K). "I said in the course of our controversy about Irish affairs and Irish agitation," Croke reported of his conversation with Mgr. Machi, "that if the Italian Bishops and priests took the same course that we in Ireland had taken, and headed the people against their infidel government, the Pope would be a free man instead of being a prisoner, and the Italian clergy respected and loved by the people, instead of being hated and despised." "This," Croke insisted, "Machi told the Pope, and that led to the result of which you know something. *That is certain.*"

Given what was at stake, Croke had every reason to be both troubled and depressed by his conduct. He was too intelligent not to realize that he would not only have to face the Irish people on behalf of the pope if Walsh was not appointed, but because of his own imprudence he would also soon have to face Walsh on behalf of Croke. On Monday, May 18, the day after he had written his long and despairing letter, he wrote Walsh again(W). "I had a long and confidential conversation yesterday," he reported to Walsh, "with Mgr. Jacobini at Propaganda in which he assured me that he knew nothing of Dr. *M*'s appointment, and that he did not believe there was any truth in the report about it." "He told me this so confidently," added Croke, who was seizing on straws, "and seemed to dislike *M*, so heartily, that I was full of courage, and since then, have come to the conclusion that yr. appointment is certain." "We are, I believe," he continued, "to have a general audience on Sunday next, 24th int., when we all hope he will tell us who the *Man* is to be." "The moment I get a glimpse of the truth," Croke assured Walsh, in obvious good humor, "I shall flash it to you." The pope, however, did not relieve the tension, as Croke expected, by naming "the *Man*," at their final audience.

Soon after Croke arrived home, he reported to Kirby that he was not only exhausted, but the worst of it was that he must immediately begin his visitations. "If the Pope," he complained fretfully in the course of this letter, on June 6, "keeps the Dublin business much longer on hand, nothing, I fear, can be done to keep the press or the people quiet—especially if they begin to believe that Dr. Walsh will be passed over"(K). "My reception in Ireland," Croke reported, taking his comfort from what he was most secure in, "was a most extraordinary one. Never was anything like it. I send you Freeman. The reception in Kingstown was quite as enthusiastic." "I spoke a great deal," he noted carefully, "and endeavoured to be as cautious as possible." The long letter Croke wrote Manning the next day, Sunday, however, was even more revealing about the troubled state of his conscience. "You must have thought it strange," he began significantly on June 7, "that I did not call on your Eminence when I was passing through London, some days ago"(C). "But, the fact is," Croke apologized lamely, "that I had not a moment to myself while there. I had a good deal of banking, and other business to transact, on Monday, and I left for Chester, at 10 o'clock on Tuesday."

"Things are looking very threatening here," Croke reported, turning from what was on his conscience to what was on his mind. "The people cannot be persuaded that the Pope has not entered into some sort of agreement with the Government by virtue of which *he* is to obtain certain privileges for Catholic minorities in India, Malta, and elsewhere." "The price paid by His Holiness, being," Croke spelled out the *quid pro quo*, "the setting aside of the popular Candidate for the See of Dublin, and the appointment instead of Dr. Moran who, I regret to say, is detested, or of some other, perhaps, less objectionable, but equally cold and colourless Ecclesiastic," "I dread this myself—" Croke confessed, "for, in point of fact, during our last interview with His Holiness, he formally sketched such a plan, and declared that 'he was not the Pope of Ireland alone but of the Universal Church'—thereby pretty clearly indicating, that Irish views on Ecclesiastical or other matters should not, and would not stand in the way of what I may call Imperial projects, or legislation." "So I am dreadfully afraid," Croke warned,

> that he may think of treading on this very dangerous ground, just now—and dangerous, indeed, it is—for, if, two years after the Simeoni Circular and the angry excitation to which it gave rise, it should turn out that English influence proved to be so potent in the Vatican as to cause His Holiness to discredit one of the foremost Ecclesiastics of the day, *simply because* he happened not to be a "persona grata" to the Government, I really fear that the Irish people at home and abroad will cease to believe in the impartial [*sic*], or to respect the person and office of the present Pontiff(C).

"This is," he assured Manning, "my solemn and sober judgement as to the situation." "I write it to your Eminence," he concluded formally, "as the highest and most influential Ecclesiastic within the realm, with the hope that you may have it conveyed to the proper quarter, and thus prevent if it not be too late one of the greatest Church disasters that have occurred within our time."

"I was glad," Manning replied five days later, on June 12, "to get your letter"(C). "I now write briefly to say," he explained to Croke, and laying down an interesting order of priorities, "that I wrote fully about Dublin pointing out"

1. The supreme danger of even *seeming* to be swayed from here.
2. The *united* wish of the Bishops.
3. The *worthiness* of the man.

"No adverse, or other decision," he reassured Croke, "has been yet come to. And you may confide in my leaving nothing undone that I can do." "Meanwhile," he advised in conclusion, "if you & Mr. Parnell can prevent outrages, a better day is near." A few days before Croke received this reassuring note from Manning, however, he had received the very disturbing news from Kirby that Moran had actually been summoned to Rome. Walsh had also learned that Moran had been sent for, and immediately wrote to inform Croke, who was in the midst of his visitations. "Your note," Croke replied to Walsh from Mitchelstown, on Saturday, June 13, "reached me *here* a while ago"(W). "Before that," he explained, "I had just got a line from Dr. Kirby announcing the same fact—so, there is no doubt about it." "If *M* has been sent for to be placed in Dublin," Croke commented bitterly, "there will be bad work, and I shall never raise hand or voice to prevent or allay the trouble—I have no time to write more." "I am very tired," he concluded wearily, "I'll make no more speeches now, and tis hard to say what else I may do, or not do—."

Errington, who had spent the whole and more of the parliamentary Easter recess in Rome, meanwhile, had returned to his duties in London shortly before the middle of May. "I leave the question," he had assured Granville on May 5, shortly before his departure, "of the Dublin Archbishopric in a hopeful state. Indeed, if it were not that the Pope is unfortunately so liable to change, I should feel now confident that Dr. Walsh will not be appointed."[29] "The Dublin archbishopric," he wrote Granville again from the House of Commons, on Friday, May 15,"being still undecided, I must continue to keep the Vatican in good humour about Goa, and keep up communication with them generally as much as possible."[30] "I am almost ashamed to trouble you again when you are so busy," he apologized, and giving good evidence of how ineffective Dilke and Chamberlain's protests had been with their Cabinet colleagues, "but perhaps on Monday you would allow me to show you the letter I propose to write." "The premature report about Dr. Moran," Errington pointed out, "will cause increased pressure to be put on the Pope, and create many fresh difficulties. The matter must therefore be most carefully watched so that the strong pressure I can still command may be used et the right moment, and not too soon or unnecesserily (for too much pressure is quite as dangerous as too little)." "To effect this," he concluded artfully, "constant communication with Rome is necessary."

[29] B, 49690.
[30] *Ibid.* This letter was also published in *United Ireland*, August 1, 1885, and is quoted in R. Barry O'Brien, *The Life of Charles Stewart Parnell* (London, 1910), p. 310. There is in the latter version, however, an important discrepancy in that "Goa" is represented as "you."

Four days later, on May 19, Errington wrote Smith explaining that he could have no idea really what a sensation the report of Moran having been recalled to Rome had caused. "Everybody, Protestant & Catholic," he generalized, "regards Dr. Walsh as such a strong Nationalist & so entirely the Nominee of the anti English faction, that they would hail any nomination which should save the country from him." After asking Smith to assure Cardinal Simeoni again that he had the complete support of the government in dealing with Portugal about Goa, Errington also asked Smith to tell the cardinal that the Irish government was disposed to make those changes the cardinal felt were necessary in the projected elementary education bill. The point about the constitution of the court to enforce compulsory attendance, Errington explained, posed no real problem, but "the other and much graver point, as to giving over the Schools partly to the controul of a *popular elective body*, offers great difficulty." The difficulty, however, did not come from the government, but "from the Nationalist Members *who insist* on introducing the *popular elective* into the controul of education." "There could be nothing more dangerous for education," Errington warned, "for if this once begins the Clergy will lose very soon all the controul they have: as you are aware under the present System while the State pays almost the whole cost the Clergy have the whole management."

"The Parnellites," he further argued, "insist that an element of popular controul should be introduced to modify the priests' absolute management. Yet the Bishops support the Parnellite views." "If the Parnellites are so devoted," Errington noted, "cannot Dr. Croke induce them to give up this attack on Clerical Management, and if so I can guarantee that Govt. will be delighted and will gladly agree: if the Parnellites will not consent to this, the only thing I can promise is that the bill shall not pass this year in its objectionable form. This shows how friendly the Govt. is." "Pray explain this to Cardinal Simeoni," he then begged Smith, "and ask him whether he thinks the Parnellites are the friends of Catholic Education." If indeed Errington was right about the Parnellites being insistent on the principle of a popular elective body being introduced into the Irish elementary education system, which is very doubtful, it did not follow that the bishops necessarily agreed with them. Moreover, if Smith did explain all this to

Simeoni, the cardinal must have certainly wondered at the relative and growing weakness of the government and the apparent increasing political strength and influence of the Parnellites. The cardinal must have also wondered whether the Parnellites would prove more useful now as friends and allies rather than enemies in the cause of Catholic education at Westminster. Further, would not a united Irish episcopate under the leadership of Walsh and the tutelage of Manning be, perhaps, the best means of both securing and containing this alliance? Errington, however, seemed oblivious of the implications he was raising in making his own case at Rome.

In the following weeks Errington wrote Smith constantly, always insisting that the appointment of Walsh would be a catastrophe for both the Irish Church and any hope for Roman-British relations. The pope, meanwhile, in early June, and after the Irish bishops had left Rome, did actually summon Moran to Rome. Whatever the pope's intentions were with regard to Moran, it was obvious the archbishop of Sydney would not arrive in Rome for at least a month. During June, therefore, Errington continued to bombard Smith with assurances that appearances were not necessarily reality. He explained on June 5, for example, that an Irish member had just asked Gladstone in the House a question about whether the government intended to establish more regular relations with the Vatican instead of the present anomalous state of things, simply to embarrass the government. "This put Gladstone in great difficulty," Errington pointed out, "for if he said yes just before the elections it would be sure to cause trouble so he replied in these words, 'Her Majesty's Govt. have not formed any intention of establishing regular diplomatic relations with the Holy See.' This is the usual in this case necessary evasion." "He merely says," Errington maintained, interpreting Gladstone a little loosely, "*the Govt. have not yet made up their minds* either way; I hope you will call on Msgr. Jacobini and explain this to him, for otherwise the answer might irritate the Pope." "I think matters look very promising," Errington then concluded optimistically, "for something being done after the elections, but it is clear that Dr. Walsh's appointment would put an end to all our noble arrangements." Smith wrote by return on June 9, to reassure Errington that there was nothing new in Gladstone's reply.[31] "The Pope and everyone here," Smith added, "knew that Mr. Gladstone never formed the intention of holding diplomatic relations with the Vatican. However I will explain the question to Monsig. Jacobini." "The Pope is still silent with regard to Dublin." Smith reported, "Monsig. Jacobini tells me that the Pope has not yet decided the person." "The Bishop of Salford," Smith noted further, referring to Herbert Vaughan and his diocesan weekly, *The Tablet*, "is working hard for Dr. Walsh. He says openly that Dr. Walsh has been unjustly treated in Rome!" "The Vaughans," Smith commented acidly, "always look after money. The Bishop wants to sell his Tablet in Ireland."

The day before, meanwhile, Errington had written Smith again from the House of Commons. "I returned to London on Friday," he reported to Smith on Monday, June 8, "political matters are in a very confused state: I think it is very probable that the Govt. may break up later in the session"(S). "Dr. Croke," Errington noted astutely, "seems to be much toned down for the present by his visit to Rome & by the Pope's exhortations: but I fear this will not last long." "The gravest interest," he assured Smith, "is still felt about the Archbishopric of Dublin. The Nationalist press this week speak in desponding terms." "I trust the Pope will be firm," Errington added, "if he appoints anybody *except* Dr. Walsh the result will be so good here that I think you will see a crusade in the English Press *in favour of diplomatic* relations with Rome; this would enable Govt. after the general election to propose sending a Minister to Rome." "But if Dr. Walsh is appointed," Errington warned, "of course the whole thing falls to the ground, for the reaction will be very severe in this country: it will be regarded as a very unfriendly & hostile act; and it will be mischievous beyond all belief to religion."

The government, instead of breaking up (later in the session) as prophesied, was broken the very evening of the day Errington wrote Smith. The ministry was defeated on an

---

[31] GR, 30/29/149. This letter of Smith's was covered by a letter from Errington to Thomas H. Sanderson, a Foreign Office official, June 13, 1885: "If convenient to you I could look in after luncheon tomorrow to finish the letters. / Would you kindly give the enclosed letter to Lord Granville; it arrived yesterday and is rather interesting—socially & otherwise."

amendment to the budget by twelve votes, in a division in which seventy-three Liberals were absent and six actually voted against the government. The following day, June 9, Gladstone resigned. "Were you much surprised," Errington asked Smith on June 17, "at the fall of the Ministry? It is announced this evening that Lord Salisbury has succeeded in forming a Ministry"(S). "Let me tell you one thing in strict confidence," Errington added, "in order to mark their feelings of gratitude towards the Pope for his kindness, the outgoing Ministry will I believe confer some slight honour on me. You are the only friend to whom I have mentioned this, & it must be kept secret until regularly published. You know the liberals are very stingy, and reward their friends very reluctantly." "I expect to be charged," he projected optimistically, "to write the Cardinal Secretary, the Pope, Propaganda, &c in Lord Granville's name; & I also trust to carry on with the next Ministry." "You see how important it is," he finally drew the moral from his lesson, "not to name Dr. Walsh to Dublin."

On Tuesday, June 23, the pope finally decided to appoint Walsh archbishop of Dublin. Kirby immediately telegraphed the news to Walsh and the appointment was published the following day. "We are all much startled," Errington confessed to Smith on June 25, "by the news of Dr. W's appointment to Dublin. How did it come about?"(S). "I expected the Pope ultimately would name him," confided Errington, "for I heard *Cardinal Manning* has been intriguing with the English radicals in this sense; but I did not think the Pope would decide so soon or so suddenly." "After all, though I still think the appointment most unfortunate on the State & Church," Errington then stoically continued, "I cannot help feeling that the delay will have had a good & quieting effect on Dr. W." "The misfortune is," he added less philosophically, "that his nomination throws the whole Irish Church & the hundreds of good quiet priests who are now painfully resisting the agitation, into the arms of the Nationalists; besides I fancy it puts an end to any chance of relations with Rome." "Gladstone," Errington then confided in a paragraph marked "private" to Smith, "has just (today) offered me a baronetcy: pray keep this strictly private till it is publicly announced." "I am glad of this," Errington confessed, "for it rehabilitates me before the public, & ought to be accepted at Rome as a compliment to the Pope. I shall write in this sense to Cardinal Jacobini: Lord Granville has given me a letter to send him, of thanks from the late Govt. to the Pope for his kindness in these 4 years of negotiations."

"We are quite easy in our mind here now," Croke wrote revealingly to Kirby from Thurles on June 30, "as Dr. Walsh has been appointed"(K). "Nobody can tell," he conjectured freely, "what would have occurred in this country and in America, if, unfortunately, the Pope had acted otherwise. But, the Spirit of God guarded him, no doubt, in this very grave matter, and his decision has given unbounded satisfaction." There was also personal and general satisfaction as well as deep relief in Dublin, as well as Thurles. "The Providence of God," the venerable dean of the Dublin cathedral chapter, Walter M. Lee, wrote Kirby that same day from Maynooth, "has brought us through a great crisis, perhaps the greatest danger the Church in Ireland ever encountered: the exclusion of Dr. Walsh would have shaken the fabric to its foundations and the result would have been worse than the infliction of the penal laws"(K). "No one thought of interfering with the freedom of the Pope," Lee protested, "but the very presence of Errington in Rome was a source of anxiety and alarm." When the news of Walsh's appointment reached Clogher, Lee explained that even though the priests were on retreat and "in the house of God there was at once an universal clapping of hands." Two weeks after the appointment enthusiasm was still general in Ireland. "I fear I am very bold," Archbishop MacEvilly, obviously still exuberant, wrote Manning from Tuam, on July 7, "and what is more, I fear I may continue so"(M). "It is this that makes me write to your Eminence," he continued, "to tell you what I dare say you know already—but it may be no harm to corroborate it—that there *never was* a more popular man in Ireland, than our Holy Father. The appointment to the See of Dublin shall never be forgotten to the H. Father by the Catholic people of Ireland." "Your Eminence," MacEvilly gratefully acknowledged, "had *a hand* in it." "The *ovations*," he then reported, "given the Bishops everywhere on their return from the See of Peter tells well. Nothing was ever witnessed here like the last demonstration." "It proves," he maintained in conclusion, "that there is still great union between clergy & people. The appointment to Dublin will be a firm bond to keep all together."

While all Ireland thus seemed to be in a state of enthusiastic joy in early July, a serious and expectant archbishop of Sydney arrived in Naples. Moran was greeted by a papal courier, who presented him with the consoling news of his elevation to the Sacred College of Cardinals. When he had received a terse telegram from Cardinal Simeoni—"*Venias Romam Quamprimum*"—in early June, summoning him to Rome, Moran was fully convinced that his heart's desire was about to be fulfilled in his translation from Sydney to Dublin. The pope had, indeed, Moran later explained, thought not only of translating him to Dublin, but of sending Walsh to Sydney in his stead. Why did the pope change his mind? According to Moran, who had an audience immediately after his arrival in Rome, the pope explained that he had reconsidered both because of the strong feeling manifested by Irish Catholics in favor of Walsh and because he had discovered the lying nature of the conspiracy against him. Further, Moran added significantly in this letter to the rector of the Dublin diocesan seminary at Clonliffe, B. Fitzpatrick, some months after the event, Cardinal Simeoni had become convinced that Walsh should be appointed to Dublin.[32]

According to Walsh, who had been requested by the pope to come to Rome for his consecration, and who wrote Croke on July 25, the day after his initial audience, the pope "spoke most freely about the opposition to my appointment, the stories about my most extreme politics, etc., but he said he had satisfied himself it was *tutto esaggerato* [*sic*], *tutto falso*"(C). "Then he spoke," Walsh reported, "at great length about the appointment being altogether his own act." "Even towards the end," Walsh added, "it was suggested to him to let the case go to Propaganda, but he said 'No: this Archbishop is to be appointed by myself.'" "Then he turned on the Errington question," Walsh explained, "—the incorrect representations made by E. and others about Irish political affairs—how he inquired, and found out they were telling him 'mensogne' [*sic*]." "'Then,' said he," Walsh continued, "'*I decided to see Errington no more*. I gave directions also to the Propaganda, and to the Secretary of State, and though, of course, they could not close their doors against him, he was made to see

---

[32] *Walsh*, p. 175. Moran's letter to Fitzpatrick is paraphrased and is dated September, 1885.

FIG. 2. William J. Walsh, Archbishop of Dublin, 1885.

that he was not wanted to prolong his stay in Rome.' " "He told me repeatedly," Walsh then emphasized towards the end of this very long letter to Croke, "that it was the strong recommendation of the Irish Bishops that had the most weight with him in my appointment—their confidence in me, and the prospect of their being more united if I were in Dublin than if anyone else were there." " 'They were,' he said," Walsh quoted the pope in conclusion, " 'unanimous, or all but unanimous, we may call it unanimous.' "

In reviewing the reasons given by the pope to both Moran and Walsh, for the appointment of Walsh, the most immediate and striking thing is the apparently crucial influence of Manning. All those points recommended to the pope by Manning, and which must have reached Leo XIII some ten days before he made his decision about Dublin—the supreme danger of even "seeming" to be swayed by English influence, the "united" judgment of the Irish bishops, and the "worthiness" of Walsh—were all tactfully introduced by the pope in his conversations with Moran and Walsh. In his interview with Walsh, for example, the pope discreetly de-emphasized the importance of Errington's influence, while emphasizing to Walsh the confidence of the Irish bishops in him. With Moran, on the other hand, the pope considerately subsumed the unanimous, or almost unanimous, opinion of the Irish bishops in favor of Walsh in the larger and less personal body of Irish Catholic opinion, while he shifted some of the responsibility for a decision he actually had reserved entirely to himself to Cardinal Simeoni. The reasons given, therefore, though tactfully tailored to Moran and Walsh's feelings and the pope's needs, were substantially Manning's. Manning himself certainly believed that there was some cause and effect relationship between his letter and Walsh's appointment. "I thought my last letter to Leo XIII," he confessed to Vaughan on June 28, "would have vexed him."[33] "We have been," he added obviously relieved, "on the brink of an enormous scandal." "Rightly or wrongly," he explained, "the feeling in Ireland about Dublin was full of danger." "I found out," he then reported, "that the Cabinet had no part in it, had never discussed it or touched the question." "It was the work," Manning noted, "of about three working outside the Cabinet with Er-

---

[33] Leslie, *op. cit.*, pp. 392-393.

rington." "Thank God," he explained finally, "that is over!"

To argue that Manning's letter to the pope was decisive in itself, however, would be to misunderstand not only the mind of Rome, but the conscience of that mind, the pope. Walsh's appointment, in retrospect, was inevitable. To argue otherwise is to maintain the pope was an arbitrary and willful despot, and this the evidence will not support. The pope was not a free agent in fact and to plead that he was so in theory is simply to beg the question. Whether Walsh's appointment, therefore, is considered from either the point of view of right or expediency, that appointment was inevitable. For, the right was as much governed by procedure as indeed the expediency was dictated by necessity. The procedure in appointing a bishop in Ireland was common knowledge: Commendation by the clergy of a *terna*, report on that *terna* by the bishops of the province, and finally recommendation by the Propaganda to the pope for his authoritative approval. When the Pope reserved the decision about Dublin to himself, he was not breaking procedure, but suspending it for cause. He was really raising a question that was implicit in the ordinary procedure and normally taken for granted—the worthiness of the candidates commended and reported. No one understood this better than Walsh. "The complications that have arisen," he wrote Manning on June 9, "have sadly embarrassed me, and deprived me of all freedom of action as to my own position."[34] "One thing is clear:" he maintained, "my Presidentship is necessarily at an end; the office is not one that could be held even for a day by anyone on whose career an adverse judgement had been pronounced by the Holy See." Since there was no doubt about either Walsh's integrity or his ability, the question of his worthiness really became one of prudence, a quality much valued among high ecclesiastics generally and even more especially appreciated in the mind of Rome. When not only the Irish bishops, but Cardinal Manning guaranteed Walsh's prudence, the pope no longer had any cause that would allow him to violate procedure in the name of the right.

The pope, however, might also find legitimate cause in his need to promote the greater good. As he explained to the Irish bishops at their final audience in late May, he was pope of

---

[34] *Ibid*., p. 392. See also C, Walsh to Croke, March 4, 1885.

the Universal Church as well as the Church in Ireland and had to consider the needs of all before the interests of the few. The Irish Bishops, however, found it more difficult to distinguish at this point between the greater good and pure expediency. Still, even if Walsh's appointment is considered from the lower limit of expediency, it becomes evident that the pope was constrained by the logic of his own recent policy. Since the Parnell Circular, the pope had been attempting to restructure his power and influence in Ireland. Further, the pope had recently taken Cardinal Manning into his confidence and the cardinal was wholly and totally committed to the Irish cause. To think that the pope would forsake the patient labor and policy of two years and alienate at a stroke the Irish Church and people, as well as Manning, without some adequate recompense is inconceivable. What indeed could the British government offer the pope that could justify his undermining his own power and influence in the English-speaking world? Diplomatic relations might have tempted the pope in terms of effecting a greater good, but he knew not only that Mr. Gladstone had formed no such intention but that Gladstone's government was tottering towards its end. "The Gladstone Ministry," Manning had reported to the pope, on May 24, "is undergoing a crisis"(M). "Four Ministers," Manning explained, "are opposing certain measures concerning Ireland." "The said four want a local administration for Ireland in all local, municipal and public interests, excluding all, in fact, that are Imperial interests; they want what the Irish Bishops want." "To these wishes of theirs," Manning assured the pope, "I heartily adhere as a Catholic and an Englishman." "The condition of Ireland," he emphasized, "is unjust and intolerable, and the proposed legislation would be just, sound, and most prudent (*prudentissima*)." Even from the point of view of expediency, then, the British government at the end of May had nothing substantial to offer the pope.

Since the pope and his advisers, therefore, were well aware by early June that both right and expediency dictated Walsh's appointment, why did they take the unprecedented action of summoning Moran to Rome? The answer, of course, was to gain time. As long as the issue was real, or at least appeared to be so, and the British government was dealing from a position of weakness, time was on Rome's rather than London's side.

The crucial thing was not to make the appointment before the ministry collapsed, and summoning Moran from Sydney would give Rome at least a month. Concessions as far as Irish education was concerned and support for the Vatican in its relations with Portugal over Goa, for example, were more likely to be conceded if the British government felt there was still something to be gained from Rome. Walsh's appointment, significantly enough, was made on June 23, two weeks after the fall of Gladstone's ministry, a week after Salisbury formed a new government, and some two weeks before Moran arrived in Rome. The timing of the appointment was masterful, maximizing Irish gratitude and minimizing English resentment. Rome of late years had not demonstrated much diplomatic skill in dealing with the British government about Irish affairs, but in the Walsh appointment she appeared to have recovered the diplomatic touch.

X. Conservative Interlude

June, 1885 - November, 1885

Four days after he had been provided to the see of Dublin, Walsh faced a minor crisis. On returning to Maynooth from Dublin, on Saturday, June 27, Walsh found a letter from Kirby explaining that it was the pope's desire that he should come to Rome for his consecration. Walsh decided immediately that he must consult Croke personally and took the Sunday morning train from Dublin to Thurles. Croke was, unfortunately, still conducting his visitations, and Walsh had to content himself with a note instead of a visit. "I will ask your Grace," Walsh wrote, "kindly to give me your opinion, not as an element that is to be taken into account in a general consideration of the case by me, but as an indication simply of what I am to do"(C). "From your knowledge of Roman ways, " Walsh appealed to Croke's greater experience, "and what weight should in such a matter be attached to Dr. Kirby's opinion, you are the best judge in the matter." "So," he then resigned himself, "I leave the decision *altogether* in your Grace's hands. My personal leaning in the matter would be in favour of acting on the suggestion. But I mention my own view not at all to influence your Grace's opinion, if you lean at all strongly the other way, but only because I think you may wish to know what my own feeling in the matter would be." "P.S.," he added hurriedly, "It is *essential* you should come to the Maynooth meeting on Tuesday. There is the greatest difficulty in securing a quorum, i.e. *seven Trustees.*"

"What an awkward thing it was," Croke responded the next morning, Monday, June 29, "that I was away from home yesterday, and thus missed seeing you in Thurles. But there is no harm done. I wired, at once, this morning, recommending you to go to Rome"(W). "I see but one *solid* objection to it," Croke explained, "the people (i.e.) the country, will be disappointed. But it can be circulated far and wide that the proposal

302

for the Roman Consecration came from Rome itself. Tis better to have this understood so as to lead to no misunderstanding." "As a rule," Croke then confided to Walsh, "I do not attach much importance to Kirby's suggestions, but his instincts are wonderfully correct; and he knows well what would please the Romans. So I go with him fully in this case." "I do not think it *possible*," Croke then excused himself, "for me to go to Maynooth as I am greatly knocked up for want of sleep. I really think I got a touch of the Roman fever, and have not worked it off yet. I have a cold on me, moreover, and so feel very much in need of absolute repose." "I had a letter yesterday from Cardinal Manning," Croke then informed Walsh, turning to happier thoughts, "congratulating all concerned on your appointment, and praising Lord Carnarvon (Ld Lieutenant) to the stars. He would wish greatly to have the 4 Archbps meet him and lay before him their views and desires as to the state of the country." "The Cardinal has been a true friend," Croke concluded loyally, "and I shall write to him one of these days in return."

That same day, Croke wrote Walsh another letter, enclosing £500 and marked "*strictly confidential*"(W). "The enclosed cheque," Croke explained, "*may* be of use to you. If so, turn it to account, and pay me when you grow rich." "I would wish you," he confided to Walsh, "to be very openhanded in Rome, and cheque would enable you to be so. Nothing takes so well in the Eternal City; and the fuel spreads like wildfire." "See Gualdi at Propaganda," Croke advised, "He is as you know Minutan for Ireland. He speaks English, for a foreigner, amazingly well, and is a worshiper of Cardinal Manning. So belaud his Eminence." Croke, in fact, wrote his promised note to the cardinal the next day. "I heartily thank God," he began his letter to Manning, on June 30, "that the Irish Ecclesiastical Crisis has come to a satisfactory ending"(C). "I thank," he then added simply, "your Eminence also." "Lord Carnarvon," he immediately assured Manning, referring to the new lord lieutenant in Salisbury's recently formed ministry, "will, I'm sure, get every fair play. I hear on all sides that he is an excellent man. But his Dublin Castle surroundings are as bad as can be, and it will be hard for him not to be contaminated by them. The whole lot must disappear before a Lord Lieutenant, however personally good and amiable, can hope for even an approach to popularity in Ireland." "I shall be most happy," he then reassured Manning, "to say and do anything in my power to secure fair play for Lord Carnarvon." "Indeed," Croke concluded significantly, "I think the Irish Party are well disposed towards him."

Walsh, meanwhile, was deeply touched by Croke's princely generosity. "It is poor thanks for me to say," he wrote on June 30, "that I cannot find words to thank your Grace for this last great act of your kindness towards me"(C). "Over and above this," Walsh added, having explained that he had no source of private income and no savings to speak of, " I prize it, as I cannot but regard it as the truest act of friendship I have ever known." " I only hope," he then concluded, "I may be able to thank you in some more substantial way than by these empty words." "When do you start," Croke asked in reply the next day, July 1,"—and how did the Maynooth difficulty get solved?"(W). "I had a note from Mori," Croke explained, referring to one of his Roman contacts, and former editor of the *Aurora*, "this morning, in acknowledgement of £20 I sent him for his letters in the Unita Catholica [*sic*]." "He tells me two things," Croke reported, "—amongst others—relating to yr. appointment."

1. that, a few days before it, he had it from one of the Pope's chief friends that Cardinal Moran would be Abp of Dublin.

2. that he (Mori), on hearing this took a note of mine just received to Cardinal Jacobini and read for him the passage in it in which I stated, that if "anyone but Dr. Walsh be appointed to Dublin, there will be bloody work in Ireland, and in America as well—"

"I wrote him that certainly." "I shut up now," Croke concluded, "I go on retreat on Monday next with Parish priests."

Walsh replied on Friday, July 3, that he hoped to leave Dublin for London on Tuesday morning, July 7, leave London on Thursday morning, and arrive in Milan on Friday evening, from where he would be guided by Dr. Kirby as to his arrival in Rome (C). "I dare say Molloy," Walsh explained to Croke, referring to the rector of the Catholic University, "will come to London," "We are," he added, referring to Parnell, "to see 'the leader.' " "After the General Meeting on Wednesday," Walsh then reported to Croke what had passed at

Maynooth, "a meeting of the Episcopal Education Committee was held at which a series of Resolutions were passed (to be published at once) insisting on our right to a fair share in what is going—and especially to a fair i.e. *proportionate* representation of Catholics, having the confidence of the Catholic body on all educational commissions, Boards etc." "There are also," Walsh added, "two Resolutions, not to be published, authorizing me and Molloy to put these before Lord Carnarvon, and to see 'Mr. Parnell and the members of the Irish Parliamentary Party,' to secure the pressing of the matter at once on the attention of Parliament & of the Ministry."

On Tuesday morning, July 7, however, Walsh was still in Maynooth. He wrote to Kirby explaining that he had been delayed because the bishops at their Maynooth meeting wanted him to bring their educational resolutions personally to the attention of the new lord lieutenant(K). "It may in future," Walsh added, "be of use that I thus met him so soon after his arrival." "As to the Archbishopric," Walsh further explained to Kirby, "I wrote at length to Card. Simeoni yesterday, explaining to H. E. that I really feel myself to be unfit for the position. Many of the Bishops are of opinion, in view especially of recent occurrences, that it would be well to have some recognised person in Rome, whose duty it would be to give trustworthy information through the newspapers as well as other sources, correcting, publicly if necessary, inaccurate statements made." "If I were in such a position," Walsh confessed, "I believe I could do much more good than in any Bishopric or Archbishopric at home or abroad. I should wish your Lordship confidentially to consider this, and to confer with Card. Simeoni, so that if advisable I should be in a position on reaching Rome at once to put my views in writing before the Holy Father." "I feel bound in every way," Walsh added scrupulously, "to act so that I shall incur *no* responsibility as to acceptance of a position such as the Archbishopric." "I know," he concluded, "I can count on your Lordship's kind counsel and good offices in this, as in all other things."

That same day Walsh also wrote Croke, explaining his scruples. "I may as well now say plainly," Walsh wrote, "what your Grace may not be unprepared to hear—that before I accept the Archbishopric, I must put clearly before the Pope my view as to the necessity of an Irish representative having the confidence etc. etc. etc., and as to my conviction that I am fit for *one* position and unfit for *the other*"(C). "Now that he," Walsh added, referring to the pope, "has put down the intrigues of the Vetoists, the Dublin question is a much simpler one than it was. I make no merit in all of this for all my personal feelings are in favour of the Roman post and against that of Dublin." "I find," Walsh had written earlier in this letter, "there is no possibility of my wanting your Grace's cheque. The amount in hand will go quite far enough for all present purposes." "You suggested," Walsh then noted, " 'openhandedness.' Kindly suggest details." "Is *Gualdi*," Walsh asked pointedly, "a man to take money? You mentioned his name in that context. Then in what form is it best to give what is to be given? Is Dr. Kirby a safe guide in such matters? What should I give him, or Verdon, when leaving . . . ?" "I should like to organise," Walsh then explained, referring to an influential Vatican newspaper, "an Irish correspondent for the *Moniteur*—a letter a week. Fr. James Daniel would write it, & some of the French College people put it into French." "A good deal of useful information," Walsh maintained, "could then be *forced* on the Romans."

Croke replied the next day, July 8, in a long, playful, and characteristic letter, indicating that the depression induced by his late Roman visit had finally lifted(W). "Yours to hand," he began briskly, "Cheque all right. Cash always on hand here, in plenty and at *Call*." "Gualdi," Croke responded, considerably modifying his earlier intimations, "is quite unknown to me, beyond having had a couple of talks with him. But I heard he was reliable, and a great friend of Cardinal Manning." "I do not think," Croke explained, "that he would take money *directly*: But, I think, that if he were employed to do a job in an ordinary way, he would be glad to get paid for it." "Start from the conviction," Croke then advised Walsh, "that Dr. Kirby is the best of men, but not fit to deal with rogues or intriguers—especially if they be high up in Ecclesia." "*I* gave Verdon £50," Croke emphasized, "when leaving: but I gave it for improvements of House. I promised £50 more, making in all for this purpose £300. I gave Kirby £10, and sent him another £10, a week, or so ago—for which I got a note of acknowledgement by this midday post." "Nothing in it new," Croke reported good-humoredly,"—all prayers which suit me now as I am *on retreat*."

"Do not be coquetting," he added playfully, "at all with the

Dublin See." "Fit or not fit, you *must* go ahead now," he warned, "or we would eat you down to the boots." "I now tell you *deliberately*," he continued, more seriously, "that Dr. Moran was called home to be appointed to Dublin, and that he would have been appointed, had we not kicked up such a row as we did. That has come to me in a way that cannot be doubted of —on inquiry, in Rome, you will find it correct." "I would not care to be consecrated by him," Croke confessed; "I hear they are thinking of it. Simeoni would suit better, and the Pope best—of course." "I saw a letter today from Rome," Croke then reported, "in which it was stated, that the idea about me in Rome is (or was) that I never attend to anything but politics. That's funny,—whereas, in reality, I never mind politics at all: but spend all my time at my Diocesan business." "Should you get a chance," he suggested to Walsh, "especially with the Pope (though, indeed, I care but little what they think of me), dispel this delusion. Even in politics I am most moderate, and have kept down many a rising wave of trouble. You will, I'm sure, drop me a line now and then stating how the cat jumps." "Retreat," Croke then noted, "going on here well. Jesuit Hayden conducting." "He is a correct and fluent talker," Croke explained revealingly, "with a good manner and accent, but he is too speculative and does not hit their Reverences sufficiently on the 'raw' for my taste." "This letter," he concluded, "will reach Rome befoɪe yourself. I direct Irish College." "P.S.," he then added merrily, if not reverently, " 'Pieces Justificatives' of your humble servant may be opportunely put *into* the Pope when you are speaking of the necessity of having an accredited representative in Rome." "Here is," he concluded amusingly, and referring to himself, "an instance of defamation of character &c &c !!!"

Walsh, meanwhile, who had set out for Rome, wrote Kirby from London, reporting on his interview of Wednesday, July 8, with Lord Carnarvon in Dublin. "It was in every way most satisfactory," Walsh explained to Kirby, on Friday, July 10; "Before coming over he made an excellent speech in the House of Lords. Mainly as the result of this, he got a really good reception from the people, with which he was naturally much gratified." "So," Walsh continued, "the preparation for the interview was of the very best."

When Dr. Molloy and I arrived at the Vice-regal Lodge, Dr.

Molloy was taken charge of by one of the Secretaries, and then on receiving me, after a few words of compliment on both sides, his Excellency at once asked me if I had any objection to speak freely with him, not merely on the Education question, but also on the state of the country generally. Of course I expressed great satisfaction at his affording me an opportunity of doing so, and I then explained to him my views as to what I consider the two most urgent points—viz. an inquiry into some of the judicial proceedings of the last few years, and a good measure to enable the tenants to *purchase* their lands. He told me candidly the difficulties in the way, but of course I said I was not in a position to appreciate these as his Excellency was, and that I merely put forward my view as to what I regarded as indispensable for the reestablishment of confidence in the law. As regards one set of convictions, those in the Maamtrasna case, I told him that after a very careful study of it I am satisfied of two things: first that one poor man who was hanged, and three others now undergoing penal servitude for life, are as innocent of all share in the murder, or of anything connected with it, as his Excellency or myself; secondly that all this will be fully established if only an inquiry be held. All this being fully believed by the people throughout the West of Ireland, is it not hard to expect them to have confidence in the law as recently administered among them?(W)

"I dare say," Walsh then pointed out to Kirby, "there will be an outrage about my going to the Viceregal Lodge, but on the other hand it is not impossible that by doing so this soon, I may have prevented the establishment of a system of dictation from the newspapers." "On the Education question," Walsh assured Kirby, "his Excellency is *with us* to a most surprising extent." "I saw a number of our M.P.'s here yesterday," Walsh reported, "—including some of the more 'advanced.' " "To my surprise," he confessed in conclusion, "they all seemed glad to hear that I had called on his Excellency, and established friendly relations with him!"

Walsh evidently made a considerable impression on the new lord lieutenant, for Carnarvon not only immediately spoke that same day to his Cabinet colleague, Lord Ashbourne, the lord chancellor of Ireland, who was preparing the government's proposed land purchase bill, but he took the additional precaution of writing Ashbourne the next day. "I doubt whether," Carnarvon explained to Ashbourne on July 9, "I yesterday sufficiently made you aware how strongly the Arch-bishop of Dublin dwelt upon"

(1) The payment of a *very moderate* annual payment.

(2) The consequent extension of time over which these annual payments may be spread with regard to a purchase bill.[1]

"This and the Maamtrasna case," Carnarvon emphasized, "were the two points which he selected to urge *very strongly* upon me when in private, adducing in support his own knowledge & experience of Irish small holders; I cannot but think that if you see your way towards accepting these principles it would be well, & as far as I can judge of such a subject there seems to me to be much reason in the proposal." "I imagine the Irish peasant," Carnarvon shrewdly conjectured, "to be exactly the person who may be tempted by a small *immediate* advantage in the terms of purchase, whilst he would be blind to prospective & more distant gains in the transaction." "But you know your countryman," he concluded wisely, "far better than I can understand them by my imperfect conjectures."

While Walsh was thus doing his best in his own industrious way through Kirby to assure the Roman authorities that he was really a moderate in politics, Croke was also attempting to rehabilitate himself at Rome. "Somehow," he complained to Kirby, on July 15, "I am always set down by the English press, and by the Irish press, as one who not only never had said anything against outrages but who actually had encouraged the perpetrators of them and this, I suppose, *was* or *is* believed of me in Rome"(K). "The fact was," Croke protested, "that I constantly denounced outrages, and, I think, had a great share in putting them down. I wish then you would kindly call the attention of the authorities to the short speech which I send you on the matter, delivered lately. Perhaps you could get it, or a substantial portion of it, into one of the Roman orthodox papers seen by the Pope." Croke then went on to explain to Kirby about the argument he had had with Monsignor Machi the day of his audience, which the Monsignor reported to the pope, and which in turn caused the pope to take MacEvilly and Gillooly rather than himself into his confidence on Irish affairs. "To be candid with you," he bravely told Kirby, "I care but little how I am misrepresented as a rule." "I value truth and principle," he insisted, a little too much, "and shall always adhere to them 'coute qui coute'—but I do not care a button for the interpretation put

---

[1] Carnarvon Papers(CAR), Great Britain, Public Record Office, London, 30/6/56.

on my words or acts, when I conscientiously believe both to be right."

Walsh arrived at the Irish College in Rome on Sunday evening, July 19, and as soon as he dined and read his letters, he visited the Propaganda where he had an interview with Cardinal Simeoni. "The interview," Walsh reported to Croke on July 21, "was substantially commonplace, owing in great measure to my great difficulty in understanding him in his mumbling way of talking in conversation"(C). "However," Walsh added loyally, "I made an opportunity of putting in as a natural digression in the conversation, a short statement of the ecclesiastical aspect of affairs in Cashel. Simeoni had introduced the topic fairly by laughing good-humouredly on my telling him that my two traveling companions, Secretary and Chaplin (!), were outside, and that one was from Rapotensis, and the other from Casseliensis." "So he launched out into an exposition of his views," Walsh noted, and referring to the speeches recently made by Croke on his visitations, "upon the speeches in the recent 'campaign'. " "They seem," Walsh assured Croke, "to have given unbounded satisfaction here—especially the numbrous and emphatic expressions of confidence in the Pope, and exhortations to the people to have full confidence in him. But Simeoni seemed to regard all this as a sort of a conversion." "So I then struck in," Walsh continued, "and said that the newspapers reported only the *political* proceedings of public interest— that the Papal aspect of the case now happened to be closely mixed up with this—but that it was notorious that in the pastoral, as distinct from the purely political, part of your ordinary course, no bishop in Ireland stood up more stoutly for the Pope than your Grace did, and no one who did more to lead the people to have confidence in him, just, I added, as there was no diocese in Ireland where there was better or more regular administration, as regards priests, nuns, churches, schools, etc. etc." "I have got notice," Walsh then reported, "of my audience for to-morrow, Wednesday, midday," "Then I go out to Genazzano," he added, laying out his itinerary, "for a few days retreat: return on Sunday: see the Consistory, etc. etc., next week: Consecration by Sydney, *at special desire of the Pope*, on Sunday, August 2d." "I will write again," he assured Croke in conclusion, "after the audience."

"I had my audience yesterday" Walsh reported to Croke on Friday, July 25, from Genazzano, in a letter in which "confidential" was underlined four times(C). "Nothing," Walsh immediately reassured Croke, "could be more satisfactory, whether as to substance or as to tone." "I was quite prepared," Walsh confessed candidly, "for a sort of homily on the necessity of observing moderation etc., but there was nothing of the kind, nothing even approaching it." "He told me," Walsh then continued, after the Pope had also told him how he had found out that the charges made against him were both exaggerated and false, "that Simeoni had gone to him with a letter of mine but that when he heard it was to raise difficulties about accepting the appointment he had refused to listen to it." The pope then went on to explain, Walsh reported, how he had for all practical purposes dismissed Errington. "At this point." Walsh informed Croke, "came the most satisfactory part of all."

> After talking a little about India, the hierarchy, etc., and the advantage of his having relations with the English Government, he said, "I know that the Irish are afraid that anything of this sort may be injurious to them, and I see that their view is reasonable." "Yes Holy Father," said I, "It is quite plain from what occurred in my own case that we are exposed to great risk of being misrepresented to you," and I then brought in what your Grace suggested about yourself, and the idea that you devote yourself to politics neglecting your pastoral work. Well, said the Pope (just as I was going to make a suggestion about a representative), "I have been thinking of a plan for some time past, I think it would meet the difficulty, but I don't know what the Irish bishops would think of it; I have not mentioned it to anyone, but I said, I will ask 'Valsh' when I have him here."
> So thereupon he propounded his scheme, consisting in the establishment of an Irish representative, fully recognized, and ecclesiastic having the confidence of the Holy See and of the Irish bishops. "We could make him," he said, "a bishop in partibus." Of course I said at once that this was the very thing we wanted, and that I had a letter from Cashel two days before, suggesting to me to see if the Holy Father would approve of it. "Oh," said he, "it depends altogether on yourself and the other bishops, so we may say it is done" (C).

"On other topics," Walsh added, after he and the pope had discussed who might suit as representative and how the technical details might be arranged, "he spoke very freely also e.g. on Moran and the suggestion made to appoint him to Dublin as he was already a Bishop of experience, etc. etc." "Putting together what the Pope said," Walsh explained to Croke, "and all I have picked up in Rome, I don't think the project of appointing Sydney went very far." "But I hear," Walsh added, "that Sydney himself came over fully satisfied that he was coming to Dublin, and that he made no secret of his annoyance when he heard at Naples that he was brought over to bring back the Hat to his Australian See." "As to political affairs at home ...," Walsh then pointed out, "going in for separation was the only political programme he seemed to object to." "I am to be consecrated," Walsh finally concluded his long and crucial letter, "by Sydney in the Irish College on Sunday, 2d of August."

Four days after his consecration, Walsh reported to Croke that he was about to leave Rome (C). They had been scheduled to leave the previous morning, but the day before that, they had received an invitation from Cardinal Pecci, the pope's brother, to dine with him. Since Walsh had been consecrated in what was technically the Cardinal's church, St. Agatha of the Goths, which also served the Irish College as its chapel, the invitation was *de rigeur*. Moran, Walsh noted, had been taken so ill after the consecration that he had not been able to attend the cardinal's dinner. The company, therefore, consisted of himself (Dublin), Kirby (Lita), and James Donnelly (Clogher), with their respective secretaries. The dinner was first-rate, Walsh explained, and they, especially Kirby, gave the cardinal full worth of it back in the right kind of information about Ireland. They had managed not only to identify the Prince of Wales and the late viceroy, Earl Spencer, with the Freemasons, but when the cardinal said that they could now look forward to having good measures passed for Ireland, Kirby had "struck in boldly about the Irish Parliament." The cardinal, Walsh observed, seemed surprised at this, but he had "assured him that it was a matter now of a very short time, 'pochi anni' at the outside etc., etc." "It is plain," Walsh further emphasized, and evidently impressed, "Dr. Kirby has the full confidence of these people; and certainly according to his lights he makes good use of his opportunities."

"Lita was confidentially," Walsh then continued, explaining why he was impressed, "sent for last night to bring me the address (autograph) sent by the Belgian bishops giving their adhesion to the Pope's letter on the excessive ultramontanism of some of the Catholic papers." "The Pope told him," Walsh reported, "that these letters of adhesion are coming in, that he will make a collection of them and print them in a volume, and that he would not like Ireland to be absent." "I suppose," Walsh suggested delicately to Croke, "we should do something to gratify H. H. as he has acted so decently towards us. He gave Dr. Kirby the Belgian letter to bring to me, as he said it indicated the general view that it would be useful to put forward." "What," Walsh then asked, "does your Grace think of this?" "What occurs to me," he further suggested, "about it is that

> (1) it would be ungracious not to do what we could, "to keep the Vatican in good humour"; (2) that in anything we write we should not omit stating that for our country fortunately, no difficulty such as that dealt with, exists—the advocate of Catholic interests and rights being, with us, thoroughly in accord with the Bishops and thus loyally dutiful to the Holy See; so that (3) we should write merely for the sake of having the voice of Ireland heard when all other countries are speaking out, that all may see that now, as has always been the case, our country is second to none in devotion etc. etc. etc.—or something to that general effect(C).

"I dare say your Grace is away from home," Walsh added, covering nearly every contingency, "but you can easily communicate with Dr. Carr, who, in conjunction with Dr. Logue (or Dr. Woodlock) as Secretaries can draw up a letter suited to the occasion that all may sign." "My first safe address," Walsh noted for Croke, "will be care of M. l'Abbé Navello, St. Moritz, Engadine, Switzerland." "I will expect," he added, "a letter there from your Grace at the end of next week." "P.S.," Walsh added characteristically, leaving little to chance, "I enclose copy of the Belgian letter. If you are at home you will find the official letters on the subject in the *Catholic Review* (New York) for July 18th. If you are in London you will find all in the *Tablet* or *Weekly Register*."

"You will be glad to hear," Walsh wrote Kirby from St. Moritz, on August 16, "that I have had a letter from Dr. Croke to say that he has written to Dr. Carr (whom I had asked to communicate, as Secretary, with the Bishops when he has the draft of the letter prepared), authorising him to attach his Grace's signature to *any* letter he may draw up on the subject"(K). "He does not seem to think," Walsh reported of Croke, "*we* are especially called upon to take up the matter." "But I know," Walsh added, in a masterpiece of understatement, "he would not make any difficulty about it from the way in which I wrote to him." "So, *Deo Gratias*," Walsh concluded, a little more piously than was his wont, "this little affair seems in a fair way of being worked out so as to gratify the Holy Father."

While Walsh was in Rome, educational matters had been left in the capable hands of Dr. Gerald Molloy, rector of the Catholic University. "As I shall be going over to London in a few days," Molloy wrote Carnarvon on July 19, "I would venture to ask your Excellency for a short interview, in reference to the question of education, on which you so kindly heard Dr. Walsh and myself previous to his Grace's departure for Rome."[2] "I do not think I have anything further," he explained, "to lay before your Excellency on the subject of University Education. But with regard to the Educational Endowments Bill, I am authorized by Dr. Walsh to express his clear opinion, in which I entirely concur, that it would be a matter of great importance to have it passed through Parliament during the present session." "I have heard from Lord Randolph Churchill," he noted interestingly, "that some opposition has been threatened by the Irish members. But if it be the situation of the Government to go on with the Bill, I think [we] should be able to use some influence to get that opposition withdrawn."

Immediately after his interview with Molloy, Carnarvon wrote Sir William Hart Dyke, chief secretary for Ireland, who was responsible for Irish business in the House of Commons. "I have this morning," Carnarvon informed Dyke, on July 21, "had a conversation with Father Molloy on the Educational Endowments Bill."[3] "Father Molloy," he explained to Dyke, "is a good representative of the R. C. party—very much bound up with the Bishops and a leading person as regards education. He was present the other day at my interview with the new Archbishop of Dublin—*altogether very important and very*

---

[2] *Ibid.*, 30/6/58.
[3] *Ibid.*

friendly." He had told Molloy, Carnarvon added, that he desired to have the Endowments Bill passed in that session and would like the block removed. Molloy intended, therefore, to put pressure on Joseph Biggar, the most obstructive of Parnell's lientenants. Carnarvon also advised Dyke that Molloy intended to ask him for an interview, and it would be wise to give him "a friendly and civil conversation." Carnarvon then reported that he had been having an anxious time in Ireland, and was not at all sure that he was yet "out of the wood." Some of his Cabinet colleagues, Carnarvon complained, did not seem to understand what he was trying to do and had become unnecessarily alarmed. They would be better advised, he concluded, in saving their alarm for the political consequences of a failure in Ireland.

What Carnarvon was really complaining about, it appears, was that his proposal for an immediate grant to the Catholic University College had been rejected by his Cabinet colleagues as politically inexpedient at the moment. What had, in fact, made it politically inexpedient was the extravagant conduct of some of those same colleagues in the Maamtrasna debate the previous Friday, July 17, in the House of Commons. Two Cabinet ministers and a member of the government had, during the debate, and in the face of their own party, made violent attacks on the late administration of justice in Ireland under Lord Spencer. Carnarvon, however, had not only nothing to do with the irresponsible proceedings of Sir Michael Hicks Beach, Lord Randolph Churchill, and Sir John Gorst, but he had, in fact, scrupulously and strenuously opposed in the Cabinet any proposal that involved a formal judicial review of his predecessor's acts, consistently maintaining that this would subordinate the administration of justice in Ireland to party politics. Moreover, the majority in the Cabinet had supported Carnarvon in that view. When Carnarvon's Cabinet colleagues, therefore, called the administration of justice in Ireland under Spencer into question, it appeared to both the House and the country at large that they must have had not only the approval of the Cabinet, but the approbation of the lord lieutenant as the member of the Cabinet responsible for Irish affairs. The conduct of Carnarvon's colleagues had also unnerved the Conservative rank and file in the House, because they were left with the impression that the leadership was cultivating an alliance with the Irish party, which if effected would certainly prove disastrous to their developing prospects in the country at the approaching general election.

When the Cabinet met, then, some days after the Maamtrasna debate to discuss Carnarvon's proposal for an immediate grant of £6,000 to the Catholic University College, they rejected it. Salisbury immediately notified Carnarvon by telegram on July 22 of the Cabinet's decision, and both Dyke and the earl of Harrowby, the Lord Privy Seal, wrote the same day explaining the decision. "The R. C. vote of money," Harrowby explained to his old friend, "is, I fear, really impossible. Already there is a growing distaste for our supposed Irish Alliance, distrust has been excited by Randolph's and Gorst's unfortunate speeches on the Maamtrasna affair (which have altered the situation since you were here)."[4] "The vote in question," he pointed out to Carnarvon, "would be considered a showing that the compact was signed, sealed, and delivered, and in addition to the horror of Ireland and Irish alliances, we should awaken the whole Protestant feeling which is only slumbering, and turn both Dissenters, Evangelicals, Scotchmen, middleclass and artisans, who are just joining us, into disappointed friends and bitter foes." "The whole Cabinet," Harrowby concluded, "you may say, *though in favour of the proposal itself*, and hoping it may be done later, is against such action at present, except Gibson [Ashbourne] and Randolph."

When Carnarvon received Salisbury's telegram on July 22, he immediately wrote Dyke, explaining that he was willing to give up the grant, but the Cabinet would now have to undertake a reconsideration of the whole question of Irish higher education. "I was really pleased," Dyke replied the following day, Thursday, July 23, "to get your letter this morning and the relief to me is great."[5] "The debate on Friday last," he emphasized again, referring to the Maamtrasna discussion, "has had a much more lasting effect than I anticipated & we should have been very roughly handled by our opponents if we had made any proposal for a grant this year." "Tomorrow morning," he then informed Carnarvon reassuringly, "I hope to see Dr. Molloy at the Irish Office, & you may be sure of my

[4] A. H. Hardinge, *The Life of Henry Howard Molyneux Herbert, Fourth Earl of Carnarvon, 1831-1890*,3 (London, 1925): p. 172.
[5] CAR, 30/6/58.

support in regard to your programme for the future." As Dyke was thus loyally reassuring him on July 23, Carnarvon was hurriedly writing Dyke another note. Since the Civil Service estimates were to be discussed the next day in the House, and since these estimates included the annual votes of money to be made to the Queen's Colleges, which happened to be the standing educational *bête noire* of the Irish bishops, Carnarvon insisted that it was essential that some guarantee be given by the ministry to reconsider the whole question of higher education as it related to Catholics, especially since the grant to the Catholic University College must now be abandoned.[6] "I propose to write in this sense," he advised Dyke in conclusion, "to Salisbury tonight and if you are in difficulties pray see him."

When one of Parnell's lieutenants, Justin MacCarthy, moved, on July 24, in the House the omission of the annual votes of money in aid of the Queen's Colleges, Sir Michael Hicks Beach, the chancellor of the exchequer, replied for the government. "I would wish to say, in the first place," stated Sir Michael, who had been chief secretary for Ireland in Disraeli's second ministry and architect of the Irish Intermediate Education Act of 1878, "that this is not a question which ought to be approached with the idea of concession or conciliation."[7] "I should wish to approach it," he explained to the House, "—and I think we would all wish to approach it—with the sole desire of endeavouring to spread as far as possible what I believe to be the great blessing of university education in Ireland, among all persons, whatever their creed, and, so far as possible, whatever their class, if duly qualified to receive it." "The lines on which it has been dealt with successfully," Beach then went on to maintain, "are those of the Intermediate Education Act of 1878 and of the Act [establishing the Royal University] of 1879, whereby it was decided that the State should pay for the results of secular education wherever given, and however obtained, quite irrespective of the circumstances whether they were gained by private tuition, in a denominational college, or in a mixed college." "We shall continue to regard this question on the principle I have laid down," Beach added, coming finally to what Carnarvon

---

[6] *Ibid.*
[7] Quoted in *Walsh*, p. 528.

thought was essential, "with the hope and the wish to do something to make university education more general and more widespread in Ireland; and if it should be our lot to hold office next session, to make some proposals which may deal in a satisfactory way with this most important matter."

Archbishop Walsh, meanwhile, who had arrived in Rome, was more than pleased with the latest Irish news from London. "The Dublin Freeman's Journal of last Saturday," Walsh wrote Carnarvon on Tuesday, July 21, "has just arrived here containing the report of the debate and proceedings in Parliament on the Maamtrasna case and the Land Purchase Bill."[8] "I feel it my duty at once," Walsh confessed, assuming a little too much, "to write your Excellency to say how deeply grateful I feel to you for your action at this critical time. At last we begin to see some prospect of a restoration of a feeling among our Irish people of respect for the law and for the maintenance of order in Ireland." "Your Excellency's personal action," Walsh added, and Carnarvon must have winced, "has, I believe, contributed more than any other influence to the bringing about of this better state of things." "I beg that your Excellency," Walsh then concluded, after indulging in some constitutional pleasantries, "will not take the trouble of writing in answer to this. It needs no answer." "I cannot refuse myself," Carnarvon replied to this small dividend on disaster on July 25, "the satisfaction of thanking you for the frank & kindly expressions in your letter of the 21st and I hail your Grace's recognition of my desire to meet the constitutional desires of all good & loyal Irishmen."[9] "Nothing," he then pointed out to Walsh, "can aid more powerfully in this than the frank & friendly spirit in which your Grace has met me." "I may perhaps add," he concluded hopefully and significantly, "that the line of action which we propose to take in Parliament on the important question of higher education is one that will commend itself to you."

In the following weeks, the Land Purchase and Educational Endowments Bills passed through their various stages and readings in Parliament and became law, respectively, on August 11 and 14. The Land Purchase Act, or the Ashbourne Act, set up a state fund of £5,000,000, which allowed tenants

---

[8] CAR, 30/6/58.
[9] *Ibid.*

to borrow the whole purchase price agreed on between them and their landlords, usually eighteen years' rental value, and repay that capital sum to the state at the rate of four per cent interest over a period of forty-nine years. If, for example, a tenant had been paying £10/year rent for his holding to his landlord, he would now, in effect, be paying an annuity of something more than £7/year for forty-nine years to the state, after which the holding became his own. Under the purchase clauses in the Land Acts of 1870 and 1881, very few tenants had been able to purchase their holdings, because they had been required to raise under the terms of those acts one-third and one-fourth of the purchase price, respectively, and there were not many tenants who could mobilize the capital necessary for the venture. This was remedied under the Ashbourne Act by simply having the state advance the whole of the purchase price to the tenant. Further, the acts of 1871 and 1881, as distinguished from 1885, were less advantageous to the tenant because the interest rates were higher, five as against four per cent per year, and the period of years, thirty-five as against forty-nine, within which the capital sum or purchase price had to be repaid was shorter. The fact that the initial grant of £5,000,000 was exhausted within three years, and a supplemental act was necessary, was ample testimony to the success of the Ashbourne Act.

The Educational Endowments Bill was finally passed on August 14, the last day of session. The act provided a commission of five, two commissioners and three assistant commissioners, to regulate the various endowments that had been made to Irish educational institutions and to redistribute in a more equitable manner those endowments which had become patently anomalous. Many of the original endowments, though granted for public purposes, had, in fact, become Protestant monopolies which had recently atrophied in Catholic areas, and it was the purpose of the commission to reallocate the income from those endowments in order that Catholics might have a fairer share. The constitution of the commission, which was the work of Lord Justice FitzGibbon and the Irish attorney general Hugh Holmes, was interesting in that either one of the two commissioners could veto any decision made by the commission as a whole. The crucial point, of course, would be the religious composition of the commission. While it was apparent from the way in which the commission was structured that one of the commissioners would be a Protestant, the real question became how many of the assistant commissioners would be Catholic.

"Our new Government," Walsh wrote Kirby somewhat bitterly from the Irish College in Paris on August 24, "after all their promises have acted badly enough in the appointment of the Commission for dealing with the school endowments"(K). "The Bishops," Walsh explained,"had passed a most reasonable Resolution asking that in all such cases Catholics should be represented in proportion to our numbers—this was intended as a protest against the half and half system of the National Board." "Now," he exclaimed,"on this new Commission they have actually put us in a minority!" "The constitution of the Commission," Walsh added, obviously referring to the veto,"is also objectionable in another way. I have suggested to Dr. Gillooly, as Secretary of the Episcopal Education Committee, that he should get out a good strong protest at once."[10] "There is a plain matter of principle involved," Walsh maintained, "which can be strongly reprobated without saying a harsh word of a single individual. Lord Carnarvon I am sure was not listened to by his Colleagues." "Could we have had a better illustration," Walsh pointed out, drawing a Home Rule moral from his parable, "of how hopeless it is to get on satisfactorily while purely Irish questions of this sort are dealt with, in utter disregard of Irish wishes, by an English legislature and administration."

Two days later on August 26, Carnarvon wrote Walsh, politely explaining that under the terms of the Endowments Act, the two commissioners, Lord Justice FitzGibbon and the former Lord Chancellor Naish, and two of the three assistant commissioners, Professer Dougherty and Dr. Traill, had already been named.[11] "May I ask your Grace," Carnarvon requested, "to recommend to me the name of the third?" "It is a matter in which," he explained, "I specially desire to make a wise choice, and one that will generally commend itself to public approval, and I know that in requesting your aid I cannot go

---

[10] G, August 18, 1885, Walsh to Gillooly. Walsh noted in this letter to Gillooly, after suggesting that a strong protest be made, that the Irish party have made no sign. "As it was I that gave the Resolution to Parnell," Walsh added, "I intend to write to him on the subject when I get time to do so."

[11] CAR, 30/6/58. FitzGibbon and Traill were prominent members of the Church of Ireland, Dougherty was a Presbyterian, and Naish was a Catholic of the Whig and "Castle" variety.

to a better authority." "I hope you have returned," he concluded solicitously,"none the worse for the fatigue of your long journey." In replying some four days later, on August 30, from northern France where he was visiting the shrine of St. Laurence O'Toole, the patron saint of Dublin, Walsh took the occasion of Carnarvon's letter to enter a lengthy and solemn protest against the constitution of the Commission.[12] "I fear," Walsh began coolly, "that in the circumstances I cannot be of much help in the very important matter about which you have been good enough to write." "The constitution of the Commission," he explained, "as regards the provision to be made for the protection of the interests of our Catholic schools is so decidedly unsatisfactory, that I cannot but regard as hopeless the prospect of its proceedings commanding the confidence of the country." "I feel, therefore," he added, "that I should place myself in an essentially wrong position, and act indeed unfairly towards your Excellency, if by putting forward any suggestion such as you do me the honour of inviting me to make, I were to imply that it would be possible, within the framework of the Act to make even fairly satisfactory provision for the protection of the interests of the Catholics of Ireland."

"Those interests," Walsh continued, "are in this matter, of a peculiarly complicated kind." "It will be necessary," he maintained, "for the Commission to hold the balance fairly between various classes of schools, as for instance

> (A) between the schools in the neighbourhood of the metropolis and those scattered throughout the country; (B) between the great schools conducted for the most part, by members of various 'religious orders,' or 'communities,' and the smaller schools, under the management of laymen or of secular priests; and (C) perhaps the most difficult and delicate point of all, between the individual schools under the care of the various religious orders such as Clongowes, Blackrock, Tullabeg, Rockwell, Belvidere House Dublin, etc. I feel it due to the confidence with which your Excellency has treated me to say at all events this—that the selection of our one Catholic Assistant Commissioner from any body or organization directly interested in the success of the schools of any particular section or class among those I have enumerated would be simply fatal to whatever chance there may be of bringing some satisfactory result out of an organization so radically defective.

---

[12] *Ibid.*

"I do not know," Walsh finally came to Carnarvon's point, "whether Dr. Molloy would accept the Commissionership. His neutral position as Rector of our Catholic University organization would keep your Excellency clear at all events of the serious difficulty to which I referred." "There is really no one else," Walsh concluded rather pointedly, "that I can think of, whose appointment as sole Catholic Assistant Commissioner would in my opinion not be open to very grave objection on this score." Several days later on September 4, Carnarvon wrote Walsh again thanking him for his letter.[13] "I understand the difficulty in which you feel yourself placed," he assured Walsh, "& thank you for the suggestion which you informally make me." "I shall hope," he added more diffidently, "to act upon it." "Personally," he concluded, "of all with whom I have become acquainted, none could be more agreeable to me than Dr. Molloy."

When Walsh received this rather short and somewhat hesitant reply from Carnarvon, he undoubtedly realized that he had gone too far in his circumlocutions about the assistant commissionership, for a week later he wrote Carnarvon inviting him and Lady Carnarvon to visit the Mater Misericordia, the chief Catholic hospital in Dublin. Lady Carnarvon had already expressed a wish to visit the hospital, which had come to Walsh's attention, but some repairs had forced a postponement. "Personally," Walsh explained to Carnarvon in a most friendly tone, on September 12, "I am indeed very glad that the necessity of postponing it thus existed, for I should wish, for more reasons than one, to have the visit take place while I am at home."[14] "It would, I think, be becoming that, if your Excellencies had no objection," he added, "I, as the Catholic Archbishop, should be there to receive you." "I am writing," he then concluded more deferentially than was his custom, "indeed with great freedom to your Excellency but I know you will not take it ill of me." Several days later, however, on September 15, Walsh wrote Kirby complaining that Carnarvon had just placed him in a very awkward situation(K). After explaining that he had invited Lord and Lady Carnarvon to visit the Mater Misericordia, and that the viceroy had accepted in "an exceedingly nice letter making my time theirs," Walsh reported that there

---
[13] *Ibid.*
[14] *Ibid.*

had appeared in that morning's newspapers a very strong speech by Carnarvon in the "most extravagant praise of the principles of Masonry!" "As I had, just the day before," Walsh noted, "publicly spoke of him in terms of praise, and as I am now committed to receive him at the *Mater Misericordia*, I am a little embarrassed."

Almost immediately after his return from his tour of the North, Carnarvon asked Molloy whether he would accept the assistant commissionership. Molloy asked for the opportunity to consult with the two commissioners in order to allay his own doubts, undoubtedly induced to some extent by Walsh's misgivings, about the working of the act. "Since I had the honour of an interview with your Excellency, on Monday last, "Molloy reported to Carnarvon on Wednesday, September 23, "I have spoken to Lord Justice Fitzgibbon and Lord Justice Naish, on the subject of the Educational Endowments Commission."[15] "I cannot say," Molloy explained, "that they have entirely removed the misgivings that I feel with regard to the practical working of the Act. But I am satisfied, all things considered, that I ought, at least, to make an honest effort, so far as may rest with me, to use the opportunity which is afforded of redressing in some degree, a long standing grievance, and of promoting the interests of Education in Ireland." "I am happy, therefore," he added, "to be able to meet your Excellency's wishes, and to accept the office of Commissioner." "Your Excellency was pleased," Molloy then continued, "to ask me to refer, in writing, to a topic which came under consideration at our interview." "I understand that," he assured Carnarvon, "so long as the Commission lasts, it will be my duty to maintain a becoming official reserve on all matters belonging to the work of the Commission, but that I shall be free to use my own discretion in speaking on other subjects, as, for example, the subject of University Education, with respect to which I hold responsible position under the Catholic Bishops of Ireland." "I mention this matter," Molloy concluded in a friendly yet dignified manner, "at your Excellency's request, but I may add that I am entirely satisfied with the explanations which you were kind enough to offer in conversation, and that, so far as I am concerned. I require no further assurance on the subject."

How is Walsh's unusual ambivalence in his correspondence

---

[15] *Ibid.*

with Carnarvon to be explained? Walsh's testiness, circumlocutions, his blowing hot and cold, were all the result of his finding himself in the awkward position described by Croke to Manning in early July. While Carnarvon personally might be a very good and a very well-meaning man, the system which he represented, and the policy for which that system was responsible, were still in force and operation. Nowhere was the dead weight and inertia which that system and policy represented more in evidence than in the area of education. "I am worked nearly to death," Walsh explained to Kirby on September 23, some three weeks after his return to Dublin, "receiving addresses; but I try to turn them to some practical account by making my reply an exposition of some important question—such as Education, and the like"(K). By the end of September, Walsh had indeed said his say on the education question. In a series of replies to addresses of welcome and congratulation on his appointment to Dublin, beginning with St. Vincent's College, Castleknock, on September 9, and ending with St. Patrick's Training College, Drumcondra, on September 29, Walsh covered the whole ground of Catholic grievance with regard to primary, intermediate, and university education in Ireland. It was truly a prodigious effort and all the more powerful because it was the fruit of more than ten years careful study and attention. The underlying and unifying theme in this comprehensive presentation was a demand for justice and equality for Catholics in matters of education. Implicit in what Walsh had to say, in effect, was that if the British government was going to insist on Irish Catholics being loyal, Irish Catholics were going to demand that the British government be fair.

In his *tour de force*, Walsh was generally careful not to indict the current ministry under Carnarvon, but rather to arraign the cumulative policy of various governments, Liberal and Conservative alike, which had evolved the present inequitable system. The issue on which Walsh chose to depart from his general line of policy concerned the one educational measure that had become law in the present ministry's term of office, the Educational Endowments Act. Further, the point at which he chose to attack the act was in the constitution of the commission, which had violated one of the episcopal resolutions passed the previous July at Maynooth, which had to do with a demand that Catholics be represented in proportion to their numbers on all public educational bodies and commissions. Walsh chose to make his stand on October 1, at Blackrock College.[16] "Three of the five commissioners," he maintained, "are to be non-Catholics, and we the Catholics of Ireland, we, the representatives of the interests of the vast majority of the successful Intermediate schools of the country, are to be in a minority of two."

> Is this equality? Is this fair play? I am told indeed, that a fair provision has been made for our protection in the appointment of two of the five members of the commission with the special powers. They are called Judicial Commissioners. One of them is a Catholic and one a Protestant; and the provision on which we are to rely is that the Catholic commissioner can effectually protect our interests, inasmuch as he has the power of veto. He can put an end to any scheme of redistribution of these endowments of which he does not approve. So far, no doubt, the scheme looks fair. But then we must remember that if the Catholic commissioner can veto the Protestant scheme, and if the Catholic scheme is vetoed, the endowment remains with the Protestants.[17]

"If any scheme of redistribution of endowments," Walsh then went on to explain, "is to emanate from the new commission, it must be the result of compromise between the two cheif representatives of Catholic and Protestant interests, each meeting the other half way." "Is this then," he asked, "the outcome of all the promises to do justice to the Catholic schools of Ireland?" "Our present Government," he noted, "is indeed lavish of promises and of fair words. Something more than promises is needed to do us justice." "Those who think that we will submit to such a settlement of our claims," he concluded with a warning, "are likely soon to have a rude awakening from their pleasant dreams."

No one, meanwhile, had been more conscious than Carnarvon of the need for something more than promises and fair words in the area of education. In late July, prior to a tour of the West of Ireland, he wrote Cardinal Manning asking him for letters of introduction to the western bishops.[18] In thanking the Cardinal for his good offices, on August 24, Carnarvon explained that foremost among the advantages of his recent

---

[16] *Walsh*, pp. 510-511.
[17] *Ibid.*
[18] CAR, 30/6/58, July 26, 1885.

tour were "the frank &full conversations which I have had at Galway with Bishop Carr and at Sligo with Bishop Gillooly."[19] "They both impressed me much," Carnarvon added, "and I hope that it may be in my power to advance some of the excellent objects which they have at heart." "It is impossible for me to exaggerate," he continued feelingly, "the admiration that I feel for some of the good work which is being done in the industrial schools in connection with the Convents which I visited. It seems to me the very saving & regeneration of the lowest and poorest part of the Irish people." Even before Walsh's warning on October 1, at Blackrock College, Carnarvon had already decided to impress on the Treasury the necessity of a grant of £7,000 for some seven industrial schools. In effect, the chancellor of the exchequer, Sir Michael Hicks Beach, on September 23, refused Carnarvon's request.[20] In pressing him again, on September 30, Carnarvon explained to Beach that he feared that "your alternative promise of legislation in a future session will be a morsel of very cold comfort to the R. C. Bishops and clergy who are principally interested in this matter."[21] "A future session," Carnarvon realistically pointed out, "is always a matter of uncertainty and we may not be in office."

"I must ask you to remember," he ironically reminded the former chief secretary for Ireland, "what a difficult task this Govt. of Ireland is." "One of the very few influences for good," he added, "at the present moment are the R. C. Bishops. A few months ago they were utterly alienated from my predecessor and wd hold no communication with him on the Irish Govt. They are now as a whole friendly and many of them in close communication with me and doing their best, though quietly to support me in the Govt. of their country." "It was only a few weeks ago," he added by way of illustration, "that by their influence a most ugly quarrel was settled in the South where at one time it seemed likely that we shd have had to employ nearly a thousand troops & police combined." "I have been applied to personally," Carnarvon then continued, "and have personally seen five out of seven cases, and if I were to offer merely the contingency of future legislation, I shd certainly do better to offer nothing." "I most wished for many reasons as I said," he then earnestly explained, noting that time was of the es-

[19] *Ibid.*
[20] *Ibid.*
[21] *Ibid.*

sence,"to have had your concurrence before leaving Ireland on Saturday, and without making too much of this matter, I am bound to tell you that the loss of this week or ten days is a very serious loss to me." "But as it is now impossible to act in the matter," Carnarvon noted, "I must postpone the arrangements of the question with you till next week."

Why Carnarvon was so concerned, of course, about losing a week, was that he had hoped to have the whole matter of a grant to the industrial schools settled before Monday, October 5, when the Irish bishops would hold their annual general meeting. Carnarvon had, in fact, hoped to forestall any hostile public declaration on the part of the bishops, inspired as they would undoubtedly be by Walsh's latest pronouncements on the education question. Without something more than promises and fair words, however, as Carnarvon suspected, the worst happened. The bishops at their meeting, pressed on by Walsh, "called on the Government to reconsider the constitution of the Endowments Commission so as to give Catholics their due proportion of representation thereon, and declared their opinion that if no action were taken to give effect to their protest the Catholic Commissioners should resign at once."[22] While in London, Carnarvon quickly convinced his Cabinet colleagues and particularly Beach as to the necessity of conciliating the Irish bishops. He immediately wrote the bishop of Galway as well as the other bishops who were also concerned, explaining that the government would make an increased grant to the industrial school in his diocese. In his reply, the bishop of Galway, Thomas J. Carr, considerately offered Carnarvon the means by which the lord lieutenant and the bishops could effect a kind of public reconciliation. "It occurs to me," Carr explained, on October 11, "that, if your Excellency sees no objection to it, I should publicly acknowledge the practical interest you are taking in the welfare of Galway,"[23] "If I had your Excellency's permission," he suggested, "to publish your letter to me, it would give point and meaning to my grateful acknowledgement. I am convinced that if your predecessors in office had acted in the same sympathetic and beneficial spirit as your Ex-

---

[22] *Walsh*, p. 512.
[23] CAR, 30/6/58. See also Carnarvon to MacEvilly (Tuam) and Woodlock (Ardagh), on October 12, 1885; to Gillooly (Elphin) and MacCormack (Achonry), on October 15, 1885.

cellency is showing, the feelings of the Irish people towards the Crown, and its representatives in Ireland, would be very different from what they are, or at least have been prior to your Excellency's arrival." "Even now," Carr concluded adroitly, "I believe that a speedy and substantial change of public feeling will be effected by wise, generous and curative legislation."

Carnarvon readily consented to the publication of the correspondence, and a *rapprochement* was soon rapidly effected with Archbishop Walsh.[24] "I know the interest that you take—& particularly in Irish educational affairs," Carnarvon wrote his Cabinet colleague, Lord Randolph Churchill, on October 16, "—& so I write one line before the post goes to tell you that I have had this evening an interesting & important conversation with Dr. Walsh, the Archbishop of Dublin, as to Dr. Molloy's position in the Commission."[25] "The Resolutions of the R. C. Bishops," Carnarvon explained to Lord Randolph, "will not be brought at present into active operation, and everything will, I hope work smoothly." "When Parliament meets," he noted in conclusion, "everything may come up for consideration, but for the present all difficulties are, I hope, out of the way, and I can carry on my general policy on existing lines." "It was very kind of you," Lord Randolph replied politely from the India Office, on October 19, "finding time to write me a line giving the result of your interview with the Irish Archbishop. I was certain that your diplomacy would make him tractable."[26] "An agreement or understanding," he surmised significantly, "between the Tory Govt. & the Bishops on the Education Question may possibly have a most powerful influence on future Irish politics." "It is the first time I can recollect," Churchill concluded, "that a Lord Lieutenant has been able to emancipate himself from Treasury shackles so as to translate generous promises into generous acts." "Burmah," he noted laconically in a postscript, "will be annexed."

A week later, Carnarvon discovered that there was a crack in the episcopal armor that had been worn with so much confidence of late by Archbishop Walsh. On October 23, Carnarvon had a long private conversation with the coadjutor bishop of

[24] *Freeman's Journal* (Dublin), October 15, 1885.

[25] CAR, 30/6/58. See also Carnarvon to FitzGibbon, October 17, 1885, returning two letters of Churchill's and one of Molloy's, which were obviously the occasion of this note to Churchill by Carnarvon.

[26] CAR, 30/6/58.

Clonfert, John Healy. In a memorandum made immediately after the interview, Carnarvon noted significantly:

(1) Evident suspicion of & friction with Dr. Walsh—who is driving the bishops as well as the Irish Parliamentary party much further & faster than they like.

The bishop complained inter alia of Dr. W's opposition to the R. University & the grounds on wh it rested—and he hinted that Archbp Croke was of the same mind in this respect.

(2) What he [Healy] desires in Higher education is briefly—

a. direct endowment to University College—Dr. Delaney—& the Jesuit Fathers and I imagine other R. Cath. colleges.

b. that the Galway & Cork Queens Colleges cd. be handed over to the R. C.

c. R. University—He accepts it for the present—though not *altogether* friendly. He criticised Dr. Walsh's objections to it & though partly agreeing in them said they were [word illegible].

Walsh's objection (as I understand it) is this—the Queen's Colleges are fully equipped—the R. Cath. Colleges are not. The students from the former compete on too favorable terms. There is "inequality though not injustice."

(3) His [Healy's] own district is quiet—very little boycotting. He is very anxious to restrain Ld Clanricard from evicting a considerable number of tenants.

(4) He is not at all a Nationalist in the sense of desiring a trial Parlt. & he evidently does not much like the Parnell party. . . .[27]

Less than a month later, on a visit to London to attend a Cabinet meeting, Carnarvon was made even more aware of Walsh's forwardness by no less a personage than Manning. "Conversation," Carnarvon noted in another memorandum, on November 19, "with Cardinal Manning. He congratulated me warmly on my success up to this time in Ireland, & assured me that the bishops and clergy were very well disposed to me."[28] "We discussed Archbishop Walsh," Carnarvon added. "He spoke of him as an eager, impulsive man who was not quite as prudent in his utterances as he cd be." "I told him," Carnarvon continued, "what had passed in

---

[27] CAR, 30/6/67.
[28] *Ibid.*

the Educational Endowmts Comn with regard to Molloy: & I could see that he was distrest." "We spoke of Higher Education in Ireland," he then noted, "& I said that I felt strongly the importance of having two Universities, a Protestant and a Cath—& not one as Dr. Walsh had indicated. He entirely agreed with me, and said he thought the great majority of the R. Cath bishops also agreed." "I asked whether," he shrewdly concluded his interview with the Cardinal, "this was also the view of Rome—viz—denominational education in all its branches, high & low, & he significantly said it was."

XI. Catholic Power
September, 1885 - January, 1886

Walsh had indeed been pressing very hard since his return to Ireland in early September, and he had undoubtedly antagonized a number of well-placed and important people. His vigorous pronouncements on the education question, however, and even more, his unreserved endorsement of Home Rule not only contributed to the rising nationalist political tide, but to his own general popularity as well. His energy, drive, and enthusiasm, moreover, generated confidence and hope, and his obvious determination to maintain the initiative he had seized in ecclesiastical and constitutional politics marked him out as a man, if not to be admired or loved, at least to be respected. Archbishop Croke, who had almost alone borne the burdens of clerical leadership over the past six years, seemed to be relieved to be able to allow those burdens to fall to his very capable and incredibly industrious younger colleague. Walsh was, in fact, as much convinced as Croke that the power and influence of the Irish Church was intimately bound up in the national aspirations of the Irish people. Since these aspirations were now constitutionally represented by the Irish Parliamentary party, he was prepared, as Croke had been, to ally the Church with the party, but not simply on the party's terms, for his own power base was made precarious by the extremely delicate situation in Rome.

No one, therefore, was more aware than Walsh that what was essential to the effective working of this alliance between Church and party was the tacit approval and good will of Rome. The best way to prevent the Roman flank from being turned against him, Walsh felt, was to provide the Roman authorities with as much energetically reasoned information as would be necessary to keep them alive to the subtleties and complexities of the situation in Ireland. Crucial, therefore, to Walsh being able to make himself effectively heard in Rome

331

was the need for a permanent official representative of the Irish bishops who should also have the confidence of the Roman authorities. In Walsh's first audience with Leo XIII, in the previous July, it will be recalled, the pope actually approved such a representative and had even suggested that the *dignus* on the Dublin *terna*, P. J. Tynan, might meet the need. While in Rome, however, Walsh had been much impressed with Kirby's obvious intimacy and influence with the pope, and his many important contacts among the Roman authorities. Before he left Rome, therefore, Walsh had concluded that in the present circumstances Kirby would indeed be the most effective representative that the Irish Church could hope for, and he arranged with the help of Cardinal Moran that some additional dignity be conferred on Kirby now that he was to be "the official medium of communication between the Holy See & the Irish Church."[1]

The pope responded handsomely, raising Kirby to the rank of archbishop, by translating him to the titular and much coveted see of Ephesus, *in partibus infidelium*. "I have just heard from Card. Moran," Walsh wrote soon after his return to Ireland, on September 11, "that the little compliment paid to your Grace has succeeded. Deo Gratias! "(K). After confessing his fear and trepidation in entering formally on his new office, Walsh added more piously than was usual with him, "I am sure your Lordship has not been forgetful of me. And I may add that I have even more faith in our Lady of Good Counsel than ever I had before. I trust too that my little visit to the shrine of our holy patron St. Laurence was not without some fruit." In his letter of the following week, Walsh more characteristically settled down to the business at hand, and thus began an eight-year correspondence that was to be as important as it was extensive. "As I telegraphed to your Grace to-day," Walsh explained energetically on September 17, referring to the promised adhesion of Irish bishops, in imitation of the Belgian bishops, to the pope's letter condemning the excessive ultramontanism of some of the Catholic newspapers, "the letter of the Bishops is on its way at last"(K). "I had

---

[1] K, January 14, 1886, Bernard O'Reilly to Kirby: "Had I seen you I could have told you that one of the very first things which Dr. Walsh told me at Maynooth on his return from the Eternal City was that you were to be in future the official medium of communication between the Holy See & the Irish Church."

some difficulty," he noted, indicating that he was early and fully aware of the danger of driving his episcopal colleagues too hard, "in taking a very prominent part in the management of it once I had put it in the hands of the Bishops themselves." "But I knew of course," he then added more firmly, "that the Bishops would not think I was putting myself unduly forward in the matter by merely doing what was necessary to get the letter sent out, especially when your telegram came. So I telegraphed at once to the two Secretaries, and also to the Primate and I have now got everything straight," "The copying of the letter," he then noted, efficiently anticipating all, "may cause the delay of a post, so I send your Grace a clean copy already made. It may be useful too, in case anything should go wrong with the other copy in the post."

Walsh then proceeded to explain to Kirby at great length the details of his reception on his return, which provided among other things an interesting insight into some of the tensions which existed in the Catholic community in Dublin. He began by noting that he had been met at the railway station by an enthusiastic crowd, and greeted officially by the Dublin Corporation with an address of welcome. "Of course," he observed tartly, "the 'Errington' and 'Castle' Catholics kept sullenly aloof." "But what I said," he declared, "at the close of my reply to the Corporation at Westland Row left them no ground to stand on. So they are all coming in. They now know that they do not in themselves constitute the Catholic body of Dublin." "Curiously," Walsh then added, "this evening, I am for the first time dining out at a layman's house, and it is Sir Richard Martin's, who is in one sense the head of all that party—he was the Baronet created on the occasion of the visit of the Prince of Wales, and like many others of his class refused to be part of the reception committee to present the diocesan address to me!" "Of course," Walsh emphasized even more firmly, "I look upon the invitation for this evening—especially when coming so very promptly—as an acknowledgement of the necessity of accepting my view as to the union of all our Catholics *as Catholics*."

"I try to find a few minutes," Walsh explained again to Kirby on September 23, in what was becoming his almost weekly newsletter to Rome, "to write to your Grace"(K). "What your Grace said to the Holy Father," Walsh then noted approvingly, and turning to the delicate question of Home Rule, "was quite right. You can tell him that Mr. Gladstone's address setting forth the Liberal programme really covers the whole ground for us."

> All Irish affairs are to be handed over to us: the only reservation in our new system (according to Mr. Gladstone's programme) would be, 1st, "The Supremacy of the Crown"; 2d "The Unity of the Empire"; and 3d *"such* supremacy of the Imperial Parliament as would be necessary for the maintenance of those two objects(K).

"The full significance of the statement," Walsh was careful to point out for Kirby, "does not seem to have been noticed by the newspapers." "I thought it well," he added shrewdly, "to bring it out incidentally in connexion with our University, in reply to an address yesterday."

"You can also say," Walsh further prompted Kirby in anticipation of his next audience with the pope, "that yesterday's Freeman's Journal contains the report of a speech by probably *the most extreme* man of the Parliamentary party, O'Kelly, M. P. (a very queer sort of man)." "In it," Walsh reported, "he went out of his way to explain that the granting of *legislative* independence, would make all people turn away their thoughts from separation—and that for his own part he would *prefer* to have us remaining a country of the Empire, to having us cut off from it, and thus becoming a satellite of France or some other such power." "This," Walsh emphasized for Roman consumption, "is a most important speech," "I have also succeeded," he then added, inadvertently explaining why some Party members might feel he was pushing them too hard, "in getting the Managers of the National League themselves to denounce the violent conduct of some of their branches, and to announce that in such cases they will cut off the branches altogether." "Please God," he concluded, "they can soon be brought round to the ways of moderation."

Three days later, on September 26, Walsh again reported to Kirby that "Mr. O'Kelly, the M. P. of whom I wrote, has made another equally remarkable speech in the same line"(K). "It is evidently," Walsh noted shrewdly, "a matter arranged with Parnell, who generally gets work done by another when there is anything that might not be fully popular with all. I will get the passage translated in a day or two and sent to you to show to the Holy Father." "I have got," Walsh then turned to the subject of the preparations being made for the selection of candidates for the forthcoming general election in early December, "the position of the priests recognised *as priests* in the County Conventions for the selection of M. P.'s"[2] "I have also secured," Walsh noted significantly in conclusion, "that the reporters will not be present at those bodies, so they will be merely business meetings." "Our new Archbishop here," Carrie Gray, wife of the owner and publisher of the influential *Freeman's Journal,* aptly summed up for nationalist admirers of Walsh at this time in a letter to Kirby, on October 3, "is winning, as you may perhaps see, all along the line—he has a wonderful hold of the people & knows how to use it *and it was wanted"*(K).

"We have just finished our annual meeting," Walsh reported promptly to Kirby, on Wednesday, October 7, "and also the meeting of the Maynooth Board"(K). "Everything," he reassured Kirby for the benefit of Rome, "passed off most harmoniously and satisfactorily." "In addition to our ordinary business," he explained, indicating that he had perhaps as great a "hold" on his episcopal colleagues as he had on the people, "we adopted a number of strong resolutions on the Education question in all its branches, in which the Bishops endorsed in the fullest way my recent declarations on the Educational question." "They also unanimously approved," he added significantly, "the line I had followed in the case of the Wicklow Convention, which emphasizes the right of the priests [to be delegates] and independent of all connection with political organisations." "The most important resolution, perhaps," Walsh prompted Kirby, "is one in condemnation of outrage and crime, now unhappily so prevalent in Kerry, and some few other districts. *It was moved by Dr. Croke, and unanimously adopted.* Kindly let the Holy Father know all this. It will no doubt be a

---

[2] Indeed, Walsh had gone even further than he had informed Kirby. See Conor Cruise O'Brien, *Parnell and His Party, 1880-1890* (Oxford, 1957), p. 129: "In his confidential instructions to his clergy—of whom he assumed, correctly, that many would deem it their duty to attend—Archbishop Walsh, with characteristic prudence, laid down four principles: (1) To help the two candidates of most satisfactory antecedents among those known in advance; (2) to block surprise candidates; (3) failing that to use every effort to secure an adjournment; (4) failing that, to withdraw from the proceeding." O'Brien is here paraphrasing a *copy* of a letter dated September 25, 1884, from Walsh to William Canon Dillon, P. P., Wicklow. For letter see *Freeman's Journal,* September 26, 1885. See also *Freeman's Journal,* September 21, 1885, for Walsh's speech at Enniskerry, on September 20, 1885, on the same subject.

comfort to him." "It may be as well also," he further suggested, "to mention that recently in a country parish in receiving an address I took occasion to denounce to the country people the outrages thus prevailing in other parts of Ireland. *There was no part of my speech more enthusiastically cheered,* although indeed the good people were most enthusiastic throughout." "Now that the people," he finally concluded, "have the sympathy of the Holy Father, and of the Bishops and priests, so long as they confine themselves to legitimate efforts, they are quite prepared to join us in every denunciation of excesses."

Some ten days later, the Archbishop of Tuam, John MacEvilly, wrote Kirby from the west of Ireland, independently endorsing Walsh's assessment of the general temper of the people. "They," MacEvilly reported, on October 18, referring to the people, "are now thank God, devoted to the Clergy & the Holy See, and we must strive as far as the Law of God & the just laws of man will permit, to keep them in this temper, by heading them in all constitutional and just efforts"(K). "The *Irish Party,*" he assured Kirby, "are decidedly Constitutional." "Behind them," he warned, "there is a *wild lot* of extremists. Our duty, by clinging to the Irish Party & sending good men to sustain them, is to render null the same efforts of the extremists & disguised Fenians. This, please God, we will do." "The times are very depressed," he noted ominously, "No price for anything, Cattle, produce &c so that the people cannot pay their rents fully." "If the Landlords," he added grimly, "insist on the pound, they cannot be paid it." "I am sorry also," he concluded dolefully, "to find the potato crop has failed in Connemara."

After the fall of Mr. Gladstone's second ministry in early June, and the appointment of Archbishop Walsh to Dublin later in that month, nationalist politics and Home Rule, naturally, continued in the ensuing months to dominate the public media, if not the public mind. While this ascendancy of nationalist politics became even more evident in the months immediately preceding the general election scheduled for early December, it was increasingly punctuated by nagging remarks about a worsening economic situation. Within the framework of a depressing slump in British trade and industry in 1885, the vulnerable Irish economy was severely shaken in July by the failure of the Munster Bank in Cork, the largest and most important financial institution in the southwest. When, therefore, a generally dismal Irish harvest, accompanied by the failure of the potato crop in the west, was added to a disastrous slump in agricultural prices for livestock as well as produce, because of foreign competition, an ugly and potentially dangerous social situation was being created in Ireland. There had been in fact during the summer and autumn an increase in boycotting, for which the local branches of the National League were often held accountable in the public mind. Since the Conservative ministry was in a minority in Parliament, and was tacitly pledged to pursue a policy of conciliation rather than coercion in Ireland, it was prevented from resorting to that kind of legislation, of which indeed its predecessors in office had made unprecedented use.

The government's dilemma was ably summed up by one of Carnarvon's best informed sources in late October. "There is a large body of public opinion," wrote M. O'Toole, on October 26, "even in the S. of Ireland, opposed to the extravagant lengths to which boycotting has been carried."[3] "But when one comes to ask—what is the best thing to be done to put an end to such a state of things," he then pointed out, "there seems to be very little light. Unquestionably, boycotting did not prevail so extensively under Earl Spencer's regime, but it would be pure folly & madness to return to the Crimes Act to stop boycotting." "Besides," O'Toole added, "the circumstances this winter are peculiar & did not exist during the period of the existence of the Crimes Act. I doubt if the same agricultural depression existed during the last few years as now prevails that the Crimes Act would have prevented boycotting." "Every class of men—even the landlords," O'Toole reported, "admit the extraordinary depreciation in the value of livestock and agricultural produce, and in the face of the teaching which the people have received during the past few years, it is folly to expect that they will tamely submit to bear the whole loss of bad times, and the landlords go scot free."[4]

---

[3] CAR, 30/6/66, October 26, 1885, M. O'Toole to H. Rochefort (copy). As Rochefort explained to Carnarvon's secretary, in sending the first of O'Toole's letters: "The writer is the Chief Telegraphist of the *Freeman's Journal*, & consequently being always in the office has ample opportunities of knowing the feelings & policy of that party—circumstances laid him under an obligation to me, & I found him so intelligent & clever & so good a loyalist, that we often correspond—& the letter I now enclose is a specimen—I need not say that I am sure it will be in safe keeping, as if it became known that he revealed any of the secrets of the Party, the consequences to him would be most damaging and unpleasant." CAR, 30/6/65, August 18, 1885. See also *ibid.*, O'Toole to Rochefort, September 4, 1885.

[4] See also K, November 4, 1885, MacEvilly to Kirby.

O'Toole had opened this letter with a discussion of the tactics that should be adopted in the forthcoming general election by those who were opposed to Parnell and his party, if they hoped to maximize their political effort. In the course of this discussion some interesting insights emerged with regard to local politics and the place of the clergy in relation to the party. "I am very much afraid," O'Toole explained, "that a rash indiscriminate opposition to Parnellite Candidates, merely for opposition's sake, will produce bad results. There are certain Constituencies where Loyalist Candidates might be run with advantage—Constituencies where disunion existed at the Convention which selected the candidates, and in which a considerable amount of friction has been caused by the bitterness with which the different factions supported their nominees." "In such Constituencies," he pointed out, "the defeated party would in many cases vent their chagrin by voting against their successful opponents. And such Conventions have not been rare notwithstanding the parade of harmony made in the National press." "At no less than 5 Conventions," he reported, "the nominees of the priests were defeated after a bitter struggle, and in the Co. Waterford Pyne's nomination was carried in the teeth of Parnell's personal opposition to him." "The whole system of governing the Convention, in fact," O'Toole argued, "has produced a good deal of discontent among intelligent Nationalists who strongly object to the wire pulling carried on to secure the adoption of certain men as Candidates without a full discussion of their claims & abilities."

"Previous to the Conventions," he explained, "a conspiracy of Silence was organized by which the names to be submitted to them were kept in the dark. Under no circumstances were the intended nominees' names to be published in the Freeman, United Ireland, or other National Papers lest it might provoke criticism & ["dissension" crossed out] discussion." "Then came Dr. Walsh's pronouncement." O'Toole continued, "that his Clergy had received instructions which amounted in short to this—that unless the names submitted to the Conventions were adopted—if any other names were sprung on the Convention—the priests were to withdraw. This pronouncement caused great excitement at the time, and not a few important and influential letters were sent to the Freeman protesting against this 'gagging,' but the word was given that the letters were not to be published, and they were not." "This," he added, "is how the 'harmony' has been secured. It only requires a favourable opportunity for a great body of Nationalists to give expression to their resentment of this policy and perhaps if they were afforded it under the cover of the ballot box, they would do so." "The Fenian party," O'Toole noted later in this long letter, "boast that they have secured the adoption of several candidates who will prove a thorn in Parnell's side if he shows the white feather but on the other hand a large number of those chosen are moderate men."

While there is substantial evidence that some of the conventions were managed with a rather heavy hand by the party,[5] and that this might have justified Walsh's foresight in attempting to preserve to his clergy their independence and influence within the new political framework, most of the candidates chosen, as O'Toole pointed out, were moderate men, and as such appear to have been generally acceptable to the clergy, high and low. Some of the friction between the clerical and lay politicians on the local level must certainly have had to do with the new and fundamental adjustment the clergy, who had been for so long politically ascendant in many places, had to make when it actually came to sharing political power with, if not indeed submitting to, their new or former lay allies.[6] The ability to adjust to this new alliance between Church and party on the local level is readily seen in the changed attitude of that former enemy of the party, the archbishop of Tuam. "Our Conventions in Galway and Mayo," MacEvilly reported to Kirby on November 4, "have got on admirably."[7] "The Irish party," he argued, in his new-found enthusiasm, "I regard as the Salvation of the Country." "I was hitherto afraid of them," he then explained, "now I am not." "But I am greatly afraid," he added significantly, "of the wild revolutionists, from whom the Irish Party, if well supported, will save us."

Walsh, meanwhile, having made his pact with the party, had fully entered into the political fray, and he took especial care to see that his position would not be misunderstood at Rome. "I write hurriedly," Walsh explained to Kirby on October 27, "amid my usual pressure of business, to ask Yr. Grace to read

[5] C. C. O'Brien, *op. cit.*, pp. 130-132.
[6] See S, October 27, 1885, William Delany, bishop of Cork, to Smith.
[7] K, November 4, 1885. See also C. C. O'Brien, *op. cit.*, pp. 131-132, for the case of P. J. Louden.

carefully my 'Swords' address in the Freeman of yesterday, Monday"(K). "I will send out a copy," he added characteristically, "in case your ordinary copy may have missed."

I regard the address as a very important one, and I have reason to know that it is already regarded by the "loyalist" faction as a very heavy blow to their cause. They have been pursuing for years a system of wholesale slander. Unfortunately for themselves, their leader—the Earl of Meath—has now committed himself to definite statements, and to proofs.

I think I will get someone to republish this address of mine in a penny pamphlet—printing in full, as an Appendix, the speech of Mr. Parnell from which Lord Meath pretended to quote.

Kindly call attention of the Holy Father in a special manner to all this. Tell him in detail the three statements of Lord Meath. Tell him that, as I have shown, there is not a particle of foundation for them. And then call his attention to the impossibility of attaching the slightest credibility to the statements of this class of people(K).

"When they have the hardihood to make such statements here at home, and in public," Walsh insisted, "what are they not likely to do abroad, in Rome for instance, where as we know, the[y] speak so much in private, and do so much to try to poison the minds of high officials." "Above all," emphasized Walsh, "call the attention of the Holy Father to the line that I took the opportunity of drawing between *legislative* and *total* independence." "I must admit," he confessed candidly, "that my main object in the whole address was to get the opportunity of bringing out and emphasizing the strong and clear statement of the M. P. I quoted." "He is," Walsh concluded, referring again to O'Kelly, "decidedly the most 'advanced' of the Irish Parliamentary Party."

"This post," Walsh alerted Kirby five days later, on November 1, with his usual efficiency, "brings to your Grace half-a-dozen copies of a pamphlet, I think an instructive one, that has been brought out—containing (1) the Earl of Meath's charges; (2) my reply; and (3) the whole speech of Mr. Parnell from which his Lordship pretended to quote in support of his calumnious charges"(K). "Will you kindly," Walsh then asked Kirby calmly, "call the marked attention of the Holy Father to it." "Direct his attention," Walsh suggested most significantly, "most especially to the masterly way in which Mr. Parnell (who, no doubt, has moderated his original views in many most important points) deals with the question of 'separation.' " "Is it not monstrous," Walsh noted indignantly, "that on such a speech as this, Lord Meath should have based his charges of anarchy &c." "Mr. Childers—Chancellor of the Exchequer in the late Ministry," Walsh explained in his thorough fashion, "... in a speech of his reported in the London Times, Octr 29th, page 12, ... has gone exactly on Mr. Parnell's line, viz., that the concession of *legislative* independence is really the safest, if not the only safe, line now to take to get rid of any desire for separation."

Walsh's energy and activity in the political arena during this critical period in national affairs was simply prodigious. He seemed to be everywhere in his vast diocese and interfering quietly in everything. "*All* our Dublin Parliamentary candidates," Walsh explained to Kirby on November 16, "are selected now: 4 for the City, 2 for the County, 2 for Co. Wicklow, 2 for County Kildare"(K). "*All are Catholics*," Walsh emphasized strongly for Roman consumption, and added significantly, "I asked to have this so." "Mr. Gray," Walsh added, even more significantly than Kirby knew, referring to the owner of the *Freeman's Journal* and M. P. for Carlow, "was to-day selected to fight the great battle by contesting the one doubtful division of the city with the Tories and so-called 'Loyalists.' " What made Gray's selection most significant was that it had been rumored earlier that Parnell himself had vetoed Gray's standing for the Dublin constituency. "Gray's return to Carlow," O'Toole had reported for the benefit of Carnarvon three weeks earlier, "has caused some surprise here because it was an open secret in Nationalist circles that he had volunteered to Parnell to contest the Stephens Green Division of Dublin against Cecil Guinness."[8] "It is now thought," O'Toole explained, "that Parnell, aware of the éclat which such a contest would bring to Gray—for he would undoubtedly fight the seat as no other man of the party could fight it—and being jealous of him as a possible rival, refused his offer—the refusal is a snub which Gray will certainly resent when the occasion presents itself." "Gray is not wealthy," he noted interestingly, "—he has no money in reserve, but he has an income of probably £6,000 per annum." "His wife," O'Toole added for good measure, "is a most ambi-

---

[8] CAR, 30/6/66.

tious & extravagant woman." If indeed O'Toole was correct about Parnell and Gray, then Walsh's personal influence in Dublin politics must have been decisive, for it seems most unlikely that Gray could have been selected for Dublin over Parnell's objections without Walsh's approval.

"I have just come in," Walsh explained to Kirby on November 29, in an incredibly long and detailed letter, "from a heavy day's work at Bray where our good Dean (Lee) has had me"

> (1) presiding at a distribution of premiums to the children of the Cathechism classes; (2) receiving an address from the Christian Doctrine Confraternity; (3) another address from the Juvenile Temperance Association; (4) another from the Association of Men in honour of the Sacred Heart. Then the scene changed to a platform erected outside the town hall, where I had to receive [(1)] an address from the Town Commissioners of Bray; (2) an address from the Clergy of the County of Wicklow (in the three dioceses of Dublin, Kildare, and Ferns) thanking me for defending them against the attacks of Lord Meath; (3) an address from the Bray branch of the National League; and (4) an address from the Adult Temperance Association of the parish(K).

"So," Walsh exclaimed, "Your Grace sees that I am incorrigible! " "At any rate," he confessed, "I cannot see our good people disappointed." "Is it not a grand thing," he asked, "to see them thus crowding around me in the very midst of their election excitement?" "Whether I am here, long or short," Walsh maintained, "I do not like to lose any opportunity of keeping our good hold of them."

"I will ask Your Grace," Walsh continued, "when you have the opportunity, to explain to his Holiness one circumstance connected with this day's work which I think will gladden his heart."

> First I should explain that about ten days ago I took occasion to speak very strongly at Wicklow against the unwisdom of the action of those people who are irritating the country by raising foolish contests merely for the sake of putting the people to expense and giving them annoyance. I dealt especially with the case of the County of Wicklow.
>
> Now the polling took place there *yesterday*. The votes are to be counted *to-morrow*. So the County is [in] the very heat of the Con-

test and excitement.

Well, on the occasion of my visit to-day, I had an address of welcome from the Town Commissioners—a body in which there are of course both Protestants and Catholics. There are even *Orangemen*(K).

"The address," Walsh reported, "was unanimously adopted." "It was *individually signed*," he emphasized, "even by those who were not present at the meeting of the Board adopting it." "And today," he exulted, in the midst of all the excitement, "*every Protestant member of the Board was present on the platform* for the presentation of the address!" "Of course," Walsh explained, "I took good care to thank them for their generous conduct, and to praise them for it." "I held it up as a model to the people of the place," he added, "to show them how they are bound to act with moderation, and with all respect for the feelings even of the smallest minorities when they are entrusted, as they soon, please God, will be with a fuller control over their local affairs." "These are the facts," Walsh suggested, "which I will ask Your Grace to put into shape for his Holiness." "I know," he finally concluded, "he will be pleased to hear them." One may well imagine Kirby, after this long letter, attempting to formulate for the pope and his cardinals the significance of this ingenious argument on the part of Walsh for moderation in the interests of toleration and minority rights.

In Ireland, meanwhile, all attention was focused on the elections. The only question was how many of the 103 Irish seats would the Parnellites win; and informed opinion was that they would return between 75 and 80 members. "There is great excitement," Robert Carbery, S. J., wrote Kirby from Miltown Park, on November 30, "in Dublin at present as the City elections are going on to-day—and the news is just being cried out that in the most Protestant district of the County (in which the polling was on Saturday) Sir Thomas Esmonde has been successful. He is, they say, the first Catholic Member of Parliament for Dublin County"(K). "We are all here," MacEvilly wrote Kirby excitedly two days later, "in the turmoil of a Election and beating down the Orange-Anti-Catholic party"(K). "In this Co. of Galway," he reported, "there were walks over, in *three* of the four divisions. In the borough, a Englishman (Protestant), who was trifling with the Catholic people got 100 votes against 2000 for the Catholic party." "Dr. Carr," MacEvilly applauded, referring to the bishop of Galway, "did his business well." "In Mayo," he continued, "two walks over, and yesterday I had a Telegram saying an Orangeman who stood for the West division of Mayo got the large No of 130 votes—the Catholic 4900. The other division of Mayo contested will, I make no doubt, be equally triumphant." "The bigots I see," he noted, "are completely beaten in Dublin. Dr. Walsh flung himself into it like a man." "I," he reported no less manfully, "had Conferences in the different portions of Mayo in this Diocese (there are two divisions of Mayo & two of Galway in Tuam Diocese) a fortnight before the Convention."

"We are," he continued, "living in very eventful times. The clergy in full accord with the *people*. There are some Landlords, calling themselves Catholic (Orange Catholic) Castle-hunters, who are the greatest enemies of our people, and who would oppose the H. See tomorrow & insult it, if their Masters so willed it." "Our support and reliance," he then argued, indicating how far the democratic leaven had spread, must be "on our poor persecuted people, who will stand by us and religion in all circumstances as they have always done." "The times," he again reminded Kirby, "are dreadfully depressed, no price for anything, the people unable to pay rents. I had charge of some charity property, and I was obliged to reduce the rent 50 per cent. Many landlords are insisting on their pound of flesh & the people cant pay." "Some of our priests," he confided, "are, in their zeal, rather imprudent. Reports were made to me by Government. I, of course, admonished them to keep within the Law, as otherwise, besides conscience, they would injure the people." "But," MacEvilly noted, "in replying to the Government official I stated, 'the people, in most instances, cannot pay the full rent and it would be *cruel* to enforce *impossibilities*.' If the Government assist in enforcing impossibilities we cannot expect peace." "I am sure," he concluded more optimistically, with Carnarvon most likely in mind, "they will do their best not to assist cruel Landlords."

"The elections are over," Croke reported with obvious satisfaction to Kirby, on December 15. "There were a most extraordinary and unbroken round of successes for Parnell and his Party"(K). "Not a Whig returned," Croke emphasized, "—not even *one*. In Leinster, Munster, or Connaught not a single Whig or Tory returned. All Nationalists, that is *Parnellites*." "Even in Protestant Ulster," Croke exclaimed, "out of 33 seats Parnell has carried 17!!" "Thus it comes to pass," Croke noted ironically, "that the man who was so bitterly assailed in the famous Roman Circular, is now the recognized leader of the Irish bishops, priests, and people, and the arbiter between the two great political parties that alternately preside over the destinies of the British Empire." "There is a profound lesson in all this," he pointed out wryly to Kirby for the benefit of Rome, "which I need not further specify." "One thing is certain at all events," Croke concluded, unable to resist a final crow, "that *my* attitude in Irish politics, for the last six years, has been amply and conspicuously vindicated." Indeed the Parnellites had won a tremendous electoral victory, capturing 85 of the 103 Irish seats, as well as one English seat in Liverpool, and confining the Conservatives to 16 seats in Eastern Ulster and 2 seats for the University of Dublin.

More than that, however, the liberals and Conservatives had returned 334 and 250 members, respectively, thus giving the Parnellites, with 86, the balance of power. "The late elections," as the bishop of Ferns, James Browne, also explained to Kirby from Wexford, on December 15, "have placed enormous power in Mr. Parnell's hands and have put an end to all dissensions amongst Irish Catholics"(K). "The Nationalists have got such a majority," he pointed out, "that no one ventures to question their supremacy. This in itself is a great advantage. We have now to join together as one man and I trust there is an end to all dissensions among Irish Catholics." "I dare say," he added confidently, "some measure of Home Rule will be given us and this must effect great permanent good for the Country. I am inclined to think that things must improve in every way among us." "Since the appointment of the Archbishop of Dublin," wrote Maurice Mooney, P. P. of Cahir, one of Kirby's simpler, but no less enthusiastic, correspondents, that same day, "our poor Ireland scarcely knows herself"(K). "She is full," he virtually bubbled, "of life and hope and gratitude. There is no doubt now of Home Rule."

"I have just received the Cabinet summons for the 14th," Carnarvon replied to Salisbury, on December 6, "and am glad that you have convened us to consider the situation."[9] "I con-

---

[9] CAR, 30/6/55.

fess," he then reported, after an astute analysis of the as yet incomplete election returns, "after much anxious considera- tion that I believe it best that we should take advantage of the Election *not* to meet Parliament, if it is clear that we cannot agree on a policy, or if for a variety of reasons we think it unwise to propose one." "I propose to send you," he finally concluded, following an extended discussion of the disadvantages in meet- ing Parliament without an Irish policy, "a mem: if possible within a day or two, on the general subject; but I cannot today command the time." He did, however, write Salisbury the fol- lowing day, explaining that he had forwarded his memoran- dum to the Foreign Office, where it would be confidentially printed in order to prevent any leak on his proposed Irish pol- icy.[10] He had also directed, Carnarvon advised Salisbury, that one copy should be sent to him as prime minister, so that he could make the final decision as to whether it should be distrib- uted to the Cabinet for the meeting on December 14.

"Whatever may be the decision of the Cabinet in reference to the elections," Carnarvon began his long memorandum, "I think it desirable to place before my colleagues, as shortly as I can, the present state of Ireland, and the opinion which I hold with regard to it."[11] "As regards the condition of the country," he reported, "agrarian crime and outrage have been and con- tinue low." " 'Boycotting,' " he then added guardedly, "has been held in check, as I said it would be, and has diminished, though it is still very mischievous and capable of development. On the other hand, the National League has lost none of its power. It has, on the contrary, acquired a remarkable organization and force." "The Roman Catholic Clergy," he further conceded, "though with reluctance on the part of the Bishops and higher clergy, have been drawn more and more under the influence of the National League and into the ranks of the Nationalist Party." "The landlords," he also acknowledged, "seem in most districts hopelessly alienated from the tenants, and without in- fluence." "To all this I must add," he then continued, "that there is a great development of the Secret Societies in the United States, an abundance of money subscribed, the closest communication existing between them and kindred Societies in Ireland, which though not active, are only waiting the signal

---

[10] *Ibid.*, December 7, 1885.
[11] *Ibid.*

to become so, and are every week growing more formidable."
"Besides this," Carnarvon added, turning from the present to
the future, "there are other most serious dangers immediately
ahead. The position of trade and agriculture is very grave. On
all sides there is a disposition to refuse rent in whole or in part.
Fresh organizations—more difficult to deal with—are constantly being formed, and at any moment we may have to face a
widespread agreement on the part of the tenants to refuse
rent." "In many parts of the country," he noted, "this is due to a
real absence of money; in the other parts, advantage is taken of
the agricultural depression. We are, in fact, enjoying a short
truce."

"The question then arises," Carnarvon then explained, finally coming to his specifics, "what in these circumstances can
be done. I believe half-measures in this case are impracticable
and dangerous, particularly to the landowners—that class
whose interests are now threatened in Ireland." "There is no
real alternative now, I fear," he maintained, "between large
concessions and repression; and a very considerable number of
men, of the greatest experience and capacity, and of un-
doubted Conservatism and loyalty, whose judgement I have
been able to obtain, have not hesitated in confidence to avow
themselves of this opinion." "There are three burning questions," he then noted, "the land, the education, and local self-
government." "And let me say here," he emphasized, "that by
local self-government is meant not the establishment of County
or District Boards, but some elective body, which shall have all
the outward form and semblance of a Parliament." "This is
what is desired," he reported, "and nothing less, as far as I can
see, will be accepted; and when a nation has passionately, however irrationally, set its mind upon this, and when all the really
influential classes (excepting, of course, a part of Ulster) are
agreed, it will be found, under our Parliamentary system, practically impossible to refuse it." "All these three questions then,"
he advised, "will have to be faced before long, but probably the
land is the most important, and must form an essential, if not
the first, part of any scheme of settlement."

"So far," Carnarvon then admitted, arriving at the political
heart of the matter, "I have considered the matter in the general interests of England, and particularly of Ireland; but it remains to consider it in the light of Party possibilities, and if it
is clear, as some think, that the Party will not endure such a

course as I have indicated, then I admit that it is a paramount duty at this crisis not to split or divide it." "But it is worth considering," he added, "whether there is any line of action which can solve the difficulty without creating discord in the Party." "I," Carnarvon posited, "can only see three courses:"

(1) To propose nothing and to do nothing, and wait till we are turned out by a combination of Liberals and Irish, which is a view I only mention to discard.

(2) The adoption of some considerable, yet comparatively minor measures in the hopes of tiding over the difficulty till the Irish party are disintegrated—which, by the way, let me say would not really settle the difficulty or, perhaps, much improve the case.[12]

"A large scheme of higher education," Carnarvon interjected here, by way of explanation, "seemed, at one time, the most likely expedient in this direction." "But events have moved too fast," he then explained, "and I am afraid that the attempt now would be too late, mainly through the action of one man. The Archbishop of Dublin, it is clear, has made an alliance with Mr. Parnell; he has publicly declared against such a settlement as I think we ought to make, and he has within the last few weeks, strange to say, apparently won over a majority of the Bishops. It is not easy to suppose that he would go back from a public utterance such as this." Carnarvon then turned to the final and most important of his three proposed courses:

(3) One last alternative remains, viz. to do something without committing ourselves as a Government to any course which might divide the Party. I wish my colleagues to consider whether it might not be possible to propose a Joint Committee of both Houses to consider the relations of Ireland and England, or the better government of Ireland, or some such general proposition, subject to the two following conditions, expressed in the most distinct language:

1. The supremacy and authority of the Crown.

2. The maintenance of the rights of minorities in religion and property.[13]

_____

12 *Ibid.*
13 *Ibid.*

"This would gain time," Carnarvon argued, "would educate the party and the country to a knowledge of the case, in which they are extraordinarily ignorant; would be constitutionally a very defensible course; would give a chance of moderate counsels prevailing; would secure the combined action of both parties; and would, if we failed to come to a conclusion through the fault of the Irish Party, leave us free to deal with the question in a much more decided manner—and all this without committing the Government in the first instance to any definite proposals." "But such a course," Carnarvon added, "if adopted, ought, I think, to have the preliminary concurrence of the Party. It would also, I think, be highly desirable, if possible, to ascertain by very private negotiation whether we should have the support of any or all of the leaders of the Opposition. The first of these modes of proceeding appears to me necessary, the second not absolutely necessary, but very desirable." "A very considerable number of people in England," he closed finally with an act of faith, "would, I believe, approve of a union of the leaders of Parties in order to solve the problem."

The Conservative Cabinet, however, which met in London on December 14 and 15, was in no mood for acts of faith, especially where Ireland was concerned. They decided, in effect, on the one course Carnarvon had mentioned in his memorandum only to discard. They further decided they would not resign, and were determined to meet Parliament, in spite of all Carnarvon's recommendations to the contrary, without an Irish policy. Carnarvon, naturally, refused to go on, and it was arranged in the interests of party unity that he would ask the queen for his release as viceroy immediately after the opening of Parliament. "On the whole," he wrote the earl of Harrowby, Lord Privy Seal, several days later from Dublin, "I think the decision as regards myself was the best practicable and as regards the Cabinet I think a resignation would *on the whole* probably have been better."[14] "But," he added unrepentantly, "I regret & shall always regret that they would make no effort—if only to feel their way—towards a settlement of this question. They have assumed that the Party wd not allow *any* movement." "I do not feel sure of this," he concluded wryly, "—anyhow I think something might have been risked: but a Cabinet is like a Council of War: it is very timid."

[14] *Ibid.*

Carnarvon had, in fact, become a caretaker within a caretaker ministry and responsibility without power, thus compounded, began to undermine even his sanguine temperament. "Difficulties of all kinds," he lamented to another Cabinet colleague on December 19, "are thickening, and I feel sure that if by chance we should get a vote of confidence (which will be a very half & half one at best) we shall be dragged into every sort of discredit."[15] "But it is now too late," he confessed, "to go back on the decision, and we must hope that Gladstone will, as he wishes, deal with this question." "But here again," he qualified himself grimly, referring to Herbert Gladstone's incredible indiscretion the day before, in revealing to the press that his father had been converted to Home Rule, "I dread the principles on which I believe he will proceed—and whatever may be the correctness of the Programme published in the Pall Mall there is enough in it to inspire very great alarm." "The publication here," he concluded despondingly, "has caused a sort of panic in certain classes, and the fall of securities, which I mentioned to the Cabinet, continues."

As Carnarvon staggered under the burdens of responsibility without power, Archbishop Walsh confidently moved from strength to strength. Walsh's long report to Kirby at the end of December, summing up the recent political achievement for Rome, was also eloquent testimony as to why Carnarvon had charged the archbishop with being the man who had done most to consolidate the clerical-nationalist alliance. "We have had, thank God," Walsh explained to Kirby on December 30, "a glorious victory. It was a foregone conclusion in the four divisions (3 of the City, and 1 of the County) where the Catholic party was known to be strong: so in each of these cases, our people won by majorities of *thousands* in each case"(K). "I should explain to your Grace," Walsh interjected, "that under the recent Act, Dublin City is divided into 4 constituencies, each returning 1 member, and that the County is similarly divided into 2 districts, each returning 1 member." "Well," he added, "the lines were drawn in the most indefensibly arbitrary manner, and quite avowedly with the purpose of carving out districts in which the Catholic and Nationalist party should be beaten." "Your Grace can then imagine," Walsh began to warm to his subject, "the delight of all when the critical division of the

---

[15] *Ibid.*, Carnarvon to Viscount Cranbrook, lord president of the Council.

County was carried by Sir Thomas Esmonde with a majority of over *1300!*" "Then came the critical division of the City," he reported with satisfaction, "with a majority for Mr. *Gray* (over Sir E. Guinness) of over *1900.*"

"The elections were really turned," Walsh explained, "by a shocking letter from Mr. Cogan—once known as a sort of Catholic Champion." "Of course," Walsh noted sarcastically, "his Championship never went beyond keeping in with the Whigs, who made him a Privy Councillor. He now shocked the Catholic feeling of the City by not only seconding the Tory candidate, Guinness, but by writing a letter in which he claimed the support of Cardinal Cullen for his action—he also wrote that everyone who was not at that side was in favour of an illegal conspiracy against the law of the land!" "The Earl of Meath," Walsh emphasized, "all over again!" "As my name was mentioned in his letter," Walsh explained artfully, "I replied in the letter your Grace has probably seen in the Freeman; and this at once roused the Catholic feeling of the city. Several of the sectional interests which would have gone against Gray forgot everything but their Bishop and priests had been attacked." "Nothing else," Walsh asserted, with some exaggeration, "could have got such a triumphant victory." "I should like you to mention," Walsh finally came to his point, "that part of the Tory case against us was that former Archbishops never allowed the priests to interfere at elections!" "Of course this was a downright fabrication," Walsh claimed, with a good deal of truth, "most especially as regards Cardinal Cullen, whom they used to attack most violently for acting just as I have acted now." "Only one of my priests," Walsh reported, "in any way committed himself. I at once interdicted him from all public writing or speaking until I am satisfied I can trust him to act with prudence. He has taken this in the best possible spirit. You might mention this also." "If the Bishops," he concluded confidently, "would act thus with the few inconvenient writers and speakers, all would be well."

By the end of December, Carnarvon's nerves were so worn by what he conceived to be a deteriorating situation in Ireland[16]

---

[16] CAR, 30/6/53, December 20, 1885, Carnarvon to Sir Henry Ponsonby. Carnarvon wrote Ponsonby, the queen's secretary, that the temper of the Irish people was reflected in the recent violent occurrences in Kerry as well as the fact that a good many of the recently elected Irish nationalist M. P.'s had had a direct connection with Fenianism.

that he was driven to write Salisbury a most uncharacteristic letter, making what amounted to a desperately unreal proposal. "The more I consider this Irish difficulty," he explained to Salisbury, on December 30, "& the form which matters have assumed by the union of the Nationalist & Clerical parties, with all the consequences to which that union may lead, the more important do I feel it to be that the Pope should correctly understand what are the objects and the relations of those two parties."[17] "There are few if any persons at Rome—as far as I know," he gratuitously informed the prime minister, who was also his own foreign secretary, "—who can now give him this information—some because they are ignorant of Irish matters, some because thay have been in Rome so long that though they knew Ireland 25 or 30 years ago, they do not know it now, some because intentionally or unintentionally they would misrepresent the facts." "But," Carnarvon insisted, "it is of incalculable importance that this information should be given—and without loss of time—even a few weeks hence and it may be too late." "What I therefore propose," Carnarvon suggested, "is that I should prepare a Mem: at once, that I should send it to you to be translated into Italian at the F. O. and that it should be then sent to Lyons to be given to the Nuncio there[at Paris] Monsig. Rendi—in strictest confidence and without saying by whom the Mem. is drawn or whence it proceeds: merely saying that it comes from a reliable authority." "I have," he further suggested, "several other channels of communication of which I could avail myself, but on consideration I believe this is the best & safest—and the more confidential the communication the better." "Please to think of this at once," he urgently begged of Salisbury, "and say whether you agree with me—for there is no time to lose—and none of these things can be done under several days to say the least." Salisbury wasted little time in making his reply. "Too Dangerous," he telegraphed Carnarvon, on January 2, "I Will Write."[18]

"I telegraphed to you," Salisbury explained the next day, "to say that I thought your scheme for communicating with an influential Person was too dangerous."[19] "Such secrets are in practice rarely kept," he noted, and added patriotically,

---

[17] CAR, 30/6/55.
[18] Ibid.
[19] Ibid.

"& foreigners are very unscrupulous in what they will communicate to the newspapers." "However," he pointed out shrewdly, "it is the one thing of which the Irish members have horror, & directly they got wind of it they would ask the question promptly. And if the step is to be of any use, they must get wind of it—because the object for which it is done is that it should have certain effects." "If it has those effects," he concluded with inescapable logic, "it will betray itself, if it has not, it is of no use." A chastened and somewhat calmer Carnarvon replied, some three days later. "The value of informing the Roman Court," he continued to insist somewhat lamely, "or rather the Pope, who, as you know, is his own foreign Minister—on the true position of Irish Parties and objects is I think almost beyond calculation at this present moment; but I admit the risks which you point out and if on consideration you place them above the advantages, there is nothing more to be said."[20] "It is I suppose," Carnarvon ruminated relatively, "like so many other such questions to be decided on the balance of pros & cons: & you can best judge this." "I thought it, however," he finally closed the subject politely, "right to give you the opportunity of considering it."

What indeed is there to be said of this last desperate bid on the part of Carnarvon to enlist the aid of Rome, in order to redress the balance of British power in Ireland, except to say that it was both a symptom and a measure of how much that power had deteriorated during his short tenure in office. Irish power was now both real and decisive: decisive, because the recent general election had set up a new parliamentary equation in which the Irish factor was determinant, and real, because a viable clerical-nationalist alliance had been evolved. That power would, in fact, remain real as long as the clerical-nationalist alliance was maintained, and decisive as long as the new parliamentary equation was not upset either by another general election or a fundamental realignment of British political parties. Carnarvon, in invoking Rome, went inexpediently to the heart of the matter, while Salisbury, in understanding that the time was not yet ripe, realized that as far as English politics were concerned the fact that Irish power was decisive must take precedence even over its being real. When the parliamentary equation was reformulated and Irish power was no longer decisive,

---

[20] *Ibid.*

then the reality of that power could be contained and perhaps, in time, even destroyed by invoking the aid of Rome.

Archbishop Walsh, however, since his appointment to Dublin in the previous June, had obviously seen the danger and had been making very great efforts not only to consolidate his power base in Ireland, but to strengthen it as well at Rome. In Ireland, Walsh had already in less than six months transformed the alliance between Church and party. That alliance, which had indeed been structured for at least a year before Walsh became archbishop, had resulted in the clergy, high and low, assuming the role of auxiliaries rather than equals in their relationship with the party. In his own diocese, Walsh had effectively recovered most of the lost initiative by insisting on his voice being heard with regard to the selection of parliamentary candidates and, more especially, with regard to securing the independence of clerical representation at the conventions. By also securing the public endorsement of his new political posture by his episcopal colleagues at their annual general meeting, he extended his influence, at least, if not his actual power, throughout the Irish Church. Walsh had astutely further strengthened his already considerable political influence, though the details are not yet altogether clear, in befriending and endorsing the influential owner and publisher of the *Freeman's Journal*, E. Dwyer Gray, in his bid to exchange his safe Carlow constituency for a more prestigious Dublin seat.

At Rome, too, Walsh had worked very hard through Kirby to preserve that confidence the pope had placed in him by appointing him to Dublin. Walsh's long and detailed letters to Kirby are a significant measure of his understanding how important it was that his position in Ireland should not be undermined from Rome. It was not simply enough, as indeed the recent experience of Archbishop Croke demonstrated, to have the confidence and affection of the Irish people and the great majority of the clergy, high and low. If the power and the influence that naturally came with this popular esteem was not to be hamstrung at every turn and eventually dissipated, Roman approval and good will were essential. The traditional educational *quid pro quo* on the part of the government, in this instance a settlement of the university question, as Carnarvon pointed out to his Cabinet colleagues, had been effectively blocked by Walsh's public declaration that no such wedge could be driven, and Home Rule was now the *sine qua non* of any settlement.[21] Carnarvon's suggestion to Salisbury, then about enlisting the aid of Rome, was simply a recognition of the fact that there was now no way but one, perhaps, either to break up or at least to mitigate the effects of the recently consolidated clerical-nationalist alliance. If indeed Salisbury's government had not already been written off by those astute connoisseurs of power in Rome as a ministry whose days were obviously numbered, Walsh's diligence and energy in keeping the authorities informed through Kirby would have certainly limited the effectiveness of any attempt on the part of the government to enlist Rome in the interest of redressing British power in Ireland.

---

[21] CAR, 30/6/67. See for a memorandum by Carnarvon on his farewell conversation with Walsh, who visited him on January 26, 1886, for a somewhat different view of Walsh's priorities at this time: "A farewell visit to explain to me how sorry he & many others were at my departure. Also to say that Archp Croke though he had not seen me & rather from his political views stood aloof also desired to express his regret that he had not become personally acquainted with me. He then proceeded to talk of the State of the Country & to say that in his opinion the settlement of the land question was at the root of everything & he went so far as to intimate that if that could be settled other questions & difficulties wd. disappear. . . . His conversation was very friendly & moderate & indeed extremely reasonable."

XII. Irish Nationalism

January, 1886 - October, 1886

"Mr. Gladstone," Cardinal Manning informed the pope on January 4, 1886, "has allowed one of his sons to publish in the press extreme opinions regarding his Irish policy" (M). "This act of imprudence," Manning explained curiously, "has provoked a very strong opposition on the part of Mr. Gladstone's principal colleagues and has thus awakened a determination to concede justice to Ireland, but only on the condition of inviolably preserving the unity of the Empire." "A few days ago," he confided to the pope, "I received a letter from Mr. Gladstone in which he says:'The Irish question predominates; and while it may lengthen my political life, it will shorten my natural life.' " "This," Manning added, "enables me to foresee the course he will pursue." "He will propose," Manning accurately prophesied for the pope, "a wider and more advanced policy for Ireland than that proposed by the present Government, with the hope of drawing to himself the Irish members." "I do not believe," he added, even more accurately, "that he will succeed, at least for the present." "I will not fail," Manning promised the pope in conclusion, "as soon as the Bill is drafted, to lay the result humbly before your Holiness."

The cardinal, meanwhile, had written Archbishop Walsh, asking him to use his influence with the Irish members in reference to a particular educational matter. Walsh took the opportunity offered by the cardinal's letter to explain that the attitude of some English Catholics was very far from satisfactory from an Irish point of view. "As to the Education question generally," he pointed out to the cardinal, on December 27, "I fear that great harm has been done by the articles which have recently appeared in some English newspapers"(M). "In the first place," Walsh noted, "we have the proposal distinctly made to subordinate the interest of the Irish movement, in support of which

356

the Irish M. P.'s have been returned, to the interests of the English Catholic body in the question of Education." "Then," Walsh complained indignantly, "we have the most scurrilous attacks made on those same Irish members and on the Irish Bishops for seeking their aid in Parliament on the Irish Education question, and no public protest is made against these attacks by the English Catholics or their representatives." "It is, in fact, generally felt over here," Walsh added candidly, "that with the exception of your Eminence and a very few others, our brethern across the water rather sympathise with those attacks than disapprove of them." "I write by this post also," Walsh concluded significantly, referring to Herbert Vaughan, proprietor of the *Tablet*, chief among the offending English Catholic papers, "to the Bishop of Salford."

"I feel that your Grace's position in Ireland," Manning replied the next day, "and, I may say, my own in England, make it of no light moment that you and I should be open with one another."[1] "With this motive I will say at once," the cardinal came immediately to the point, "that I know of no one who desires to subordinate the Irish movement to English education." "And you may rely on me," Manning then reassured Walsh, "for refusing to subordinate the Irish movement to any English question, as I believe you would refuse to subordinate the Irish movement to your own Education." "I know that I labour under the '*peccatum originis*,'" he added good humoredly, referring to his being English, "but if you can trust me, and you seem to say so, let us lay aside all mistrust, for if you and I are of one mind we may better serve Ireland and the Church than if we were doubtful of each other." "As to the newspapers," Manning noted, "I read with indignation only less than yours the language of most of them." "I am glad," he then added approvingly, "you have written to the Bishop of Salford, for I suppose your words in some degree include the *Tablet*. Let me ask you always to let me know what you find amiss in it. I will always do, as I have always done, my best to correct it." "I have written, my dear Lord," Manning reassured Walsh, in conclusion, "*aperto corde*—for I have no hidden thoughts."

While Manning, perhaps, had no hidden thoughts, he did have some very serious reservations about what constituted Home Rule, and he was also very much aware that the Irish

---

[1] *Walsh*, pp. 262-263.

bishops were being pushed much farther along by Irish lay politicians than they had been willing to go in conference with him in London the previous spring. Some three weeks after his initial letter on the subject of Home Rule, Manning again wrote the pope, explaining that English public opinion was rising strongly against the proposal of a parliament in Dublin. "The imprudent language," Manning boldly maintained, on January 24, "of some English politicians, among them a son of Mr. Gladstone, has awakened the strongest and almost universal opposition of English public opinion to the demand of some Irish for a Parliament in Dublin"(M). "They openly declare themselves," Manning reported aghast, "in favor of the union of the two countries, and the integrity of the Empire, but assert that a Parliament in Dublin is compatible with the integrity of the union of the two countries—a thing which seems to me incredible." "The dualism of Austria-Hungary survived the first conflict," argued Manning, ". . . but an Anglo-Irish dualism between nations so divided and mutually antagonistic, subject to a perpetual flux of Irish-American sedition and conspiracy, cannot last. Civil war, as in the United States, will be inevitable." I will repeat," Manning then reiterated with emphasis, "that the widest and most extensive local administration with the power of making laws for this purpose must be granted, but a Parliament—No!" "A Parliament," Manning explained, and discussing his favorite subject, the nature of power, "is an independent and absolute thing. '*Suprema potestas sese disolvere potest, sese ligare non potest*.'" "Every attempt," he added, "to bind the Parliament in Dublin would always be a source of conflict."

"The Irish Bishops," Manning reminded the pope, deftly turning to the more practical consideration of power, "perceived these dangers last year, but the Irish Members frequently speak of a Parliament. The Bishops themselves are in great difficulties, but they have acted with much prudence and loyalty concerning the wishes of your Holiness." "I must especially praise," the cardinal noted most significantly, "the conduct of Monsignor Croke. From time to time some words fall from the lips of others, and my countrymen will greatly exaggerate them." "The situation in Ireland," he shrewdly added, "has not really grown worse, but as the legislative crisis approaches, the agitation seems more acute." "Excuse me," Manning concluded, politely acknowledging where supreme power really lay, "for repeating that the four Archbishops united, under the supreme control of your Holiness, that same control will successfully guide the rudder."

Before this letter had even time to reach Rome, however, the legislative crisis Manning had warned the pope about came to a head. On January 26, the Conservative government was defeated in the House of Commons on an amendment to the queen's speech by a combination of Liberals and Irish. Salisbury submitted his resignation to the queen, and Gladstone undertook the task of forming his third ministry. In this momentous crisis, Archbishop Walsh took Manning at his word, regarding the offer of mutual confidence, and thus began another correspondence which was to be as vital as it was intensive and which would only end with the cardinal's death some six years later. "As I have seen Lord Ripon's name mentioned in connexion with the Irish Viceroyalty," Walsh wrote Manning, on January 29, "it occurs to me that I ought to write to your Eminence to say to you that in my opinion such an appointment just now would be simply *disastrous*"(M). "The great difficulty here," Walsh explained, "is twofold. There is the religious difficulty, and that of 'property.' " "As to what is called 'Home Rule,' " he noted, "I believe there would be practically unanimous concurrence of opinion in Ireland in favour of it if the landowners and the Protestants of the country could feel assured that there was no fear of a general confiscation of property on the one hand, and of the establishment of an intolerant Catholic ascendancy on the other." "Everything," he added shrewdly, "that goes to foster either apprehension tends to emphasise and perpetuate the present lines of division in Ireland." "The appointment," Walsh came finally to the point about Ripon, "of a Catholic Lord Lieutenant would plainly have this effect."

There does not seem to be any evidence that Gladstone was seriously considering Ripon for the post of lord lieutenant. In any case, a comparative political novice, the earl of Aberdeen, a Presbyterian, accepted the Irish post without a seat in the Cabinet, as the more seasoned Ripon took over the Admiralty. Gladstone had obviously decided that, since Ireland was to be the crucial issue in the next Parliament, he wanted real power vested in the chief secretary, who would not only be of use in the Cabinet, but who would also be able to defend the government's Irish policy in the House of Commons.[2] Gladstone, therefore, offered the crucial post to John Morley, a prominent English radical, who accepted. Morley, however, was not only an advanced Radical, but a militant agnostic and an avowed enemy of denominational education to boot. Unfortunately, when his appointment was announced, the *Fortnightly Review* had just published an article by him in which he had some very uncomplimentary things to say about the Church. "The Church," Morley had written, "it has been truly said, has broken with knowledge, has taken her stand with ignorance, and is striving might and main, even in countries where she has no chance, to use the machinery of popular government to keep back education."[3] "The worst enemy of science," Morley had added, "*c'est le clericalisme*."

Archbishop Walsh, naturally, could not allow this to pass without comment. "Wise and well-informed as Mr. Morley thinks himself to be," the archbishop noted, among a good many other things, in a public speech on February 4 in Dublin, "and as in many fields he undoubtedly is, we may surely say of him, and I wish to say it without offense, that on one subject at all events, he has something yet to learn."[4] "Mr. Morley," Walsh pointed out, "is coming to Ireland in very special circumstances." "He is not coming to govern us," the archbishop added, significantly noting that Home Rule was the overriding consideration, "He comes to lend his help in carrying out the scheme of Mr. Gladstone to set us free, within limits, to govern ourselves." "In these circumstances," Walsh concluded these very careful remarks about Morley, "the Chief Secretary ought to be received by us with no unfriendly greeting." "In almost any other circumstance," he qualified himself, "the appointment should be protested against by every Irishman who sets store by the preservation of our Christian and Catholic people."

The following week, the influential Vatican weekly, the *Moniteur de Rome*, published Walsh's comments on Morley. The Roman correspondent of the London *Standard* sent the follow-

---

[2] Gladstone, who also perhaps anticipated that Hartington would take a large number of Whigs and Chamberlain an even larger number of Radicals with them in opposition to his Home Rule policy, by appointing a Radical as chief secretary, hoped he might be able to hold a good part of the Radical line against Chamberlain.

[3] *Walsh*, p. 202. See John Morley, "Sir H. Maine on Popular Government," *Fortnightly Review*, N.S., 230 (February, 1886).

[4] *Ibid. Freeman's Journal.*

ing telegram, which appeared in the *Irish Times* on Thursday, February 18:

> Rome, Tuesday night
> The Moniteur, the mouthpiece of the Vatican, publishes Archbishop Walsh's recent address on the subject of the appointment of Mr. John Morley. This address is in direct opposition to the Pope's urgent injunctions and warnings. The truth is that the Pope is absolutely powerless over the Irish Clergy in matters touching Irish nationalism.[5]

Not knowing what the *Moniteur* had published, Walsh immediately telegraphed Kirby to forward him a copy(K). Three days later, he wrote Kirby explaining the situation. "The enclosed telegram from Rome," Walsh noted February 21, "was published *on two successive days* in our Dublin 'Irish Times' endeavouring of course to make out that I have been condemned at Rome!"(K). "I am quite sure," Walsh eloquently laid down the line for Kirby to take at Rome, "that of all the occasions on which I had to speak in public, this was the one on which what I said was most fully on lines that would be approved—condemnation of secret societies, protest against Mr. Morley's offensive 'anti-clericalism,' practical respect for him as Chief Secretary, praise of Mr. Gladstone, declaration that we want nothing outside the lines of the constitution, hope of reconciliation between the two countries, and recognition of our duty as a nation, to give thanks and honour to God."

"Dr. Donnelly," Walsh explained, referring to his auxiliary bishop, "gets the *Moniteur*. He gave it to me yesterday"(K). "To me," he continued, "it seems quite plain that the insertion of my address was in no way condemnatory, but quite the contrary." "Could we get any expression of opinion," Walsh asked, "to this effect that might be of use in silencing the misrepresentations of the Protestant correspondents of London newspapers?" Walsh, however, it appears, was becoming a firm believer that Rome best helps those who help themselves. "I had an interesting letter a few days ago," he wrote Kirby a month later, "from the Editor of the *Moniteur de Rome*"(K). "I now get that paper," he reported, "and the *Osservatore Romano* regularly." "I noticed several friendly articles," Walsh explained,

---

[5] *Ibid.*

"on Irish affairs in the *Moniteur*, so I had some papers sent to the Editor with important passages marked." "He now writes to say," Walsh noted, obviously pleased, "that he will be always ready to insert anything we send him from here. He also asks me to get an arrangement made with the *Freeman's Journal*, for a regular 'exchange' of the two papers. This is now arranged." "It is no doubt," he added pointedly, "most important that the editor of so prominent a paper should be regularly supplied with authentic information from your side." "May I ask yr. Grace kindly," Walsh then politely suggested, "to see if the *Freeman's Journal* I get sent by my Secretary each day reaches Cardinal Simeoni regularly. We *mark* anything that may seem of special interest." "I hope yr. Grace," Walsh concluded politely, "is getting special prayers for our public interests now. Everything is in a most critical state." "I am in *direct* communication." he confided impressively, "with a member of the cabinet, and I know there is grave reason for uneasiness."

There was indeed grave cause for concern, as Walsh had good reason to know through his very discreet contact in the Cabinet, H. C. E. Childers, the home secretary.[6] On the very day, March 26, that Walsh was writing Kirby from Dublin, Joseph Chamberlain and G. O. Trevelyan resigned from the Cabinet, thereby virtually assuring the defeat of any extensive measure of self-government for Ireland. Both Chamberlain and Trevelyan had, in fact, been on the verge of resignation ever since Gladstone had introduced some two weeks before his Irish proposals in the Cabinet, and they had only held their hands in the hope of being able to work out a satisfactory compromise. Walsh's growing uneasiness was, of course, a result of the fact that he had in recent weeks deeply committed himself and the Irish hierarchy to Home Rule; and it was daily becoming more apparent that Gladstone would not be able to hold the Liberal party together on the question of Home Rule.

While nearly all the Irish bishops, though in varying degrees, were in favor of Home Rule, they had never corporately expressed their opinion on the subject. When, therefore, the four Irish archbishops, each attended by two of their suffragans, met in Dublin in the third week in February to prepare the preliminaries for the forthcoming national synod, which had been discussed and approved in Rome the previous year, they also

---

[6] *Ibid.*, pp. 205-206.

made their meeting the occasion for a public pronouncement in favor of Home Rule.[7] They had, undoubtedly, been prompted in their pronouncement, which was made in February 16, by the publication in the press that same day of a letter by Gladstone to Lord de Vesci, an Irish peer. In his letter, Gladstone maintained that the three great Irish issues facing the ministry of the day was self-government, the land question, and social order.[8] He then added that he was open to suggestion from any quarter which would help him satisfy "the wants and wishes of the Irish people." The bishops, therefore, wrote Gladstone the following day, February 17, offering him their considered opinion on the three heads of proposals in his letter to De Vesci.

"As regards self-government or Home Rule," the bishops emphasized, maintaining the line they had publicly taken the day before, "it is our firm conviction—a conviction based, as we believe, on the fullest, most varied, and at the same time the most reliable information—that it alone can satisfy 'the wants and wishes of the Irish people.' "[9] "As regards the settlement of the 'Land Question,' " they declared, "we have no hesitation in stating that, in our opinion, it now imperatively calls for a final solution, and that this cannot be better effected than by some such measure as the purchase by the Government of the landlord interest in the soil, and the reletting of it to tenant farmers at a figure very considerably below the present judicial rents." "We desire to have it perfectly understood," the bishops studiously emphasized, "that the Irish people do not aim at the confiscation of any species of property, but only ask for fair play as between man and man, in what has been described as the right to live and thrive in their native land." "As regards 'social order,' ... " the bishops added turning to the last and knottiest of the issues, and arguing from strict economic causation, "every disturbance of social order that has occurred amongst us for years has arisen from a sense of wrong entertained by a large majority of the occupiers of the soil, owing to the remorseless exactions of needy or extravagant landlords." "Even now," the bishops added, noting that the struggle had

---

[7] Conor Cruise O'Brien, *Parnell and His Party, 1880-1890* (Oxford, 1957), p. 184, n. 3.

[8] *Walsh*, p. 203.

[9] See C, February 17, 1886, for draft of this letter. See also *Walsh*, pp. 203-204.

taken on the aspect of class war, "the peace of the country is seriously imperiled by the fact that very many landlords have entered on an ill-conditioned course of eviction against their unfortunate tenants." "We would, therefore, earnestly urge that pending the final settlement of the Land Question, the power of eviction be suspended in Ireland; at the same time that in the more impoverished districts some provision, in the shape of remunerative labour, be made out of the public purse to support the starving poor in the present, and help them on to better times."

"We sent from our Meeting," Walsh reported to Kirby, on February 21, "a most important letter to Mr. Gladstone, as he asked for information from all Irishmen"(K). "I have just now received," he added, "a very nice letter from him." "All," he concluded, "will appear in tomorrow's *Freeman*." A week later, on February 28, Walsh wrote Manning explaining that he had found the new viceroy and his wife, Lord and Lady Aberdeen, all that the cardinal had led him to expect(M). Walsh also noted that Lord Aberdeen had been with Gladstone when he received the bishops' letter, and that it had made a good impression on the prime Minister. Not only, Walsh added significantly, was the whole of the letter edited by Croke, but two thirds of it was written by the archbishop of Cashel. Only the week before, Walsh had written the cardinal that the *Tablet* was again getting out of hand(M). "I have always," Walsh explained, "studiously avoided any unfriendly reference to the *Tablet*." "But," he then warned, "I really cannot see how I can any longer hold aloof from making common cause in the matter with the Archbishop of Cashel and others of whom it has from time to time written in so unfriendly a spirit."

To make matters worse, several days later the leading English Catholic layman, the duke of Norfolk, in a speech to the "Primrose Dames," declared that the recent action of the Irish bishops in publicly supporting Home Rule had caused him "special grief and shame."[10] "Has your Eminence," Walsh indignantly asked Manning on February 23, "seen the extraordinary speech of the Duke of Norfolk on the Catholics of Ireland?"(M). "To me," he confessed, "it seems one of the most unprovoked attacks upon the people of this country that I have met with for a very long time." "This is the sort of action," Walsh

---

[10] *Walsh*, p. 211.

then warned, "that really embitters the relations between the Catholics of the two countries." "There is a view, " Walsh continued, trying obviously to be constructive, "of the Irish case which I should wish your Eminence to take into consideration, if you have not already done so, as affecting the interests of the Church in England." "It is generally felt, I believe," Walsh suggested delicately, "by English Catholics that the granting of Home Rule, to whatever extent it may be granted, means to the same extent a weakening of the force now available for the protection in Parliament of Catholic interests in England. But, there is another side to the question." "Does not the continuance," he then asked, somewhat unconvincingly, "of the present state of affairs involve the presence of a powerful disturbing element in the election contests of very many English boroughs?" "And supposing the Irish difficulty done away with," he suggested artfully, "would not the Parliamentary force of English Catholicity become far more available than it now is even when aided by the somewhat irregular help given by the Irish M. P.'s in the House of Commons?" "Mr. Morley, for instance," Walsh pointed out in conclusion, "would have had absolutely no chance of election last time but for the Irish vote. In other circumstances, that vote could be turned against him."

"You will say," Manning replied two days later on February 25, "that the good Duke of Norfolk is old enough to be more guarded in speech."[11] "But," Manning added, attempting to reduce the archbishop's temperature, "he is both young and surrounded by those of whom you complain. In public life he has had little experience. In this way I understand what I very much regret. In Ireland he will be regarded as the English laity. It is not so." "In the time of my predecessor," Manning explained, referring to Cardinal Wiseman, "there was a great breach between English and Irish Catholics. For twenty years, I have laboured to heal it. It is unhappily again open. But the English Catholics are few. The mass of our people are Irish and united with Ireland." "Michael Davitt first suggested to me," Manning then noted, astutely accepting the premise in the archbishop's letter, while rejecting the argument based on it, "the risk of losing forty or fifty Catholic members from the Imperial Parliament. It is obvious." "It is a Catholic and a world-

[11] *Ibid.* Also Shane Leslie, *Henry Edward Manning* (London, 1921), p. 415.

wide danger," he concluded significantly, "I hope justice will reign in Ireland without this danger."

In this crucial exchange, Manning made it perfectly clear, notwithstanding Walsh's clever debating distinctions, that without the solid phalanx of Irish Catholic members at Westminster, English Catholic political power dwindled as to nothing. He also understood, in the age of the democracy, that what little political power might remain to English Catholicism was numerically and therefore fundamentally Irish. From the beginning, therefore, Home Rule which would result in the Irish members being excluded from Westminster was in the cardinal's view bad Home Rule. Manning was, however, astute enough to understand that real power now rested with the Irish bishops and that the levers of that power had been vested by them in the very able hands of the archbishop of Dublin. The cardinal, therefore, was careful not to disturb the public impression that he was at one with the Irish bishops on the question of Home Rule. This posed no real problem, in fact, as long as Home Rule remained a vague and undefined term. Since Gladstone, however, would soon define what he, at least, meant by Home Rule, in introducing his measure in the House of Commons, the moment of truth for the cardinal was perhaps not far off.[12]

The Irish bishops, leaderless and divided the year before, had indeed at that time allowed the power initiative to fall to the cardinal, especially as their intercessor at Rome. In the interim, however, with the rising political tide and especially after the emergence of Walsh as effective head of the Irish Church, they had regained their confidence and were less willing to submit to an English lead, even if it came from so venerable and proven a friend as the cardinal himself. Indicative of this new self-confidence was the attitude that their pastoral rights were being infringed upon if the various letters and instructions which came from Rome were translated or promulgated for Ireland by any other authority than their own. When Walsh

---

[12] See the curious entry, however, in Wilfred Scawen Blunt's diary, *The Land War in Ireland* (London, 1922), for February 23, 1886, pp. 31-32: "To London, and lunched with Cardinal Manning.... The Cardinal's view about Ireland is like mine, but he makes some exception to a Parliament at Dublin as not suited to the Irish. He wants them, however, to govern themselves, and his objection is not [sic] against the principle of separation."

received notice, therefore, through Manning's secretary of the announcement of the Jubilee celebrating the pope's fiftieth anniversary of his priesthood, he wrote the cardinal gently protesting the mode. "I trust," he explained, on February 28, "there may be no soreness of feeling, but I know that some of our Bishops will dislike anything that may look like intermediary intervention between them and the Holy See." "At our meeting on the 16th," Walsh went on to inform the cardinal, "I took advantage of the presence of so many Bishops to get what I considered a satisfactory arrangement made for the translation of all such documents. The arrangement was unanimously approved. It is just coming into operation." "The translation," Walsh then concluded, "is officially entrusted to the President of Maynooth, who is also editor of the I.[rish] E.[eclesiastical] Record."

Only the week before, Walsh had written Kirby a long letter, explaining in detail what had happened on the sixteenth at the episcopal meeting in Dublin(K). "I have also got an arrangement made," he had reported, on February 21, after outlining the preparations that had been made for the holding of the proposed national synod, "which I trust will work satisfactorily, for the publication of an official translation of all Encyclicals and such documents in future." "Thus we shall try," Walsh promised, artfully noting that in Ireland the theme was unity, "to keep clear of the disedifying disputes that I see going on in England & America about the translation of the Encyclical *Immortale Dei*."[13] "Until I had this meeting," Walsh pointed out prudently, "my position in such matters was, I felt, a somewhat delicate one. I know of course the kindly feelings of all our Bishops toward me, but I could not tell but some might not think I was taking too much on myself if I moved in advance of the others in a matter equally affecting all." "I [will] now," Walsh added, "proceed to publish the Jubilee. Very few Bishops were about to do so until toward the close of the year." "But they all agreed," Walsh concluded, again emphasizing unity of action, "that it would be well to move together, and to publish it generally at the beginning of Lent." Meanwhile, Cardinal Manning was, of course, too astute a politician to be over-concerned about form when the substance of power was at

---

[13] This Encyclical had been published in English as "On the Christian Constitution of States," on November 1, 1885.

stake. No "soreness," therefore, appeared on his side, and his correspondence with Walsh continued to flourish "*aperto corde*" as before. Tension elsewhere, however, began to mount as the Cabinet meetings got under way in London.

Soon after the first Cabinet meeting of the new ministry on March 13, rumors were afloat that the government was in serious trouble. "Things seem to be going badly with the Government," Wilfred Scawen Blunt noted in his diary in London, on March 16. "Chamberlain is likely to part company with them, not on the question of Home Rule itself, but of the hundred and fifty millions to be paid to the landlords."[14] "If he leaves the Government on that gound," Blunt surmised, "many will go with him." Gladstone had, in fact, opened the Cabinet meeting with a scheme for land purchase in which the state would advance a gigantic loan of some £120,000,000 at three per cent to enable the Irish tenants to buy out their landlords. Chamberlain then shrewdly asked whether the £50,000,000 which was to be floated immediately, as the initial installment in Gladstone's scheme, was to be advanced to a part of the United Kingdom or to what might soon be an independent nation. Gladstone was thus forced to outline his Home Rule proposals, which he had hoped to reserve until the Cabinet had agreed to his proposals on the land question. Chamberlain and Trevelyan then demurred, on hearing what Gladestone proposed on Home Rule, and said they must resign. Gladstone argued they should at least wait until they heard his proposals in extenso, and the resignations were held over until March 26, when the Cabinet would again meet to consider Home Rule.

"We are all very anxious, " Walsh confided to Manning on March 26, the day of the crucial Cabinet meeting, "over here about the success of Mr. Gladstone's scheme"(M). "As to his project of buying out the landlords, " Walsh noted, "it is no doubt very chivalrous of him to embarrass himself for the sake of a class of people who are so bitterly hostile to him and to his prospects. They seem quite blind just now." "I have no doubt," he prophesied all too accurately, "that if some reasonable settlement be not made this time, the people will take the Land question into their own hands and solve it by a general refusal to pay

---

[14] Blunt, *op. cit.*, p. 36.

rent." "It will be a sad result," Walsh continued, obviously somewhat depressed, "coming on us at a time when everything seemed so hopeful for a thoroughly constitutional settlement of all our difficulties." "I know," he concluded hopefully, "that we can always count on your Eminence's help in every way."

When the *Tablet* published the next day, March 27, a letter by Viscount Bury, an English Catholic peer, Walsh was furious.[15] Bury had replied to the earl of Ashburnham, another English Catholic peer and a founder of the British Home Rule Association, who the week before had remonstrated with the duke of Norfolk for his speech before the "Primrose Dames." Bury's letter, among other things, claimed that the support the Irish bishops and clergy were giving to Home Rule was "political and withal treasonable." "The Catholic bishops," he went on to assert, "teach Rebellion. . . . Rebellion is punishable by the law of the land." "The matter is not one of faith or discipline," Bury further argued, "and the Pope, if he took a side unasked would do a thing very unusual among foreign powers." "His action," he added, referring to the Pope, "would justly be resented as an interference with the domestic economy of another nation." Walsh immediately wrote Manning, on March 27, asking whether there was anything that could be done to stop this sort of thing(M). There was something more serious involved, Walsh argued, than even "the vile language regarding the Irish bishops," for Bury openly denied "the jurisdiction of the Pope in a manifestly spiritual matter." It would be less harmful, Walsh then suggested, to have action taken at the English rather than the Irish side. "We have," Manning replied two days later, on March 29, "Nemesis and Erinyes hanging over us."[16] "I am weary of remonstrating," he added, "but I will do so again by this post." "The Bishop of Salford," he observed, delicately making a suggestion of his own, "is not absent."

Walsh took the hint and wrote Vaughan, protesting the publication of Bury's most offensive and lying, and even heretical, letter in, the *Tablet*. "We live in a plague of lies," the bishop of Salford commiserated pointedly, "and you, as being so very active and prominent, are the most violently attacked."[17] "There is one thing," he continued, abruptly changing the subject,

---

[15] *Walsh*, pp. 249-250.
[16] Leslie, *op. cit.*, p. 414.
[17] *Walsh*, pp. 250-251.

"which I do not know how to answer, and I should be very grateful for an answer that would satisfy my own mind." "The question is asked." he noted for Walsh, unctuously adding insult to injury, "—Why do not the bishops speak out more plainly and also frequently against crime?"

> The reproach of being *"dumb dogs"* dates from the beginning of time, and human nature often deserves the reproach when silence is pleasanter than speech. I should have thought that the pursuance of O'Connell's plan of continually denouncing the man who commits a crime as the enemy of his country would have told well in every way. I know that if the bishops were loud on the side of virtue and order—I mean if they denounced evil—they would stand better on this side of the water.[18]

"There must therefore," he concluded offensively, "be some strong reason which renders the contrary policy the more desirable one. I should much like to understand it." There does not seem to be any record that Walsh dignified this patently malicious probe with a response.

In any case, Walsh and all Ireland were soon caught up in the excitement of Gladstone's introduction, on April 8, of his Home Rule proposals in the House of Commons. Typical, perhaps, of the general feeling was the reaction of the usually taciturn nationalist bishop of Clogher, James Donnelly. "Your Grace's letter," he wrote Kirby, on April 11, from Monaghan, "arrived here the same day as the Newspapers bringing Gladstone's Home Rule proposals—a great and never to be forgotten day"(K). "God grant," he prayed, "that his proposals may be enacted." "Oh!" he added, unable to contain himself, "What a day for Ireland! The dawn of a glorious era, which you & I scarce ever expected to see—Hurra! Hurra!!" While nearly all shades of Irish nationalist opinion were agreed on the principle embodied in Gladstone's proposed measure that a domestic legislature to deal with partly Irish as distinguished from imperial affairs was fundamental, there were a good many varying opinions as to how the distinction between what was Irish and what was Imperial should be made. The crucial question, of course, was what was to be done about the Irish members then sitting in the imperial Parliament. Gladstone and his Cabinet decided that the only possible workable solution was

---

[18] *Ibid.*

the total exclusion of the Irish members from Westminster, except for the purpose of revising the organic statute. The further question as to whether the powers of the Irish legislature should be limited in terms of what the legislature might do or what it might not do, was decided in favor of the latter mode. All questions, therefore, that had to do with defense or the armed forces, foreign and colonial matters, the law of trade and navigation, of coinage and legal tender, as well as the integrity of charters and the sanctity of contracts, and the endowing or establishing of any particular religion, were reserved to the imperial Parliament.[19]

"As regards Mr. Gladstone's Bill,"Walsh wrote Manning on April 14, and coming immediately to the point, "I think I ought to say to your Eminence that to me it was a great puzzle why Mr. Gladstone should have attached such importance to the exclusion of the Irish Members, and why the opponents of the Bill should have concentrated their fire on what seems so easily alterable a provision"(M). "For my part," he confessed, "I must regard the Amendment of the Bill in this respect as an improvement in every way." "It takes from us," he explained, "nothing that is given to us in any other part of the scheme. It gives us an additional power over and above those already given." "Then for the English Catholics (little as they, as a body, deserve it)," he added, undoubtedly thinking particularly of the bishop of Salford, "it is a decided advantage, and one of which I would be sorry to see them deprived." "How is it," he concluded somewhat ironically, "that no one has put forward the claim of the English Catholic body to a set of 'guarantees,' such as are now to be provided for the Irish Protestants?" "Your comment," Manning replied the next day, April 15, "on Mr. Gladstone's Bill is altogether my conviction."[20] "As I came out," he reported, "after hearing his speech, I found myself in the midst of your members, and I said, 'you must all stay here.' " "I have many reasons for this opinion," Manning assured Walsh, "and I shall hold it all the more confidently knowing that you and, I take for granted, your colleagues are of the same mind."

When Walsh received this reply from Manning, he undoubtedly immediately wrote H. C. E. Childers, the home secretary, and his contact in the cabinet, for Childers noted hurriedly in

---

[19] John Morley, *The Life of William Ewart Gladstone* **2** (London, 1906), 547-548.
[20] Leslie, *op. cit.*, pp. 416-417.

reply on April 17, "Thankful for your note."[21] "I don't feel at all easy about the Bill," Childers confided, "but the language used by Mr. Gladstone, about the representation at Westminster, makes the chances of success somewhat greater." "The compromise you suggest," he added, "as to the number of Irish members being proportional to the Irish contribution seems very fair; but their exclusion from debates on English and Scotch affairs is practically very difficult to work out."

> If the Imperial Parliament and the legislature of Great Britain met at different times, and if the Imperial Government and the Government of Great Britain could be more distinct bodies there would be less difficulty. But the 570 members for England and Scotland might be by a small majority Conservative, while the fifty Irish members might be by a large majority Liberal. Thus there might be a liberal majority in the Imperial Parliament and a conservative majority in the legislature of Great Britain. Of what colour would His Majesty's Ministers have to be?
>
> On the other hand, if they always sat together, the Irish members might carry English and Scotch measures which without them might be negatived, and *vice versa*.[22]

"Home Rule," noted Childers, "to be logically perfect, must be applied to the three Kingdoms. Of course, we never are logical, and find rough and ready solutions; I hope we may do so now." "It was a great misfortune," he then lamented, "that the two Bills (the Home Rule Bill and the Land Purchase Bill) had to be separated: as the Land Bill contains proposals affecting both."

The Land Bill had, in fact, been brought in and passed its first reading the day before, April 16, immediately after the debate introducing the Home Rule Bill was over. Parliament then adjourned for the usual Easter recess and, when reconvened, the Home Rule Bill was given its second reading, on May 10, when a full-dress debate which continued for some sixteen nights, and carried into early June, followed. During the whole of this critical period, Archbishop Walsh worked hard to make both the bill and Mr. Gladstone's way easier, in Ireland, England, Rome, and Parliament. On the crucial question of the exclusion or inclusion of Irish representation in the Imperial Parliament, Parnell and most of the Irish party favored exclusion. Walsh, of

---

[21] *Walsh*, p. 206.
[22] *Ibid*.

course, understood that the proposal to exclude the Irish members from Westminster was not only unacceptable to Cardinal Manning but would give a handle to those who argued that exclusion was tantamount to separation. Moreover, Walsh also understood that the feeling in the Irish party for the exclusion of Irish members was bound up with the need to soften the antipathy of those extreme and irreconcilable nationalists who were indeed in favor of separation.

The key man in this delicate balance of constitutional and revolutionary forces was William O'Brien, editor of *United Ireland*. O'Brien was a master of the pseudo-revolutionary gesture and his inflammatory language in *United Ireland* had won for him the reputation, at least, of being on the extreme left of the constitutional movement. "I send enclosed." Walsh, who had crossed over to London, wrote Manning on May 19 from the Charing Cross Hotel, "a copy of Mr. O'Brien's speech"(M). "Of course," Walsh noted for the cardinal, "it is for the *tone*, rather than for the view put forward or some points of detail, that I think it worth being looked through by your Eminence." "I chanced to meet Mr. O'Brien to-day," Walsh reported, "in the House of Commons, and I told him he should have called on your Eminence long ago." "Strange to say," Walsh added, "he is somewhat timid, awkwardly so. He did not venture to call, not knowing whether it would be right of him to do so. I am sure he will not be much longer in default, and I trust he may be so fortunate as to find your Eminence at home. I think you will not find him at all *irreconcilable* on the question of the Irish representatives at Westminster." "Indeed I was surprised at how readily he fell in with my view to-day," Walsh noted, while suggesting to the Cardinal the line to be pursued with O'Brien, "which I put to him thus:"

(1) That just now we need not trouble ourselves about the abstract question as to whether it is really better for Ireland, our M. P.'s should be at Westminster or not;

(2) That taking the crisis as it stands, we should willingly fall in with the view of those who are for Home Rule, but also for the Westminster representation always of course provided that

(a) Our M. P.'s are to be here for Imperial purposes only, and

(b) Our Irish "legislature" is not on this account to lose its control over *Irish* affairs(M).

"I find that my suggestion," Walsh informed the cardinal in conclusion, obviously still referring to O'Brien, "of an 'Instruction to the Committee' proceeding on those lines is thought to have something in it."

Manning, indeed, had some very serious doubts about the Home Rule Bill prior to Walsh's visit to London. In writing to a godson of his Protestant days, Manning refused to allow him to make his current opinions on the Home Rule Bill public. "No," he wrote Sir Howard Vincent, on May 13, "my words yesterday, unless they were fully explained, would be fairly misunderstood."[23] "I am," he explained, "a firm and large-handed advocate for giving to Ireland a power of self-administration in all matters affecting Ireland alone. And I would give this to Ireland more largely than to Scotland for two reasons: first because England and Ireland are heterogeneous, but England and Scotland are homogeneous; and secondly because we have wronged Ireland for three hundred years." "We owe," he then added, "justice, retribution, and separation [*sic* reparation], and in this I go as far as these three words can reach." "But," he noted, making the important qualification, "They all stop short before the integrity of the Imperial Parliament." "My criticism on this Bill," he further explained to Vincent, "would sound as if I were not in the largest possible sympathy with Ireland. But, I must wait my opportunity, not make it." "Therefore," he concluded, "keep my words to yourself as a filial godson."

Walsh's London visit, therefore, obviously resulted in a *modus operandi* being worked out between the archbishop and cardinal. Manning persuaded Walsh, for example, to deemphasize the word "parliament," with its sovereign implications, and substitute the term "legislature," when referring to the new law-making body to be set up in Dublin. Walsh again, explicitly and in writing, reassured the cardinal that he was for the integrity of the empire and against separation by acknowledging that he was in favor of including the Irish members at Westminster and, moreover, was using his best efforts to have the bill amended in that direction. Manning, meanwhile, with Walsh's assurances made, could well afford to bide his time. For, if the bill passed its second reading, it would then go into committee, where the various proposed amendments

---

[23] Leslie, *op. cit.*, pp. 407-408.

would be considered; and the attitude of the Irish members, if successfully influenced by Walsh, would be crucial. If the bill was defeated, on the other hand, then Home Rule would certainly be postponed. The proposal to exclude the Irish members had, in fact, been fast losing ground ever since April 8, when Gladstone had introduced his measure. "I frankly admit," Gladstone confessed to Granville on April 30, towards the end of the Easter recess, "that I scarcely see how a Cabinet could have been formed, if the inclusion of the Irish Members had been insisted on."[24] "And now," he confided, "I do not well see how the scheme and policy can be saved from shipwreck if the exclusion is insisted on, as an absolute preliminary condition." "Not that I think for a moment," he concluded significantly, "the cabinet will so insist."

William O'Brien was not, however, the only molder of public opinion cultivated by Walsh during this period. Edmund Dwyer Gray, owner of the all-important nationalist daily, the *Freeman's Journal*, and recently returned for South Dublin with Walsh's approval and support, was drawn more and more to the archbishop. Gray had asked the archbishop to use his considerable influence at Rome in favor of his petition for a private oratory in which to keep the Blessed Sacrament. The privilege of an oratory was becoming rarer in Ireland and, indeed, in the world at large, as the Church became less and less interested in identifying itself with the upper classes in the age of democracy, and Rome, therefore, had begun to frown very seriously on new petitions. "I am sorry," Walsh wrote Kirby a little stiffly, on April 10, after explaining that he had little time for letter writing since Archbishop Croke was with him, "you see any difficulty about the oratory"(K). "Whatever may be the theory," Walsh rejoined, "the *fact* is that there are *many* instances in Ireland, and not a few in Dublin, where the privilege is enjoyed by persons who have no other claim to it than they are *well-to-do*." "Our friends," he added, referring to Gray and his wife Carrie, "about whom I wrote have rendered for years most important services to religion, the gentleman by the extent to which the paper is freely at our disposal, the lady by her personal action in works of charity." "*Both*," Walsh emphasized, "have been for

---

[24] Agatha Ramm (ed.), *The Political Correspondence of Mr. Gladstone and Lord Granville, 1876-1882* **2** (Oxford, 1962): p. 445.

weeks past most actively cooperating with me in the establishment of a new home for the recovery and reformation of girls
who have fallen but who have not become really depraved."
"About a fortnight ago," he continued, "I arranged for an *exchange* of the *Freeman's Journal* daily with the *Moniteur de Rome.*"
"Fr. Daniel," Walsh explained, "is to get the *Moniteur* every
evening. He then is to contribute articles out of the material
thus supplied." "But," Walsh noted, and very significantly, "it is
still more important that for some time past Mr. Gray has been
urging on me the importance of establishing a really *Catholic*
paper." "I think," Walsh confided, "we may soon see our way to
this. But for the present it is of course *absolutely confidential.*"

In this long letter, Walsh was not forgetful to be mindful of
Rome and its needs. "As for the Encyclical," Walsh noted, referring to *Immortali Dei*, which had not yet been published in
English in Ireland, "it requires careful explanation on account
of the Protestant prejudices here." "I hope soon," he promised,
"to write some few pages on it." "At our last Meeting of
Bishops," Walsh again, and with greater emphasis, explained
to Kirby, "we made all arrangements for translating and publishing it, but in about a week, we all received *from Cardinal
Manning* bundles of copies of an *authorised* translation which *he*
was directed by the Holy Father to send to the Irish Bishops."
"*This is very strongly resented,*" Walsh underlined heavily, "*in certain quarters and most naturally so.*" "It is directly contrary," he
added emphatically, "to what was arranged last year in Rome!"
After Easter, and nearly three weeks later, Walsh again turned
to Rome and, more especially, to its needs. "If you see to-day's
Freeman," Walsh charged Kirby on April 29, "—I know it goes
regularly to the Irish College—you will see we have made a beginning, and, I think, under good auspices, as to the Jubilee of
the Holy Father"(K).

"The fact is," Walsh continued, "the Freeman is *completely* at
our disposal but great discretion has to be exercised as to the
time and mode of bringing out certain views." "Mgr. Jacobini,"
Walsh added, referring to the Secretary of Propaganda, "sent
me the numbers of the 'Giubeleo Sacerdote.' " "I will get the
project," he promised, "well written up in the Ecclesiastical Record." "But in all these matters," he warned, "I am always (as I
know the late Cardinal was) afraid of imperiling in any way the
solid steady *yearly* contribution of Peter's Pence from this diocese." "I do not like," he explained, obviously referring to a

comment by Kirby with regard to his reticence about the Jubilee, "to say anything personally about the H. Father's Jubilee until this year's Peter's Pence collection is over. / And I believe that next year the best plan will be to make it the occasion for a special 'whip.' " "I think I asked Yr. Grace before," Walsh continued, "to find out for me whether the Freeman reaches Cardinal Simeoni regularly." "I have posted it to him," Walsh pointed out, "—at Yr. Grace's suggestion—every day." "It goes from here," he reported, "my chaplain first looking over it, and marking anything likely to be of special interest." "We have never heard," he complained in conclusion, "of it reaching safely."

All Irishmen, however, soon found their interest focused on Westminster as Parliament reconvened after the Easter recess for the second reading of the Home Rule Bill. "We are very quiet here in Ireland now, thank God," Michael Logue, the bishop of Raphoe wrote Kirby from Donegal, on May 9, the day before the second reading, "with the exception of a occcasional war note from the Orangemen which means nothing"(K). "The National party," he reported, "are leaving Mr. Gladstone and his followers to fight the battle, and are making no objection to anything he proposes. The Nationalists certainly deserve the praise of moderation for their present attitude." "I trust," he concluded optimistically, "this circumstance will bring about a speedy and satisfactory settlement of the questions at issue." "We are," MacEvilly prophesied for Kirby, about a week later, on May 15 from Tuam, "on the eve of great changes"(K). "Our poor suffering bleeding country," he then lamented, "has long been robbed of her rights, and our poor people cruelly oppressed by Landlords because they were Catholics & devoted to the See of Peter." "It is hard to say," he added, less prophetically, "how Mr. Gladstone's bill will turn out. I fervently pray successfully." "At present," MacEvilly reported, "great peace prevails, and will surely, if Mr. Gladstone's measure pass. If not, I could not say, I would tremble for consequences." "God grant," he concluded piously, "it may all turn out for the best."

"Your Grace will know the fate of the Home Rule Bill," Walsh wrote Kirby, on June 6, "before this reaches you"(K). "At present," he noted, "all is uncertain," "My own view is," he explained, "that it would be better in the end to have the Bill beaten now by a *small* majority than to have it carried by a *small* majority (and there is no chance of a big one)." "I went over to London," Walsh reported, "and spent three or four days there about a fortnight ago, when I saw Mr. Gladstone and found him full of confidence." "Mr. Parnell too seemed confident," Walsh added, commenting incidentally on what makes for leadership, "but almost everyone else at our side seemed to have made up his mind for a defeat." Indeed, two days later, in the early morning of June 8, the Home Rule Bill was defeated 343-313, with some 93 dissentient Liberals voting against the government. Gladstone immediately decided to appeal to the country on the Irish issue and Parliament was duly dissolved, with the general election scheduled for early July.

Rumors and false reports were again soon rampant. The anti-Home Rule press carried a report in mid-June that the pope had been critical of the Irish bishops and clergy for committing themselves to a political party. The occasion for the report was a resolution on the part of the Tuam clergy in support of Mr. Gladstone, the Irish party, and Home Rule. "I send you [a] copy," MacEvilly wrote Kirby on Saturday, June 19, "of the 'Irish Times,' an Orange Rag, which contains a Telegram *purporting* to come from Rome having reference to a wise resolution passed by the Tuam Priests at wh I presided"(K). "It has taken the round," he reported, "of all the Orange Anti-Irish Papers. The Irish & Catholic Papers have taken no notice of it as it is regarded as a bogus business." "If regarded as genuine," he warned, "it would do a world of mischief as it would be construed into a censure on Gladstone, and at this crisis of dissolution a help to the Tory Elections, a thing Rome in its supreme wisdom would never do. It would be construed into doing the very thing it *purports* to censure in us, viz. taking part with a political party & that a party hostile to Ireland, Rome, and the Catholic interests." "Indeed," MacEvilly expostulated in conclusion, and since the letter was more carefully written than was usual it was obviously meant for presentation to the authorities, "after the exposure of the insult offered by Errington to the Pope & the Vatican which he was 'keeping in good humour'—it is monstrous to suppose the Vatican would sanction such a thing, especially after the numerous proofs of Paternal good will & deep interest of our Great Pontiff toward his Irish & devoted children."

In his own quick and energetic way, however, Walsh had al-

ready written Kirby three days before, asking him to take effective action. "I write now," Walsh had explained on Wednesday,
June 16, "in extreme haste"(K). "I have of course," Walsh replied to a letter of Kirby's received the day before, "been noting
the thoroughly friendly and sympathetic tone of the *Moniteur*
and *Osservatore*." "I assume, then," he added, "that the enclosed
is a pure invention. But, it is of the utmost importance that I be
able to contradict it formally and efficiently." "There is of
course," he noted, "nothing in what is stated as coming from the
Holy Father but what everyone would cheerfully endorse."
"But," he qualified himself, "the saying of it to us just now
would necessarily be regarded as conveying a reproof to the
great body of the Bishops who by their present and recent line
of action have done so much for the peace of the country."
"This letter will reach Y. G.," he informed Kirby, and referring
to the annual spring meeting of the bishops, "on Saturday, I
shall then be in Maynooth, where I shall be bound to remain
until the following Wednesday or Thursday. Your Grace will
see there is not a moment to be lost." "If Cardinal Simeoni,"
Walsh suggested, "would authorize the sending of a *telegram*
directly contradicting the statement as utterly devoid of foundation this would enable us to act at once." "Our Dublin Peter's
Pence Collection," Walsh shrewdly concluded with a special fil-
lip, "will be held on the 1st Sunday of July, and it may be useful
to give the people a little stimulus to special generosity, such as
would surely be afforded by such a contradiction."

Meanwhile, that formidable political warrior, Cardinal
Manning, was preparing his ground on the English Catholic
side and laying down the battle line to the most difficult and
reluctant of his captains. "The Dissolution," he firmly wrote
Herbert Vaughan, on June 11, "is on one issue."[25] "We cannot
evade it," he advised the bishop of Salford in military staccato,
"We cannot put Education before it. The Irish vote in England
would be lost by doing so. We should seem to oppose Ireland.
We should hopelessly divide our own people." "The Education
Question," he further maintained, "would not be listened to
apart from Ireland. We can speak on both, but not on Education alone." "I have hitherto been silent," he explained, "except
that vague letter to N. Wales. But now I cannot be silent." "I will

[25] Leslie, *op. cit.*, p. 408.

not make an occasion," Manning warned Vaughan, "but I must take it when made by others. And my words will be, 'The integrity of the Imperial Parliament and a legislative power in Ireland for all home matters not Imperial.' " "Also," he added, indicating that he was leaning more and more towards a Federal solution, "I should desire the same for Scotland and Wales." "I feel," he warned Vaughan again, "I cannot longer be silent, but how, when and where I may say it, I cannot yet decide. Education cannot be helped at this election, nor do I think it will be hindered." "This," the cardinal concluded, leaving the bishop of Salford little room for maneuver, "will need much thought and counsel, but it is inevitable."

Some three weeks later, on July 6, in the midst of the general election, the cardinal chose to break his long silence in a lengthy letter published in the London *Times*.[26] The occasion was a reply to an American friend who had called his attention to a declaration by William Arthur, a prominent Belfast Methodist minister, who had maintained that it was to him "a moral mystery how any friend of religious liberty could consent to hand over Ireland to Parnellite rule." With that biting irony of which he was a master, Manning, after making much of Parnell's Protestantism and England's historic role as the defender of religious liberty in Ireland, invoked the authority of Leo XIII as recently expressed in his encyclical, *Immortale Dei*, on the teaching of the Church with respect to liberty of conscience and religious toleration. It was in his last paragraph, however, that the cardinal finally came to his real point. "In your majestic Union (American)," he noted fulsomely, "there is a central power which binds all your liberties and legislatures into one Commonwealth." "England, Ireland, and Scotland," he argued, emphasizing a federal solution, "must, in my belief, all alike have Home Rule in affairs that are not Imperial." "The growth of Empire," the cardinal further maintained, "and the fullness of time demand it." "But," he added, referring to Parliament, "there is an august sovereignty of a thousand years, the centre of a world-wide Empire, standing in the midst of us. England, Scotland, and Ireland can be handed to no man and to no movement; neither can they wrong one another, or put fetters on the liberties of any member of our great Imperial Com-

[26] London *Times*, July 5, 1886. Manning's letter was to a Mr. Hulbert and is dated July 1, 1886.

monwealth." "The sovereignty," he boldly asserted, "prevades all its parts, and will even restrain and promptly redress all excesses of delegated powers." "I wish," he finally concluded somewhat archly, "I could have written a shorter reply, but on a subject near my heart I hardly know when or where to stop."

"As to your *Home Rule* letter," Walsh noted hurriedly, on July 12, "I send by this post a copy of 'United Ireland' "(M). "It gives expression," he added gratefully, "to what we all feel." Indeed, the cardinal's letter was one of the few bright spots in the Home Rule cause as the results of the general election became known. The returns, which came in over a period of two weeks, proved a disaster for Gladstone and the Home Rule Liberals, as they were reduced from some 327 to only 191. While the Irish party held their own at 85, losing only one seat, which they would shortly regain, the Conservatives gained nearly 70 seats, increasing their numbers from 249 to 316. Since the Conservatives would be supported by some 78 Liberal Unionists on the Irish issue, the final figures gave a conclusive majority of 118 against Home Rule in the new Parliament. Manning's letter, therefore, was doubly appreciated by the Irish because it came precisely in their hour of need. The cardinal had proved himself loyal at the critical moment and won, thereby, not only the affection of the Irish in Ireland but what, perhaps, was more important from his own point of view, the hearts of the Irish in England. No one seemed to notice, moreover, that the cardinal had not really committed himself to much more than a vague form of federal devolution. His very use of the phrase Home Rule, however, which was significantly stressed by Walsh, was more than enough for the Irish at home and abroad to identify him as one of their own. "I do not," the cardinal reassured Walsh, on July 14, while at the same time sticking to his last, "interpret this election as a refusal to Ireland, but as a rejection of the mutilation of the Imperial Parliament by the removal of the representatives of Ireland."[27]

On July 24, and three days after Lord Salisbury had formed his second ministry, Walsh wrote Manning asking him if he had read an article by Robert W. Dale of Birmingham on Home Rule in the June issue of the *Contemporary Review* (M). "I am surprised," Walsh confessed, "it has attracted so little

---

[27] Leslie, *op. cit.*, p. 417.

notice. To me, it seems to give the outline, with indeed a good deal of detail, of a very fair settlement of the whole case." "It gives us," he then informed the cardinal, "all that Mr. Gladstone gives, but free from all that lacked finality in his scheme." "When in working order," Walsh maintained in conclusion, "improvements could easily be made, and made with general concurrence." What made Dale's proposals even more significant was that he was a friend and supporter of Joseph Chamberlain. In brief, Dale's proposals amounted to a system of federal devolution. Great Britain or, if more desirable, England, Scotland, and Wales, as well as Ireland, would be given local parliaments, while all would also send representatives to the imperial Parliament. Manning, of course, who had recently been leaning more and more towards a federal solution, naturally agreed with Walsh that Dale's proposals were sound, since they would not only guarantee the sovereignty of the imperial Parliament and be a safeguard against separation, but would also maintain Catholic representative power in that imperial Parliament.

Walsh had even more reason to be optimistic about the Roman as the home front, for the annual Peter's Pence Collection, which had been held on Sunday, July 4, was a resounding success. "I send you enclosed," Walsh informed Kirby, on August 11, "a cheque for £1,720, the Peter's pence offering of the Archbishop, Auxiliary Bishop, Priests, and People of Dublin"(K). "You will know," Walsh advised delicately, "how to present it in suitable form to the Holy Father. I will ask you to explain to his Holiness that the Diocesan Collection which is always made in Dublin on the Sunday within the Octave of the Feast of SS. Peter and Paul, happened to fall this year on a day of naturally great political excitement—the day immediately preceding the polling day for the city of Dublin." "At first," Walsh explained, "I thought of postponing the Collection. But, I made up my mind eventually that it was better it should go on as usual, as I felt convinced that our good people would not allow their anxiety or excitement about their political affairs to impede in any way their expression of devotion to the Sovereign Pontiff and to the Holy See." "The result of the collection," Walsh noted, "is really marvellous. This is a year of great depression, yet the amount is fully up to the ordinary standard." "Explain to his Holiness," Walsh emphasized, "that with us the offering is a *yearly* one. Others which come in only at large intervals may naturally be larger in amount."

The defeat of the Home Rule Bill and the losing of the general election by such a large margin, however, naturally dampened that buoyant political optimism that had been so apparent among the Irish at home and abroad in recent months. Whether the extreme nationalists would now gain at the expense of the constitutional movement became a very serious question. In more recent years in Ireland, extremism had tended to find its focus in the land question, while abroad, and especially in the United States, the focus had been more political than agrarian, with the object remaining traditionally an Irish republic and the means being revolution. In Ireland, however, besides the recent political disappointments, the situation was further aggravated by deteriorating economic position, which by the summer of 1886 had become precarious. The harvest of the previous year had not only been deficient, but agricultural prices had continued depressed, and the winter had consequently been very hard on the small farmer.[28] What had made matters even worse was that the spring had been extremely wet and the planting and sowing had been very late.[29] The prospects, therefore, for a good harvest, which was all that now stood between the small farmer and ruin, were greatly reduced. In brief, then, whether extremism would gain in Ireland seemed to depend largely on the coming harvest.

As far as the extremists abroad were concerned, Parnell had been alarmed by a conversation with one of them in London in the spring which left the Irish leader with the impression that the American irreconcilables were out for blood. The Irish National League of America, which had fully endorsed Parnell's leadership and recently contributed large sums of money to fight the two recent and costly general elections, was scheduled to open its third annual convention on August 18 in Chicago. How the irreconcilables in that organization would take the new Irish-Liberal Alliance, especially after the recent reversals, caused Parnell and his colleagues no little concern and anxiety. In order to forestall the extremists at the conven-

---

[28] See K, MacEvilly to Kirby, January 6, 1886.
[29] K, MacEvilly to Kirby, May 15, 1886. See also Blunt, *op. cit.*, p. 53, March 31, 1886.

tion, Parnell dispatched three parliamentary colleagues, led by the inimitable William O'Brien, to Chicago and asked Michael Davitt to accompany them. O'Brien was, of course, reputed to be about as extreme as it was possible to be and yet be part of the constitutional movement, while Davitt was still the generally acknowledged leader of the agrarian left in Ireland.

Before O'Brien and Davitt left for America, however, they obviously consulted with Walsh about the best means of steadying Irish public opinion at home and abroad. For, as Walsh explained at great length to Manning on Friday, August 13, "Not withstanding many refusals in answer to similar requests, I have consented to have myself 'interviewed' "(M). "I did so,"Walsh reported,

> "mainly for two reasons: first that as your Eminence concurs with me in a general approval of Dr. Dale's scheme, and as you, with all your opportunities of forming a judgement as to what is right and prudent, think that an expression of my opinion in favour of it may be of use, I feel it a duty to give that expression of opinion, and to do so in the most public way open to me; secondly, that I think the time has come to give a solenm warning to the new Ministry as to the terrible difficulty that is ahead if the Irish landlords are allowed to 'do what they like with their own,' as their favourite phrase is, in reference to their dealings with their land and their tenants(M).

"My interviewer," Walsh further explained, "is an official of the American Syndicate. The interview is 'cabled' across, and appears simultaneously in a leading newspaper in every great city of the U. States and in the *Freeman's Journal* here." "The first instalment," he added, referring to August 11, "appeared last Wednesday: I sent a *Freeman* to your Eminence. I thought it judicious to have the matter thus divided." "Next Monday," Walsh continued, and referring to Augst 16, "when the Irish M. P. Delegates to the Chicago Convention arrive at Chicago, and interest is fully aroused, the second instalment will appear." "I advocate strongly," he advised the cardinal, and referring to the Ashbourne Act of the previous year, "a good measure of Land Purchase, on the lines of the present (Tory) Act, and a measure on the lines of Dr. Dale's scheme for the settlement of the Irish Government question." "It is hoped," Walsh finally concluded, "that all this may help the M. P.'s who have gone over, in their work of steadying the Chicago Convention, and keeping things within bounds."

"It seems to me of much moment," the cardinal replied approvingly on Tuesday, August 17, "that you should distinctly and fully declare yourself."[30] "And I have carefully read," he noted, "the two reports of the 'interview' in the *Freeman's Journal* with much pleasure." "If your Grace and the Bishops do not speak out, and first," he warned, "others will take the lead and the due order will be reversed. In the last year I have noticed that the Bishops are guiding the question. This seems to me vital." "If I rightly understand your meaning," the cardinal assured Walsh, "and I think I do, I fully agree in what you have said. If you can put before the Holy See and the English people, such an outline as you have sketched, with the concurrence of the Bishops, its success is certain." "I have read with much satisfaction," the cardinal then noted, "Michael Davitt's speech in America. It is the sure way to gain what Ireland needs. Justice is working widely here, if imprudence does not wreck it." "I know what Henry George means by 'nationalisation' of the land," the cardinal concluded most significantly, "but I am not sure of your meaning unless it be that the Irish people shall re-enter into the possession of their own soil. The garrison must give way to the nation."[31]

O'Brien and Davitt, meanwhile, did their work well in Chicago as a united and harmonious convention on August 20 cordially endorsed Parnell and his policy. In Ireland, however, the incessant rain was creating an ominous situation. "Still," Michael Verdon, Kirby's vice rector, who was once again in Ireland trying to collect some badly needed funds for the Irish College in Rome, reported optimistically, on August 27, "the country looks well and if fine weather came even at the eleventh hour the harvest would be fair"(K). "Prices are exceedingly low," he added, entering an important qualification, "and farmers are in very bad circumstances. Very few rents will be paid in full this year for many cannot pay and some who could pay, won't pay." "However," he added, even more optimistically, "the country is quiet and likely to remain so. Politicians are satisfied to play the waiting game for they are confident that they

---

[30] *Walsh*, pp. 226-227.
[31] See M, December 28, 1886, for Walsh's reply.

will get all they want within the next two or three years." "Dr. Walsh and Dr. Croke," Verdon observed with obvious satisfaction, "are in good spirits."

Two weeks later, on September 9, at their annual general meeting, the Irish bishops led by Walsh and Croke, and in imitation of the resolutions passed by the newly elected Irish party, meeting in Dublin on August 4, renewed their own declaration in favor of Home Rule, as well as demanding temporary measures dealing with land crisis, "while awaiting permanent remedies in order to prevent the outrages and disorders which they apprehend. . . . "[32] Parnell, meanwhile, on August 25, shortly after the opening of Parliament, had moved an amendment to the queen's address, pointing out that unless something was done immediately about the land crisis, social order in Ireland would be seriously endangered. A month later, Parnell introduced a tenant's relief bill, the main clause of which expediently empowered the Land Court to suspend evictions, if the tenant paid fifty per cent of his rent, pending the investigation of his case. When the Conservative government opposed the bill, Parnell, with its rejection inevitable, on September 25, asked the Irish National League of America for support in establishing an anti-eviction fund to fight the landlords during the coming winter in Ireland.

Immediately after the bishops' meeting on September 9, Archbishop Walsh crossed over to London on his way to the continent for a well-earned holiday. By the time he returned to Dublin in the middle of October, however, it was only to find the land crisis more critical than when he left. The reports from the various parts of Ireland had, in the meantime, been most disquieting. "I am sorry to say," William Hutch wrote Kirby sadly from Fermoy in East Cork, on September 23, "the prospects for the winter are extremely gloomy. We have had a bad harvest, the payment of the fall rents is an utter impossibility, and the landlords seem disposed to evict the poor people from their little holdings without the slightest mercy"(K). "It is religion alone," he explained, "that gives our poor people the patience to endure their hard lot." "No other people in the world," he maintained in conclusion, "would stand it with such resignation." Some ten days later, on October 4, the less literate parish priest of Ballyhooly, Robert

---

[32] C. C. O'Brien, op. cit., p. 199.

Foran, reported to Kirby from the foot of the Galtee Mountains in northern Waterford, explaining that besides a bad harvest, the fall in prices had beggered the tenant farmers. "Early during the land agitation," Foran pointed out, "when [the] land bill was passed, I induced all who had no leases to go into [the] land Courts and have their rents fixed"(K). "The land Commissioners," he maintained, "have unsettled and ruined the farmers being altogether in the Landlords' interest. They fixed the Judicial sum on the tanants [sic] improvements so high that if there was no fall in prices it would be difficult to pay them—but now that prices of almost every kind have fallen, the rents are become impossible and the Land Lords will make no allowance but are pressing in all cases for rents." "The tenants," he noted further, "are here ruined, beggared, some of them are so naked that they can't send children to school. There is an almost absolute drain of mony [sic] and several of the farmers are hundreds of £ in debt to shopkeepers in towns." "Now that," Foran warned in conclusion, "[the] Landlord party is in power there is much danger of excitement amongs [sic] tenants in parts of the Country."

The accounts from the West and Northwest, where the margin of subsistence was at its narrowest, were ever more distressing than from the relatively well-off South. "Owing to the sad condition," MacEvilly lamented to Kirby from St. Jarleth's College, Tuam, on October 10, "of some parts of this Diocese I was obliged to give up the Collection for the H. Father, always made by me, last year"(K). "I am to have it this year," he added somewhat surprisingly, "tho, indeed, owing to the grinding rapacious exactions of bigoted, Orange Landlords, our people are oppressed even beyond endurance. This is done in a great measure in *odium religionis*." "I have had to hear," MacEvilly then reported, "of sad cases of great oppression in my late visitation. The Landlords are maddened, and I fear the present Government are hounding them on." "The Rosary," he concluded piously, "thank God, is taken up very fervently, and *she* will baffle them." "We are looking forward with some anxiety," Bartholomew Woodlock, bishop of Ardagh, explained to Kirby, on October 29, from Longford, "to the coming winter on account of the hardships which, we fear, may be in store for our poor people, especially our tenant farmers"(K). "Still I hope," he added piously, "Almighty God may preserve us from all danger through the intercession our Imm. Mother & of St. Patrick & St. Bridget." "Your Grace," Woodlock noted, brightening up a little, "will be happy to hear that during this year of the Jubilee we have had missions or Retreats in 21 out of our 41 Parishes—we shall have them, Please God, in one or two more before Christmas. In all these places the Exercises have been attended with the most abundant fruit, all the people with scarcely a single exception approaching the Holy Sacraments—so this has indeed been a year of grace for us." "May God be praised," Woodlock concluded, "& may He preserve the fruits."

Not all the distress in Ireland in the summer and fall of 1886, however, was due simply to natural or economic causes. "We have had a sad time of it in Belfast during this summer," the bishop of Down and Connor, Patrick McAlister, reported to Kirby, on September 2, "in consequence of the Orange riots"(K). "They are over, Thank God," he exclaimed, obviously relieved, "but we have about 500 families out of work & in great want. Several have been killed & many badly wounded and abused." "The Commission of Inquiry into the Riots," McAlister again reported to Kirby, some two months later, on October 24, from Belfast, "is coming to [a] close"(K). "The sworn evidence," he noted with obvious satisfaction, "has brought confusion to the Tory & Orange party. The government magistrates and police officers have given an almost unanimous testimony to the peaceful disposition of the Catholic people and the extreme violence of the Protestants; and to the valuable assistance given by the Priests & respectable Catholics in keeping the peace." "How much good may result from the inquiry," McAlister confessed, "we cannot yet say: but the Orange party have been foiled in their designs." "The Catholics," he pointed out bitterly, "have to endure continuous insults from them." "To insult them," he added by way of example, "they whistle in their faces a tune called, 'Kick the Pope,' & cry 'to Hell with the Pope.' " "The Catholics who all love his Holiness," McAlister noted grimly, in conclusion, "have great difficulty in restraining not only their feelings but their hands under such provocation."

A year before, in the autumn of 1885, the worst economic and social effects of a generally dismal harvest had been diluted in the politically hopeful Parnellite victory in the gen-

eral election of late November and early December. A year
later, however, there was no political excitement to take the
sting of despair out of an even more dismal harvest. Many of
the tenant farmers were already in serious debt, and since
there had been no improvement in agricultural prices in the
interim, they would not be able to pay their rents. Once again,
as in 1879, the farmers were faced with eviction, and the
laboring poor with starvation or emigration. Yet there was
profound difference between a desperate peasantry fighting
for survival in 1879, and a politically conscious and united
Irish nation demanding its social and political rights in 1886.
The difference, of course, was that in 1886 the Irish tenant
farmer was not only formidably organized in the Irish National League, but possessed a leadership that was both experienced and confident in its ability to defend his interests.

Since Parliament, however, had refused to sanction in the
autumn session any remedy or relief in the face of low prices
and the dismal harvest, and since the tenants were scheduled
to pay their half-yearly rents in November, the constitutional
leadership in Ireland was obliged to produce an effective
agrarian policy in order to forestall the evictions which now
appeared to be inevitable. If, indeed, they did not take up the
cause of the tenants, it was certain that the tenants, as they
were already doing in Kerry and Clare, would take the law
into their own hands. In the third week of October, therefore,
the leadership of the constitutional movement produced the
famous "Plan of Campaign," which would not only effectively
check evictions, but also contain the worst effects of agrarian
outrages in Ireland in the next five years. In producing the
plan, moreover, the constitutional leadership insured that
Irish political rhythms would never again depend simply on a
good or a bad harvest, and Irish agrarian agitations would
never again escape their political harness. In a word, Ireland
had, indeed, been politically transformed in the eight years
between the death of Cardinal Cullen and the defeat of the
first Home Rule Bill.

Epilogue

This has been the tangled and complex story of a struggle for power in Church and state in Ireland between 1878 and 1886. By 1878, Paul Cardinal Cullen had indeed come to symbolize all that was real about Roman power in Ireland, while Parnell was giving an early promise of what was soon to be no less real and a good deal more enduring: the embodiment of Irish power at home and abroad. Their quarrel, which symbolically transcended them in death and life, had actually to do with how they would share in the affections of the Irish Church. What further complicated their quarrel, however, was that the Irish Church had already found a secure and comfortable home in the British state, the temporary guardian of which was Mr. Gladstone. Moreover, this residence, at least, if not the relationship, was heartily approved by Rome in the interests of the Irish Church's Holy Mother, the church universal. Parnell, however, who was successfully constructing a new home in the Irish state, found the old arrangement increasingly intolerable, and insisted that the Irish Church must forsake the house of her temporal stepfather, even if it meant the outright defiance of her spiritual mother. He did, in fact, have his way and much more, for both Roman and British power were eclipsed in Ireland, and the Irish Church did come to live in the house which he built. Furthermore, the terms on which she took up residence are still essentially the terms on which she lives there today.

The decline of Roman power and influence in Ireland, between 1878 and 1886, was both continuous and inevitable. What made it continuous as well as inevitable, of course, was Rome's deliberate decision to pursue the resumption of diplomatic relations with the British state in the face of a developing and dynamic Irish nationalism, which was finding its focus in Parnell and which he would soon crystallize in a *de facto* Irish state. For nearly three years before she issued the Parnell Circular in May, 1883, Rome had been resolutely pursuing the resumption of diplomatic relations with the British government, while at the same time attempting to invest the archbishop of Dublin with the requisite authority to conserve her rapidly diminishing power, even if he was unable to effect her will. The failure of Archbishop McCabe, however, to respond to the responsibility laid upon him by Rome had perhaps more to do with the impossible nature of the burden than with even his evident inability to shoulder it. The *rapproachement* of an estranged Irish Church with Rome following on the Circular, which Rome cultivated by a series of episcopal appointments culminating in the succession of William J. Walsh in June, 1885, to Dublin, only masked the effects of what was certainly more fundamental in the undermining of Roman power and influence in Ireland—the clerical-nationalist alliance inaugurated in the autumn of 1884. With the establishment of that alliance, the Irish Church had, in fact, divided her allegiance and presented Rome with a *fait accompli.*

Ironically enough, the responsibility for the undoing of Cullen's achievement lay with Leo XIII. What then was Leo XIII attempting to achieve that would justify the sacrifice of Roman power and influence in Ireland? His aim, of course, was to restore the temporal power of the papacy. Leo's concept of the temporal power, however, was not that of his predecessor, Pius IX, who had conceived of that power in terms of the geography of the papal states and who, when deprived of his patrimony in 1860, attempted to compensate by constructing a more effective ultra-montane control of the various national churches. Leo XIII endeavored, instead, to resurrect the temporal power on another level, the diplomatic, by either restoring or reinvigorating relations with all the great powers. His efforts with the heterodox German and Russian empires were promising, while his encouragement in France of a policy that would eventuate in the *ralliement* in the 1890's was less productive; but his signal failure was in his inability to persuade Great Britain to resume diplomatic relations. Among Polish and French Catholics, if not among German Catholics, he paid a considerable price for his grand design. Among Irish Catholics at home and abroad, however, the price paid, not only in terms of affection but in obedience, was extremely high. Whether indeed Leo's vision of a papal equality so necessary, in his mind, to the dignified functioning of the vicar of Christ among the powers of this world was worth the sacrifice of so much of that Roman power and influence bequeathed to him by his predecessor is, of course, a moot point. What is less debatable is that the calculated risk resulted in no real corresponding gain, and Roman power and influence in Ireland and in the world at large at the end of the pontificate of Leo XIII was certainly a good deal less than it might otherwise have been.

Whatever may be said about the continuous decline of Roman power and influence in Ireland after 1878, there is little doubt that the parallel decline of British power was both precipitous and complete. Precipitous because British power in Ireland, if taken in perspective, had been real for nearly two hundred years, and complete because the process finally became irreversible. What indeed Leo XIII was to the decline of Roman power in Ireland, Mr. Gladstone was to the eclipse of British power there. The death knell of British power in Ireland was sounded, in fact, when Gladstone was obliged to suspend the Constitution to maintain law and order there. Not only were *habeas corpus* and due process of law virtually suspended and civil liberties seriously curtailed, but recourse was also had to Rome through the informal representations of George Errington. When Parnell was then arrested and the only effective alternative to "Captain Moonlight" thereby removed, Gladstone came to realize that Britain might indeed rule in Ireland, but only at the price of being eventually ruined. What Gladstone understood, of course, was that this resort to extra-constitutional means on the part of the government could only be justified in terms of expediency and that if they were not efficacious, there would have to be a basic reconsideration of the Irish question in the light of fundamental liberal principles. What Gladstone further understood, and perhaps more clearly than anyone else, was that the most fundamental of those principles was freedom.

When Gladstone, therefore, finally agreed to the terms of the "Kilmainham Compact" with Parnell in May, 1882, the first momentous step was taken in the actual transfer of British power in Ireland. Over the next three years, British preoccupation elsewhere, particularly in Egypt, and with domestic political reform, the general responsibility for the maintenance of order in Ireland came increasingly to depend on Parnell as he confidently gathered all the various strands of nationalist power into his own hands. The very real control he had quietly acquired in those years both in the country and over the party was made evident when Salisbury's caretaker Conservative government allowed the Coercion Act for Ireland to lapse as the price for Parnell and his party's support in helping to bring Gladstone's government down in June, 1885. When six months later in December after the general election, Parnell finally became the arbiter between the two great British political parties, Gladstone decided to take up the cause of Home Rule. In making his decision, Gladstone not only made what was a situation in fact inevitably legal, but he also guaranteed that the British two-party system, which was threatened in the emergence of the Irish party, would be preserved while waiting for what was now inevitable to be legalized. By opting for Home Rule, Gladstone had, in effect, incorporated the Irish party in the Liberal party. Furthermore, in choosing to fight a general election in July, 1886, on that issue alone and deciding after losing that election to persevere politically in leading the Liberal party to an expected victory at the next general election, Gladstone effectively bound the Irish party to the Liberal for as long as the question of Home Rule remained undecided.

Meanwhile, the Irish Church had not only sworn allegiance to the Irish state, but the Church had also defined its relation to that state. The clerical-nationalist alliance, which was informally concluded in October, 1884, had been in the making, of course, ever since Archbishop Croke had committed himself to the defense at home and at Rome of the Land League. It was Rome, in fact, which had inadvertently contributed as much as anyone to the making of that alliance by first issuing the Parnell Circular and then insisting that the Irish bishops exert themselves by bringing pressure on the British government to defend Propaganda's property *vis-à-vis* the Italian government. The Roman Circular provided the Irish clergy, high and low, with a clear example of how very dangerous it was for their own power and influence with their people to cut across rising nationalist expectations, while in the affair of Propaganda's property, the bishops were made particularly and painfully aware that their real power was rooted in their influence with the people through their priests, and the only way to make that power effective and preserve that influence in both their own and Rome's interest was to come to an understanding with the Nationalist party.

The fact that the clerical-nationalist alliance was based on an understanding rather than on a formal agreement certainly obscures its terms though it does not make them any less real. As far as the bishops were concerned they understood they had an explicit undertaking on the part of the party that the initiative with regard to the education question on all its levels would rest with them. On the other hand, the party was implicitly assured in the bishops' formal request for their support in the education question that all doubts were now removed—about either the party's constitutional character or its aims with regard to achieving Home Rule and the settlement of the land question. Those bishops and priests, therefore who were inclined to commit themselves to the party and its program were completely free to do so. What Home Rule meant specifically or what might be a satisfactory settlement of the land question was, in fact, only worked out pragmatically in the next few years. By the fall of 1886, however, the bishops had, under the energetic and able leadership of Archbishop Walsh defined their position both with regard to the party and its program. They had not only endorsed the party's lead on the question of Home Rule, and approved the system of purchase as a final solution to the land question, but they had also established their individual right to be consulted as to the suitability of the parliamentary candidates to be selected by convention within their spiritual jurisdiction as well as spelling out specifically their clergy's role as clergy in the approval of those candidates in convention.

In that short decade, then, between 1878 and 1886, the Irish Church had a very considerable hand and part both in the making of the Irish state and in defining its place in that state. In doing so, the Church contributed very materially not only to the character of that state, but to its stability as well. That the new state must be essentially Catholic was obvious. By 1878, in fact, Irish and Catholic were already as interchangeable as Nationalist and Catholic, and Unionist and Protestant, were to become by 1886. Ironically, it was Parnell who understood best perhaps that the Church must be accommodated in order to create a stable Irish state. He further understood that it was possible to coerce the Church through the people, but his real genius lay in his realization that the effectiveness of this tactic must decline with its use. His strategy, therefore, was to court the clergy constitutionally, and eventually come to terms with them in the clerical-nationalist alliance.

In accepting its constitutional place in the Irish state, the Church, in effect, prevented that state from being eventually turned into the worst kind of autocracy by either the leader or the party. In the development of a concept of leader a one-party system, a mass machine organization, a controlled press, and a single-plank National program, Ireland was certainly not unique among those nations struggling to become states in the modern world. In Ireland, moreover, because that revolution was constitutional rather than violent, the politics of dissent gave way to the politics of consensus rather than to the tyranny of the general will. What saved the Irish state from the tyranny of the "Leader," the "Party," and even the majority, was that in the last analysis the Church had enough real power and influence within the consensus to resist effectively any attempt by either the "Party" or the "Leader" to overrule the consensus.

The consensus was real, therefore, because none of its constituent elements, the "Bishops," the "Party," or the "Leader" was a law unto itself and none had the power to impose its will on the others. In thus helping to preserve the politics of consensus to the Irish state in this critical period between 1886 and 1921, the Irish Church made an important contribution both to the making of democracy meaningful and to the survival of representative institutions. With the establishment of the Free State in 1921, for example, it was much easier to begin the return to the politics of dissent from within the framework of the politics of consensus than it would have been from the tyranny of the general will. Why the Church, therefore, has had and continues to have considerable power and influence in the Irish state is simply because the basic terms of the original concordat worked out by Archbishops Croke and Walsh and Parnell and his party still stand. That agreement, and the resulting consensus, in fact, has been fundamentalized in the constitution of the Irish State, written and unwritten, and is basic to the politics characterized in Ireland today by the effectiveness of its democracy and the success of its representative institutions in preserving and guaranteeing liberty.

Bibliographical Note

The sources for this study were mainly archival, and the printed materials used were few in number. I have not, therefore, listed the books, articles, and newspapers in a formal bibliography because the reader will easily find what is pertinent in the footnotes. Two works which have been liberally used in the writing of this volume, however, deserve especial mention. One is Conor Cruise O'Brien's *Parnell and His Party, 1880-1890* (Oxford, 1957), and Patrick J. Walsh's *William J. Walsh, Archbishop of Dublin* (Dublin, 1928). The first is what may be termed a basic book, which no scholar or student of the period can do without, while the second contains a considerable amount of original material, sometimes unfortunately inaccurately quoted, which has either been lost or is now unavailable to scholars. The archival materials consulted are to be found mainly in Dublin, London, and Rome.

In Dublin the main bodies of material consulted were:

1. The Papers of Edward Cardinal McCabe. Dublin Diocesan Archives, Archbishop's House, Drumcondra.
2. The Papers of William J. Walsh. Dublin Diocesan Archives.
3. The Papers of Thomas William Croke. Cashel Diocesan Archives, Thurles, County Tipperary. Microfilmed and on deposit in the National Library of Ireland.
4. The Papers of Laurence Gillooly, C.M. Elphin Diocesan Archives, Sligo, and have been microfilmed.

In London the main bodies of material consulted were:

1. Foreign Office Papers for Italy and Rome. Public Record Office, Chancery Lane.
2. The Papers of the Earl Granville. Public Record Office.
3. The Papers of the Earl of Carnarvon. Public Record Office.
4. The Papers of Arthur Balfour. British Museum.
5. The Papers of Sir Charles Dilke. British Museum.
6. The Papers of Henry Edward Cardinal Manning. Archives of the Church of St. Mary of the Angels, Bayswater.

In Rome the main bodies of material consulted were:

1. The Papers of Tobias Kirby. Archives of the Irish College.
2. The Papers of Michael O'Riordan. Archives of the Irish College.
3. The Papers of Bernard Smith, O.S.B. Archives of St. Paul's Basilica Outside the Walls.

397

Index

Standard (London),148-160n, 218, 360

Stead, W. T., editor of *Pall Mall Gazette*, 257

Stephens' Green, 193

Stuart, Robert, 148

Sullivan, A. M., M.P., Meath, 101, 102n, 105

Sullivan, Mrs. A. M.,101

Sullivan, Edward, lord chancellor, 246

Sullivan, T. D., M.P., Westmeath, 92, 276

Sydney, archbishop of, see Moran, Patrick Francis

Tablet, 175, 245, 248, 293, 313, 357, 364, 369

Talbot, Captain, chief commissioner of Dublin metropolitan police, 243n

Taylor, Helen, 119

Telegraph (Daily), 68

Tenant farmers, xx, 28, 91-93, 109, 111, 113, 120, 123, 131, 134, 161, 164, 165, 235, 237, 319, 363, 364, 386, 387, 389

Tenants' Defense Associations, 23

"Three F's" (Free Sale, Fair Rent, and Fixity of Tenure), 91, 110n

Thurles, 50, 105, 128, 210, 223, 295, 302

Times (London), 57, 102, 257, 341, 380

Tipperary, 114, 229

Toronto, archbishop of, see Lynch, John

Tory, 95, 241

Tory press, 27, 45, 50, 52, 91, 293, 309

Traill, Anthony, assistant education commissioner, 320

Trappists, 229

Trevelyan, G. O., chief secretary for Ireland, 154-156, 240n, 362, 368

Tuam, 132, 197, 295, 377, 378

Tullabeg, 321

Tynan, P. J. Rev., secretary to Cardinals Cullen and McCabe, 10, 32n, 182, 183, 263, 266, 267, 332

· Ulster, 124, 344, 345, 347

Ultramontaine, xx, 3, 8, 15, 88, 89, 152, 205, 313, 332, 392

United Ireland, 242, 271, 275, 290n, 338, 373, 381

United States, 32, 277, 285, 346, 358, 384

Vatican, see Rome

Vaticanism, 223

Vaughan, Herbert, bishop of Salford, England, 57n, 68, 85-87, 96, 97, 99, 100, 105, 107, 151, 175, 244, 245, 279, 295, 298, 357, 369, 371, 379, 380

Verdon, Michael Canon, rector of Clonliffe College, and vice rector of Irish College (Rome), 3, 32, 119, 120, 204, 219, 220, 233, 306, 385, 386

de Vesci, Lord (John Robert William Vesey), 363

Veuillot, Louis, 96

Victoria, colony of, 32

Victoria, Queen, 58, 220, 247, 255, 272, 277

Vincent, Sir Howard, 374

Vincentian, 181

Vinegar Hill, 34

Visitations, 115, 116, 228, 290, 302

Voltaire, 60

Waldron, James, P.P., Annagh, Tuam 115

Wales, 257, 379, 380, 382

Walsh, William J., president of Maynooth, archbishop of Dublin: question of appointment to Dublin (1883), 201, 206, 207; appointment to Dublin (1885), 254-256, 261-263, 265, 268, 269, 272, 273, 275, 276, 281-285, 291-296, 299, 336, 392; consecration in Rome, 302, 306, 310, 311;relations with Parnellites, 271, 329, 348, 386; relations with Croke, 232, 250, 264, 266, 267, 270, 274, 278, 287, 288, 290, 298, 303, 304, 307; relations with Kirby, 313, 332-334, 350, 355, 364, 365, 367, 376, 377, 379; relations with McCabe, 241; relations with Carnarvon, 323, 324, 328; relations with Manning, 368, 369, 371, 374, 384, 385;Educational Endowments Commission, 305, 308, 309, 314, 318, 320-322, 325-327, 331, 335, 356; election of 1885, 338, 340-344, 351, 354; opposition to Morley, 360, 361; Home Rule Bill of 1886, 359, 362, 366, 372, 373, 375, 378, 381, 382; clerical-nationalist alliance, 395, 396; other references, 370

Walshe, James, bishop of Kildare and Leighlin, 24n, 168, 235n, 265

Walshe, Nicholas Canon, V.G., P.P., SS.